AN ELUSIVE COMMON

A volume in the series
Cornell Series on Land: New Perspectives on Territory, Development, and Environment

Edited by Wendy Wolford, Nancy Peluso, and Michael Goldman

A list of titles in this series is available at cornellpress.cornell.edu.

AN ELUSIVE COMMON

Land, Politics, and Agrarian Rurality
in a Moroccan Oasis

Karen E. Rignall

CORNELL UNIVERSITY PRESS   ITHACA AND LONDON

Copyright © 2021 by Cornell University

All rights reserved. Except for brief quotations in a review, this book, or parts thereof, must not be reproduced in any form without permission in writing from the publisher. For information, address Cornell University Press, Sage House, 512 East State Street, Ithaca, New York 14850. Visit our website at cornellpress.cornell.edu.

First published 2021 by Cornell University Press

Library of Congress Cataloging-in-Publication Data

Names: Rignall, Karen E., 1970– author.
Title: An elusive common : land, politics, and agrarian rurality in a Moroccan oasis / Karen E. Rignall.
Description: Ithaca [New York] : Cornell University Press, 2021. | Series: Cornell series on land: new perspectives on territory, development, and environment | Includes bibliographical references and index.
Identifiers: LCCN 2020057795 (print) | LCCN 2020057796 (ebook) | ISBN 9781501756122 (hardcover) | ISBN 9781501756139 (paperback) | ISBN 9781501756146 (pdf) | ISBN 9781501756153 (epub)
Subjects: LCSH: Land use, Rural—Political aspects—Morocco. | Land use, Rural—Social aspects—Morocco. | Land use, Rural—Economic aspects—Morocco. | Globalization—Political aspects—Morocco. | Globalization—Social aspects—Morocco. | Globalization—Economic aspects—Morocco. | Morocco—Rural conditions—21st century.
Classification: LCC HN782.Z9 C665 2021 (print) | LCC HN782.Z9 (ebook) | DDC 307.3/30964—dc23
LC record available at https://lccn.loc.gov/2020057795
LC ebook record available at https://lccn.loc.gov/2020057796

For my mother and father

Contents

Note on Transliteration and Translation	ix
Introduction	1
1. Custom and the Ambivalent Romance of Community	37
2. Political Pluralism, Local Politics, and the State	77
3. Land and the New Commoning	104
4. Environmental Politics and the New Rurality	133
5. Making a Living on and off the Land	161
Conclusion	203
Acknowledgments	209
Glossary	213
Notes	215
References	225
Index	245

Note on Transliteration and Translation

I transliterate place-names as they appear in official records in Morocco or are otherwise commonly written. I adopt the transliterations people use for their own names or, when I could not ascertain individual preferences, use the dominant spellings, which usually follow French conventions (*ou* for a long *u*, for example). For other words in Tashelhit, the local Amazigh language, and Arabic, I use a simplified version of the *International Journal of Middle East Studies* transliteration system (namely, using diacritical marks only for the letters ʿayn and hamza and removing indications of long vowels and the doubled letter for the *shadda*). All translations are mine.

AN ELUSIVE COMMON

INTRODUCTION

Moha ou Lahcen owned the last traditional café in the mountains overlooking the Mgoun Valley. He called it traditional and so did others I asked about what made his café different from those in Kelaa Mgouna, the market town at the bottom of the steep road linking the mountains to the lower valley. In Kelaa, as the town was usually called, the two main streets were filled with ordinary cafés: small round tables and plastic chairs spilling onto the uneven sidewalk where travelers, market goers, and other patrons caught up with friends and relatives from across Morocco's southeastern oases. Moha's café, by contrast, was tucked into the first floor of his adobe home in the village of Imzilne, right outside a weekly market significantly smaller than the sprawling regional market in Kelaa. His café seemed to be a holdover from a time when people would travel overnight by pack animal to the weekly market from villages higher up in the Atlas Mountains. They required hosteling services like a place to stay, warm food, and a paddock to secure their animals. A series of private rooms where travelers would take their meals and sometimes stay the night opened onto a central courtyard where the footsteps of customers coming in for a glass of tea were hushed by the soft earthen floor (figure 1). The corrugated plastic roof that protected the courtyard from rain and dust storms filtered the light and gave the clay water pots leaning against the rough-hewn beams a warm glow. Moha said his café reflected "our customs—the way we used to live," but the café was not simply a relic of the past. In addition to providing respite for weary travelers, it served as a staging ground for his other enterprise: he baked and delivered bread to small corner stores in the villages dotting the arid, windswept plateau, using the aged Renault his brother in France had driven down

FIGURE 1. Moha ou Lahcen emerges from the kitchen in his café.
Photo by the author.

for him one summer. The café indexed a half century of transformation in the valley and surrounding mountains. Like Moha, residents of Morocco's southeastern oases had negotiated their integration into the modern Moroccan state and global markets to refigure agrarian life, the meaning of land, and community. These negotiations produced a "new rurality" rooted in creative—though contested—approaches to governing social and political life (Hecht 2010), approaches that I describe in this book as a new politics of the commons.

When I first visited Moha it was market day. Outside the café, donkeys and mules were corralled separately from the rocky expanse where transit vans and pickup trucks transported market goers to and from the mountains. The vehicles were heavy with building materials, sacks of produce, and other supplies. Moha was busy serving tagines (a stew prepared in a blackened, conical clay vessel) and small tin pots of sweetened green tea and rosemary. At the end of the day, Moha sat with me and my research assistant, Saïd, to reflect on the changes he had seen over the decades. He had a unique vantage point. In addition to running his café and bakery, Moha served as Imzilne's collective-land representative, adjudicating access to the village's communal lands and advocating for their interests in disputes with outsiders. There was pressure on land throughout the valley because labor migration, capitalist transformation of the livestock sector, environmental change, and other shifts in livelihoods had spurred resettlement from the mountains down toward the steppe around the market town. The plateau where Imzilne was situated fell midway between the high peaks of the Atlas Mountains and Kelaa.

When I asked Moha if new residents had been moving into Imzilne as part of this resettlement, he laughed. "Why would people come here? There is no water, no work. Even people who are from here do not want to stay." They faced similar obstacles as small farmers and other rural residents throughout North Africa and the Middle East—namely, global market demands, government disinvestment, and environmental pressures, among others. However, they also challenged their exclusion by forging new economic and political arrangements crafted from existing local governance institutions and land-use practices. I saw in subsequent visits to Imzilne that, Moha's sardonic comment notwithstanding, many people *were* staying and asserting their attachment to place in increasingly political terms.

This book tells the story of how small farmers and other residents in Morocco's southeastern oases actively engaged with broader economic and political processes to invest new resources and meaning in their rural roots. These investments defied the pessimism about the viability of rural life that had marked dominant narratives and government policy since the French colonial period (1912–1956). In the 1960s, large-scale migration to Europe and urban Morocco allowed many to escape the chronic poverty and rigid social hierarchies of oasis society. Even for those who did not migrate, integration into the national polity and capitalist transformation reshaped rural life. However, this integration did not signal the death of agrarian livelihoods. In Imzilne, migrants labored abroad and in Moroccan cities but also sent money back to plant trees after drought in the 1980s and 1990s had decimated the walnut and almond groves that supplemented the income of this historically subjugated community of Black metalworkers. As work dried up elsewhere, especially in the aftermath of the 2008 global recession, or migrants became too old to work urban construction sites, many came home to maintain their fields and otherwise earn a living in the valley (figure 2). These changes played out differently in the heterogeneous social and agroecological landscape of the valley. Water scarcity, distance from markets, and other economic pressures limited agricultural possibilities in the mountain plateaus, but outmigration permitted new kinds of agrarian livelihoods to emerge in areas with adequate land and water. This facilitated upward mobility for many but also created new inequalities as groups without access to remittances or other resources were excluded from economic opportunities.

When Moha declared that "no one wanted to stay," he raised an apparent paradox at the heart of the region's transformations: How do we reconcile the pressure to leave with the labor Moha and many others like him have devoted to place? Life here was hard and produced constant mobility as residents searched for work, yet the Mgoun Valley was in little danger of losing its identity as their rural *tamazirt* (homeland). However, what constituted the tamazirt was, as Katherine Hoffman (2007) explains, a subject of intense contestation among Imazighen (Berbers, sing.

FIGURE 2. Fields of wheat in the Aït Hamd plateau.
Photo by the author.

Amazigh) both present and absent. Multiple forms of inequality affecting women, racially Black Imazighen, the poor, and outsiders excluded from collective land rights informed different groups' efforts to either preserve or contest historical privilege.[1] Historically, political and economic domination were rooted in a racialized form of indentured sharecropping, tying many to the land but at the same time excluding them from political and natural resource governance.[2] New labor relations unfolded as migration, other wage labor, and a reconfiguration of livestock production and oasis farming introduced alternatives to agriculture, especially between the 1980s and the first decade of the twenty-first century. These emergent relations sustained the importance of land but dramatically shifted its political significance and the viability of agrarian livelihoods. Land represented a form of social insurance that activated networks of support in times of need, a store of wealth, and a political tool for challenging historical repression and inequality.

In the Mgoun Valley of southeastern Morocco, people used land not only to make a living in new ways but also to assert new political claims. Formerly marginalized groups challenged their historical exclusion from landownership by reshaping inequitable customary land tenure institutions (the practices and governing bodies that regulated landownership and use) rather than rejecting those institutions. Their goals were broader than securing access to land; formerly marginalized groups also sought to refashion how collective life was governed.

Communal governance in the form of *jma'at* (customary councils) at the village and regional levels historically managed both private and collectively owned property and otherwise exercised political power. Rather than dispensing with customary practices and institutions, formerly marginalized groups advanced a "distributive politics" that reimagined communal governance as guaranteeing their subsistence rights and other political claims (Ferguson 2015). Their efforts to reinvent commoning as a framework for governing agrarian livelihoods, social life, and rural politics formed the basis for the Mgoun Valley's new rurality. These transformations did not dismantle the inequality that historically marked communal governance in the region but rather managed old and emergent inequalities to sustain a communal basis for rural life.

Aims of the Book

This book places land at the center of the question: What does it mean to live a rural life at this juncture in the twenty-first century? Through an ethnography of land, labor, and community, I explain how small farmers and other residents crafted a *new rurality* in one oasis valley in southeastern Morocco. They did this by using their global engagements to invest in place—in agriculture, other economic activities, and social relations of reciprocity and dependence. They also crafted a new rurality by reshaping the institutions that govern collective life. This *politics of the commons* drew on a tradition of legal and political pluralism in the Mgoun Valley, offering new visions for communal governance while also producing contestations over belonging, political representation, and subsistence rights.

These contestations offer a lens into how agrarian politics are changing in marginalized rural zones around the world. Living a rural life today means surviving on "one of the decisive battlegrounds of neoliberal globalization" (Moore 2008, 54). Agrarian landscapes are the site of intensifying contradictions in the ecological processes, labor relations, and capital flows associated with globalized agriculture. Governments around the world have scaled back expenditures and services in rural areas while concentration in global agrofood systems has increased corporate pressures on agrarian livelihoods, especially those of small farmers and agricultural laborers.[3] The 2008 financial crisis raised the stakes of these contradictions, precipitating food price spikes, land speculation, and other disruptions that accelerated the restructuring of agrarian economies (Horlings and Marsden 2011). The pressures are not only economic. A global food system powered by fossil fuels links these processes inexorably to environmental change (Weis 2010). Land and food sovereignty advocates warn that the basic fabric of rural life is being frayed as deepening economic pressures compound long-standing political marginalization (see, for example, Holt-Giménez 2009). These advocates emphasize how peasants or small farmers nurture diverse, sustainable agrarian systems based on social cooperation and communal approaches to managing natural resources.[4] But "does it even make sense to speak or write of 'peasants' today" (Veltmeyer 2006, 445) when the pressures of global capitalism threaten to overwhelm the livelihoods and life ways of small farmers?

A New Rurality

Attending to the quotidian practices and politics of rural life in southeastern Morocco demonstrates that it does make sense to talk of peasants today. We do, however, need to broaden our analysis from a traditional focus on peasants as farmers to consider the diverse economic and political strategies that take shape in rural spaces (Fabricant 2012; Hecht and Cockburn 2010; Kay 2008). Land and small farming remain central to rural life, but they are also the object of new struggles as residents negotiate shifting livelihoods, environmental change, and ongoing political repression (Hecht et al. 2006). In resisting a productionist focus—the small farmer as paradigmatic rural actor—this book also resists the notion that peasants are relics, holding on to a way of life that contemporary capitalism has rendered obsolete. Residents of the Mgoun Valley were not purely defensive in the face of external pressures but rather used their global engagements to advance projects for sovereignty over their land and livelihoods.

Considering rurality on its own terms, rather than an "other" to the urban or a relic of the past, underscores the distinctiveness of struggles for economic and political autonomy in marginalized rural zones such as the Mgoun Valley (Rignall and Atia 2017). These struggles challenge a long-standing orthodoxy in development theory and policy that privileges the urban over the rural as *the* site of innovation and productivity. Mainstream economists have complicated the simplistic "stage" models of 1950s modernization theories that posit the diminishing importance of agriculture and rural out-migration as necessary steps in a teleological movement toward industrial growth (Cooper and Packard 1997). However, the underlying premise of the rural as an outmoded condition to be superseded continues to drive development funding and economic policy (Rignall and Atia 2017; Watts 2003). Even for rural development programs, dominant paradigms such as the Alliance for a Green Revolution in Africa promote technical, market-based solutions imported from corporate agriculture as a replacement for the diversified and stubbornly persistent small-farming sectors throughout Africa, Latin America, Asia, and as this book demonstrates, North Africa and the Middle East (Kerr 2012). In many cases, these small-farming sectors are not on the margins at all. They continue to feed and employ a substantial portion of their countries' populations and sustain vibrant rural societies with manifold connections to urban areas and the global economies. In the Middle East and North Africa, "more than 80 percent of some annual and perennial crops and livestock species is provided by the small-scale family farming, and nearly 75 to 85 percent of agricultural land holdings is held by family farmers" (Marzin et al. 2016, ix). Notions of development that cannot accommodate alternative models for economic and social organization dismiss these rural spaces as unproductive and in need of improvement.

However, essentializing notions of the rural as inherently stagnant are not limited to proponents of development orthodoxy. Similar assumptions can also mark social movements and scholarship from critical or radical traditions. Hardt and Negri, for example, assert that "metropolitan life is becoming a general planetary condition" as "circuits of communication and social cooperation are becoming generalized" across the globe (2009, 252–253). For them, the extension of metropolitan life means that "rural life is no longer characterized by isolation and incommunicability," offering new hope for emancipatory politics and a radical ethics of the commons (253). This stance discounts the possibility that the rural might constitute a viable site on its own for the elaboration of such politics. The emergent rurality I describe is not a simple projection of a metropolitan imaginary. Instead, it engages with both rural dynamics *and* global processes to offer alternative, cosmopolitan visions for negotiating economic, cultural, and political change.

While it is important to question overly pessimistic assessments about agrarian life, we must also challenge the assumption that a rurality rooted in smallholder farming is by its very nature socially just and environmentally sustainable. This assumption is common in agrarian solidarity movements that uphold the peasant farmer as "capital's other," emblematic of an environmentally and socially harmonious rurality (Bernstein 2014, 1032). Sounding the alarm about the urgent challenges confronting rural zones can lead to essentializing images of the past and possible future of agrarian life. These images evoke romantic—what Raymond Williams called "warmly persuasive"—accounts of a mythic, egalitarian community rooted in agrarian systems that are inherently sustainable, diverse, and equitable (Altieri and Toledo 2011; Williams [1976] 1985, 76). In this formulation, peasant livelihoods represent an ideal past to which we can return through rural social movements and a transformation of the global food regime. Yet as Tania Li notes for food sovereignty discourse more generally, these virtues "don't necessarily cohere: sustainability, proximity, sufficiency and democracy may pull in different directions" (2015, 206). Like other farming systems, peasant farming is a fundamentally *social* relation, marked by labor and other inequalities that shape how these agrarian formations interact with broader political and economic processes (Hecht and Saatchi 2007).

Assumptions about peasant farming's inherent sustainability and justice can also obscure the complex, sometimes uncomfortable, forms political agency takes in rural zones. Peasants do not necessarily adopt the anticapitalism of many social movements and may support authoritarian populism, currently witnessing a global resurgence (Edelman 2005; Scoones et al. 2017). Many rural residents "simply struggle to get by with a range of different livelihood strategies" (McMichael 2008, 207). Tania Li describes how indigenous highlanders in Central Sulawesi (Indonesia) attempted "to join the march of progress" by embracing capitalist property relations (2014a, 2). This had the troubling result of dismantling communal governance and unraveling the highlanders' networks of social support. However, this outcome is not a foregone conclusion. The example of Mgoun indicates that capitalist relations do not always destroy reciprocity or the potential for agrarian livelihoods even as they transform rural life. Residents of the Mgoun Valley did not articulate anticapitalist goals or ally themselves with transnational food sovereignty movements, but their strategies nonetheless produced upward mobility for many and forged new communal arrangements.

The economic and political strategies that unfolded in the Mgoun Valley were a response to capitalist pressures but also formed part of a *longue durée* of agrarian change that included shifting relations with the *makhzan*, long-standing racial and economic inequality, and other dynamics that can be neither divorced from nor reduced to these pressures.[5] Former indentured sharecroppers or marginalized Black residents like Moha ou Lahcen used their improved economic status to contest the historically trenchant hierarchies of agrarian life; they often elicited resistance from elite families and from others who had not experienced the same success. The conflicts produced by this upward mobility complicate the common assumption that peasants seek to preserve traditional farming and resource management systems in their efforts to secure land or food sovereignty. Some may be doing just that, but marginalized groups in Mgoun strove for economic and social autonomy by reworking rather than preserving tradition. They introduced new labor relations that integrated cash wages but sustained other noncommoditized relations such as women's unpaid agricultural work. They also reoriented customary land tenure to meet new priorities—for example, using traditional irrigation and land-use rules to facilitate the introduction of small-scale commercial agriculture. Following these strategies ethnographically shows how the viability of agrarian rurality does not necessarily rest in protecting tradition but in recognizing peasants' ambivalence toward that tradition.

My fieldwork beginning in 2010 documented how different groups mobilized customary governance institutions like the jmaʿa to influence the everyday conduct of rural politics and experiment with new livelihood and land-use strategies. The ongoing importance of customary institutions may, on the surface, seem like continuity with the past. But this apparent continuity took work and was highly contested, which in turn infused those institutions with new meanings—what Guyer terms the "changing shape" of persistence (1992, 483). In the Mgoun Valley, these contestations took the form of everyday practices on the land, a refashioning of customary governance, and occasionally, formal political claims for land. I term these practices an emergent politics of the commons, innovative governance arrangements that were often invisible to government officials or other observers who only saw a decline in communal life and agrarian rurality. This official invisibility belies the importance of such governance arrangements—a new politics of the commons—in rural zones around the world.

A New Politics of the Commons

In arguing for an agrarian rurality constituted through rather than cordoned off from global engagements, I also question assumptions about the kinds of politics that can promote land and food sovereignty. The oppositional politics accompanying Mgoun Valley's new rurality did not hinge on individual rights-based claims or a straightforward defense of communal institutions. Formerly marginalized groups in the Mgoun Valley contested the historical iniquities that protected the privilege of rural notables, but they also used political and legal pluralism—the presence of multiple systems for governing land and political life—to retain the communal orientation of customary governance institutions. The vision of the commons produced through this negotiation defies dominant understandings of what communal governance, or commoning, should look like. During another visit to Moha's café in Imzilne, he explained to me the communal logic that informed these emergent political claims. This time, I was asking his opinion about a judgment I frequently heard from local government officials in the valley: villages were dividing up their communal lands because of the decline of customary institutions like the jmaʿa that historically governed land, natural resources, and other aspects of social life. Moha responded to my question with another question: "What do you mean? Our customary institutions are working just fine! Look outside there, look at those walls, look at how we have been able to work together!" He swept his hand in front of the window to indicate the grid-like arrangement of adobe walls enclosing the hard earth outside the perimeter of the Imzilne market. Moha explained that the placement of the market outside Imzilne in the 1960s was politically charged, involving multiple successive appropriations of the village's land—land that could be taken because they were Black metalworkers with little power. The local *commune* (county government) was controlled by rural notables who had regularly invoked the power of eminent domain to seize Imzilne's land. Over the coming decades, the area around the market became the site of the commune offices, housing for commune employees, an agricultural extension office, the local middle school, and a dormitory for children attending the middle school from their remote mountain homes. All these structures were built in Imzilne's collective lands, and the village was neither consulted in the decision-making process nor compensated for the appropriations. As Moha, Imzilne's collective-land representative, conceded, "There was no way to say no," a succinct characterization of centuries of domination coming from the marginalized village's most respected community leader. However, Moha saw emergent political possibilities in using customary rules to challenge that domination, not to return to "traditional ways" but to forge new forms of common action.

In the summer of 2010, the local Ministry of Interior official announced plans for a new *qiyada* (ministry office) in the plateau. The office was to be placed in the same complex of government buildings that had encroached on Imzilne's collectively owned land. Residents knew this would probably herald yet more encroachment, so they decided to find a way to say no, or at least, no more. The form of refusal they chose was to formally divide Imzilne's collective lands. Doing so would prevent seizure because with its transformation into *mulk* (private property), this newly divided land would not be subject to the same eminent domain procedures as when it was collectively owned. Imzilne residents had talked about dividing their land before, but the final impulse came when they saw contractors begin work on the new government building. As Moha asserted: "If we do not divide our land, they will just come and keep on taking more and more. At least if individuals own and signal [*'alam* in Arabic] their land, the government cannot take anymore." So, in a matter of weeks, the sound of cement mixers on the Ministry of Interior construction site merged with the sound of Imzilne residents pounding the wet clay of the adobe walls going up around their newly allocated plots (figure 3). The political message was clear as the successive appropriations of previous decades had now been answered by the quiet enclosure of Imzilne's remaining lands. While scholars might interpret such actions as dismantling the commons and the communal sensibilities that go with it, Moha's narrative underscored the importance of that enclosure for asserting Imzilne's (albeit limited) sovereignty.

The division of communal property could signal the vitality of customary tenure institutions because new rights in land were nested in collective governance arrangements. There was, in other words, a fundamentally communal logic to Imzilne's land division since residents or rights holders could not simply dispose of the land as they pleased. Property was still subject to collective rules about transferring ownership and use. Such hybrid property forms and social arrangements complicate ideas of the "new 'commons'" (McCarthy 2005, 10): the groundswell of popular movements and scholarship that counters the relentless drive to neo-

FIGURE 3. Moha ou Lahcen and his son prepare the adobe walls for their allotment.

Photo by the author.

liberal privatization with "the positive project of building an alternative vision of the good life" (Reid and Taylor 2010, 4). The extensive literature on the new commons aims to nurture the "suppressed praxis of the commons in its manifold particularities, despite a millennium of privatization, enclosure, and utilitarianism" (Linebaugh 2008, 19). This praxis regards commoning as much more than a collectively owned natural resource. It is a broader struggle for the "commonwealth," social cooperation that rejects the exclusions of private property in favor of collective well-being and justice (Hardt and Negri 2009). Commoning therefore represents the struggle for the *just*, not just good, life rather than a straightforward property form defined by collective ownership.

This book embraces such an expansive approach but pushes back against the "romance of the commons" (evoking Joseph 2002) that is often implicit in scholarly and social movement work. As Lauren Berlant argues, "The commons concept has become a way of positivizing the ambivalence that saturates social life," threatening "to cover over the very complexity of social jockeying and interdependence it responds to by delivering a confirming affective surplus in advance of the lifeworld it's also seeking" (2016, 395). The pervasiveness of the commons as both strategy and goal for anticapitalist struggle today signals, in Berlant's estimation, a profound need for belonging and a way out of contemporary capitalism's radical individualism. I assert that this has produced a romance of the commons in contemporary social theory that supersedes the "romance of community" as an antidote for the anomie and dispossession of capitalism (Joseph 2002). Social theorists have long been critical of the regressive possibilities for community as a putatively organic, natural, or spontaneous form of human relatedness (Joseph 2002, viii). This may be a long-standing theme of scholarly critique, but, as Joseph argues, celebrations of community "relentless[ly] return" in popular imaginings of a more meaningful social life (2002, xxxii). She posits that community represents a "supplement to capital," a distinct product of capitalist modernity designed to legitimate inequality and remove responsibility for collective well-being from the state or any social body (Joseph 2002, 172). In the context of suspicions about community as an egalitarian or emancipatory space, the commons emerges as a theoretical object of desire in its stead—a site for progressive political possibility. To sustain its analytic coherence, however, the commons needs to be grounded in a political economy that can accommodate different property forms and political claims that do not always articulate resistance to capitalism.

In the Mgoun Valley, marginalized groups eschewed nostalgia for tradition as they experimented with different forms of common action. They simultaneously invoked and undermined tradition, pursuing private property forms or new market-based livelihoods while embracing the norms and institutions of communal governance. David Harvey (2011), one of the most prominent theorists of contemporary enclosure, acknowledges how this complexity can unsettle expectations about how commons should work, warning against a simple binary view that opposes privatization or enclosure to collective ownership. He sardonically observes that "the whole issue has been clouded over by a gut reaction either for or against enclosure, typically laced with hefty doses of nostalgia for a once-upon-a-time, supposedly moral economy of common action" (101). Harvey notes the possibility of antienclosure activism that foregrounds private property or some form of exclusive ownership as one way, sometimes the best way, to preserve valued commons (103). Others have also resisted interpreting moves to private or individual property forms as necessarily opposed to these new ethics of commoning. Wendy Wolford (2010) describes how northern Brazilians joined the Landless Workers Movement but did not share the movement's leaders' interest in collective land, preferring instead individual property regimes.

In taking seriously the proposition that enclosure could enable residents to, in Moha's words, "work together better than we ever have," I argue that these mobilizations represented a "latent commons" hidden in unrecognized forms of communal action (Tsing 2015, 135). Anna Tsing likens the latent commons to subjugated knowledges because they are not immediately apparent to the dominant. I take the latent commons to mean practices, ideas, and forms of solidarity that may organize collective action but remain obscured, either because they are self-evident to practitioners or because they could be the subject of repression. They are not reducible to "hidden transcripts," James Scott's (1992) term for modes of resistance that escape the notice of the powerful, because they embody the expansive communal ethics I have described as characteristic of the "new commoning." Tsing reminds us that while latent commons may be "ubiquitous, we rarely notice them," in part because they move in "law's interstices . . . catalyzed by infraction, infection, inattention—and poaching" (2015, 255). The latent commons of the Mgoun Valley and surrounding steppe were difficult to discern because they too were not always institutionalized. Participants in land conflicts sometimes made overt political claims, but most often they worked directly on the land itself, occupying and refashioning the landscape because they were excluded from formal political spaces. Their sense of the commons was also rooted in a profound attachment to place and each other—the communal orientation that shaped the way people organized their labor, farming practices, migration patterns, and social relations, even if those relations were rarely egalitarian. That the latent commons may sometimes turn to private property forms indicates that enclosure does not always signal the death of the commons in the face of encroachment or repression. What mattered to the residents of Imzilne was communal governance, not the property form.

An Elusive Common

The title of this book refers to the potentially latent character of the commons. The commons were elusive because they were often hidden, embedded in customary law and governance institutions that nonetheless articulated new political and subsistence claims. The commons were also elusive because in important respects, they never actually existed. Idealized notions in the anthropological literature and popular imagination that emphasize democratic approaches to self-governance in the Amazigh southeast downplay the exclusions that historically marked Morocco's collective lands.[6] The new politics of the commons advanced by formerly marginalized groups critiqued the fact that the commons had never truly operated for the collective good. Raymond Williams (1975) has to keep looking back in the English literary tradition to earlier and earlier evocations of "community" and the "country" in search of the time when those ideal types may actually have existed. He never finds it. The commons were just as elusive to the residents of the Mgoun Valley as they were to the poets and novelists plumbing

England's past for a rural idyll they could never quite reach. Chapter 4, for example, details how the commons were folded into the state apparatus when the French colonial state assumed *la tutelle* (tutelary authority) over collectively owned lands in 1919. Mahmood Mamdani (1996, 2012) and Pauline Peters (1994, 2004), among others, have described this strategy as integral to colonial rule in Africa, where European authorities codified customary rule over collectively owned resources to circumscribe communal authority or expropriate resources outright. This legacy continues to ramify throughout postcolonial Africa and the Middle East. Scholars have documented how customary law and tenure institutions as an instrument of colonial rule have been repackaged in the form of neoliberal reforms, community-based natural resource management, participatory development, and decentralization initiatives (Berry 2004; Chanock 1991; Geschiere 2009; Mamdani 1996; Obarrio 2010, 2014). These reincarnations of custom sustain or even create social differentiations rooted in historical inequalities.

At the same time that they were reconstituting custom, French Protectorate officials and scholars of Morocco developed narratives that customary governance institutions were in a state of inexorable decline and hence required colonial intervention. These narratives about the decline of rural life in Morocco's peripheral zones informed the discourses I heard in 2010 about the dissolution of community in the Mgoun Valley. International donors, Ministry of Agriculture officials, and other government representatives often asserted that customary tenure regimes could no longer safeguard what they termed the "fragile environment" of the steppe. They developed a story, detailed in chapter 5, about the relationship between institutions governing land-use practices and environmental degradation: corrosive individualism eroded the social solidarity underlying these institutions, requiring the state to restore a version of the commons that would remain subordinate to government authority. These visions of the commons deployed nostalgia to rewrite the history of how the state itself undermined tribal sovereignty over collective lands.

Residents countered these narratives of decline not simply by resisting government authority but by engaging state actors in a pragmatic effort to advance their claims. The Moroccan case shows how commoning does not exist in a timeless, egalitarian space where people assert their rights against enclosure, expropriation, or a neoliberal state. Rather, the commons represents a historically specific site of contestation where different actors—state agents, customary leaders, and marginalized groups, among others—negotiate hierarchy as an inescapable element of social life. McCarthy reminds us that exclusion and inequality are inherent to commoning: "To assert a commons at one scale is almost necessarily to deny claims at another" (2005, 19). To successfully govern collective life, commoning in the Mgoun Valley had to manage this inequality, but it produced new exclusions and social tensions in the process. As new forms of collective governance took shape in Imzilne and the other places featured in this book, residents invoked customary law to delimit who could participate in and benefit from the commons. Such uses of tradition are widespread. The anthropological scholarship on belonging illustrates how laying claim to an authentic past based on autochthonous identities can become a mechanism for policing boundaries and producing exclusions (see, for example, Geschiere 2009; Geschiere and Jackson 2006). Even a distributive politics aimed at dismantling historical privilege could have the effect of reinscribing inequality in southeastern Morocco. However, axes of difference shifted from traditional sources of prestige—land, livestock, saintly authority, and "wealth in people"—to money as a primary source of wealth and power, although land and livestock were still important (Guyer 1993; Miers and Kopytoff 1977).

The repurposing of customary law and communal governance therefore produced contradictory effects. This was due in part to the malleability of customary institutions—what Guyer calls their ability to sustain performative repertoires (2004, 98). Guyer's work in West Africa shows how European colonial encounters with diverse economic systems could undermine state efforts to "fix" economic practice and produced yet more diversity instead: a "historical tendency . . . toward elaboration rather than reduction" (66). This increasing elaboration raises the possibility that codifying custom does not always simplify or fix identities. It can also mediate new meanings, throwing up uncertainties that people sustain rather than eradicate to make "marginal gains" both literal and metaphoric (Guyer 2004). Guyer describes how these "transactional institutions" systematically play with the interface between capitalist and noncapitalist economies by linking, yet maintaining a difference between, diverse exchange systems and registers of value (98). This applies as much to political rule as to regimes of value. In the Mgoun Valley, political pluralism—customary authority, an authoritarian state, rights-based claims, and emergent oppositional politics—enabled various actors to draw on or negotiate different sources of power. Discourses of custom ran up against civil society activist demands for liberal government that would replace political pluralism with the rule of law. At the same time, marginalized populations excluded from or unmoved by this discourse of rights turned to commoning as an alternative language of politics.

The commons may be elusive, but it still nurtures the possibility for a transformative politics, especially for marginalized groups. Berlant (2016) and Joseph (2002) use their critiques of the romance with the commons and community as a springboard for imagining what emancipation might look like given the "unbalanced load of desire that the commons claim now carries" (Berlant 2016, 398). In other words, how can we draw inspiration from critiquing this romance to fulfill the political potential of the commons and acknowledge unconventional forms of commoning, such as the ones described in this book? Scholars and activists are trying to "undo static notions of the commons (as pre-social natural resources or pre-given natural order)" in favor of a dynamic approach to the commons as the "substantive grounds of collective life" (Reid and Taylor 2010, 12, 19). The commons here is fundamentally processual—Linebaugh (2008, 279) calls for resurrecting the term's usage as a verb, "to common"—and not simply property owned or governed collectively. Linebaugh warns us, however, about the danger of such a sweeping approach: in celebrating all that is held and done in common as potentially emancipatory, a critical political economy of the commons might slip away. This book attempts to hold the two approaches—an expansive theoretical understanding of commoning and a critical political economy of the commons—in balance with each other, arguing that they need each other to sustain the analytic and political power of the commons concept. The way I use commoning throughout this book does not require a natural resource to be at the center of a communal management system, but it does require a "political economy."[7] Commoning as I define it, then, is both an approach to governing communal resources (tangible or intangible) *and* a site for negotiating conflicting interests and social inequalities. Rather than see inequality as deforming the possibility marginalized residents of Mgoun found in new approaches to commoning, however, I understand the management of inequality as integral to their senses of hope. I challenge utopian approaches to agrarian rurality and commoning as *the* answer to contemporary capitalist exploitation, emphasizing instead the pragmatic and sometimes problematic viability of rural people's own visions for their collective life.

A Socioecological Introduction to the Mgoun Valley

Viewed from satellite photographs (figure 4), the Mgoun Valley stands out as a thin emerald ribbon wending its way through the brown, jagged topography of the southern foothills of the High Atlas Mountains. The valley stands in the rain shadow of the Atlas and is considered part of the pre-Sahara because the arid steppe surrounding the river represents a transition from the mountains to the hyperaridity of the desert (Joly 1954, 1979). Precipitation from rain and snow in the high mountain plateaus and gorges (averaging six hundred millimeters annually) fills the rivers and karstic aquifers essential to the production systems of the pre-Saharan oases farther to the south (Diekkrüger et al. 2010, 63).[8] The waters descend from the area surrounding Ighil n'Mgoun (Mt. Mgoun)—at four thou-

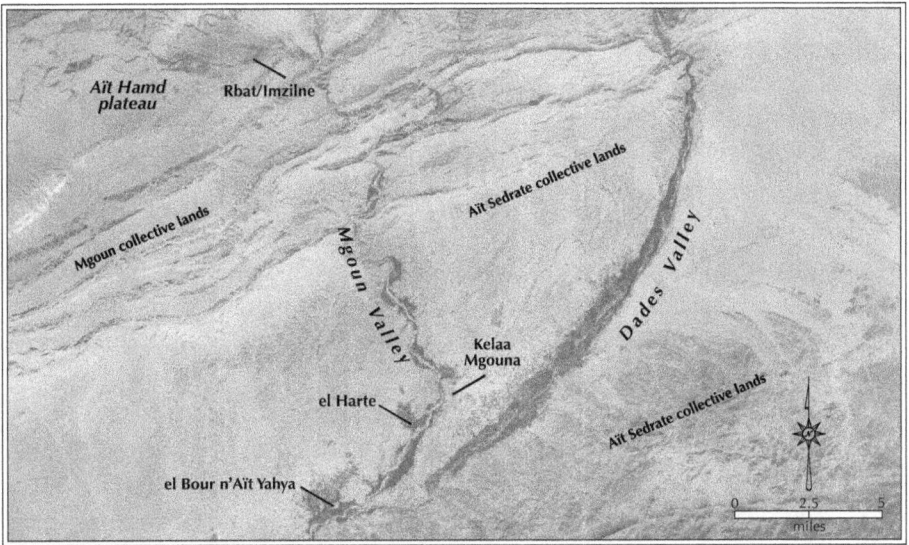

FIGURE 4. Aerial view of the Mgoun and Dadès Valleys. SPOT image, January 11, 2008; image accessed through Google Earth March 22, 2012, and processed by Richard Gilbreath.

sand meters one of the highest peaks of the Atlas—and pass through the Aït Hamd plateau (Attar 1994). *Bour* (rain-fed agriculture) has long been a feature of higher-altitude cultivation, but residents of the plateau reported to me that bour cultivation had not been possible since the droughts of the late 1990s. Just south of the plateau, waters from a number of high mountain valleys converge to form the Mgoun River, which then works its way south to Kelaa Mgouna at an altitude of fourteen hundred meters. There, average annual rainfall calculated over a twenty-year period hovers around 150 millimeters, too little for rain-fed agriculture (Centre de Mise en Valeur Agricole 2010). Just south of Kelaa, the Mgoun River joins the Dadès River, the main source of water for the more affluent but also more water-stressed Dadès Valley to the east.

The Mgoun River is one of the few in the region that continue to run all year, enabling residents to rely primarily on surface water for agriculture.[9] The rugged topography in the higher elevations limits the possibility for converting steppe land to cultivation, while the higher availability of surface water and favorable topography in the area around Kelaa Mgouna have sustained oasis farming and even some expanded cultivation with minimal use of mechanized pumping (Attar 1994). Higher water availability has dampened draws on groundwater and mitigated the impact of frequent droughts. My field research revealed that even with increased areas under cultivation, the availability of surface water meant that villages in the lower valley did not have to enforce customary rules that rationed irrigation water since the drought of 2001; farmers were irrigating when and as much as they needed with no reports of scarcity in the villages surrounding Kelaa. By contrast, residents of Dadès, the neighboring valley to the east, have relied heavily on groundwater pumping from aquifers fed by mountain runoff to meet household needs, a growing tourist sector, and oasis farming (de Haas 2001). This has dropped the water table, a concern throughout the southeastern oases and the Souss (Barathon, El Abbassi, and Lechevalier 2005; Houdret 2012). Agricultural extension officers in Kelaa reported that since the early part of the first decade of the twenty-first century, many fields in Dadès have lain fallow for the summer crop rotation because of diminished water flows.

Such marked spatial variation extends beyond water availability to define the broader climatic and ecological dynamics of drylands such as the Moroccan pre-Sahara. While some ecologists have emphasized the fragility of arid environments, others have documented their resilience and how socioecological systems—the ways human and ecological systems coproduce one another—have adapted to the wide climatic variability in the region (Reynolds and Smith 2002; Blondel 2006; D. Davis 2016). Over the past three decades, range ecologists have interpreted this variability as evidence that dryland ecosystems are not equilibrial systems that naturally tend toward stable states in terms of vegetation cover or other ecological processes (Behnke, Scoones, and Kerven 1993; Scoones 1999). Foundational research in political ecology has also detailed how assumptions about the fragility of arid lands and their tendency toward desertification have been used to justify repression of pastoralist land uses (Bassett and Crummey 2003; Fairhead and Leach 1996, 1998; Leach and Mearns 1996), with Diana Davis documenting how this has unfolded in Morocco (2005, 2007). Historical, ecological, and social science research has debunked those assumptions, showing instead that dryland dynamics are disequilibrial and that stochastic events and climatic variability have a greater impact on arid and semiarid ecologies than grazing (Scoones 1994).

These theories of disequilibrium have also contested assertions that the Sahara is inexorably marching toward desertification (D. Davis 2016). Scholars adopting the disequilibrial paradigm do not dispute the impact of climate change on contemporary agroecologies in the region, but climate change effects across time and space are complex and debated. My acquaintances in Kelaa were certain that higher temperatures associated with climate change were forcing residents of Zagora, in the Dra' Valley farther to the south, to spend their summers in Kelaa to avoid the heat; some Kelaa residents complained that the influx of summer visitors raised local housing prices. Research on North Africa predicts that over the coming century and congruent with widely held popular expectations, annual precipitation will likely decrease, more extreme weather events like floods will occur, and temperatures will increase, with the greatest impacts in the High Atlas and other mountain zones (Karmaoui and Balica 2019; Schilling et al. 2012; Zereini and Hötzl 2008). Hydrological and climate models for the Dra' Valley and surrounding catchment (which includes the Mgoun Valley) also project higher temperatures and shifting precipitation dynamics at this smaller regional scale (Fink and Reichert 2009).

Both pastoralists and oasis farmers have crafted highly productive land-use systems that use mobility and sophisticated risk management strategies to adjust to these long-standing climatic uncertainties and emergent socioecological pressures.[10] Although some researchers have described the dissolution of customary resource management institutions (Bourbouze and Gibon 2000), others have pointed to different dynamics: that mobile pastoralism is less vulnerable to drought than sedentary livestock production (Freier, Finckh, and Schneider 2014) and that customary management regimes can adapt to these evolving challenges (Auclair, Aspe, and Baudot 2006). However, the increasing practice of trucking herds to find favorable forage sites, economic dynamics that favor large herd owners, pastoral development programs that have sedentarized mobile pastoralists and produced unintended vulnerabilities, and the integration of pastoral zones into the national and global economies have transformed livestock production in the region.[11] This book places these dynamics in relation to oasis agriculture, which has historically formed an integrated regional system with more extensive land uses.[12] In this system, seminomadic or transhumant pastoralists seasonally moved herds from summer pastures at higher altitudes down to winter pastures in the lower-elevation Saghro Mountains or steppe around Kelaa Mgouna.[13] Land-use agreements between farming and pastoralist groups, trading relationships, regional governance structures, and diversified households with members participating in different livelihood systems indicated the many ways extensive and transhumant livestock production was imbricated with oasis agriculture.

This book resists treating oasis farming and transhumant pastoralism as discrete livelihood and land-use systems, but I focus more on oasis life in the lower valley than on areas where higher concentrations of residents were involved in transhumant pastoralism. Insights from dryland ecology are nonetheless as important to the highly anthropogenic landscape of the oasis as they are to the surrounding steppe. Global estimates indicate that approximately 150 million people live in oases, from the high-altitude cold-weather oases of China to the Saharan oases that have captured European and American imaginations for centuries (de Haas 2001). This small number belies the renown of the archetypal oasis farming system in the Middle East and North Africa: the tiered structure whereby trees produce dates, olives, fruit, and nuts and offer a microclimate through their cooling shade, grains and fodder provide sustenance to humans and livestock, and vegetable cultivation produces a variegated landscape and diverse diet. Intricate networks of irrigation canals and dirt pathways produce a patchwork of irregularly shaped fields, some only a few meters in area and yet all intensely cultivated with great care. But there is so much diversity among oasis farming systems that the simplistic three-tier image of production obscures as much as it clarifies (de Haas 2001). The riparian oasis of the Mgoun Valley is too high and cold to support the iconic date palm usually associated with Saharan oases, although similar principles guide the farming system. Historically, tree crops such as almond, olive, pomegranate, peach, apricot, fig, and quince, along with walnut and apple in the higher altitudes, were dispersed throughout fields growing a wheat/barley and maize rotation. Kitchen gardens yielded fava beans, turnips, carrots, squash, and other vegetables. While intensive livestock production had assumed greater importance, it was always integrated into oasis farming systems, with cattle, donkeys, goats, and sheep providing manure for cultivation, animal traction, and a ram to slaughter every year for the religious commemoration of *'aid al-kabir* (the major religious holiday).

Although colonial authorities foregrounded farming as more productive and civilized than pastoralism, they still caricatured oasis farmers with Orientalist narratives that simultaneously romanticized the timeless beauty of oases while decrying farmers' inability to modernize (Battesti 2005; Bencherifa and Popp 1990). These narratives carried into contemporary discourses I encountered during my fieldwork. One agricultural extension agent declared to me: "You cannot say that our farmers know agriculture; it is not modern," because oasis farming bore little resemblance to the technicist approaches promoted by state agricultural policy and the institutes that trained ministry officials. His characterization revealed a common modernist bias against smallholder agriculture. As in rangeland ecology, however, agroecological scholarship on oasis farming has critiqued dominant assumptions about productivity, experimentation, and the role of diversity in dryland farming. This literature details how production techniques integrate "cultivated, natural, and semi-natural ecosystems" through highly ordered, intense cropping and the active management rather than suppression of microenvironmental variation—an effective form of risk management in these uncertain agroecologies (Ater and Hmimsa 2008, 107; Brookfield 2001; Jennan 1986). These analyses acknowledge contemporary pressures on oasis farming, such as the long-term effects of disease affecting the date palm, labor availability, water scarcity, water logging and salination, and economic obstacles (Côte 2002; De Haas 2001; Fusillier, El Amami, and Le Gal 2009; Sedra 2015). But in highlighting the expertise and artistry in oasis farming, agroecological research focuses attention on oases as an agro-biodiversity hotspot that contributes to global food security and our collective agricultural heritage. That the United Nations designated the

North African biome more generally a globally important biodiversity site confirms what Moroccan and other North African scholars have documented for decades: complex farming and natural resource management systems not only have adapted to the region's challenging agroecology but also have helped to constitute the diversity of that agroecology in the first place and are crucial to its sustainable management (Blondel 2006; Koohafkan and Altieri 2011). I use these accounts of both transhumant pastoralism and oasis agriculture as a basis for theorizing how transformations of the previous half century shaped the agrarian rurality I encountered in the Mgoun Valley.

Tracing History on the Landscape in the Mgoun Valley

Signs of these socioecological transformations were visible on the landscape. When I first traveled the national road to Kelaa Mgouna in the early 1990s, I was struck by the apparent emptiness surrounding the oasis towns along the two-lane national road that wended its way through the dramatic geological formations and open spaces of the red-clay steppe.[14] I saw transhumant pastoralists guiding herds of goats, sheep, and camels across the road down to winter pastures. Occasionally, a man or elderly woman would stand on the side of the road, waiting for a passing car or taxi to provide transport. It was difficult to imagine where they could have walked from, but the visible emptiness belied the intense sociality of this space. Villages nestled in the foothills had long used this land to pasture their herds and as a gateway to livelihoods and social ties throughout the valleys that open onto the plateau. Now they used the road to get to market towns, the hospital, or their jobs in the city.

Every bit of this land was social, governed by diverse institutions that regulated land use for transhumant pastoralists and smallholder farmers. Tribal confederations, termed "ethnic collectivities" by the French, established rights of way for livestock and otherwise managed the collectively owned steppe.[15] Pastoralists have historically been the most politically powerful groups in the Moroccan southeast, with confederations such as the Aït Atta to the east of Mgoun asserting dominance over settled oasis populations. Although the Aït Mgoun confederation was loosely allied with the Aït Atta through a *tada* (pact) signed at the end of the nineteenth century, the relationship between pastoralism and oasis agriculture was slightly different in Mgoun, reflecting the valley's intermediate position between the more extensive systems on the edge of the Sahara and the transhumance dominant in the High Atlas Mountains (Aït Hamza 2002b, 11). In the Mgoun Valley, the Mgoun confederation settled along the banks of the river, with many households assigning different members to cultivation and transhumance. Like the Aït Atta, though, pastoralism represented the major source of wealth and prestige. A sharecropping system that indentured both racially Black and poor White Imazighen meant that few households could actually field herds on the range (Aït Hamza 2002b; El Manouar 2004). Mobility was still important to these historically marginalized populations, but theirs was not the mobility of transhumant pastoralism; many had fled famine, drought, or repression in other southeastern oases (Ennaji 1994). Such movements were not in the distant past. I conducted several interviews with people my age whose parents had come from the Draʿ or Ziz Valleys to escape destitution and seek the protection of the local saintly brotherhood.

Hierarchy is therefore integral to understanding the region's agrarian economy. Excluded through customary arrangements from owning land, subjugated populations were also excluded from full political participation. Customary governance among the tribal confederations of the southeast has been labeled egalitarian because leaders were chosen through consensus (Hart 1981). However, only racially White, male Amazigh landowners had the right to constitute that consensus. Black sharecroppers were indigenous and ethnically Amazigh, but not usually described as such even if Tashelhit was their native tongue.[16] A substantial literature dating from the colonial period traces the racial dynamics of southern Morocco through time and space (de Foucauld 1888; Ilahiane 2004; Jacques-Meunié 1958; Silverstein 2010). Although Morocco historically participated in the slave trade and enslaved people lived throughout the country, the indentured, racially Black groups of the Mgoun Valley did not have slave origins (El Hamel 2013; Ennaji 1994; Ensel 1999; R. Goodman 2013). They formed part of a heterogeneous social landscape, living among mobile and settled Amazigh populations, saintly Arab groups, and Jewish communities in arrangements that differed substantially from one valley to the next (Boum 2013). The racial hierarchies to the east of the Mgoun Valley—for example, in the Ziz Valley described by Ilahiane (2001a, 2004) and the Goulmima area described by Silverstein (2010, 2011, 2015)—were more rigid than Mgoun, which represented a transitional zone between the oases ringing the Sahara and the Atlas Mountains. The lower Mgoun Valley, in particular, evinced the racialized hierarchies of other oasis systems, but farther up the valley, White Imazighen were also indentured by the powerful families that mediated between the confederations, the central sultanate, the *qaʾid*s (customary leaders who transitioned to become Ministry of Interior representatives post-independence) who served as agents for the French Protectorate, and the modern state.

These relations of inequality and repression formed the backdrop to the region's variable relationship with a central government since chroniclers first described the pre-Saharan oases in the early Islamic period. Although few mentions of the Dadès and Mgoun Valleys appear in written sources, the region has a cosmopolitan history (Dunn 1977). The Moroccan southeast has figured importantly in the political and economic life of the sultanate for over a millennium: in the seventh century, silver from the Imider mine 150 kilometers to the east of Kelaa was minted as currency, the region was an important staging point for the trans-Saharan trade, and the Tafilalt oasis is the natal home of the current dynasty (El Manouar 2004; Rivet 2012). Although the Aït Mgoun's origins are obscure, the Aït Sedrate tribal confederation surrounding the Mgoun Valley moved into the region over five centuries ago under the mantle of Moulay Idriss, the founder of the current Alawi dynasty; the Aït Sedrate have subsequently been known as a "makzhan tribe" (Aït Hamza 2002a). Even if the region was never directly ruled by the sultan, then, ties with the central government were both thick and contested. Tribal confederations exercised sovereignty over land and people, but this sovereignty was not completely independent of the central government (Bouderbala 1996). Thus, when the French Protectorate elevated the brutal Glaoua qa'ids to serve as their proxy rulers, it was not the first time that agents repressed local populations for the benefit of external actors. French colonial ambitions did, however, elicit fierce resistance from tribal confederations in the region.[17] The 1933 battle of Bougafer, when the French defeated the Aït Atta tribal confederation in the last resistance to colonial rule, took place two full decades after the protectorate was established.

Southeastern Moroccans' efforts to assert autonomy continued in various forms during and after the protectorate. Just after independence, an armed insurrection in the southeast challenged the newly consolidated power of King Mohamed V, one of several rural uprisings around the country that brought a severe military response (Hart 2000; Leveau 1985; Silverstein 2011). Since then, an authoritarian monarchy that alternately uses patronage and violence to pacify rural zones has elicited popular resistance (Hammoudi 1997). In a valley near Mgoun, for example, I learned from acquaintances how a popular uprising against the king during the 1960s precipitated a pass system that, much like the colonial era, required residents to receive official permission to travel beyond the valley. That system was only revoked in the early 1990s. In the contemporary period, land conflicts figured in regional political dynamics both as an object and an idiom of protest, although disaffection with central government control did not produce demands for territorial sovereignty or autonomy in a formal sense. Rather, protests took various forms that challenged national land tenure policy, decried the lack of economic investment, or denounced restrictions on political expression and representation.

These protests have at various times and places been framed as struggles for Amazigh rights, but their claims cannot be characterized as a straightforward indigenous rights movement. This is in part a reflection of the changing relationship between Imazighen and Arabs throughout Moroccan history.[18] It is, for example, difficult to quantify the Amazigh population when the definition of the category itself is so historically specific; Amazigh identity has been variously understood as an ethnic, political, linguistic, or cultural category ordering identities and social formations in different ways (McDougall 2010). Estimates of the percentage of the Moroccan population who use an Amazigh language in their daily life range from 30 to 50 percent, but this obscures the diversity of linguistic and other cultural practices that may make one identify as Amazigh (Maddy-Weitzman 2011). Colonial taxonomies aimed for pure distinctions between Arab and Berber, writing cultural and religious differences into the legal code and famously sparking the formalization of anticolonial resistance into a nationalist movement in the early 1930s (Berque 1962; Joffé 1985). Nationalist ideological commitments of cultural and religious unity subsequently suppressed the expression of Amazigh identity as a component of Moroccan national identity. In the postindependence period, predominantly Amazigh areas have been marginalized through the Arabization of government and education, low economic investment, and political erasure (Maddy-Weitzman 2011). These areas, which are significantly poorer and politically repressed because of historical resistance against the central government, map onto the rural periphery (Hoffman and Miller 2010). While there is debate about whether Imazighen experience discrimination because of their Amazigh identity or their rurality, Amazigh rights groups have expanded their demands for cultural recognition to include more explicit claims for political rights and investment in rural zones (Feliu 2004).

Although the Mgoun Valley was decidedly Amazigh, social movements were not politically prominent in the region. Mgounis themselves described to me how the Dadès and Todgha Valleys to the east were more politically active in the Amazigh movement because they were wealthier and had more college graduates. People often learned the language of indigenous rights at universities in urban centers, and few residents in the Mgoun Valley had access to higher education (Crawford 2005; Feliu 2004). Claims for Amazigh cultural recognition and other rights were therefore more pronounced elsewhere, even if many youth and civil servants in the Mgoun Valley expressed admiration for the activism of Goulmima, Tinghir, and the Todgha Valley (Silverstein 2010, 2011). For the people I knew, Amazigh identity was self-evident, experienced more as habitus than as an explicit cultural identity or political commitment defined in opposition to Arabness (Ilahiane 2001a). While Amazigh identity may not have motivated political resistance in overt ways, residents of the valley were well aware of their historical subjugation at the hands of the state and of traditional elites. One farmer I knew in el Harte encapsulated this relationship with state: "We only see the state once every ten years, and when it comes, all it does is take and take and take." A similar suspicion was reserved for the rural notables who had repressed sharecroppers and served as agents for external patrons or the sultanate.

Uneven Development in the Rural Southeast

These histories of repression meant that when the opportunity to migrate to Europe presented itself to residents in the Mgoun Valley, many people were eager to take the risk. In the early 1960s, a French labor recruiter enlisted thousands of single men from throughout rural Morocco to work in French and other European coal mines (de Haas 2009; Iskander 2010).[19] Nearly eighty thousand men from the rural southeast joined this labor exodus at the same time that domestic migration to urban Morocco became an important economic outlet for this chronically poor region (de Haas 2005; de Haas and Plug 2006; Gallina 2006). Beginning in the 1970s, migration remittances from France, the Netherlands, and Belgium (with Spain and Italy becoming significant destinations only since the 1990s) became an important source of income, representing a diversification of livelihood activity in and of themselves but also financing new forms of diversification, such as small-scale commercial agricultural production, small businesses, new transportation networks, and other commercial activity centered on the market towns (Aït Hamza 1993). By the 1990s, migration had become pervasive, with most households sending at least one member to work in urban Morocco; a smaller but wealthier minority had access to higher, consistent remittances from jobs in Europe.

Beyond migration, however, a range of factors transformed rural life in the region. The expansion of state power into rural Morocco, integration of the region into the larger economy and into international markets, and capitalist transformation of the agricultural sector all shaped the direction of change in Mgoun. Commoditization and the legacy of colonial policies restricting pastoral mobility meant that after the severe drought of the 1990s many pastoralist households were no longer able to continue livestock production as their primary livelihood (D. Davis 2007; Gertel and Breuer 2007). Although villages along the Mgoun River had enough water to sustain their populations through a combination of wage labor, cultivation, and transhumance (although fewer households fielded herds on the range), the neighboring Imaghran confederation was more geographically isolated and experienced more severe, lasting effects from the drought. In the 1990s, Imaghranis began to move down to the steppe in large numbers to be closer to wage-labor opportunities. These households tended to be smaller and depended almost exclusively on unskilled wage labor either in the region or in urban Morocco. With no native land rights in the steppe (because they were not from Aït

Mgoun or Aït Sedrate, the other major tribal confederation in the region), these new arrivals had to purchase land to build housing but could rarely access land for agriculture. Despite this limited access, most households engaged in some farming, even if it meant planting just a few olive and almond trees in a kitchen garden, a practice that offered economic benefits and deepened claims to the land.

These changes remade the landscape that surrounded the national road I initially traveled in the early 1990s. Taking that road again in 2010 to begin my field research, I saw the same landscape dotted with small patches of green where people had found a water source close enough to the surface to sink a well, build a house, and plant crops. Approaching Kelaa Mgouna, these irregular attempts to settle in collective lands gave way to two commercial farms visible from the road. These farms were known as *firmas*, a derivation of the French word *ferme* (farm), although here it connoted a type of commercial holding that used "modern" agricultural techniques. The road became almost suburban after that. It was hard to distinguish where one village ended and the next began with the agglomeration of houses, gas stations, and tourist cafés that gravitated to the national road. The agricultural fields seemed crowded out by the sprawling expanse of adobe and cement housing compounds extending into the steppe. At Kelaa Mgouna, the national road became the de facto town plaza, as people from surrounding villages and new housing tracts vied with the cars, trucks, and buses just passing through. Children made their way to school on the road, women walked in groups to the health center, men rode into town on bicycles or motor scooters, and donkeys carried produce to market. On the road that broke off the main artery to carry goods and people into the mountains, other landscape changes came into view (figure 5). The angled turns of the road revealed villages clinging to steep riverbanks, but the empty hillsides and plateaus I had seen in the early 1990s were not so empty anymore. Piles of dried brush collected for cooking fires dotted the landscape outside the domestic compounds. Adobe walls marked off large geometric enclosures with no construction inside, while villages with room to grow were ringed by newly constructed homes with small gardens and young tree plantings. In villages dividing their collectively owned lands, the household allocations surrounding established settlements were marked by piles of rocks laid in regular increments, olive saplings, or newly pounded adobe walls. These actions on the landscape represented land claims—placing rocks or brush, or establishing use rights—and reflected new economic dynamics that valorized land for cultivation and housing around villages and the market town.

To government statistics and many of the officials who visited the region, however, the Mgoun Valley was an undifferentiated space of poverty. One of the wealthiest families I came to know in the village of el Harte still earned only a few dirhams above the national poverty line. By various measures the pre-Saharan southeast

FIGURE 5. Kelaa Mgouna viewed from the mountain road leading to the Aït Hamd plateau, with the abandoned qsar of the village of Mirna in the foreground.

Photo by the author.

continues to experience high levels of inequality both within the region and in relation to the rest of the country. Morocco is a middle-income country with such striking disparities that economic and demographic profiles consistently place the country in the lower third of the Human Development Index, a sensitive political issue in the country. In 2011, the per capita gross national income was $4,190, placing Morocco in the rank of 130 out of 187 countries listed by the United Nations Development Programme (UNDP 2011, 130). This statistic tells us little about actual income dynamics in the country: the government estimated that in 2006 the wealthiest 20 percent of the population earned 52.6 percent of total income, while the poorest 20 percent of the population earned only 5.4 percent (Royaume du Maroc 2006, 147). Beyond income disparities, however, inequality is marked by lack of access to basic infrastructure, services, and employment in rural areas.

The tenacity of this inequality began to worry the government when the structural adjustment program initiated in the 1980s ushered in a period of increasing poverty and low growth. Morocco's adjustment measures were typical: subsidy cuts, fiscal austerity, reduced income supports, and privatization of state-owned companies, to name a few. As in many other countries, the policies—combined with other grievances—spurred political unrest and did little to address the structural roots of Morocco's inequalities: the economic primacy of the littoral plains, wealth concentration among the monarchy and a small group of elite families, and the bifurcated structure of Moroccan agriculture. The 1990s continued this pattern. Unemployment remained high, successive droughts depressed agricultural production, and falling phosphate prices reduced foreign exchange receipts, among other pressures (Royaume du Maroc 2006). It became clear to national policymakers that persistent poverty and the tendency of economic growth to track high rainfall years meant the status quo would increase economic and political instability (Royaume du Maroc 2006, 8; World Bank 2006, 2). The entrenched interests of an elite centered in the Casablanca-Rabat corridor, however, led to a growth strategy that in the years 2000–2009 focused on further liberalization, high-value export agriculture, and tourism, a strategy with few prospects for addressing persistent poverty, especially in rural areas (Akesbi, Benatya, and el Aoufi 2008). Despite this, rural areas have remained an object of concern and intervention, as government efforts to track the spatiality of poverty rendered the rural hinterlands legible to national poverty programming (Marei et al. 2018). In 2007, the government developed a poverty map by combining census data with the results of the Household Living Standards Measurement Survey (Litvack 2007). Ouarzazate province (in which Kelaa Mgouna was included before being redistricted as part of Tinghir province in 2010) was the sixth-poorest province (of sixty-one), registering a poverty rate of 18 percent; two of the poorer provinces were also in the southeast (Zagora and Tata), while the remaining three were in the northern Rif Mountains, another historically marginalized rural enclave (Royaume du Maroc 2010a, 6).

The rural character of this economic marginalization has deep historical roots. During the colonial period, the division of Morocco into *utile* (productive) and *inutile* (unproductive) sectors bifurcated agriculture into "modern" and "traditional" categories, a discursive construction that continues to guide contemporary investment patterns and agricultural development. Massive irrigation perimeters were formed in the littoral plains around consolidated tracts devoted to mechanized agriculture, while rain-fed agriculture, irrigated oases, and pastoral areas received little government support or were actively repressed. This duality became more pronounced after independence in 1956 (Swearingen 1988). King Hassan's policy of a "thousand dams" inaugurated a massive infrastructural effort to direct water to industrial agriculture with "not a drop of water to the sea" (36). The policy benefited large landowners, not least the state itself, which became the country's largest landowner (holding approximately one million hectares) when it folded formerly colonized lands into state-owned enterprises (Courade and Devèze 2006; Pascon 1986). Beginning in the 1980s, Morocco adopted a suite of neoliberal agricultural policies aimed at privatizing collective lands in large irrigated perimeters. This internationally sponsored program intensified agricultural production, especially for export, in land primarily used for pastoralism. The agricultural investment codes of 1994 and 1996 demarcated agricultural development, pastoral improvement, and soil conservation zones that became subject to state control, including the obligatory exploitation or improvement of this land (Davis 2006). Additional laws (33–94 and 34–94) in 1995 aimed to create "the necessary conditions for an integrated development of a modern and productive agriculture" in bour and irrigated perimeters by making agricultural investments, cultivation, or other "exploitation" in designated zones obligatory (Van Buu 1995, 691).

Since the colonial period, then, the "modern" and "traditional" sectors were reified along spatial lines, with rain-fed uplands, mountain regions, and the pre-Saharan oases marginalized in agricultural development plans. This spatial differentiation was reaffirmed with the 2008 Plan Maroc Vert (Green Morocco Plan, or PMV), a comprehensive agricultural development program designed by McKinsey, the international consulting group. As one ministry official described to me, the PMV was "more than just a policy"; it was "a philosophy of governance" that included subsidies, public-private partnerships, and incentives to attract private investment into agriculture. The goal was to transform agriculture into the "principal motor of growth for the Moroccan economy" (Ghiche 2009, 2). Places like Mgoun, however, were on the margins of the PMV, slotted into the category of "solidarity agriculture" that involved modest support for what was deemed subsistence cultivation. The plan was designed without farmer consultation and ended up reinscribing the paternalistic approach to agricultural development in the country's rural periphery (Faysse 2015). Although only a small number of well-placed farmers in the Mgoun Valley had any hope of participating in the program, the PMV had implications far beyond those who actually received funding. The policy divided the national territory into agroecological regions from which new kinds of value could be extracted. It reimagined land in the arid periphery as a huge untapped resource to be mobilized for national growth, opening the vast collectively owned lands to new forms of valuation and investment.

Collective lands are the focus of this book, but they form part of an extraordinarily diverse land tenure system in Morocco, from mulk, *habous* (religious endowment land), *guich* (land historically conceded by the sultan to tribes offering military service), state-owned, and varying forms of collective ownership (see Bouderbala 1999 for an overview of Moroccan land tenure). The plural regimes governing land throughout Morocco are in part an expression of the sultan's historical practice of building political alliances through land concessions as well as frequent conflicts between tribal confederations. In chapters 1 and 3 especially, I explain the land tenure system as it was practiced in the Mgoun Valley, which did not have all the forms of land tenure (such as *guich* lands) present in Morocco. The political, legal, and agroecological dynamics surrounding these different

TABLE 1. Distribution of total land area of Morocco by legal status

STATUS	AREA (HECTARES)	%	MANAGING AUTHORITY
Collective lands	12,000,000	41.6	Ministry of Interior (Direction of Rural Affairs)
Private freehold (*mulk*)	8,000,000	27.7	NA
Precolonial royal concessions (*guich*)	210,000	0.7	Ministry of Interior and Ministry of the Economy and Finance
Religious endowment (*habous*)	100,000	0.3	Ministry of Endowments and Islamic Affairs
State owned (including forestland)	8,565,000	29.6	Ministry of Equipment, Ministry of the Economy and Finance, High Commission for Water and Forests
Total	28,875,000	100%	

Source: Banque Mondiale 2008, 6.

categories of land, and even within categories, vary significantly across time and space. Within land held by ethnic collectivities, land use and governance reflect diverse agroecological conditions, the specific history of each zone, and the economic value of land. Of the 12 million hectares of collectively owned land in the country, 10.5 million are rangeland and only 1.5 million are suitable for cultivation (El Alaoui 2002, 2). Table 1 shows the distribution of land area for each major category of land, along with the governing authority for that category, although this simplifies overlapping jurisdictions. In the Mgoun Valley, the dominant land tenure dynamics reflected a dialectic relationship between communal ownership at varying spatial and geopolitical scales and private ownership. Land could shift back and forth between both legal statuses, and the tensions over which authority—customary institutions as well as different institutions of the state—should govern land tenure framed many of the conflicts described in this book.

Overview of the Methods

This book is an ethnographic inquiry into the political ecology and economy of rurality in the Mgoun Valley. I weave together stories of the land and portraits of people's lives—how history shaped their possibilities, how they negotiated the politics and social complexities of life in the valley, and the ways their strategies articulated with broader processes.[20] My fieldwork took place over twelve continuous months from December 2009 to December 2010. I have returned for month long fieldwork trips every year since, occasionally returning twice a year. I chose the Mgoun Valley (map 1) for scholarly and personal reasons. Acquaintances from

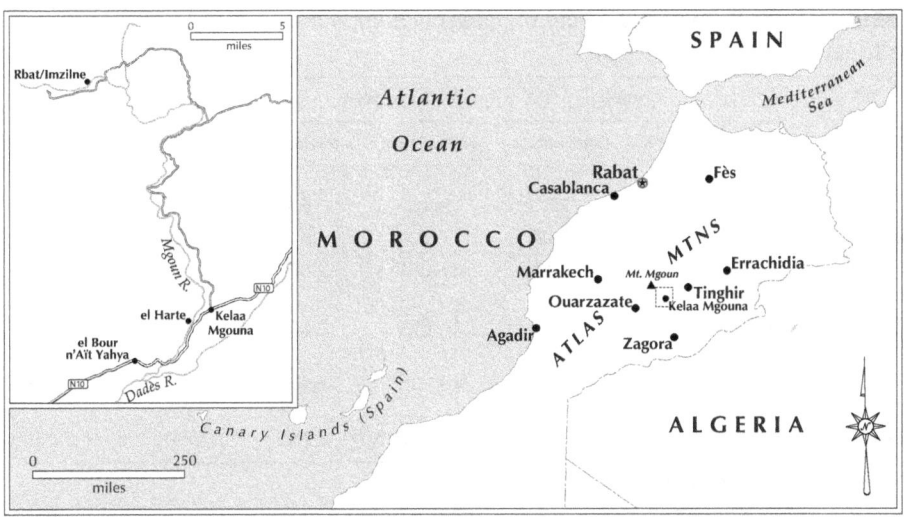

MAP 1. Morocco and research sites (southern part of the country truncated for legibility).

Map by Richard Gilbreath, independent cartographer.

my previous work in the region facilitated introductions to civil society activists and community leaders who welcomed me into their networks.[21] I began with key informant interviews with those leaders, municipal officials, local representatives of the agriculture and interior ministries, and civil society activists, among others, to orient myself to the transformations of the past half century: especially cultivation expanding into the steppe, a growing market town, and population movements into and out of the valley.

My initial interviews facilitated the selection of field sites in three communities, each with a different relationship to these transformations so that I could develop a regional perspective. Population statistics for the five communes (equivalent to counties) composing the Mgoun Valley and surrounding steppe are presented in table 2. Kelaa Mgouna served as a home base to facilitate access to my field sites, and I alternated time in each on an informal basis. I spent the most time and developed the closest relationships in el Harte, a village of approximately one thousand people adjacent to the market town and the epicenter for a localized surge in commercial agricultural production fueled by out-migration.[22] El Bour n'Aït Yahya, a fifteen-minute drive from Kelaa Mgouna, was the second site—a relatively new settlement of over five thousand people established in the late 1970s on the steppe. In the early 1990s, el Bour became a receiving area for intraregional migrants who had left higher-altitude mountain villages in search of wage-labor opportunities. My third site was the twin villages of Rbat and

TABLE 2. Population and number of households for five communes in the Mgoun Valley and surrounding steppe

	1994		2004		2014	
	POPULATION	HOUSEHOLDS	POPULATION	HOUSEHOLDS	POPULATION	HOUSEHOLDS
Ighil n'Mgoun	17,707	2,292	19,182	2,509	22,010	3,093
Aït Ouassif	6,717	788	7,591	855	8,238	1,134
Aït Sedrate Sahl el Gharbia	11,650	1,401	13,082	1,800	15,327	2,369
Aït Sedrate Sahl el Sharkia	12,211	1,565	14,864	2,110	17,376	2,856
Kelaa Mgouna (municipality)	10,524	1,672	14,190	2,438	16,956	3,171
Total	58,809	7,718	68,909	9,712	79,907	12,623

Source: Royaume du Maroc 1994, 2004, 2014.

Imzilne, located in the mountains an hour and a half drive (forty kilometers up the mountain road) from Kelaa. I considered them as one field site because, with a combined population of five hundred and fifty, they were intertwined through historical relations of domination. For hundreds of years, one prominent Amazigh family dominated the racially Black metalworkers of Imzilne, the poor White Imazighen of Rbat, and the region beyond. In each field site, I conducted initial censuses and introductory interviews as I began the participant observation typical of ethnographic work.

Participant observation served as the backdrop for extended case studies of twelve households, chosen to reflect different social positions in terms of their income or wealth, landownership, social status, and migration experience, among other characteristics. By collecting detailed information on family histories, landownership, migration experience, livelihoods, land use, agricultural practices, education, housing, assets, income, consumption, and expenses of a select group of households, I could use the experiences of specific households and contextualize those experiences to tell a larger story of transformation in the valley.[23] Three case study households were from Rbat and Imzilne, five from el Harte, and two from el Bour n'Aït Yahya. This distribution reflects the relative amount of time I spent in each community; the dispersed spatial and social organization of el Bour made it difficult to conduct sustained research with more families there. I conducted multiple interviews over many hours with the household head at the time and other members of his or her household and family. I also participated in social gatherings and occasional work in their fields. I collected reports and data from local and provincial government offices, along with contracts and manuscripts held by individuals and the local saintly brotherhood, although as I discuss in chapter 1, residents in Mgoun largely relied on unwritten customary law. Overall, I conducted over one hundred and thirty formal interviews during this extended fieldwork, not including the regular conversations and meetings with civil society activists, local officials, and other research participants that I documented in my field notes. My ethnography draws on these case studies, conversations, and the insights gleaned on the margins of my interviews. I bound the narrative with the past tense to avoid the problematic implications of the ethnographic present. I do not describe a persistent truth about the Mgoun Valley so much as account for how processes of change produced the conjuncture of social, political, and economic relations I first encountered in 2010.

I complemented my initial period of extended fieldwork with additional research using mixed quantitative and qualitative methods. From 2013 to 2015, I conducted a survey with 306 households in partnership with Yoko Kusunose, an agricultural economist, and the Réseau des Associations de Tinghir pour le Développement et la Démocratie, a regional civil society group. Survey households were selected through stratified random sampling; communities were chosen to represent the region's diverse agroecological zones. Within those communities, households were chosen randomly from each village association's list of households receiving potable water (which were verified and, in some cases, modified for accuracy and completeness). The resulting data include (1) *historical* details regarding the origin, relative wealth status, land uses, land rights, and livelihoods of households, (2) *contemporary* household location, income, asset ownership, land uses, land rights, and livelihood activities, and (3) *retrospective* data on large investments, spatial movements, and other major household changes over the intervening fifty-year period. Although I include data from this survey in the book, I resist the implication that the survey confirms or validates my qualitative fieldwork, considering the results instead as complementary ways of producing knowledge and interpreting developments in the valley. My ethnographic findings were essential to adapting the Haut Commissariat au Plan's household living standards measurement survey for our own survey in the Mgoun Valley.

Although my research focused on three rural communities, my residing in Kelaa Mgouna had the effect of turning the market town into a fourth field site. I observed how people throughout the valley interacted with each other and with the town as an economic, political, and social crossroads for the region. Kelaa is a municipality as well as the seat of a rural qa'id responsible for five of the surrounding communes. My fieldwork in Kelaa (primarily participant observation) was deeply influenced by the fact that I brought my spouse and two young children with me. It was in Kelaa that I waited with other parents in front of the preschool to pick up our children, shopped for vegetables in the weekly market, attended local municipal council meetings, chatted with women as we scrubbed our respective children in the *hammam* (public bath) owned by our landlord, and conducted the business of life with repairmen, pharmacists, bakers, electronics merchants, and the myriad other people who found their niche in this regional economic center. Some of these people were originally from my rural field sites, giving me insight into the multiple identities they enacted in their villages and in the slightly more anonymous environment of the market town.

Bringing my family with me for fieldwork simultaneously opened new spaces and placed practical limits on my research. My status as a married woman whose spouse and children were well known in town facilitated a social and spatial mobility unavailable to me when I originally spent time in the region as a young, single woman. This social status—and the fact that respected local figures introduced me to each field site—enabled me to interview men with little difficulty, especially since I always had a research assistant with me during formal interviews.[24] However, my social relationships were with women, and I would regularly visit female friends and participate in daily village activities, especially in el Harte. Most of these relationships did not figure in my formal interviews. I would assist friends in harvesting and other agricultural activities, accompany them to doctor's appointments, cook meals with them, clean wheat, attend village social occasions, and bring my children for visits. If having small children facilitated new social connections and insights into rural life, it also imposed pragmatic constraints. Elsewhere I have described the balance I tried to strike in conducting the work of ethnography (Rignall 2013). Family commitments limited the opportunity to develop my Tashelhit skills: I arrived in the region with Arabic and French but little Tashelhit, the Berber language that dominates social intercourse throughout the valley. Although my Tashelhit improved markedly through formal study and friendly tutoring in the course of my social interactions, I relied on assistants for interviews with people who were not comfortable in Arabic.

Plan of the Book

Each chapter of the book focuses on a different set of processes that shaped how people negotiated rural life in the Mgoun Valley and how their experiences informed a new politics of the commons. Chapter 1 introduces the three main fieldwork sites by relating how different groups' efforts to reimagine communal governance simultaneously drew on and challenged customary tenure practices. Customary land tenure was historically central to sustaining social hierarchy and defining political participation. As migration and other changes transformed agrarian rurality in the region, I argue that customary land tenure remained a key site for contesting these historical inequalities and negotiating new approaches to communal governance. In chapter 2, I broaden this account of rural political life to detail how state involvement in the valley sustained political pluralism as a central feature of local politics and social mobilizations. I trace how the colonial history of indirect rule shaped contemporary state strategies for asserting authority in marginalized rural zones. These strategies buttressed land and communal identity as the basis for rural governance and collective action. Civil society activists challenged this approach to state rule by adopting rights-based discourses that did not, however, have the same relevance for residents marginalized from both formal politics and customary governance regimes. These marginalized groups articulated an emergent politics of the commons, described in chapter 3. This chapter traces the genealogy of collectively owned lands in Mgoun to argue that the division of the commons might represent a new form of communal action. Throughout Morocco, there have been a wide range of efforts to divide collective lands among individual members of the ethnic collectivities or tribes that own them. Critical land scholarship has examined these kinds of divisions in other parts of the world as land grabs by outside interests or a shortsighted dismantling of the commons. I propose an alternative possibility: marginalized residents pursued hybrid private-property forms in an attempt to forge new kinds of "common action" that challenge assumptions about the death of the commons in the face of neoliberal encroachment (Harvey 2011).

The second half of the book relates these alternative visions of communal governance to different dimensions of the Mgoun Valley's new rurality, specifically environmental change, livelihood transformation, and agrarian practice. My aim is to show how the politics of the commons extended beyond a narrow definition of the commons to include the communal governance of multiple domains. Chapter 4 traces how different perceptions of communal governance produced competing environmental narratives about the causes and consequences of new land-use practices. Official discourses and development projects framed land degradation as the result of the decline of customary resource management regimes and advocated preserving customary regimes as "patrimony," much like a nature preserve. Such an idea was politically palatable because state territorialization projects had divorced these regimes from their wider governance roles, obscuring the political economy of shifting land-use practices and how residents reconfigured customary land tenure regimes to manage new economic and social imperatives.

Chapter 5 explores the profound transformation in the meaning and practice of labor—on and off the land—over the previous half century as the Moroccan southeast was integrated into capitalist markets. This transformation informed people's affective and economic investments in land, farming, and communal life.

I link an ethnography of work to agrarian practice, tracing how new labor relations simultaneously transformed and sustained the social reciprocity that undergirded moral economies in the valley. Rather than simply eroding the communal basis for Mgoun's agrarian rurality, new forms of laboring on and off the land represented sites for negotiating relations of dependence, obligation, exchange, and autonomy. The book concludes by situating a half century of transformation in the Mgoun Valley in global debates about supporting rural livelihoods and social life at a time of unprecedented political, environmental, and economic pressures. By attending to the quotidian complexities of rural politics and land conflict, this book also contributes to rethinking political agency and common action in rural North Africa and the Middle East.

1

CUSTOM AND THE AMBIVALENT ROMANCE OF COMMUNITY

Haj Hsain was an elderly notable who spent his days receiving visitors in a richly appointed salon overlooking the oasis gardens of Qlaʿa, a dense patchwork of fields planted with wheat, alfalfa, and a mix of fig, apricot, pomegranate, almond, and olive trees.[1] I passed by his home almost daily as I walked from the town of Kelaa Mgouna where I lived, across the footbridge over the Mgoun River, and wended my way through the village of Qlaʿa to get to el Harte, my primary research site (figure 6).[2] Qlaʿa had an imperious reputation only heightened by the haj's large adobe *qasba* (fortified residential structure) looming over the hard dirt path leading into the village. Before the French Protectorate (1912–1956), Qlaʿa was an important political center, producing the Amazigh *imgharn* (leaders, sing. *amghar*) that historically dominated the lower Mgoun Valley (Aït Hamza 2002b). The imgharn allied with the protectorate when colonial authorities placed a military outpost just across the river from Qlaʿa.

Shortly after establishing the outpost in the 1920s, the French proposed building a road through Qlaʿa and el Harte to support their military campaign against the last remaining resistance in the southeast of the country (Aït Hamza 1993). Qlaʿa's notable families, led by Haj Hsain's father, refused to allow the road. As Haj Hsain told me, the families did not want strangers to be able to "see our women," shorthand for their various concerns about opening the community to the inevitable flow of *idd barra* (outsiders). The notables were worried about outsiders' gaze compromising women's propriety, but they also wanted to shield themselves from the disruptive activities of the market and an emerging administrative center. Their power resided in the land, and so they worked to preserve

FIGURE 6. View of el Harte and Qlaʿa from across the river.

Photo by the author.

the physical and social landscape of the oasis as it was. The French accepted the notables' decision and routed the road across the river from Qlaʿa. That road now runs through the center of Kelaa Mgouna and remains the central artery connecting the region to the rest of Morocco's national road system. In 2010, the dirt path that would have become that road still wound through el Harte and Qlaʿa and ended at a wooden footbridge linking the two communities to the now-bustling market town of Kelaa Mgouna (map 2).

In the 1940s, the French moved the region's weekly market from el Harte across the river to Kelaa (Aït Hamza 1993). The growing garrison town had become the economic and political center of the valley, and the French wanted the market to be accessible by the road they had constructed a decade earlier. Noting the relative prosperity of Kelaa in the contemporary period, I asked Haj Hsain if he regretted his father's decision to oppose the road. He had no regret. His family had done well regardless of where they put the road. However, moving the market had profound implications for the majority Black residents of el Harte. Their livelihoods had centered on provisioning the market with bread, reed mats, hosteling services, and other goods. Moving the market removed that economic activity and forced many el Harte residents to begin sharecropping for high-status families such as Haj Hsain's (Attar 1994). The French had reinforced the political power of the notables, further entrenching a racial hierarchy that historically indentured Black residents to White Amazigh families in villages like Qlaʿa.

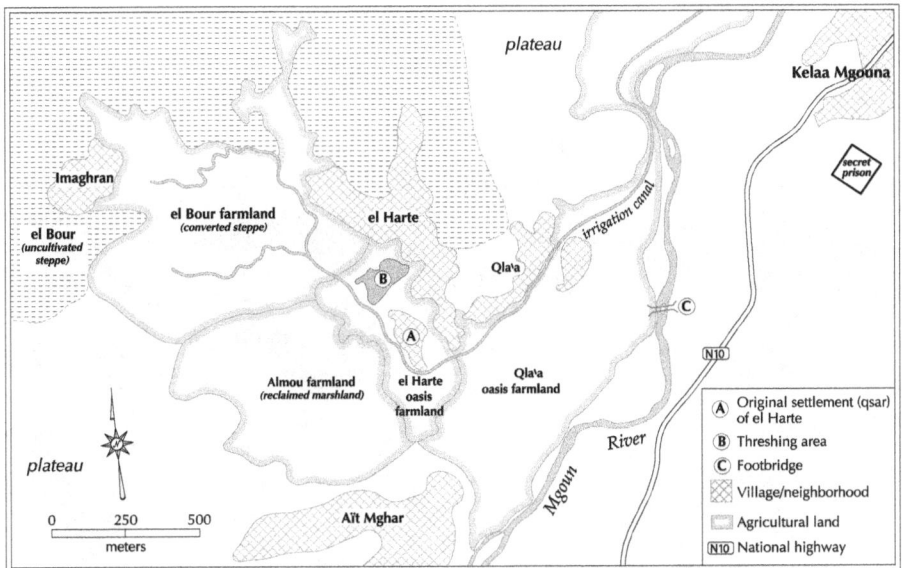

MAP 2. El Harte and Qla'a.

Map by Richard Gilbreath, independent cartographer.

By the time I arrived in 2010, this hierarchy had been upended by a series of changes that gathered momentum in the 1960s, when labor out-migration began on a large scale. These changes were evident in the daily rhythms on the dirt path that passed in front of Haj Hsain's house. That path was now crowded with mules from el Harte carrying produce to the weekly market across the river. The mules, laden with cilantro, turnips, squash, and other vegetables, carefully navigated the steep incline down to the river and stepped across the rocky riverbed. The animals could not negotiate the precarious, wood-planked footbridge with their loads (figure 7). El Harte had emerged as a regional center for small-scale commercial agricultural production, and the footbridge hindered residents' efforts to get their produce to the market in Kelaa. Since the early 1990s, el Harte's residents had petitioned government authorities to build a road through Qla'a and a bridge over the river to allow vehicles to cross between el Harte, Qla'a, and the market town. Qla'a leading families, led by Haj Hsain, blocked the road project. Several people in el Harte told me that those families *said* they did not want outsiders to "see their women," echoing debates about the French road nearly a century before. El Hartis asserted, however, that leaders in Qla'a really did "not want to see Black people from el Harte passing in front of their homes." As one man surmised: "They do not want to see us move forward. They are jealous of our success and they want to stop us, but we show them that we do not need them—that we can

FIGURE 7. The bridge of Qla'a, moments before being washed out by a flash flood, 2010.

Photo by the author.

be successful even without the bridge." The footbridge, and the narrow path that linked el Harte to Kelaa Mgouna, had become a metonym for the way social and economic mobility challenged entrenched relations of power in the valley.

This chapter documents what changed between the time Qla'a's notables rejected the French request to turn the village path into a road and the time, nearly a century later, when the residents of el Harte began to use that same path to transport their goods to market. The micropolitics of the path offer a window on the larger transformations throughout the Mgoun Valley. These changes played out differently in el Harte, Rbat and Imzilne, and el Bour n'Aït Yahya, reflecting the social dynamics of each community and the spatially differentiated possibilities for investing in agriculture and pursuing other livelihoods. Despite these differences, land remained a central object of political struggle and economic aspiration in all three communities. For historically elite families, land remained a source of political authority rooted in their traditional dominance, while for upwardly mobile families—many but not all of whom were formerly subjugated sharecroppers—land became a way to challenge inherited hierarchies and claim new kinds of authority. Each group invoked customary governance regimes to advance their claims. Their contestations ensured that customary land tenure and related governance institutions would become more, not less, important as the region's political economy was transformed.

By considering the different ways residents of the valley invoked customary tenure in their struggles over collective life, I complicate a common perception that integration into capitalist markets represents a "powerful solvent of the ties that connect locale and 'community'" (Bernstein and Woodhouse 2001, 319). Community as a sociospatial construct facilitating the governance of people, resources, and land did not dissolve in the valley, but it did not show straightforward continuity with the past either. In refiguring customary governance institutions, community became an "expression of modern rule" that shaped the political and social dimensions of the commoning practices I describe in the second half of the book (Watts 2004, 197). Customary land governance was central to defining community membership and how emerging markets for land and labor would be integrated into a changing rural landscape. Customary tenure was also the basis for a new politics of communal governance that oriented the local jma'a away from old hierarchies based on race and ethnicity but nonetheless erected new forms of exclusion based on native origins and economic privilege. Any commons, whether based on the collective management of a natural resource or the more expansive commons described in this book's introduction, operates in a complex legal and political field that informs how different groups assert power and legitimacy. In what follows, I provide an overview of customary governance, especially as it relates to land tenure, in the Mgoun Valley as a way to introduce this legal and political field. I then trace how different groups in the three communities in which I conducted fieldwork invoked customary governance as they navigated the transformations of the previous half century.

An Overview of Customary Law and Land Tenure

When I began my research, I felt I had to find *the* document that served as the authoritative source on a given village's *azref* (customary law) because written sources are available for customary law elsewhere in Morocco (see, for example, Berque 1940; Ilahiane 2004; Mezzine 1980–1981; Skounti 2012). The presence of rich oral traditions in the southeast, where literacy rates were historically low, does not mean that written records were unimportant. In fact, low literacy levels gave the written word "almost liturgical" importance (El Manouar 2004). Many families in the region carefully guarded manuscripts, *rusum* (contracts), and other documents that could shed light on customary law (El Manouar 2004). However, written versions of customary law were difficult to find in the Mgoun Valley. This overview is largely based on oral sources (interviews with the keepers of that law such as collective land representatives and irrigation managers) and on published research that is itself largely based on oral sources. When I asked el Harte's customary land representative if the village had written down its customary law, he pondered for a minute and said, "Well, yes, it has been written down. I think we registered it with the qa'id thirty or so years ago, but I do not really know where it might be. That does not matter. We do not need to write it down. It is what we know."

Hassan Rachik accommodates the written and the oral in his definition of customary law as "the ensemble of constraining rules developed by customary institutions to organize the management of their collective goods" (2016, 23). This includes customary land tenure, "the tenure usually associated with indigenous communities and administered in accordance with their customs as opposed to statutory tenure usually introduced during the colonial periods. . . . It often includes communal rights to pastures and exclusive private rights to agricultural and residential parcels" (Food and Agriculture Organization 2002, 44). The breadth of these definitions underscores the difficulty of defining custom in formal legal terms; it constitutes an "archive of wisdom" rather than a delimited body of law.[3] Customary law has a particularly politicized history in Morocco, a legacy of the French colonial project of selectively codifying custom as a counterweight to the perceived dominance of *shari'a* law in predominantly Arab zones—a project that culminated in the infamous Berber Dahir.[4] As Wilson notes, however, custom may "accommodate a variety of distinct and potentially contrasting legal and normative orderings" (2015, 73). The French articulated a distinction between customary and Islamic law that most people I encountered in Mgoun rejected. They considered all their practices to be in conformity with an Islamic legal tradition that they did not see as static or defined authoritatively in distant centers of jurisprudence.

Beyond the framework of legal traditions, customary land tenure could also include practices and norms that had not been explicitly integrated into *azref*. The emplacement of collected wood in a communal spot in a village, land-use zoning, and emergent practices of land entrustment or exchange, among others, were not necessarily elaborated in customary law but nonetheless guided land access and use. These practices were part of *'ada* (custom) more broadly, what many people described to me as the "way we do things."[5] In general, different kinds of customary law had jurisdiction depending on how land was categorized, with the state playing an irregular and ill-defined role in adjudicating legal regimes. This diversity produced a legal pluralism that muddied the boundaries between three broad jurisdictions for customary land tenure: collectively owned lands at the regional or tribal confederation level, customary law as it was practiced within the boundaries of villages, and customary approaches to managing land within households, families, and extended social networks.[6]

Collectively Owned Land at the Regional Scale

It was a dramatic gesture that introduced me to customary land tenure in the collectively owned steppe spanning the southeastern foothills of the Atlas Mountains. Soon after arriving in Kelaa Mgouna, I asked Haj Ouchtou, the collective-land representative for the Mgoun tribal confederation, for an overview of land tenure in the valley. A commanding figure with one of the area's largest herds on the range, the haj had a rough-hewn face framed by a *razza*, the tightly wound yellow turban common in the region. His role as collective-land representative was to manage Mgoun's collectively owned lands, defending the interests of tribal members vis-à-vis the state and neighboring confederations. When we sat down in a café overlooking the Mgoun River on a clear winter day, Haj Ouchtou swept his hand across the horizon. "Our land extends from there," he said, nodding his forehead in the direction of the snow-covered peak of Mgoun dominating the northern horizon, "down here to the asphalt at my feet," the national road in front of the café that skirted the southern boundary of the Mgoun Valley. He had radically simplified the various land tenure regimes in the region for effect, but he was well aware of their complexity. By "our land" he was referring to the land collectively owned by the Aït Mgoun, a grouping of twenty-five villages that coalesced as a tribe or "ethnic collectivity" some three hundred years ago (Aït Hamza 1993). The shared identity that marked these communities as "Mgoun" derived not from an origin story of a fictive ancestor, as is true for many other tribal confederations, but more pragmatically from a natural resource management and governance structure that developed around their control of the Mgoun River and adjoining rangeland (El Manouar 2004). Historically, such management involved providing security and otherwise governing the vast steppe and mountain pastures used by transhumant pastoralists. The confederation, governed by a jma'a of "free," property-owning Amazigh men, developed access rules, negotiated rights-of-way, policed agreements with neighboring confederations, or waged war to gain access to rangeland, water points, or other resources (Ilahiane 1999; Skounti 2012). Access to specific winter and summer pastures was governed by rules regarding the timing and location of pasturing in the *agdal* (collectively managed pasture), the location of corrals along transhumant routes, and ownership of manure.[7] These lands were not conducive to private ownership in part because the agroecology of the steppe promoted flexible, extensive use, but they were nonetheless subject to highly elaborated use and governance regimes (Léfebure 1979).

Rules regulating rangeland use formed part of the confederation's historical role in governing other aspects of social and economic life. The Mgoun confederation was allied with the larger Aït Atta confederation, the famous last holdouts against colonial rule, and with their defeat, the overarching structure of a grand amghar elected from constituent fractions dissolved.[8] The protectorate retained many officials in existing government roles—the roles of qa'id and *shaykh* (superior to a qa'id) among them—while using administrative reorganization to orient populations to the central state (Courageot 1934). Existing mechanisms for governing territory were labeled as "customary" in the context of colonial efforts to codify land tenure as statutory property law, what Burke (2014) terms the "ethnographic state." The imgharn of tribal confederations were absorbed into an emergent bureaucratic structure as collective-land representatives whose role was now limited to preventing illegal appropriations of collective land, resolving disputes in the steppe lands, and vetting outside investors who requested allotments from the tutelary council established during the protectorate era.[9] Collective-land representatives at the confederation level did not have direct jurisdiction over communal lands within the customary boundaries of villages, where local collective-land representatives adjudicated the relationship between communal and privately owned lands independent of the tribal confederation.

Negotiations between village and tribal confederation authorities over who had jurisdiction were overlaid by the state's role in authorizing customary practices at the tribal confederation level. Many land conflicts resulted from or were exacerbated by the bureaucratic and legal ambiguities surrounding who had authority to govern collective land, especially the process of dividing communal land to be allocated to confederation members (usually households) of the ethnic collectivity.[10] I learned of several villages in the valley that divided their collectively owned land, and in the case of Imzilne, I witnessed the process firsthand. When I met Haj Ouchtou again later in my fieldwork, I asked him about these allocations of collectively held land to individual households that could then treat them as private property, although there were still restrictions on transfer and use. He answered immediately and definitively: "There have been no land divisions in Mgoun since 1980." I was puzzled. I had seen these divisions; there was simply no question that they did not exist. "No," he said, "we do not divide our land." I looked at my research assistant for guidance but knew by the haj's tone to press no further.

In a formal sense, Haj Ouchtou was right. To officially divide land, a tribal confederation needed to petition the tutelary authority, the Rural Affairs Directorate of the Ministry of Interior, using a procedure outlined in 1957 (Zirari-Devif 2009–2010). Historically, tribal confederations used different methods for periodically dividing collective lands for cultivation, use of forest products, or other usufruct rights (Pascon 1980). This diversity was narrowed to one homogenous procedure under the protectorate that was nonetheless rife with ambiguities, prompting ten clarifications in subsequent ministerial circulars into the postindependence period (Zirari-Devif 2009–2010). For one thing, ethnic collectivities, the formal owners of collective lands, needed to elaborate a list of *ayants-droits* (rights holders) who had the right to an allocation, a politically fraught process that also varied significantly among tribal confederations. When the Ministry of Interior issued a circular in 2007 calling for lists of rights holders in all ethnic collectivities to be drawn up, the provincial office in Ouarzazate reported plaintively that this goal was unrealistic: "Local authorities say [that drawing up lists] is not necessary, and the presence of non-natives in the region, transhumance, emigration, and other conflicts make the task nearly impossible" (Mousaif 2008, 2). The difficulty of developing a list of rights holders meant that many people opted for unofficial appropriations or allocations of land rather than attempt a formal division, even if, legally, "all land in the possession of rights-holders, with the exception of those divisions effected according to the law, are considered illegal appropriations" (2).

In Mgoun, land division was further complicated by the tribal confederation's status as "delimited," a form of title clearing. Delimitation involved the Ministry of Interior formally mapping the boundaries of a tribal confederation's land and resolving any outstanding claims or opposition to those boundaries; it was intended to serve as a form of collective title parallel to private titling (Mousaif 2009). The goal was to provide a legal basis for tribal ownership given that collective lands were not a formal category of Islamic law.[11] However, as of 2008, only 40 percent of collective lands in Ouarzazate province had been delimited (approximately 800,000 hectares out of a total of 1.8 million hectares), and only two out of the twelve delimited zones had their titles cleared (*homologuées*, cleared of all counterclaims) (Mousaif 2008). This was a higher percentage than national statistics: out of the 12 million hectares of collectively owned land in the country, only 2.1 million had been delimited since the original 1924 *dahir* (decree) establishing the procedure (El Alaoui 2002, 2). Mgoun had been delimited in 1980, but an outstanding claim from another government ministry, the Ministère des Eaux et Forets (Ministry of Water and Forests), had never been resolved (Mousaif 2008). The issue with this status, apart from the legal limbo, was that all land within the delimited zone was considered collectively owned, ignoring the approximately 3,800 hectares out of a total of 140,000 hectares in Mgoun that was mulk as well as the collectively owned land within the customary boundaries of villages (the extent of which is unknown), which did not fall under the jurisdiction of the confederation (Centre de Mise en Valeur Agricole 2010). The Rural Affairs Directorate was aware of this problem. Officials fielded constant complaints from individuals seeking titles to their land but unable to do so because of the legal peculiarity that denied official private title in a zone subject to collective title. The head of the directorate reported being "reproached" by the provincial cadastral service for absorbing village communal lands, rivers, and private property into the zones delimited as collectively owned, thereby impeding the cadastral service's surveying and registration work (Mousaif 2008).

What this meant for my question to Haj Ouchtou—how collective land was being divided in Mgoun—was that land divisions were bureaucratically impossible but in practice happening all the time. Although there was another established procedure for investors to request a collective-land allocation from tribal confederations, village-level land divisions or allocations proceeded without the collective-land representative's or the Ministry of Interior's formal administrative overview (Wizara al-Dakhiliya 2008). There were, indeed, no land divisions in Mgoun in a formal legal sense, but informal practice complicated Haj Ouchtou's mission as the Aït Mgoun confederation's collective-land representative. Although he extolled a sense of shared identity rooted in collective ownership of tribal lands, I encountered few other people who articulated this shared identity as readily. It was not that tribal confederations were anachronistic—they served as important cultural referents and continued to define many aspects of resource access and regional governance—but customary legal regimes at the village level played a greater role in determining land access for most of the people I interviewed. These tenure arrangements were distinct from and yet also entangled with the larger Mgoun confederation.

Customary Law within Villages

At the village level, customary land tenure involved collective management of land and water and rules governing inhabited, productive, and symbolic or ceremonial spaces. I learned about these rules walking through the fields and sitting on the edges of irrigation canals; each minutely defined space had acquired layered histories broadly known by residents. Early on in my fieldwork in el Harte, however, I understood that women knew the history of the land better than anyone. With detailed satellite photos of the tree-lined oasis plots in hand, I ventured with two friends, Fatima and Zeinab, and a smattering of young children to walk the land and mark up the photos with the names and purposes of each *hay* (neighborhood), as they called different land types. We took these photos to Lalla Rqia's home. She was the widow of a village notable and revered as a repository of history. Everyone knew that when Lalla Rqia was ready to receive visitors in the morning, she would open the bright blue metal door leading into her courtyard. On three separate occasions, we waited on the irrigation canal across from the door until Fatima and Zeinab had to leave to attend to their work. During those periods of waiting, they explained the rules governing each category of land. The fourth day, the door finally opened.

Lalla Rqia welcomed us in a courtyard enclosed by thick adobe walls, laying out a plastic mat and blankets for us to sit on while we cleaned the stones from a sack of wheat berries she placed in the center. She explained how each area of the village got its name. *Talburin* (a lot of el bour) was a section of land converted to cultivation in the past fifty years; *Amjad* (bald) was also in the new extensions but represented an area where trees did not grow well; *Igunan* (fields enclosed by walls) was an area of the village with plentiful water; *Idiul* was, well, "who knows what that refers to? It is just the part of the fields near the qsar"; *Taw el Harte* (below el Harte) referred to the cultivated zone below the main gravity-driven irrigation canal; *Taw targwa* (below the [minor] canal) was another zone topographically well suited for irrigation; *Idarfan* (terraces) indicated an area carved from an incline; *Imizar* were the fields on the edge of the village where shepherds from Ighil n'Mgoun used to spend the winter with their herds, a practice that stopped in the 1940s and yielded to cultivation in the 1980s; and *Igiz* (a lot of water) indicated a well-irrigated zone fed by a water source reputed to begin up in Ighil n'Mgoun (difficult for me to imagine since that was at least eighty kilometers away as the crow flies). This list is not exhaustive. There were more categories of land that formed part of the physical and symbolic geography of the village, each with its distinct social meaning and each embedded in rule systems guiding its transfer and use—regardless of whether they were privately or communally owned (Mendes 1988).

The jma'a constituted the locus of customary law and tenure regimes. Composed of property-owning, notable men, the jma'a historically held authority over most aspects of village life: resolving disputes, organizing collective projects and work duties, and overseeing land tenure. Despite an apparent continuity with the past, the jma'a I encountered reflected a markedly different social reality than just a generation before. The property-owning, notable men serving in 2010 were often poor or politically disenfranchised in their youth for racial or economic reasons or both. And contrary to idealized accounts in the segmentary literature, membership did not always rotate according to democratic principles; sometimes it did not rotate at all as influential families cycled through positions with pro forma elections (Montagne 1973; Pascon 1980). I was told many times that customary law was not as important as it used to be, but I consistently saw its application through the jma'a and other institutions. Most villages had an *amghar u igran* (leader of the fields; also called *bu igran*, boss of the fields), who guarded against theft of crops, residue, and even weeds, although harvesting residue and weeds from others' fields after the harvest was acceptable. The amghar ensured that rules limiting development or land improvements on each type of land were respected and imposed a *ghurm* (fine) for any infraction (Attar 1994). As in any legal system (formal or customary), some paid the fine and others used their influence to skirt accountability. Alongside the amghar u igran was the *amghar u aman* (leader of water or irrigation manager), who ensured that everyone kept to their *nuba* (turn) by irrigating their fields at the allotted time and otherwise respected rules for water use. Not every village honored these positions, but many did, especially those (like el Harte) that had seen a rise in commercially oriented agricultural production; for them, these customary rules were far more important than Ministry of Agriculture policies or directives in shaping the commercial dimensions of the farming system. Throughout the valley, customary authorities' knowledge of landownership constituted a "real land tenure registry" and was considered authoritative even though they usually did not exist in official documents or other written form (Aït Hamza 2002b, 34).

The jma'a therefore governed both collective and privately owned land within a village's customary boundaries, as well as usufruct arrangements on land of any tenure status. Most property in the oases—the villages and the intensively farmed agricultural lands around them—was mulk as defined in the Maliki school of Islamic jurisprudence dominant in Morocco.[12] The agricultural extension office estimated that in its service area (which included parts of the Aït Sedrate tribal confederation on the Dadès River), there were 4,300 hectares of mulk land out of 295,000 total hectares; the remaining 290,700 were steppe or mountain slopes (Centre de Mise en Valeur Agricole 2010). Individuals (either men or women) could buy, sell, or pass along mulk through inheritance. People were not completely free to dispose of this land as they pleased, however, since communal resource management of water, farming systems, and the emplacement of housing constrained people's land-use practices regardless of ownership. Each community was also surrounded by a *hurm* (protected space, pl. *hurum*), a communally owned buffer zone separating villages from the open range. These rangelands belonged to tribal confederations and were subject to the collective tenure regime described in the previous section. Although in theory, Mgoun's delimited status gave Haj Ouchtou authority over all the land within its formal boundaries, customary practice vested that power in the village jma'a.

These collectively owned lands in the hurm were the site of many of the changes detailed in this book: conflicts, new investments in cultivation, and new communal initiatives to govern changing demands for land. The approach each village took to manage its land reserve differed according to geographic location, social dynamics, and economic prospects. As I detail in chapter 3, villages had long allocated or divided communal land for communal projects or individual requests; customary law still subjected those divided lands to communal governance, and allocated plots reverted to the collective if a family abandoned or did not transfer that land to another native of the village. Some villages had taken the step of dividing what remained of their reserves among native households, while others had no communal lands left or decided to continue managing remaining lands communally. In the household survey I undertook in partnership with Yoko Kusunose and the Réseau des Associations de Tinghir pour le Développement et la Démocratie, we conducted a community-level questionnaire in eighteen villages that assessed the status of collective lands (these included the three field sites for my initial fieldwork). Twelve had not formally divided their land; among them, six had reserves that could be used for expanding cultivation, two had a hurm that was strictly guarded from construction or cultivation to preserve the village's groundwater supply, another had communal lands that could not be used for anything other than pasturing, and three others were situated on the river and hemmed in by other villages. This limited their land base, and the latter three villages reported no communal land left; two had actually seen five and two hectares, respectively, "eaten" by the river during flash floods since 2006 (this represented up to 20 percent and 15 percent of their cultivable area, according to the imgharn u igran, although I could not get firm estimates). El Bour n'Aït Yahya could also be considered as not having divided land, but this new settlement never had communal land to allocate. Five villages had divided their land under differing circumstances. Two had done gradual allocations over the previous decades and reported no collective land left; three divided land in a single operation. One had divided in 2000 and another two in 2010.

There is no official documentation of these divisions as they occurred through customary mechanisms without involving the Ministry of Interior or the tribal confederation collective-land representative. No one did formal surveying in the valley because of its delimited status; the only cases of formal surveying were in Kelaa Mgouna, where it was possible to petition for a title to privately held land because of the town's status as a municipality. However, customary authorities—and other residents, too—all knew the size of an 'ashir (local land measure equivalent to 1/40 hectare), customary boundaries, and the extent of land involved in land divisions. Among our sample of eighteen villages, the size of the hurm could range from just a few 'ashir for the villages hemmed in by the river or other settlements to two hundred hectares for villages situated next to the open steppe. The amount of land involved in the divisions also varied widely, from irregular allocations of a few 'ashir at a time to Imzilne's land division of six hectares in 2010.

However, the overall amount of land held in common by a given community was not as important as the lay of the land, availability of water, and types of activity possible on that land. Having a significant hurm raised the value of land in el Harte because of the potential for expanded cultivation, while the hurum of thirty-five to two hundred hectares in the Aït Hamd plateau or at the edge of the Saghro Mountains were limited in their alternative uses by lack of water.[13] Customary authorities were closely involved in managing land markets both in the historical oases and in divided lands—all land was subject to customary legal frameworks. Land transfers outside of inheritance had always occurred to a limited extent, but markets had only developed in the 1980s when the valley's economy began to be fully monetized and integrated into the national economy. Markets did not operate in the same way even in the limited space of the valley; land transfers and disposition varied according to the location and economic situation of a given village.

Customary regimes operated with significant autonomy, but the ambiguous relationship with local government institutions produced conflict as well. The central government never officially set the boundaries of villages; what defined a *douar* (village) was the assignment of a *muqaddam* (local Ministry of Interior representative), but the land borders between villages were known through custom, not official edict (Aït Hamza 2002b). The jmaʿa did not have official status as an organ of local government, but colonial property law did establish a position of *naʾib* (collective-land representative), which was subsequently formalized by the postindependence state as accountable to the Ministry of Interior (although unpaid and not an official functionary). This representative was charged with adjudicating customary land tenure, although the ministry did not specify any tenure rules and only in 2008 did the ministry publish a guide for representatives. The guide outlines relevant laws, beginning with the 1919 dahir establishing their position, and suggests best practices for using customary law to govern land tenure at the local level (Wizara al-Dakhilya 2008). In effect, the collective-land representative joined the amghar u igran and amghar u aman as a member of the jmaʿa, although he had a special mandate to preside over collective land, underscoring how authorities could move between and sometimes combine customary and official roles.

Legal pluralism in land governance meant that there was no systematic way to determine which authority should govern a particular situation or resource. In some cases, *all* authorities governed. In the village of Imzilne, for example, I examined an irrigation agreement between tribal fractions in the precolonial period; the agreement was renegotiated under the aegis of the local French Direction des Affaires Indigènes officer when conflict broke out during the protectorate. That agreement was reportedly archived with the state but renegotiated repeatedly in subsequent years—members of the Imzilne jmaʿa pointed to the reference document as the handwritten agreement kept by a village elder, not the one registered with the state. Agreements were often negotiated, sometimes only in verbal form, by the amghar u aman without consulting the ministry at all. Even with this autonomy, customary law never occupied a separate legal or political space but always worked in relation to other sources of authority, whether they were elected officials or the local Ministry of Interior.

Customary Law as Mediated by Households and Social Networks

The customary legal and tenure regimes that operated at the regional and village levels were always mediated through families, households, lineages, and other social formations. One did not experience a right or exclusion as an isolated individual but as a gendered member of larger social and familial networks. Although women were often represented as guardians of custom, especially for men who had migrated and developed a nostalgic imaginary of the tamazirt (Hoffman 2007), they were among the most mobile and disenfranchised groups. Women shifted households upon marriage, which could involve moving across the village, the valley, or beyond. In a patrilineal system, such movement did not threaten continuity in lineages as social identity and property largely passed through the male line. Land, however, challenged this unity between the male line and the transmission of property (Crawford 2008). If women leave their natal village or become part of another family line, how can they maintain landed property without eroding their natal family's holdings or social status? Historically, customary inheritance practices in the region resolved this dilemma by not distributing land to women, in formal contravention of Islamic law, which holds that daughters should receive half the allotment given to sons. Nor did women inherit livestock. The dominant patrilineal system also meant that women gained access to collectively owned resources through their membership in a male-headed household or lineage and did not themselves qualify as ayants-droits in collective land. These exclusions have, since midway through the first decade of the twenty-first century, produced a national movement of women demanding change in how members of a confederation or tribe are defined and claiming their rights to land and resources, although this movement has not been active in the Mgoun Valley (Aït Mous and Berriane 2016; Berriane and Rignall 2017). When I asked customary authorities about how they handled inheritance, they stated that in the past women may not have received their inheritance, but people now followed Islamic law and ensured women received their inheritance.

Customary law as living practice, however, complicated this image of a seamless transition from custom to Islamic orthodoxy. Many women did receive their inheritance, but households and families represented sites for manipulating legal regimes for the transfer and control of resources (Crawford 2003). Few people would outline these strategies to me explicitly, but they became apparent over the course of my fieldwork. The same day Fatima, Zeinab, and I finished gathering information about place-names from Lalla Rqia, we made our way back to the center of the village on the main path linking el Harte to Kelaa and the weekly market. We encountered Safiyya, an elderly and much-loved divorced woman, leading a plump goat on a rope leash. We each took turns kissing her hand in the usual greeting for older women, but Fatima hardly waited for the greetings to be over before asking about the goat. Safiyya explained that she purchased it for 900 dirhams from the weekly market with money she saved from washing clothes and working in the fields of other el Harte residents. When she had divorced some years ago, she did not want to return to her brothers' house. She would have lived well as they were a prominent family and willing to accept her back into her natal home, but she was older and wanted to remain on her own. Fatima and Zeinab later described how el Harte was an easy, or at least easier, place to live if you were a woman alone because if you wanted to work, people would find ways to employ you. Few people had the money to hire others to do their laundry, but this was understood as a way of helping Safiyya and many made an effort to include her in their agricultural work parties or in occasional tasks, like the annual washing of blankets in the river—a huge collective operation. People sympathized with her not just because they cared for her or because they still adhered to norms of social reciprocity. There was more to this story. Safiyya was due a substantial allotment of land when her father died, but her brothers decided not to "divide" or go through with the inheritance division as a way to keep their land together. They continued living in the same compound and maintained their holdings as one family, but for Safiyya, this desire to maintain the integrity of family land came with the price of her dispossession. The ramifications for Safiyya were marked and long-standing.

Many resented Safiyya's brothers for their choice. While most in the village lauded the idea of keeping land together after the death of a patriarch, the idea of impoverishing one's sisters to do so was broadly disparaged. One critic of the family told me: "Sure it was their right to do this, but you can see they are just using customary law to their own advantage. But they are powerful, and no one can challenge them." While many households decided to stay together upon the death of a patriarch (that is, not divide according to Islamic legal principles), inheritance transfers were still the primary way in which land was acquired and transferred. In our survey of the valley, 54 percent of households reported inheriting land.[14] Although households could acquire land in multiple ways, 30 percent of the total sample reported inheritance as the *only* way they had acquired land

(29 percent purchased land, while 5 percent received collective-land allotments, likely an underestimate because of widespread confusion about the official legality of these allotments or the desire to minimize scrutiny of the actual amounts allotted). Customary land representatives played a central role in adjudicating these transfers, serving as de facto probate judge as few families ever went through a formal legal procedure to preside over inheritance. When patriarchs did have a plan for disinheriting a family member or otherwise adjusting the standard inheritance distribution, they often began dividing land and allocating resources before their death. Death does not always come as planned, of course, and the collective-land representatives would step in to interpret the deceased's wishes for the estate in the context of broader legal injunctions. Women rarely spoke up in these cases of unorthodox inheritance settlements and, as a result, often lost out. Even conflicts over inheritance or land division rarely ended up in court; some were resolved through customary mediation practices, while others simply simmered for years.

This is not to say that customary legal regimes simply erased or excluded women. As David Crawford (2008) notes, even women's limited landownership influences how property moves across households and shapes inequality between lineages or families within lineages. Marrying "into" a village was also a way for outsider men to establish community membership and gain access to land—at least to farm, if not to own. Despite a rhetoric of social cohesion that tied community membership to native status, there were well-established ways for mobile populations fleeing political instability, famine, or other hardships to at least partially integrate into a new village (Berque and Pascon 1978). Upon marriage to an outsider, women would, in theory, retain ownership of their land but often de facto and then de jure ownership passed to their husbands and became part of the patrilineal family's holdings. Whether this happened usually reflected the social standing women built on their own accord in the village. One of the largest landowning households in el Harte was headed by a widow who had lost her husband in a car accident when their children were very young. Without any brothers-in-law in the home, she kept her family together on her own, using her deceased husband's other holdings—Kelaa's first photography studio among them—to finance continued agricultural production on their land. Even as her sons grew up, she was able to use her high standing and strong personality to stave off the division of her husband's assets. She joked: "My sons [now adult] work for me" on their consolidated holdings. This was rare. Women, younger brothers, outsiders, and other marginalized individuals often experienced customary law as a site for obscuring their exclusion behind narratives of family and social cohesion.

Customary Land Tenure, Landownership, and Distribution

This snapshot of customary law and land tenure hints at how customary governance mediated the transformations of the previous half century, serving as a site of contestation for different groups trying to secure their positions. On the face of it, though, customary governance seemed to have sustained a continuity in landownership patterns, with inequality remaining stubbornly high (table 3).

Landlessness here does not include the plot, often quite small, on which a household constructed its home. All respondents reported owning their own home and the land it was built on, an important social marker of rootedness that was within reach of even very poor households. The only rental housing was in Kelaa, although creative arrangements of "guarding" a relative's home or otherwise entrusting property did exist in rural villages. The fact that nearly 15 percent of households did not own land and that a further 56 percent owned less than ten 'ashir (a quarter hectare) indicates marked inequality in property ownership. Such a small amount of land not only made significant agricultural production difficult but also indicated a lack of social standing and served as a proxy for poverty more generally. Some of this inequality can be accounted for by the influx of migrants from the higher mountain elevations who could not access land, and indeed, our survey showed that mean landownership by households' native status

TABLE 3. Landownership distribution in the Mgoun Valley and surrounding steppe (306 households), 2014–2015

LAND ('ASHIR, 1/40 HECTARE)	PERCENTAGE OF HOUSEHOLDS	CUMULATIVE PERCENTAGE
No land	14.4	14.4
0.5–5	35.9	50.3
6–10	20.7	71
11–15	12.6	83.6
16–20	6.3	89.9
21–30	4.8	94.7
31–40	2.2	96.9
41–50	0.8	97.7
51–60	0	97.7
61–70	1.2	98.9
71–80	0	98.9
> 80	1.1	100
Total	100	100

Source: Household survey, 2014–2015 (author in partnership with Reseau Associatif de Tinghir pour la Démocratie et le Développement).

(indicating whether they had land rights) was twelve 'ashir for native and seven 'ashir for nonnative households (Kusunose and Rignall 2018, 100). This inequality also had roots in the hierarchical sharecropping system that historically dominated the valley.

To understand this seeming stability in ownership distribution, we traced landownership over time through a modified longitudinal analysis of landholding. We asked household heads to estimate their landownership at the baseline date of 1960 (chosen because it was immediately before large-scale migration to Europe) and then triangulated those data with other household members and with the amghar u targwa and igran at the village levels. We found levels of inequality to be broadly consistent over the fifty-year period covered in our survey, as seen in the Lorenz curve in figure 8. The straight line indicates perfect equality in landownership; the further out the curve bows, the more unequal the landownership distribution.

The distribution of landownership therefore changed little over the previous five decades. Our data could be interpreted as supporting a notion of custom as essentially conservative, preserving existing land tenure and attendant relations of power. However, the social reality I encountered told a very different story. Apparent stability in land inequality masks a remarkable "churning," with some

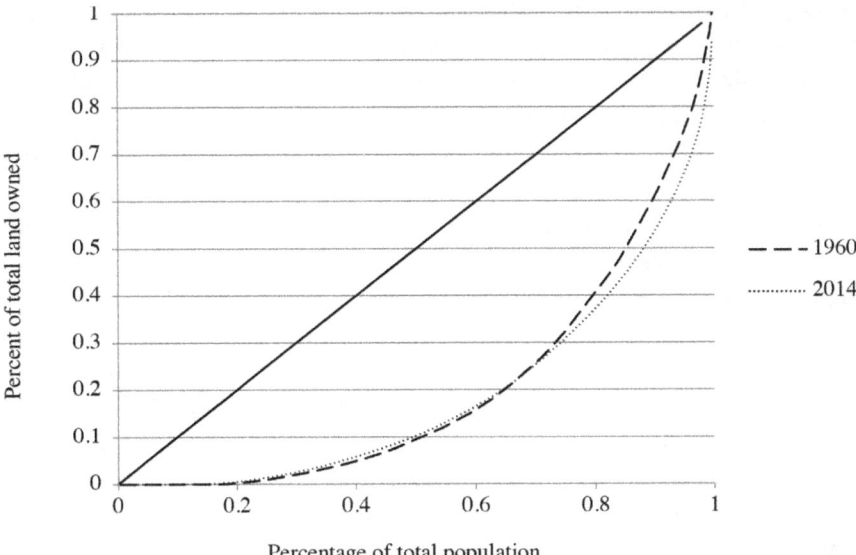

FIGURE 8. Lorenz curve of landownership distribution for 306 households in the Mgoun Valley and surrounding steppe, 1960 and 2014. Household survey, 2014–2015 (Author in partnership with Reseau Associatif de Tinghir pour la Démocratie et le Développement).

households acquiring land as part of their upward mobility, others selling or dividing land to diminish their holdings, the most marginalized experiencing continued land poverty, and the influx of new migrants not having any land at all. Customary governance did not shield the valley from the influences of new markets in land and labor, integration into the national economy, and migration remittances, but rather served as a site for either challenging social hierarchies or trying to preserve privilege in the face of change. I turn to ethnography to make sense of how customary governance figured in this churning in landownership and social transformation more generally.

El Harte: Migration, Custom, and a New Agrarian Rurality

Most people in the valley pointed to labor migration as the catalyst for the profound social and economic transformations over the previous half century, but el Harte was a particularly notable example. Although only six migrants from the village left in the recruitment drive that sparked the initial wave of out-migration in the early 1960s, their departures paved the way for other forms of migration abroad and to Moroccan cities (Attar 1994). These migrants did not simply find work elsewhere: they left with the aim of returning to challenge their historical exclusion in a place that many observers since the colonial period had written off as hopelessly incapable of sustaining an agricultural base. The emergence of small-scale commercial agriculture in el Harte indicates the important role customary governance played in managing the political and agroecological transformations of the migration era.

El Harte was a historically Black community. Residents had come from throughout the southern oases over the past few centuries, escaping poverty and subjugation to offer allegiance, in a typical arrangement, to the *shurufa'* (saints, sing. *sharif*) of the major Islamic brotherhood in the area, Zawiya Aït Ba 'Amran (Ennaji 1999). This protective but subservient relationship with the brotherhood meant that residents were not formally subjugated to the White Amazigh families from the neighboring village of Qla'a. However, formal freedom from indenture to Imazighen did not mean that landownership was a right most el Hartis could exercise. Those who did own land had very little because of their history as immigrants escaping indentured status elsewhere (Attar 1994). With small plots of their own and few avenues for mobility, they often still worked as sharecroppers or laborers for others. Haj Ahmed, the collective-land representative of el Harte and one of the village's most prominent farmers, described his own youth of desperate poverty. His father supplemented their meager agricultural production with commerce, buying peaches, figs, walnuts, sugar, and candles from itinerant traders to sell at the weekly market, which was then based in el Harte. As a young man, Haj Ahmed himself "worked for God and it was God who paid." In other words, payment was more in the form of *baraka* (blessing) for their labor because landowners offered so little: meager crop shares or handfuls of barley, wheat, or maize for day labor. In my oral histories, people in el Harte and throughout the Mgoun Valley emphasized the hunger and deprivation that many suffered until the 1960s and 1970s. Haj Ahmed echoed a common refrain: "We worked only to eat, and many times, we could not even eat."

With the advent of out-migration in the 1960s, sharecroppers began withdrawing their labor (table 4 presents household migration experience for the 306 households in our survey sample). Many used their remittances to buy land in their natal communities. Depending on its suitability for farming and susceptibility to drought, this land could be used for production, housing, or kept as an investment. In many parts of the valley, commercially viable farming was not realistic, but el Harte had more options. Proximity to the market town of Kelaa, abundant surface water supplied by gravity-based irrigation, and a topography favorable to extending cultivation into the steppe positioned the village to take advantage of a changing regional economy. Despite its overtly rural character, el Harte was essentially a peri-urban satellite of the market town, which offered a ready market for even small producers. Many migrants from the village used their remittances to buy agricultural land or otherwise invest in their farming operations. While they were away, they charged their families with working the land and even hired occasional agricultural labor, creating a local commercial agricultural sector and wage-labor market for the first time. Although migrants to Europe were a minority of those who left, they had an outsize impact on the regional economy

TABLE 4. Household migration experience for the Mgoun Valley and surrounding steppe, past and present (as reported in 2014–2015)

MIGRATION EXPERIENCE	HOUSEHOLDS	PERCENTAGE OF HOUSEHOLDS	INDIVIDUALS	PERCENTAGE OF MIGRANTS, INDIVIDUALS (IN THE SURVEY SAMPLE)
International migration	47	15	82	16, 4
Internal migration	199	65	417	84, 20
No migration	60	20	1561	NA, 76
Current migration	165	54	304	61, 15
Returned from migration	29	10	195	39, 10

Source: Household survey, 2014–2015 (author in partnership with Reseau Associatif de Tinghir pour la Démocratie et le Développement).

because they consistently sent back larger remittances for longer periods of time (Kusunose and Rignall 2018). Beginning in the 1970s, many more migrants started traveling periodically to Moroccan cities for work and they too sent remittances. This combination of labor migration and upward mobility provoked an agrarian transformation with far-reaching political implications that became apparent to me in the dueling historical narratives of Haj Hsain, the elderly Amazigh notable who opened this chapter, and Haj Ahmed, el Harte's collective-land representative.

Sitting in his salon overlooking Qla'a's oasis gardens, Haj Hsain recounted how he had established a farm in *el Bour*, the uncultivated expanse outside el Harte, when he returned from working in France in the mid-1970s. People thought he was odd to claim nearly eight hectares of land (a huge tract by local standards) in the uncultivated steppe surrounding the agricultural fields of the village. At that time, he added, "the people of el Harte did not want land—they were not farmers," eliding their history of sharecropping. It was common for families from Qla'a and other Amazigh villages to own land in el Harte with el Hartis serving as their sharecroppers. Haj Hsain himself worked his newly claimed tract in el Bour with the help of one sharecropper from el Harte, a desperately poor young man who grew up to become Haj Ahmed, el Harte's most powerful figure when I met him in 2010.

When Haj Hsain established his farm out in the steppe, he convened a lunch with el Harte's jma'a to propose a communal effort to extend the irrigation canal that ran through Qla'a and el Harte into the steppe. This was the customary mode of seeking permission for a project with communal benefits. Although the canal would flow through private land, it was considered a collective resource; and even if community members in el Harte did not contribute financially, they still needed to approve the extension. They did approve, but only a handful of people volunteered to join him in the effort. Only when they saw his success, Haj Hsain remarked, did people in el Harte begin to join him in the steppe. But by the time residents of el Harte started farming in the steppe in the 1980s, Haj Hsain's wife had died and he decided to return to Qla'a. He sold his land in increments to migrants from the Imaghran tribal confederation who had begun to leave the mountains in search of better livelihood prospects. The sale of such a large tract to outsiders evoked the ire of many in el Harte. They felt that Haj Hsain did not have the right to sell his land to the Imaghran and that, if he left, he needed to return that land to the community of el Harte, as customary law normally dictated.

Haj Hsain disagreed. He asserted that he had "*created* this land" by extending irrigation into the uncultivated steppe historically used for pasture. In his view, expanding el Harte's agricultural base was a service to people who did not even want to farm. He resolved to dispose of his land as he pleased. The dispute ended up in the courts and dragged on for years, long after the former farm had been settled by the Imaghran. The case was eventually decided in Haj Hsain's favor, a surprise to no one given his stature. The sale of the land to the Imaghran would stand even if the customary leaders of el Harte did not want Amazigh migrants moving into their village. The residents of el Harte had tried to invoke customary law to prevent the notable from selling land to outsiders, and although they lost this particular dispute, the long-term outcomes turned in el Harte's favor. Haj Hsain had not only created that land by extending irrigation into the arid steppe; he had created the land in a political sense by opening a new agricultural frontier and creating the possibility for el Harte's economic and political independence from the powerful notables of Qla'a.

By the time I conducted my fieldwork in 2010, the dispute had been legally resolved for years. People in el Harte still talked about it, though, because Haj Hsain's former sharecropper, Haj Ahmed, had become an important regional figure in his own right. He shared his own counternarrative with me in his expansive adobe compound. The compound had once been on the frontier between el Harte and the uncultivated steppe of el Bour, but by 2010 it was in the thick of a thriving agricultural landscape. Haj Ahmed described how his family was the first to move out of the *qsar* (the fortified part of the village that historically offered residents security, pl. *qsur*). Back in the early 1970s, Haj Ahmed tried to persuade others to join him in farming the uncultivated steppe, but they recoiled at the suggestion; he recounted other el Hartis as saying: "The steppe outside the village is wild, full of wild animals. You escaped from the security of the qsar. Why should we join you?" Haj Ahmed never mentioned Haj Hsain or that he first moved to the steppe as Haj Hsain's sharecropper. Others in el Harte explained that given Haj Ahmed's high stature, they would not expect him to discuss his previous experience as a sharecropper, a designation still tinged with shame. However, the sense of pride that Haj Ahmed felt in his mobility depended on a narrative arc that began with intense hardship and ended with regional prominence. Haj Ahmed was explicit about the oppressive dominance of Qla'a's leading families—how they had coerced labor from el Harte and other villages and seized lands with impunity.

Migration challenged the dominance of Amazigh notables without a direct challenge to the social order, subverting sharecropping instead of rebelling outright. Over time, migrants withdrew their labor from their overlords, driving up the share given to the sharecroppers from one-fifth in the 1960s to one-half of the harvest by the 1990s (Ilahiane 2001a). This is what Haj Ahmed did. Although he never migrated, all his brothers had. Their remittances enabled Haj Ahmed to stop sharecropping for Haj Hsain and strike out on his own, maintaining a unified homestead on behalf of himself, his brothers, and their families. When Haj Hsain stated that he "created the land" in el Bour, then, he signaled more than the literal conversion of land for farming. Opening a new agricultural frontier had inadvertently enabled the upward mobility of his former sharecropper and many others like him. Haj Hsain had *made* Haj Ahmed, not in the beneficent sense of helping him strike out on his own but by valorizing the land through which Haj Ahmed could construct economic, and eventually political, autonomy.

A similar dynamic unfolded throughout the southeastern oases. Ilahiane describes how racially Black groups in the Ziz Valley used remittances to buy land as "more than just a simple economic index of accumulation.... Land serves as the very basis for changing the political relations of subordination, as well as a vehicle to their emancipation" (2001a, 380). Former sharecroppers claimed a place in local village councils, contested elections, and otherwise used their improved status to engage in "various hidden and voiced forms of social struggle" (Ilahiane 2001a, 385). In the lower Mgoun Valley, the lead families of Qla'a ceded much of their political control when they began selling their land in the 1970s. Given the strong cultural injunctions against selling land and its ongoing importance for social status—only eighteen households, or 6 percent of our household survey sample, reported ever having sold land—these sales reflected the marked change produced by labor shortages. By the 1990s, households that historically based their agricultural operations on sharecroppers had to resort to a combination of family and wage workers when the last of their sharecroppers quit. As one former overlord quietly noted to me: "People find work in the cities so they do not have to serve us as sharecroppers anymore. The amount they make in one year as sharecroppers for us they now get in two to three months of working in the city." When the Imaghran began moving from the mountains into el Harte, some of the old Amazigh families from Qla'a hired the new arrivals as sharecroppers, an interesting twist on old social hierarchies. Black sharecroppers had quit, and while the Imaghran may have been White Imazighen, they were forced by poverty to work as day laborers or sharecroppers and became the lowest-status workers in the region's changing agricultural labor markets.

The residents of el Harte sustained agriculture as a viable livelihood strategy and remade the political landscape not by dismantling customary institutions but by appropriating them for new ends. Lunches such as the one in the 1970s that inaugurated Haj Hsain's effort to extend irrigation into el Bour were still being held in 2010. Community leaders in el Harte periodically gathered at the home of a petitioner who made a formal offering of couscous, *tajin* (the staple stew), and fruits from oasis trees as a precursor to a request for an allocation of communal land or approval for a project that had implications for the rest of the village. This practice joined many other procedures, rituals, and routines that maintained, and even extended, the reach of customary institutions into the social and political life of the village.

Customary institutions could become more, not less, relevant in the migration era because they offered an archive of resolutions to the challenges of managing such marked social change. For example, customary land tenure paved the way for small-scale commercial agriculture in part by setting the boundaries of the market and preventing the full commoditization of land. In the 1990s, el Harte's collective land representatives decided not to divide the village's remaining collective land as some other communities in the valley had done. Refusing to allocate the communal reserves to individuals as mulk protected the leading agricultural families that had begun developing freely allocated land in the early 1980s. They had paid for only a portion, sometimes a small portion, of their holdings and they wanted to maintain nonmarket means of land acquisition to preserve this low-cost advantage. This decision also buttressed labor regimes perpetuating the dependence of poor, landless family members or clients on their land-rich patrons. Large landowners benefited from land poverty among their extended relatives because it freed up those relatives to work on their land in uneven exchanges, a topic to which I return in chapter 5. The result was landownership inequality that was even more marked than for the valley as a whole, with 68 percent of el Harte households owning less than ten ʿashir, compared with 56 percent for the valley as a whole (table 5). However, the el Harte families constituting the land-owning elite had acquired their land only in the past fifty years.

In el Harte, this inequality was woven into discourses of customary governance that emphasized social reciprocity. One man described how el Harte "still does things the old way, helping each other and working together in the fields; no one here goes without food or work. We are the only village that really stays with our traditions in that way. Places like Qlaʿa do not want to work in agriculture anymore. They do not follow custom in the same way." But what defined this "old way" and who constituted the members of this community were contentious issues. The Imaghran, often referred to by native el Harte residents as the "mafia" for their reported insularity, were largely blocked from joining this community. The two collective-land representatives and the jmaʿa served as the ultimate arbiter of belonging, preventing outsiders from entering the market and undermining the dominance of el Harte's leading farm families. The jmaʿa would approve or disqualify private sales if there was a question about the status of buyers as *idd barra* (outsiders). This right of preemption was flexibly enforced—an occasional outsider would use their influence to skirt past the rule—but was still central to how custom simultaneously sustained communal sentiments and policed the boundaries of community. As migrants from Imaghran began to buy land down in the steppe, custom ensured these new arrivals could not participate in el Harte's

TABLE 5. Landownership distribution for the village of el Harte, 2010

LAND ('ASHIR, 1/40 HECTARE)	NUMBER OF HOUSEHOLDS	PERCENTAGE OF TOTAL HOUSEHOLDS
0	62	46.6
	Non-native: 44	Non-native: 33 (of total)
	Native: 18	Native: 14 (of total)
1–5	14	10.5
6–10	17	12.8
11–15	9	6.8
16–20	4	3.0
21–30	11	8.3
31–40	4	3.0
41–50	2	1.5
51–60	3	2.3
61–70	2	1.5
80	5	3.8
Total	133	100

Source: Author's fieldwork.

emergent agricultural economy. Although nonnative households throughout the valley earned a larger portion of their cash income from farming than native ones (a mean of 800 dirhams per year versus 140 dirhams for native households in our survey), it was as sharecroppers and agricultural wage laborers, not as landowners or entrepreneurial farmers.

These exclusions not only applied to the Imaghran; even residents who had been in the village for decades might not enjoy native status. I saw the continuing rancor this could produce when talking with Mohsin, an official in the Ministry of Habous and Islamic Affairs who still lived in his natal village. He was born into an Arab merchant family that had settled in el Harte nearly a century ago, and although he was clearly a respected community leader, he was always conscious of his outsider status because his family did not have a right to allocations of communal land. A normally restrained and quiet man, he became agitated when he told me: "The government says we are from el Harte. It is written on our identity card that we are from el Harte no matter what community leaders say!" The jmaʿa had denied Mohsin's request for a communal allocation to build a new home until friends with political standing pressured the jmaʿa to give his family a small lot where a half-constructed home now stood.[15] He resented the political battle. I asked Mohsin if he or the Imaghran would ever be considered *aït el Harte* (native residents). Shaking his head, he assured me they would always remain outsiders: "People here really hold onto the idea that immigrants are foreign while they are the people el Harte. That even includes me, which is why I cannot get the same land as my neighbor even though I have been here all my life. You see how I know our history, our entire village. Yet I am an outsider." The state may have said that outsiders were from el Harte on their identity cards, but customary tenure institutions still had the power to determine who could secure access to land.

This power ensured that community would operate as much to exclude as to bound together. The same man who earlier described el Harte's commitment to custom noted: "There is much improvement in our lives, especially in the spirit of our community. Before, we only thought of getting enough to eat. Now, we think about improving, about getting profits from our agriculture." For this man, as for many others, strengthening the "spirit of our community" and "getting profits from agriculture" were a complementary assertion of collective autonomy against the former prerogatives of the Imazighen in Qla'a. However, an egalitarian ethic did not necessarily figure in this "will to improve" (Li 2007). Customary governance secured greater economic and political autonomy for some by sustaining the exclusion of others.

Rbat and Imzilne: Scarcity and the Politics of Custom

The dramatic silences, expansive sky, and relative isolation of the Aït Hamd plateau (map 3) contrasted with the bustle of el Harte, offering an apparent foil to the changes the lower valley had experienced. The government was in the process of paving the harrowing mountain road that led to the plateau during my year in the valley. The asphalt stopped at the feet of a group of elderly men who gathered each evening at the entrance to the village of Rbat to catch up on the day's events. They looked small among the starkly beautiful vistas. However, the impression of isolation here was deceptive. The plateau was as implicated in the social and economic changes of the previous half century as el Harte, although the outcomes were quite different. Commercial agriculture had few prospects for success here. Water availability was a constant concern, villages were small and dispersed, and the droughts of the 1990s had made transhumant pastoralism precarious for the smaller herd owners who could not afford to truck their livestock to distant pastures (Gertel and Breuer 2007; El Alaoui 2002). Pessimistic narratives from colonial sociologists to contemporary scholars predicted the region would empty because of out-migration (Bencherifa 1991; Berque and Pascon 1978; Montagne 1952). The region, however, did not depopulate; in fact, migration enabled households to stay and contributed to the reworking of social hierarchies. As in

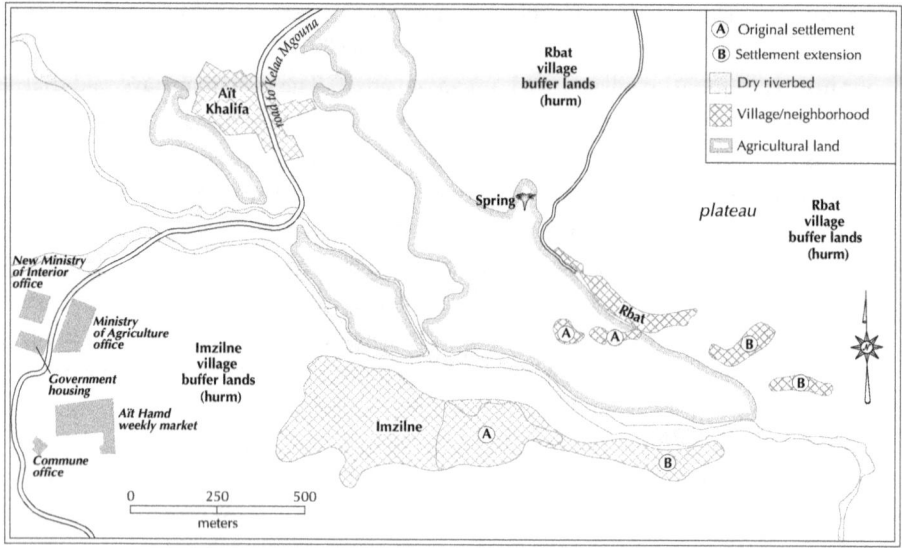

MAP 3. Villages of Rbat, Imzilne, and Aït Khalifa, Aït Hamd plateau.

Map by Richard Gilbreath, independent cartographer.

the lower valley, land remained a political flashpoint, with groups invoking customary tenure to advance their political and economic prospects.

These struggles represented a marked shift from the plateau's historical prominence as the seat of the Aït Zahirs, a family that had ruled as imgharn of the upper valley for three centuries. The political and economic orientations of contemporary Morocco placed Aït Hamd in the national, even regional, periphery. Although the plateau was no longer a political center, the Aït Zahirs remained powerful. Some members of the family had moved down to Kelaa Mgouna to be near the valley's new seat of power: the market town and municipal offices. The Aït Zahirs nonetheless kept a political interest in Rbat Aït Hamd. A family patriarch who had moved to Kelaa decades earlier served as commune president and traveled up the mountain road every Friday afternoon to spend the night in the family's historical seat and conduct official business at the Saturday market. The family maintained their fields and large adobe qasba, which had served as their granary in centuries past. During periods of famine, the family distributed grain from their vast stores and other times traded "handfuls of barley," as one man told me, in exchange for the land of the starving. The last famine occurred in the late 1930s, but memories of the Aït Zahirs' role in both sustaining individuals and seizing their land were still raw. This history of dispossession meant that others in the village often served as sharecroppers for the Aït Zahirs or lived in dire poverty despite their status as racially White Imazighen. The Aït Zahirs remained the upper valley's largest landowner.

Many of the Aït Zahirs' sharecroppers also came from Imzilne, the historically Black community of blacksmiths across the seasonal stream that fed into the Mgoun River.[16] Blacksmithing was the marker of an ascribed low status but also offered a certain degree of livelihood autonomy for Imzilne; community members kept their own plots to grow subsistence crops and historically traveled the region to serve their clients. However, they were excluded from transhumant pastoralism because of their marginalized social status and supplemented their livelihoods through sharecropping. This changed when out-migration began in the 1960s. Our household survey documented how four men from Rbat (out of twenty-one households) and eight men from Imzilne (out of thirty households) left for France, the Netherlands, and Belgium in the initial wave of recruitment for the coal mines. They had an outsize impact on the economic life of their villages. In Imzilne, these migrants became a lifeline for households facing dwindling demand for traditional blacksmithing. As overseas migration opportunities dwindled in the 1990s, virtually every household sent at least one member to work in Moroccan cities. Many periodically returned, some came home to retire, and others continued to support their families from afar. New cement housing, a newly constructed water tower, and the emergence of businesses around the weekly market indicated the extent of people's commitment to place.

As in the lower parts of the valley, migration eroded the power of sharecropping to indenture and subjugate large groups of people. However, the ways in which this process was racialized varied. Sharecropping was, in fact, widespread throughout Morocco—as in many parts of the world—and did not carry the same political valences across time and space, although Moroccan jurists historically expressed discomfort with the religious propriety of the practice (Berque 1940). The institution could also be a way of sharing risk and developing lasting partnerships in areas less associated with racial inequity (Pascon and Ennaji 1986; Robertson 1987). In transitional zones such as the foothills of the High Atlas Mountains, many sharecropping arrangements were not as clearly racialized as in the oases farther south and east (Gregg and Geist 1988). Migration was as liberatory for the impoverished Imazighen compelled to sharecrop for powerful families as it was for the racially Black groups who had been indentured (Pascon and Ennaji 1986).

This was evident whenever I spent time in Taleb's busy compound on the edges of Rbat and saw his obvious pride in the activity surrounding him. The son of a sharecropper, Taleb did not have the stigma of being from a racially subjugated group but still grew up in extreme poverty after his father's desperation sale of their minimal holdings during the last famine left them landless. As a youth,

Taleb had worked as a shepherd for a livestock owner farther up the mountains, a hard and isolated life that helped his family (he still maintained warm relationships with his former employer's family) but did not assuage their poverty. Taleb was seventeen when he left in 1969 to work in the mines of Calais, and he spent eighteen years there. He shook his head every time he described his work in the mines. Many of the migrants could not tolerate it, he said, and left after a few months, even days: "Every day in the mines was like being in a war." But his time as a youth alone in the mountains helped Taleb persevere, and every year he remitted money to his brothers to buy a plot of land or some sheep, building up their holdings in small increments. His close involvement in managing family affairs and annual trips to Rbat enabled Taleb to return when he retired and head a flourishing household with large landholdings, a stable of cattle, and a herd on the range. As we talked in the sparely appointed room where he received guests, his young toddler would frequently waddle in. Taleb affectionately scooped her up in his arms. Taleb's first wife had died, and so in addition to his adult children, he had four younger children with his second wife. He clearly reveled in his new fatherhood and expressed gratitude for his second wife's help in running their sprawling household. Taleb conceded that the work was hard, but migration had brought the family a level of prosperity he never could have imagined as a youth. He had achieved everything he had hoped for when he left for France in 1969; he had paid his dues during that difficult eighteen-year period, for sure, but he was happy.

The only time I saw Taleb's face cloud over was in talking of his relationship with the Aït Zahirs. Some years after Taleb migrated, the family's economic security enabled his father to stop sharecropping for the Aït Zahirs. Their experience of exploitation inflected Taleb's investment choices with a political calculus as much as an economic one. In addition to the land he purchased over the years, Taleb had acquired an equal amount by improving land in the hurm outside of Rbat. According to customary law, this was his right, but he recounted how the Aït Zahirs did not like his growing clout and used customary law to challenge him every step of the way. He made a formal request to the jma'a to extend the irrigation canal that issued from the village's valuable water source, a cement-lined 'ayn (spring) next to the Aït Zahirs' qasba. The Aït Zahirs used their influence to deny his request. They said the village spring could not accommodate additional water draws, but Taleb felt it was his upward mobility that was the real issue. He circumvented the customary injunction by digging two wells and installing motor pumps, which precipitated a physical altercation with one of the Aït Zahirs even though the placement of the pumps did not affect the spring that served as the primary water source for village fields. The enmity had continued to harden over the years and their personal conflicts ramified throughout the politics of the Aït

Hamd plateau, from whom various partisans supported in local elections to what infrastructure or local development projects people would support, among other issues. The Aït Zahirs could not completely stop Taleb—he remained a successful farmer and livestock owner—but their hold on regional politics had enabled them to retain their control over customary and official governance institutions alike.

The former sharecroppers of el Harte patiently cultivated a subversive power by claiming political access through customary institutions from which they were formerly excluded. Taleb's experience represented a more equivocal example of custom as a site of contestation. The Aït Zahirs had used customary law to try to prevent challenges to their historical authority. However, customary institutions were no more a relic, a holdover from a time of putatively traditional governance, in Rbat than they were in el Harte. It was, in fact, the increasing importance of customary land tenure institutions in the region's contemporary political landscape that made these institutions such a flashpoint between Taleb and his rival. When the colonial and then postindependence state bureaucratized many governance functions of customary authorities, communal land representatives were left as the most important political figures in many rural communities. The importance of these representatives increased as land values climbed throughout the Mgoun Valley, giving them often unchecked power over one of the region's most valuable resources. Land values increased regardless of the potential for agricultural production. In Rbat, the closely guarded spring sustained large canopies of walnut trees and two annual crop rotations, while across the dry riverbed in Imzilne, the lack of water meant that no one could produce enough grains to cover subsistence needs and vegetable production was minimal. Yet land was no less important there than in Rbat.

There may not have been enough water to sustain a vibrant agricultural sector in the Aït Hamd plateau, but there was certainly enough to enable households with access to external wage labor to maintain their tamazirt. Land was therefore important for housing and as an investment; it also sustained its symbolic meaning as a marker of belonging and political power. I began this book with an account of how Imzilne's communal land representative used customary tenure to challenge a decades-long precedent of land seizures from the historically subjugated community. Just as Taleb and the Aït Zahirs struggled over customary rules regarding the extension of irrigation canals, the village of Imzilne used customary rules to resist government land seizures and the history of domination those seizures represented. Hence, when residents of el Harte or the Aït Hamd plateau emphasized their commitment to customary tenure, they displayed a traditionalist reasoning as opposed to a traditional one. This reasoning recognized land as central to challenging historical forms of exclusion *and* to securing a place in the new political order. Even if other forms of customary governance had diminished, customary tenure had become synonymous with power in local politics.

El Bour n'Aït Yahya: Creating Custom Anew

Customary tenure institutions were important to local authority even in places where they did not previously exist. El Bour n'Aït Yahya was a new settlement, with no precedent of customary tenure to govern its diverse immigrant population. This made my own research challenging. Because el Bour had no clear social hierarchies or customary governance system in place, I could not use the same fieldwork strategy that I used in my other sites: having a respected acquaintance with ties to the community introduce me and vouch for my character with the jma'a. El Bour, I thought, would represent a counterexample to those communities where customary authority still held sway. In some respects, this was true. I met an elected official eager to support my work, and he took me to meet families he knew as possible research participants. They had few ties to other families in the settlement or to each other. If anything, they seemed to regard their life in the steppe as transitory, describing their jobs in the cities as a way to remain connected with family members in the mountains. No one described el Bour as their tamazirt even if it was clear they were never going home. Yet I found that even in el Bour, discourses of custom were mobilized to police and sometimes fashion new social boundaries. Rather than using custom to remake the social space of community as had happened in el Harte, Rbat, and Imzilne, residents in el Bour invoked custom to create community anew. Various groups in the settlement were working to fashion the social and political order I had found in other established communities by instituting customary leadership positions.

Like Rbat and Imzilne, the settlement of el Bour gave an impression of isolation even though it was situated on the open steppe only fifteen kilometers to the west of Kelaa Mgouna (figure 9). Because of the settlement's high-walled domestic enclosures and few agricultural fields, people were rarely visible in the streets and there were no common agricultural or social spaces, beyond the mosques, that brought residents together as in the historical oases. El Bour's silence was broken only by the call to prayer and the sharp winds that blew off the steppe and whipped through the alleyways between the cement-and-adobe compounds. An occasional clanging from a closing metal door only emphasized the atomized social life of the settlement. Four decades earlier, immigrants began arriving from the surrounding mountains. By 2010, there were upward of five thousand residents in the settlement, and it was growing every day.

FIGURE 9. View of el Bour n'Aït Yahya from the national road.
Photo by the author.

It was an accident of history that brought the immigrants to el Bour. Two tribal fractions disputing the land approximately a century ago resolved their conflict by ceding it to a local Islamic brotherhood, Zawiya Abdel Malik. The brotherhood's informal archivist, Moulay Taher, showed me the *rasm* (contractual agreement) that formalized the transfer. Formerly collectively owned steppe land used by transhumant pastoralists in their spring and fall passages, el Bour became the private property of the brotherhood, although the saints still allowed pastoralists to use the land. There was little else to do with it; it was too far from the river or existing irrigation works to bring it under cultivation. Eventually, the dwindling fortunes of the brotherhood's saints led the founder's direct descendant to begin selling off the land in small parcels to settlers arriving in the region. The relatively cheap prices attracted some residents from villages in the area, and they were soon joined by households from the mountains. Our household survey indicated the diverse origins of the migrants settling in el Bour: from areas in the commune of Iknioun (on the edge of the Saghro Mountains) especially hit by the droughts of the 1980s and 1990s to Zaouiat Ahansal (in the province of Azilal, on the northern side of the High Atlas from Ighil n'Mgoun), Aït Toukhsin and Aït Daoud (in the High Atlas plateaus traditionally controlled by Aït Mghad and currently in Tinghir Province to the north and east of Kelaa Mgouna), and Ikandoulne, Taoujgalt, and Kantola (of the Imaghran tribal confederation to the north and west of

Kelaa Mgouna). Those migrants were already leaving their mountain villages, sometimes settling in regional cities like Ouarzazate or Khenifra on the southern and northern foothills of the High and Middle Atlas, respectively. For many, el Bour was more appealing than these cities because land was affordable and closer to their natal homes.

Creating a settlement de novo produced the locally incongruous situation of strangers living right next to each other in a rural context. Many people remarked to me that el Bour was "like a city." Such urbanization of the rural had caused concern up and down the national road. Villages were gravitating to the road away from their historical concentration along the river, building housing to be close to the *goudron* (asphalt) (Aït Hamza 2002a). El Bour was an extreme example of this: an unplanned community where individual households bought land without zoning or other provisions for public services (map 4). Services such as water and electricity were extended when enough residents had occupied an area to make a collective petition. This put stress on those services. One family I came to know well was required to pay an onerous fee for a water hookup, but an inadequate pump meant that they never actually saw a drop of water in their home on the outskirts of the settlement.

El Bour n'Aït Yahya represented an anomalous case in the region not only because strangers lived next to each other but also because households there re-

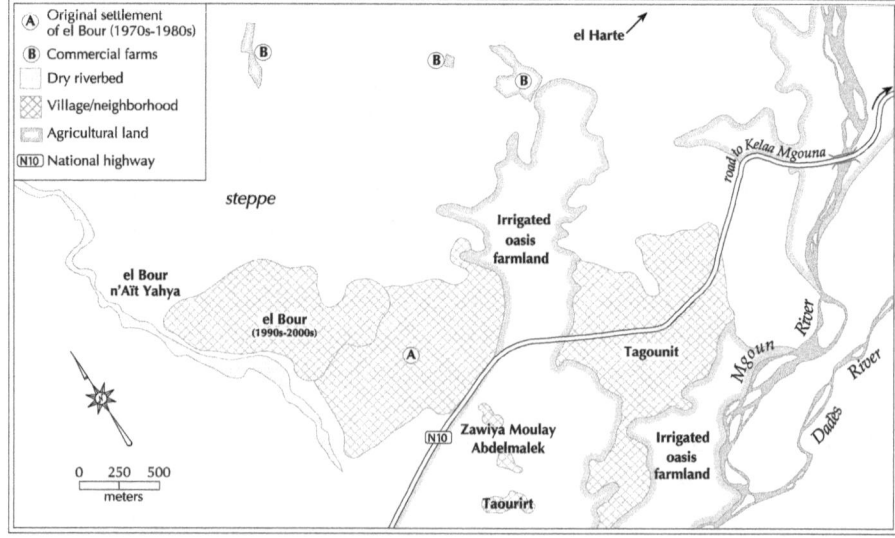

MAP 4. Settlement of el Bour n'Aït Yahya.

Map by Richard Gilbreath, independent cartographer.

lied more heavily on wage labor than did oasis residents. In the oases, most families had members working in the city, but they usually owned or had access to at least some agricultural land. This was not true in el Bour, where most residents bought a large enough plot to build a house but did not have the land or the ability to sink a well to begin agricultural production there. Only two investors, an Arab from Casablanca and a local notable who had amassed assets from his time in the Netherlands, had been able to establish farming operations with the help of deep wells. Some women in el Bour worked for them or did periodic tasks for in-kind or cash wages on lands in the historical oases. For these women, working for wages in the mountains was unimaginable, not only because of the tight economy but also because of cultural injunctions against women working for money. In el Bour, the greater anonymity and economic need combined to neutralize that injunction, even if work opportunities for women were still limited. For the most part, however, women were not drawn into daily contact by working in the fields, and so they searched for other ways to build social connections. Passing by the two mosques in el Bour, I would occasionally hear peals of laughter from women taking part in daily literacy classes. They offered a common space where women from disparate backgrounds could congregate and begin developing social networks to replace those they left behind in their natal homes. I wondered how, when women in this region worked so hard, these women were able to spend up to two hours a day in literacy courses. But they explained that without agricultural work and the large family compounds they were used to, they were left with little to fill up their days. The literacy courses gave them a feeling of accomplishment and helped them feel connected in the isolating environment of el Bour.

These classes proved to be the best way to meet people in the settlement, and I began to attend regularly. It became clear to me that I would have to tell the story of el Bour not from the vantage point of communal history. Even if the narratives of belonging in other oasis communities were contested, they still invoked a communal referent. In el Bour, by contrast, narrating place always began with an account of a given household's movement from the mountains and the year they purchased land in the settlement. I met two women whose family experiences exemplified the divergent trajectories embedded in these narratives. The first, Itto, preferred that I interview her husband, Youssef, although I spent time socially with her in the literacy classes and her home, where sounds echoed off the hard surfaces of the largely empty cement construction. The couple was from Aït Toumert, a group of villages on the edge of the Aït Hamd plateau, past Rbat and Imzilne on the road from Kelaa Mgouna. Youssef had never spent time on the range, but his family had roots in transhumant pastoralism. In a common arrangement, his uncle moved the family herd between summer and winter pastures while his father managed their agricultural lands in the village. When Youssef's grandfather died, they divided the inheritance by giving his uncle the livestock; eventually, his uncle and cousins stopped practicing transhumant pastoralism altogether. People wanted to "live better now," Youssef explained. "Transhumant herding is a very hard life. My uncle and cousins were no longer willing to accept the living conditions." Youssef's father inherited the family's agricultural land, but an ever-growing family—Youssef reported forty people in the household when he was young—could not live on a mere ten ʿashir. So, Youssef and his brothers struck out in search of new livelihoods. As a young man, he dug wells near Casablanca, but eventually returned to the area to take charge of the family and become the collective-land representative for his village in Aït Toumert.[17]

In what turned out to be a remarkably good investment, his father bought a substantial holding of twenty ʿashir down in el Bour n'Aït Yahya in 1992; and in 2006, Youssef made the definitive move to el Bour with Itto and their children. He bought a van and made a comfortable living as a regional livestock merchant, looking for opportunities in Mgoun but going as far as Marrakech, the Atlantic coast, or the border with Algeria to buy livestock for resale in Kelaa and vice versa. He also cultivated the twenty ʿashir in el Bour, planting winter wheat and fallowing the land during the summer for lack of water. He still had a brother up in Aït Toumert, and they maintained their land there, too, even if production was limited to almonds, walnuts, and cereal crops for home consumption. During harvest season, Itto and the other women in his family would wrap their *tamghurt* (hand sickle) in their *tajdat* (the local overdress worn by women) and load up in the van to harvest crops in the mountains and family plots dispersed throughout the valley. As Youssef said: "There is no difference between here and there. I will not move back, but I am from there until I die." Youssef made the one- to two-hour trip back to Aït Toumert about twice a month to check in with the family and the land there and to fulfill his duties as collective-land representative. Living in el Bour ensured Youssef a secure livelihood while keeping him close enough to Aït Toumert to maintain his prominent role in village governance. Youssef and Itto were not typical. Few people could afford to buy twenty ʿashir even in 1992, much less a van and the fuel to operate it. But it was the specificity of their situation that led me to see how people living right next to each other in the "city-like" environment of el Bour often negotiated radically different pressures.

When I visited Youssef and Itto, our conversations always took place around a bowl of fresh butter churned from the milk of their cows and honey collected from family hives in the mountains. I would take advantage of my visits there to spend time with Fatima, another research participant, who lived a few hundred meters down the hard dirt road from Youssef and Itto. Honey was out of her reach. At 400 dirhams (US$50) a liter, treasured mountain honey was far too expensive for people who could not keep their own hives. Fatima, like Youssef, was from the neighboring tribal confederation of Imaghran and had moved from the mountains in 2005, but her situation was markedly different. She managed her small family, three young children, by herself while her husband worked on commercial farming operations in the Souss, a four- to five-hour bus ride away. He returned twice annually for a couple of weeks, leaving her in charge of the family finances and other affairs; she had no family or anyone else to help in el Bour. She also had an older son, Driss, who at twenty-one had already spent four years in Casablanca learning the plaster trade and sending home wages to complement his father's earnings. In the summer of 2010, Driss returned home for Ramadan and to study for his driver's license, an intense monthlong effort that was an important livelihood investment for many literate men in the area. It cost 2,500 dirhams (US$310)—over two months' salary for Driss—to study and sit for the exam. The ability to drive opened new work opportunities, though, and he envisioned a job as a chauffeur for the Casablanca elite who needed to shuttle their children to private school. The family was completely dependent on wage labor in Morocco's urban centers and agricultural heartland. Like Youssef, Fatima's husband had roots in transhumant pastoralism. She recounted how only two weeks into her marriage, Fatima joined her in-laws on the range and began tending the herd while her husband returned to a job digging wells in the north. The family's herd of one hundred or so animals was decimated by a drought in 2001, and they abandoned livestock production. They also divided what little remained of their agricultural land. Fatima's husband sold that land in 2003 to buy a 30 × 30-meter parcel in el Bour. He and his son built their house there and planted six almond trees. They rented a small plot of land to grow alfalfa for the five or six goats Fatima kept in the home's carefully tended courtyard. They struggled to get by.

Fatima's was one of many marginalized households that had to abandon their livelihoods in the mountains. Imaghran's location in the water-scarce plateaus to the west of the Mgoun Valley meant that many pastoralists had to sell off their herds in the droughts of the 1980s or 1990s (El Alaoui 2002). Cultivable land could not sustain their growing households. When I began my research in el Bour, the dominant pattern was immediately apparent: women maintained nuclear households with no agricultural land in el Bour while their husbands traveled to work as manual laborers in Morocco's major urban centers. Settling in el Bour was a good option for these families. With limited assets, they could not afford to buy homes or land even fifteen kilometers away in Kelaa Mgouna, which, as a small regional town, was significantly cheaper than moving to a larger city. The location of el Bour along the national road also afforded easy access to transport to their jobs in the city. Labor migrants could therefore return home more often, depending on their work situation, than if they lived up in the mountains. But it was still a lonely and isolating social existence for many. For those without customary support mechanisms, livelihood insecurity could easily slip into destitution. Fatima openly expressed her fear about this: "My husband has asthma; we worry that he won't be able to work with the pesticides and dust in the fields of the Souss much longer. What will we do?" For households such as Fatima's, intraregional migration was a coping strategy, but for others, it could represent a path to mobility.

In the past decade, other residents from the region who were not necessarily fleeing poverty in the mountains also began buying property in el Bour to set up members of their households. The relatively wealthy branch of a large household from an oasis village could have a compound next door to a vulnerable family surviving on a few dirhams a day earned in a distant city. And yet to say that el Bour was a simple example of rural proletarianization would be inaccurate. Mgoun experienced what de Haas calls "rural urbanisation," a process whereby migrants returned to or invested outside their natal villages but still within the region (2009, 1583). New poles of attraction for regional migrants emerged as populations coalesced around market towns, but migration also allowed people to stay in the region. Rather than depopulating the three major migration "belts" (the southeastern oases, the southwestern Anti-Atlas Mountains, and the northern Rif Mountains), migrant outflows enabled family members to stay in the village or at least in the area (de Haas 2007b, 39). Both out-migration for work and regional migration down from the mountains reconfigured population settlements and reshaped the meaning and value of land. Even if agricultural production was not possible for households with limited assets or access to cultivable land, owning a plot was an anchor for livelihoods now based on wages in distant cities or on trades such as carpentry and car repair in the growing market town of Kelaa.

The notion that el Bour was a straightforward example of rural proletarianization was inaccurate for another reason: some in the settlement actively sought to establish customary institutions. In 2011, I learned that officials from el Bour n'Aït Yahya had submitted a formal request to the Ministry of Interior for permission to appoint collective-land representatives. At first glance, this was an oxymoron. As a new settlement constructed entirely on land purchased piecemeal from a private landholder, el Bour had no collective lands and certainly no tradition of customary governance, land tenure or otherwise, to uphold. But the elected officials and other community leaders from el Bour saw the utility of having collective-land representatives—of creating a customary institution anew—to interface with the state and advocate for settlement residents on land issues. What would be the basis for this customary law that the collective-land representative would uphold? No one I spoke to could answer that question, emphasizing, as one elected official from el Bour did, that "you cannot have a community without customary leaders." It was, in fact, custom that signified community and the "collective form" of organization to intercede with the state, giving greater legitimacy to residents' claims (Chatterjee 2006, 56). Perhaps el Bour had no communal past, but it envisioned a communal future through the creation of a customary tenure institution. This counterintuitive move made sense in a plural legal landscape that maintained the relevance of customary law in contemporary rural governance.

Conclusion

Examining how land tenure intersected with local governance throughout the valley revealed the different ways in which groups and individuals invoked custom to police the boundaries of community. Taken alone, each community told a unique story of how migration, livelihood transformation, and integration into broader markets, among other processes, remade the social and economic landscape of the valley. Taken together, a regional picture emerges of how changes in one area influenced the way other parts of the valley experienced change. Customary institutions both enabled collective governance of these changes—a "stabilizing" effect—and represented a site of contestation that could fuel disputes lasting for decades (Guyer 2004, 127). Conflict, as in the animosities between el Harte and Qlaʿa, could be seen as reactivating community, promoting a sense of collective identity among upwardly mobile farmers against their former overlords next door. The notion that custom could reactivate community, however, implies a stable, preexisting social formation that just needs to be "woken up" to confront new political and social realities. The distinct histories of the three communities in this chapter challenge this assumption, illustrating how community was as much a product of transformation as the new concrete houses and freshly paved roads.

For Miranda Joseph (2002), preserving community as a space for governing individuals and groups in the face of a retreating state is largely a regressive project. Her influential analysis posits community as functional to contemporary forms of governmentality and capital accumulation. This capital accumulation does not always involve global corporate interests or financial flows. As David Harvey notes: "The molecular processes of capital accumulation can and do create their own networks and frameworks of operation over space in innumerable ways, using kinship, diasporas, religious and ethnic bonding, and linguistic codes as means to produce intricate spatial networks of capitalist activity independent of the frameworks of state power" (2003, 90). Those networks can support individual capital accumulation on a very small scale, as in the methodical investments migrants from southeastern Morocco made in land acquisition, livestock, and agricultural production. These molecular processes also informed new approaches to communal governance, allowing some groups to use global connections *and* a mastery of custom to carve out spaces of autonomy. Migrants' investment in place, however, could not be reduced to political resistance or to a radical critique of the capitalism that drew migrants into European coal mines. The transformative mobility of former sharecroppers was an effort to secure autonomy "with" rather than "from": with global labor circuits rather than a rejection of them, with noncapitalist practices that integrated commercial agriculture into oasis farming instead of resisting market involvement, with customary tenure regimes that invoked a putatively authentic tradition while challenging racialized hierarchy. In the Mgoun Valley, then, discourses of custom and tradition provided the political and economic infrastructure for a new rurality that liberated some but continued to exclude others. The new rurality ushered in a calculus of power that refigured the relationship among customary institutions, state power, and other claims for political representation—a political pluralism that is the subject of the next chapter.

2

POLITICAL PLURALISM, LOCAL POLITICS, AND THE STATE

Approaching Kelaa Mgouna from the national road, one of the first landmarks to come into view is a large adobe complex surrounded by a high wall. If it were not perched on top of a hill, isolated and distant from other settlements, I would have thought it was a domestic compound (figure 10). The complex was a secret prison, one of the many sites for the long-term imprisonment, torture, and disappearance of political prisoners during the "years of lead" of King Hassan II's reign.[1] It was right there at the entrance to the town, overlooking the local government offices and municipal park, defying my sense of what "secret" meant. For twenty years, this particular prison held Marxists, supporters of Western Saharan independence, and Islamists (Deback 2010, 39). Various people in Kelaa recounted to me how they knew something was going on up there, but there were only rumors that it held Saharan seditionists who wanted to destroy Morocco. Only military personnel were allowed on the premises, I was told, except for local craftsmen occasionally brought in to repair the adobe. I knew one man in el Harte whose uncle was one of those workers; they were instructed not to speak to anyone about what they saw. The prison was closed in the early 1990s when King Hassan II ushered in a wave of reforms and scaled back human rights abuses, some say in recognition that illness would soon end his reign. The regime allowed greater freedom of the press and inaugurated a restitution process for victims of the abuses. King Hassan II also implemented measures intended to promote greater political participation and an active voice for opposition parties, one of which he invited to lead the government in 1998.[2]

FIGURE 10. View of Kelaa Mgouna's secret prison from the national road.
Photo by the author.

The foundation was laid for Mohamed VI, King Hassan II's son who rose to power when his father died in 1999. Mohamed VI expounded a new philosophy of governance, a "politics of efficiency, based on the principles of proximity and participation" (Royaume du Maroc 2010b). Through decentralization, democratization, economic modernization, and "good governance" the state would become more responsive to its people and foster economic growth (Maghraoui 2012). How this philosophy of governance actually played out in rural, out-of-the-way places like the Mgoun Valley, however, did not represent such a marked break with King Hassan II's strategies of rule. Nor did it interrupt the long history of contestation between diverse centers of power in Morocco: from the central sultanate, to the modern territorial state, local proxies for the central government, religious brotherhoods, customary authorities, and various oppositional currents.[3] The secret prison in Kelaa Mgouna stood as a metaphor for this plural political landscape, marking the changing presence of the state and the unique relationship of rural areas like the Mgoun Valley to larger national debates about political participation and government accountability.

In this chapter, I use an ethnography of everyday politics in the Mgoun Valley to show how *political pluralism* sustained, and was sustained by, the communal identities shaped by the *legal pluralism* described in chapter 1. The emergent politics of the commons in the valley invoked custom to refashion belonging and challenge existing hierarchies, but it did not seek a life beyond the state.[4] Rather, groups and individuals mobilized diverse strategies to engage local state institutions or actors alongside customary practices and other sites of authority.[5] Incorporation into the central state was something to negotiate, not resist outright. Attending to residents' quotidian strategies for managing this pluralism illustrates how commoning does not always oppose peasants against a repressive state in a straightforward way. Most accounts of the commons emphasize the role of the state in enforcing or promoting enclosure, with commoning as a strategy of the dispossessed to resist the state and the private property form, although there are many forms such oppositional politics could take. James Scott uses southeastern Morocco as an example of how "barbarians by design"—residents of peripheral, mountainous zones—historically crafted livelihood, governance, and cultural practices to "thwart incorporation into nearby states" (2009, 8). Tracing the genealogy of contemporary politics in the Mgoun Valley, however, suggests that the "art of not being governed" may involve a pragmatic willingness to move between different sites of political authority, including the central state, rather than a desire to avoid incorporation (Scott 2009).

Conversely, states can engage with peripheral rural zones in ambivalent ways; states are not always trying to incorporate rural populations as fully legible subjects. Although implanting a territorializing modern state in Morocco certainly involved dismantling many aspects of communal governance, this chapter argues that state actors often seemed as invested as many nonstate actors in preserving the political pluralism of the rural southeast, including nonstate forms of communal authority. In fact, the actors and institutions of local government I encountered operated more like a "nonrecording state," selectively eschewing legibility as a "deliberate strategy and important modality of state making and nation making" (Kalir and van Schendel 2017, 2). Officials sometimes actively resisted the formalization of government, which I take to mean bureaucratic routinization and state attempts to render populations legible through mapping, resource management and control, and other signifiers of state presence (Rose 1999; Scott 1998). In the Mgoun Valley, state actors often refrained from getting involved in land governance, worked through informal channels to deliver services or resources, and turned to customary leaders to resolve many challenges of everyday government. This disengagement was not a failure of the state; the government's ability to collect massive amounts of data and intervene in so many aspects of Moroccans' lives belies that notion. Rather, it was a strategy the contemporary state had adapted from the colonial period to exercise a flexible but nonetheless authoritarian power.

In what follows, I use primarily oral histories to trace how indirect rule during the colonial period helped produce contemporary political pluralism by integrating communal identities and affiliations into local government. French colonial authority simultaneously implanted a modern state with territorializing ambitions and cultivated selected customary governance institutions to preside over key aspects of life in peripheral zones like the Mgoun Valley. This "logic of legibility" did not represent "a uniform toolkit of simplifying, flattening, and homogenizing policies . . . [but] usually entailed preserving, codifying, and at times inventing, ethnic, religious, and regional heterogeneity" (Wyrtzen 2015, 23). I then describe how after independence in 1956, the practice of cultivating heterogeneity continued to inform state strategies for control and shaped the quotidian political life I observed. In municipal planning meetings and civil society workshops, state and nonstate actors alike mobilized national policy initiatives, development discourse, and "rights talk" in their contestations over local governance. While many state actors resisted attempts to formalize local government, civil society activists demanded the rule of law, although they were realistic about the prospect for meaningful democratic participation in local politics. Amid this jockeying between civil society and state actors, communal identities rooted in customary governance continued to represent an important means by which the state interpellated rural populations. The result was a plural landscape where individuals and groups moved between different sites of political discourse and action. However, these sites still excluded many of the most marginalized residents of the valley. Their claims for a distributive politics served as the ground for a new commoning, the subject of chapter 3.

The Colonial Origins of Political Pluralism

Hamid welcomed two elderly visitors wrapped in their *silham*, expansive woolen cloaks that protected them from the wind that swept into the adobe room (figure 11). Hamid's salon opened toward the sun to gather warmth in the thin winter air, offering a modest but inviting respite from the cold. Hamid was the oldest blacksmith in the community of Imzilne—his son said he was over one hundred—but he was still among the most active metalworkers in a village known for its forging tradition. The visitors had just arrived from farther down in the valley, carrying satchels with hand sickles for repair before the next agricultural season put new demands on them. Together, they recounted the history of the Aït Hamd plateau that included Imzilne, Rbat, and a few other villages: life under colonialism, the grinding poverty punctuated by occasional famine, and the richness of a social world that brought people together through simple interactions such as getting one's tools repaired. They surmised that they were the last generation that would travel hours to personally bring their tools to their blacksmith and stay the night to catch up on each other's news. Now, they said, people just drive down to the weekly market in Kelaa Mgouna, dropping off their tools to be fixed while

FIGURE 11. Hamid, an accomplished blacksmith from Imzilne.

Photo by the author.

they buy their vegetables. Hamid's daughter-in-law, Touda, listened as she spun wool around a wooden spindle. When the elderly men paused, she theorized that modern transport had damaged social relations because "before, you used to walk everywhere and had to stop in the villages along the way to visit people." Now, people took *transits* (collective vans) that whisked travelers from Kelaa up the newly paved road that ran right to the entrance of Imzilne, passing by the villages they used to visit for a meal or some tea. Trajectories that comprised voyages of two or three days a generation ago were now just over an hour. People were both closer and farther apart. Touda felt the loss.

For the men reminiscing about life as youths under the French Protectorate and for Touda's experience of more recent changes, such transformations were about incorporation into states and economies that refashioned their social worlds. These changes occurred during the elderly men's lifetimes. They could remember a time before central government became a daily presence. Although the current dynasty had ruled Morocco for nearly four centuries, historically, the makhzan was an irregular presence in the rural periphery, where ties between the sultan and local elites were often symbolic or activated by the latter's assertions of independence (Montagne 1973; Tozy 1999). Residents of the region were not, however, isolated: they had always been mobile, connected to broader networks of all kinds (Dunn 1977). The blacksmiths of Imzilne were excluded from participation in transhumant pastoralism because of racial hierarchies, but they traversed the whole region, repairing and selling metal tools at weekly markets and through regular stops in dispersed villages. Others were mobile because famine, political insecurity, or other hardships forced their search for more stable livelihoods (Rosenberger 2001).

The colonial period had contradictory impacts for these mobile populations. When, in 1929, the French built the adobe storage depot that would become Kelaa's secret prison, they had not yet "pacified" the valleys and steppe farther to the east. The depot held supplies for the forces tasked with quelling the last resistance against protectorate rule (Aït Hamza 1993). French forces finally conquered the south in 1933 in the battle of Bougafer a couple hundred kilometers to the east of Mgoun, a battle the Aït Atta tribal confederation could not win against strafing from French warplanes (Ilahiane 2006). The French retained the same proxies, the Glaoua chieftains, that had amassed regional power before the protectorate—Madani Glaoui was named *khalifa* of Todgha, Tafilalt, and Fayja by Moulay Hasan I in 1893 (Park 1996). As colorfully described by Maxwell (1966), the Glaoua enjoyed wide berth to execute their own often violent manner of tax farming, primarily in the form of agricultural levies, market-based taxation, and conscription. This enabled the French to "keep their hands clean," in the words of one of Hamid's guests, but it was also a pragmatic strategy for exercising nominal power over rebellious zones difficult to control, much less tax or otherwise subject to expropriation (Hoisington 1995). In the Dadès and Mgoun Valleys, French Direction d'Affaires Indigènes officers established what Hamid's visitors described as a more congenial outpost. The goal was to separate hostile tribal fractions and bring stability to the chronically insecure region (Aït Hamza 2002a). As in oases elsewhere, people began to move out of the fortified qsur, where historically houses had been grouped for safety (Attar 1994; Ilahiane 1999; Naji 2001). Working in the fields became less dangerous with the end of raiding and other violence that had been a feature of daily life.

The Glaoua in turn relied on local proxies to impose their will. These proxies were embedded in the long history of repressive sharecropping that existed alongside the putatively democratic institutions of Amazigh tribal governance (Dunn 1977; Hart 1981). During the colonial period, powerful families in the Mgoun Valley that had built up land holdings, in some cases over centuries, had their positions enshrined as *shaykhs*, an appointed leadership position, under the Glaoua. Memories of their absolute power were still raw for many in the valley. As Taleb, the returned migrant from Rbat introduced in chapter 1, described: "[The local proxies] had all the power then. If you did not listen to them, you went to jail. You could not even walk in the village. If Shaykh Aït Zahir [who still retained this semiofficial title when I interviewed the very elderly notable in 2010] saw you, he made you turn around and work in his fields. You could not say no." For Taleb and others with similar experiences, colonial oppression could not be expressed as a simple binary opposing French occupiers and a more legitimate Moroccan sovereign (Dunn 1977). Lines of authority blurred among the French indigenous affairs officers who played a sporadic role in local governance, the Glaoua and their proxies ruling oppressively through a more direct involvement in daily life, and customary governance institutions, such as those described in the previous chapter.

This blurring was an explicit strategy of colonial rule, allowing the French to position themselves as mediators and benevolent providers while implementing bureaucratic measures intended to control restive populations (D. Davis 2007; Hammoudi 1997; Rivet 1988). The men visiting Hamid's blacksmithing shop described how the *état civil* (identity card system) was introduced in the valley around the time of the "Year of Rice," the devastating drought-related famine of 1937 that dispersed populations north to Marrakech and other cities (Berque 1962). The French tried to keep populations put by distributing rations, the first time many had ever tasted rice or had their identities registered on cards. This was around the time that the French introduced permit requirements for leaving one's village. "It was not so bad," Hamid recounted. "You just gave your name, your father's name, and your village of origin." Pass laws may not have been particularly troubling for Hamid because, as a blacksmith from a subjugated community, he would not have had livestock on the range. The pass laws were devastating for many others, who found their livelihoods curtailed by French security measures grouped under a Charte de la Transhumance (Transhumance Charter) (D. Davis 2007; Skounti 2012). Regulations restricting mobility formed part of a broader suite of policies that contained populations and imposed the modern state as a permanent presence in the region.

The fact that this state did not territorialize its power by direct administration does not mean that central authorities were uninterested in bringing rural zones under their control. To the contrary, advocates of indirect rule—most commonly known as *association*, as opposed to colonial assimilationist ideologies—extolled it as a more cost-effective and politically expedient way of implanting and legitimating the colonial state (Betts 2005; Hoisington 1995). A foundational premise of indirect rule as elaborated by the protectorate's first resident general, Hubert Lyautey, was to cultivate communal identities as a basis for governance, especially in the rural periphery.[6] This was the general strategy of indirect rule across British and French colonies that eschewed settler colonialism or simply had to work with tighter budgets from the metropole: to produce "a social space of nonfreedom" where ethnicity and group identity structured the operations of government (Mamdani 1996; Subramanian 2009, 16). How much decision-making authority the customary authorities charged with adjudicating these communal identities actually held varied enormously. Burke notes that in the regions of early colonization, "French bureaucrats made a show of respect for the royal person and the principles of indirect rule" but really made all the decisions themselves, concluding that "Morocco was never an example of indirect rule" (2014, 195). However, in the south, the French colonial strategy consisted mainly of subsidizing the rule of the "grand caids," allowing them free rein to expropriate resources from oppressed populations (136). Oral histories describing the quotidian exercise of power in Morocco's rural periphery revealed a complex amalgam of governing strategies. Indirect rule retained a role for customary institutions that enabled the state to cement its control while absolving itself of responsibility for everyday government.

Indigenous affairs officers positioned themselves "above" communal life, mediating disputes and resource access but otherwise leaving the daily management of these resources to customary authorities. I was shown several documents from the 1940s and 1950s that detailed irrigation and other resource management agreements between rival tribal fractions brokered by French indigenous affairs officers. The jma'a, the customary local governing councils, still played an important role in local governance, but the new supremacy of the French *procès verbal*, or *p.v.* (official minutes), as official legitimation of negotiated resolutions established a new hierarchy of authority: the state as neutral arbiter that hovers above the plural and parochial structures of local governance.[7] When the Direction des Affaires Indigènes was folded into the Ministry of Interior after independence in 1956, aspects of this approach to rural governance endured.

The Ministry of Interior's roots in its institutional predecessor were visible in everyday rituals and practices of government I encountered in 2010. Every year, the qa'id in the mountains announced the opening of the agdal and submitted an official *procès verbal* to mark the event, a continuation of the protectorate practice instituted by Direction des Affaires Indigènes officers. Like their predecessors, local Ministry of Interior representatives stood above the fray of politics while also maintaining a close watch on local affairs. I was struck by one qa'id's excited response when, during my obligatory introductory visit to his office, I described my research project. He expressed interest in studying anthropology because he felt the work he did was essentially the same; the qa'id had adjudicated so many disputes that he had a bird's-eye view of the valley's cultural dynamics. He may as well put it to use, he told me, for the sake of scholarly inquiry. This, too, had antecedents in colonial rule: the renowned scholar of rural Morocco, Jacques Berque used his position as a French indigenous affairs officer in the High Atlas Mountains as a springboard for anthropological fieldwork (Pouillon 1997; Rachik 2012).

In the contemporary period, Ministry of Interior officials adjudicated disputes using discretionary power set apart from the formal legal or bureaucratic systems. The qa'id described his role as stepping in when customary mechanisms for resolving problems did not work. This seemed to happen quite a lot. One illustrative dispute took place in el Harte and pitted Mbarak, my research assistant, against one of el Harte's customary leaders. I often enjoyed an extended lunch with Mbarak and his family before we set out for interviews. During these interviews, I saw the wide respect Mbarak's family enjoyed, but I also learned how leading families sometimes took advantage of Mbarak's precarious social position as an outsider, born in the village but one of two el Harte families with Arab ancestry. One day, a backhoe started excavating a hole on Mbarak's property during one of my lunches there. The din immediately caught Mbarak's attention, and he disengaged himself from the low-lying banquette to peer out the window. His normally calm demeanor clouded over with anger and he darted outside. Waving his hands to stop the backhoe, he immediately knocked on his neighbor Lahcen's door to demand what was going on. Mbarak knew that the backhoe was there on Lahcen's behalf, digging a hole for an electricity pole that would run a line across Mbarak's property to supply Lahcen's newly rebuilt home. "We have been through this before!" Mbarak shouted. Lahcen had previously asserted the line had to run through Mbarak's land, but Mbarak came up with an alternative route that he proposed to the jma'a. He thought he had their agreement for this solution.

However, Lahcen, as an established community leader, felt emboldened to make a unilateral decision to the contrary. He assumed his extended family and peers on the jma'a would not challenge him in favor of an Arab outsider, however well liked Mbarak's family was. I kneeled on the banquette with Mbarak's wife to observe from inside as the qa'id was summoned and his Land Rover came to an abrupt stop in front of the arguing men. Standing with his hands on his hips and surveying the hole, the qa'id listened to the argument for a while and waved his hand in a gesture for silence. I wondered why the qa'id would make a direct intervention in what seemed like a parochial dispute; the qa'id's line of questioning also indicated that he felt the men should have been able to sort this out. But they had not, and to Mbarak and Lahcen's frustration, the qa'id deferred a final decision by mandating a feasibility study to determine where the electric wire should run. The dreaded feasibility study. Lahcen and Mbarak groaned in unison. They knew this would take months, with potentially inconclusive results, but their hands were now tied by the qa'id's involvement. Lahcen rerouted the line before a decision was ever handed down, because he was tired of waiting to install electricity in his new home.

I began to notice the qa'id's Land Rover all over the valley: parked outside a village to investigate complaints that women were appropriating property by drying brush on communal land, next to a mosque to hear why an imam was being threatened for taking sides in a property dispute, and by the river to verify whether a diversionary dam for one village's irrigation canals had been deliberately sabotaged by a rival village, among other conflicts my acquaintances (and sometimes the qa'id himself) told me about. The Ministry of Interior's role in adjudicating disputes that customary institutions could not resolve was an explicit and widely recognized assertion of state power. Securing a monopoly of power would, ironically, undermine that role. Resolution of these disputes could be deferred, perhaps indefinitely, but even those extended periods of indecision represented an expression of this power—a strategy of distancing the state from the governance of everyday life while creating a space for the irregular but nonetheless intrusive involvement of the Ministry of Interior in local affairs.

The Limits of Indirect Rule

This combination of irregular yet intrusive government was fundamental to the legacy of indirect rule. Even state efforts to render populations legible through modern bureaucratic structures that undermined tribal institutions retained communal identities as a category for organizing local government. This was evident in the administrative reordering of rural zones that began early in the protectorate, when colonial policies fixed tribal boundaries and otherwise contained local sovereignty in the service of a "control of proximity" (Boujrouf and Elmostafa 2008, 41). The French drew lines up and down the Mgoun Valley between various groups, transforming a sociospatial form of sovereignty into an exclusionary model of governmental authority. Demarcating neatly defined territories ignored or suppressed the multiple forms of sovereignty historically negotiated, and often violently contested, on those lands (Bouderbala 1996). As detailed further in chapter 3, indirect rule undermined tribal sovereignty and reconstituted the "tribe" as a category of identity by fixing tribal territories and incorporating elements of tribal institutions into the bureaucratic apparatus. This process is very real—and ongoing—for residents of the valley, who continue to sort through the constant *découpage administratif* (administrative redistricting) that began with French colonialism and has redrawn territorial units of local government repeatedly since then.

Soon after independence in 1956, King Mohamed V repurposed the French logic of *emboitement* (nesting hierarchies of administrative units) to stamp out resistance to central monarchical control (Boujrouf and Elmostafa 2008, 41). The goal was to geographically produce "political consensus at various scales" by structuring administrative units around regional markets (42). The stakes were high in the late 1950s: rebellions in the rural north and southeast threatened the monarchy's monopoly on governing authority (Hart 2000; Leveau 1985). In this context, individual identity cards shifted from noting tribal affiliation to listing one's place of birth—one's geographic, not social, home (Hoffman 2000). Periodic reorganization of local administrative units reoriented people's bureaucratic lives from the governing authority of tribal confederations to the ever-changing seats of local government. Communes established in 1959 were organized again in the 1970s, 1980s, and 1990s. Sometimes the new administrative units corresponded to tribal territories, such as the communes of Aït Sedrate West and East (in the steppe surrounding the Mgoun Valley) that represented territory historically controlled by the Aït Sedrate tribal confederation (Skounti 2012). However, many people in the Mgoun Valley saw the state as taking a different tack with their confederation, trying to break up its power and keep the valley "backward." One schoolteacher I knew in Kelaa attributed the valley's poverty relative to the neighboring valleys of Dadès and Todgha to a state strategy that, over the years, divided Mgoun from one commune into four. He noted that the Aït Mgoun had never been a makhzan tribe like the Aït Sedrate, with the implication that they refused subservience. By bisecting their territory, the government could undercut the confederation's power and cohesiveness (El Manouar 2004).

In 2010, a new *qiyada*, a local administrative unit of the Ministry of Interior headed by a qa'id, was created in the Aït Hamd plateau, reorienting people's administrative affiliations once again. As soon as word got out about a possible new qiyada, villages in the lower valley initiated protests and sit-ins at the old qiyada outside Kelaa Mgouna. They were angered at the prospect that every time they would need a testation of residency or other document, they would have to take a transit an hour and a half up the mountain rather than simply walk to the qiyada outside of town. Their protests were unsuccessful, and the new offices opened in 2011. At the same time, the palace announced the creation of a new province that would encompass the valley and surrounding region, carving Tinghir province out of portions of Ouarzazate and Errachidia provinces. No one could explain to me the reasons for this move: in the words of one civil society activist, the reasons were "at a high level, by the King and his councilors; they say it is to bring the government closer to the people, but the real reasons are kept secret." He and others I spoke with thought it was a response to high levels of political activism in and around the city of Tinghir, the new provincial capital. A new province could simultaneously better control populations and direct more resources to placate them.

In the postindependence period, then, measures to create progressively smaller units of government reflected the partial transformation of rural populations into individuals legible to the state. But these measures also retained a communal referent that had real implications for governing resources and village life in the contemporary period. Although the French Protectorate fixed tribal boundaries in the southeast, it did not do the same for villages. To this day, the boundaries between rural communities, as well as between rural communities and collectively owned lands belonging to tribal confederations, are unofficial in the Mgoun Valley. They are certainly known but often subject to contestation because of the changing footprint of farming, new settlement patterns, and other reconfigurations of the landscape. When I began to research land use in my field sites, I turned first to official maps, which depicted rural communities with clear boundaries. The local Ministry of Agriculture extension agents quickly told me to disregard those maps; they were correct topographically but irrelevant for understanding political units. Land within the customary boundaries of villages was under the jurisdiction of the jmaʿa. These "non-state spaces" were, in many respects, produced by the state itself when it stopped short of delimiting village lands and left them under the jurisdiction of the jmaʿa (Scott 2009).

Not fully dismantling the architecture of indirect rule actually enabled the independent monarchy to entrench state power. As Silverstein notes, the history of popular "threats to the territorial integrity of the state continues to haunt the Moroccan regime," producing a pervasive security apparatus (2010, 85). The "omnipresent character of the state," however, relies on disengagement alongside overt displays of power (Pascon 1980, 28). Several scholars have described this dual strategy of state control and distance as a defining feature of Moroccan state formation in the twentieth century, an attempt to place the king above partisan politics but squarely in control of the country (Bourqia and Miller 1999; Hammoudi 1997; Waterbury 1970). By serving as the arbiter of Morocco's diverse social forces, all three postcolonial kings deftly played these forces against each other to sustain a power base rooted in clientelism and monarchical favors (Leveau 1985). Under King Hassan II, this strategy included an authoritarian program of arbitrary imprisonment and disappearances, creating an archipelago of prisons such as the one that loomed over Kelaa Mgouna. This strategy did not rely purely on repression; it also drew on colonial "logics of legibility" that engaged, managed, and even produced communal identities as a basis for rule (Wyrtzen 2015, 64).

These political dynamics took on new valences when King Mohamed VI came to power in 1999. He inaugurated a governing philosophy of decentralization that dovetailed with the notion of proximity—bringing government closer to the people—embedded in earlier administrative reforms. However, proximity could also suggest surveillance and control, a continuing role for the Ministry of Interior as an extension of royal power. On the face of it, royal power had rebranded itself as a rejection of arbitrary rule in promoting participatory development and social welfare programs. Some called it a rule of charity. Ten years into this reign, Mohamed VI had become known to some critics as the "great inaugurator," constantly visible in the public eye cutting ribbons at rural health centers, day cares, and youth sports complexes (Benchemsi 2010). Many of these projects were funded by the National Initiative for Human Development (known widely by its French acronym, INDH), a highly publicized and well-funded effort begun in 2005 to address poverty and rural-urban disparities. Implementation rested with the Ministry of Interior and bypassed elected government in what many perceived as an explicit attempt to marginalize elected officials (Benchemsi 2010).

In this analysis, Mohamed VI reinscribed himself as the sole legitimate authority in Moroccan society by presenting the monarchy as savior of the poor while corrupt and ineffectual elected officials squandered public trust.[8] A royal strategy to undermine elected institutions of government in favor of the unaccountable Ministry of Interior perpetuated the existence of parallel state apparatuses: a modern liberal state with elected officials, local governments, and formal bureaucratic procedures and another, based in the Ministry of Interior and the makhzan, that many saw as holding the real power (Bergh 2012). Mohamed VI's strategy was a way to deepen state presence in areas historically suspicious of the central government, but it did so by relying on the legacy institutions of indirect rule, especially the Ministry of Interior officials who both kept a close eye on local affairs and left many aspects of local governance to customary authorities. In the contemporary period, then, the logic of indirect rule allowed the state to engage and even manipulate customary institutions to buttress the power of selected government ministries. Conversely for rural residents, customary institutions simultaneously represented a way of seeking autonomy from the state and a way of engaging that state. One Amazigh activist asserted to me: "We try to stay as far away from the state as we can. We solve our problems ourselves, using our own institutions." But in important respects, those institutions had developed in symbiotic relationship with the state; their autonomy represented less a space outside or beyond the state than a negotiation between plural sources of political authority.

The Legacy of Political Pluralism: Everyday Politics in the Contemporary Period

The tensions this plurality produced were evident in the quotidian dynamics of local politics that I witnessed in 2010. These dynamics were, as Koenraad Bogaert emphasizes in his treatment of social protest in Morocco's small towns, not simply local or "particularistic" (2015, 125). They continued a historical pattern of contestation over what kind of governing authority should predominate in the rural periphery: a liberal state modeling the rule of law, clientelist politics, customary governance, or a distributive politics that could address the region's historical marginalization. These contestations unfolded in the micropolitics of meetings, plans, and programs that circulated in Kelaa Mgouna. Programs branded with such clarity in the national media and central ministries of Rabat became a vague, overlapping mix of funding streams and repurposed steering committees by the time they filtered down to the overburdened local government officials tasked with implementing them. Different groups used these programs—poverty alleviation in the form of the INDH, human rights reconciliation in the form of the Consultative Council for Human Rights (CCDH), agricultural policy in the form of the Green Morocco Plan (PMV), and participatory decentralization in the form of a new local governance charter—to advocate for their own political visions. Local politics are always messy, but the way these various initiatives became intertwined reveals how political pluralism operated in people's everyday lives and helped lay the groundwork for a new politics of the commons.

The frequent planning meetings to coordinate the various national programs that "arrived," as one official termed it, at the local level were usually held at Kelaa's municipal offices. The modest offices stood at the bottom of the hill where the shuttered prison loomed. The building had been neglected for some time in anticipation of moving into the much grander municipal complex under construction in the empty lot next door; chairs were piled up in the corner of the large conference room where voices echoed because of the cement block construction and terrazzo floors. I often attended meetings when I had no interviews scheduled. I would run into the friends who had facilitated my arrival in Kelaa, sitting at a café as they waited for a meeting at the *baladia* (the municipality). They invariably asked if I wanted to tag along, noting that although they thought they knew what the meeting would be about, who knows what the agenda would actually involve. When I could, I accompanied them to see how the conduct of politics in the villages I had come to know compared with these theoretically more formal sites of bureaucratic and political practice.

In addition to local officials, a core group of older community leaders and younger civil society activists—all men—regularly attended the meetings. A small minority were the same elderly customary leaders I encountered in fieldwork in the surrounding villages. Others were returned migrants from France, visible in Kelaa because of their auto-parts business or their habitual seat in front of their rose products store. Still others were civil society activists: small business owners, schoolteachers, or other civil servants, often but not exclusively from notable families. The consistency in this group of "regulars" meant that issues from one meeting would often meld into another. Occasionally, the president of the commune (akin to a mayor) would summon them to a meeting they were told was for one purpose, only to find a completely different agenda. No one was fazed, for instance, when the commune president convened a meeting to coordinate local input into the national environmental charter and a team of foreign consultants presented recommendations for the local development plan instead. Sometimes, attendees would express frustration at this seeming lack of organization, but in general, they operated with a shared understanding that a given meeting was as good a forum as any for acting on the various initiatives they were all working on anyway. Nor did participants seem fazed that the meetings always began late, sometimes hours late, because the commune president was tied up in another engagement or presiding officials needed to wait for their superiors' official convocation of the gathering. Although initially exasperated by the seeming waste of time, I came to see the important purpose of these extended periods of milling about. Much of the work of local politics was conducted during the apparent inactivity and small talk before actual meetings began.

All the nationally prominent policy initiatives of 2010 seemed to converge during one particularly lively meeting in late March. It was an especially busy time: women had completed the rose harvest, and men had just begun preparing the soil for summer maize and vegetable cultivation. The large conference room at the municipality nonetheless filled with the regular local political figures who took advantage of the meeting's delayed start to share their assessments of the recent rose harvest festival—there were always stories to tell about petty crime, organizational missteps, and the drain on municipal services. Eventually, the commune president arrived with a folder under his arm. When he took his seat, he theatrically ushered in a group of human rights officials from the regional CCDH office in Ouarzazate. The president announced the objective of the meeting as a report on CCDH activities. When the regional representative of the CCDH, Ziyad, took the floor, he politely corrected the president: they were there to solicit project ideas for a new cooperative agreement between the CCDH and the Ministry of Agriculture that would direct human rights reparations to agricultural development programs in the valley. The CCDH was an autonomous state agency created in 2004 to offer individual and collective reparations for human rights abuses committed during Hassan II's reign, signaling the new government's break with the past (Slyomovics 2005). Residents from the Mgoun Valley had not been imprisoned, but the collective reparations program included communities whose reputations suffered because they were known as the locations of previously secret prisons (Slyomovics 2009). Ziyad introduced the community reparations program as an innovative model for reconciliation in the Middle East, even globally. Locally, however, few residents understood the conceptual link between the prison and community reparations in the form of small-scale development initiatives. Well-defined goals crafted by advocacy groups or agencies in the capital could become muddied in their bureaucratic voyage to rural outposts such as Kelaa.[9] Even more informed participants in local political debates tended to talk about community reparations as just another source of funding loosened from its original attachment to human rights. The reparations joined other funding initiatives—agricultural development projects, European Union decentralization funds, infrastructure programs, among others—to become a site for contesting the terms of local governing authority.

The commune president looked up from the papers he was signing when Ziyad explained that they were there to discuss new funding for local development programs. This would create new opportunities as well as obligations for the commune president, who had built his reputation on not only getting projects funded but actually implementing them. Ziyad, however, was more intent on explaining the political importance of collective reparations. But they did not have much time—the community reparations program was ending two years later, and so they needed to develop a plan for CCDH funds based on existing priorities for agricultural development. Ziyad posed a rhetorical question to explain this timeline: "Why is the program ending? Because it is only supposed to rectify opportunities lost because of the past. The priorities we establish today are not things we 'ask' from the state but are our rights. This—this respect for humanity, for democracy—is the basis for community reparations." They had a deadline for the program because reparations could not go on forever. They represented a delimited restitution for a specific wrong.

Ziyad therefore asked attendees to come up with turnkey recommendations: agriculture initiatives that were already identified as priority needs in the valley. He opened the floor for recommendations. Despite Ziyad's best efforts to remind meeting participants of the program's purpose, they began to discuss the human rights commission in the same terms as development funders or other central government initiatives left to local communes to implement. A returned émigré known for his commercial farming operation spoke up with a lengthy critique of how the Ministry of Agriculture did not deliver the support he needed. Ziyad stopped him short and said: "Wait. We—the CCDH—are not the state here. We are citizens asking for our rights, not just for this or that project that the state will 'give' us. Who has the responsibility of improving the state? It is us. Every CCDH project here will have a sign marking it as 'community reparation' so that everyone knows that the state now shows this respect for human rights, for humanity." Ziyad moved the discussion away from complaints about the state to needs and claims: the need for better infrastructure so that flash floods would not wipe out fields and irrigation canals, for marketing assistance so that the minimal cash crops grown in the region could receive better prices, and for programs to increase agricultural productivity so that families would not need to migrate in search of work.

Eventually, Ziyad reined in the discussion, noting: "We need to be realistic. We cannot do everything here. Our funds are meant to make a statement about the government's commitment to human rights, not change everything." And then he returned to the program's central purpose: "Maybe people here did not know about the prison when it was open, but now the reputation of the area is marked by the prison. So, we want to do something to try to shift the focus away from Kelaa's past as a place that hosted a secret prison. We know that every ministry has its program, so by supporting the Ministry of Agriculture we draw attention to agriculture and not to Kelaa: 'place for secret prisons.'" Ziyad pulled out a piece of paper and distilled the two-hour debate into a list of three possible programs to fund: an investment center, an agricultural cooperative, and an irrigation association. The meeting adjourned, and no further word was heard about human rights funding for agricultural development. But there was a result. The agricultural cooperative listed at the end was eventually taken up by the commune president, who had lifted his eyes in curiosity at the beginning of the meeting when he understood the potential for funding. He explicitly presented his proposal for a new cooperative as the outcome of that community reparations meeting. A board was constituted, and bylaws were established to access INDH funding—the other signature program of Mohamed VI. I learned on a return trip to Kelaa in 2013 that the cooperative was stalled by a land dispute over its proposed offices.

Perhaps this outcome of a stalled cooperative was an inevitable result of a confused mandate. The idea that the human rights commission, an agency created by the state, albeit an officially autonomous one, was "not the state" compounded the difficulty of explaining the purpose of reparations to people who may not have directly suffered from abuses but still held strong ideas about the state's neglect of the region. Taken in the context of the region's history, however, this confusion made sense as an extension of modern state-making strategies that played legibility and opacity off one another to deepen royal power. Human rights had been "rendered technical," transformed from a set of political claims into another bureaucratic funding stream alongside the government programs charged with local development (Li 2007, 7). By most accounts, community reparations did do something: they served as a catalyst for some programs, directly funded other existing initiatives, and made a powerful political statement (Slyomovics 2009). However, in the Mgoun Valley, the overlapping themes—and people—in these various programs meant that human rights as a guiding ethic for contemporary governance was diluted and depoliticized for many of the actors involved. Those programs drew on a shared discourse of participation, decentralization, and rule of law, but the result was to strengthen the Ministry of Interior's role as an arbitrating force in local governance. Although the CCDH was an autonomous state agency, funds for local initiatives invariably seemed to pass through the Ministry of Interior (the inheritor of Morocco's legacy of indirect rule) and were controlled minimally or not at all by elected officials. At least in the Mgoun Valley, this role for the ministry shifted the focus of community reparations from the collective harms and systemic nature of human rights abuses to communal identities as a basis for accessing resources and engaging with the state.

My fieldwork experience of local politics resonates with analyses of the INDH, the royal poverty alleviation program run by the Ministry of Interior. Scholars and Moroccan journalists alike argue that "despite the widespread rhetoric linking the INDH to the grounding of 'participatory democracy' in Morocco . . . it has in fact strengthened the power of the Ministry of the Interior's representatives at the expense of local governments, . . . served as a vehicle to co-opt regime friendly NGOs and local associations, and . . . led to the fragmentation and weakening of local (political) accountability" (Bergh 2012, 412). Situating the INDH, human rights reparations, and other government programs in the *longue durée* of rural relations with the state led me to a different emphasis: these state initiatives did not *produce* "fragmentation and weakening of local (political) accountability" so much as *sustain* a tradition of fragmentation rooted in a history of pluralism (412). The trajectory of that adobe complex on the hill from colonial storage depot to prison to source of human rights funding reflected both change and continuity in state strategies for engaging populations in the rural periphery. Viewed in this broader context, the conceptual confusion of the human rights meeting I attended was neither a failure of the state—an inability to effectively implement democratic reforms—nor a straightforward power grab, an effort to undermine democratic reforms by sabotaging them at the local level. Rather, the confusion about community reparations reflected a long-standing tension between different modes of rule within state institutions themselves. Even as initiatives like human rights reparations promoted the rule of law based on individual rights, the ways they were "vernacularized" undermined rights-based discourse in favor of a more familiar, uncodified state, one that refused formalization in the tradition of indirect rule (Merry 2006).

The cooperative initially proposed in the context of collective reparations stalled until the qa'id stepped in to resolve the land dispute that had prevented construction for nearly four years. I saw the same Land Rover, now driven by a different qa'id than the one I knew in 2010, parked in front of the disputed land in 2014. He had negotiated a settlement so that local leaders would be able to conduct a ribbon-cutting ceremony for the new cooperative when the provincial governor and the minister of agriculture came to visit Kelaa Mgouna to promote yet another government program, the Green Morocco Plan. The meaning of the cooperative had shifted from a symbol of human rights reconciliation to a marker of the region's agricultural potential, bending to the political imperatives of a new moment. The cooperative may not have met its original objectives, but this did not necessarily signal its failure. One civil society activist recounted his misgivings about the twists and turns the cooperative took but insisted: "You have to see what we were able to accomplish. We now see human rights language in local government, not just royal speeches. We see that more people than ever recognize the importance of rule of law and ask for their rights. That is something we did not have ten years ago. And it means something." For this man, the ways that national initiatives—human rights, agricultural development, poverty alleviation, and others—filtered down to the local level were both a reflection of the Ministry of Interior's persistent hold on power and an opportunity to create new spaces for political maneuver. Activists' efforts to pry open these spaces represented a claim for rights-based participation in government that stood in uneasy relation to other modes of contestation based on customary governance and communal identities. But all these forms of political contestation engaged in some way with a state that, since the colonial period, refused to fix its own political identity.

Making Claims on the State: Civil Society Activism in Local Politics

Civil society activists in the southeast were familiar with and often articulated a critical reading of local politics that ascribed overwhelming power to the Ministry of Interior. They were aware that ministry officials often appropriated initiatives and diluted their meaning. And they were aware that discourses of participation and decentralization could evacuate politics of its substance. These discourses, drawn from global development language but adapted to the political imperatives of rural Morocco, seemed intended to transform politics into bureaucratic processes rather than inclusive deliberation over priorities for local development (Li 2007). Yet these same civil society activists continued to attend planning meetings and debate funding streams. Even though they were clear-eyed about the possibilities for reform, the activists worked to change what they perceived as the impoverishment of electoral politics—from the limited room for policymaking accorded the national parliament to the absence of meaningful contestation at the local level. They tried to find those spaces where an ethical engagement with questions of rights, welfare, obligation, or representation might make a tangible difference. Activists used a liberal language of civic participation and transparency in contrast to the communal orientations of customary institutions and the new politics of the commons addressed in chapter 3. However, all these discourses were fundamentally relational, developing in response to one another and to the region's plural political environment.

Armed with their pragmatic understanding of local politics, civil society activists continued to militate, as they termed it, for greater participation in local government and economic development planning. A cynical interpretation might see their continued participation as naïveté or, worse, a self-serving effort to access funds and increase their own local prestige. Perhaps this was true for some. Silverstein (2010, 2013) documents how Amazigh activists in a nearby valley adapted transnational discourses of indigeneity and human rights to gain traction in more localized disputes. They had reframed assertions of privilege over formerly subjugated groups as indigenous claims along the lines of threatened autochthonous peoples participating in global social movements. Their goals, however, included limiting resource access for Black former sharecroppers. In the Mgoun Valley, activists downplayed Amazigh rights discourse in favor of the language of civil society movements. They developed a savvy strategy for making claims on the state that recognized the realities of how power was distributed—in effect, pushing the state to formalize itself by making good on stated goals for decentralization reforms, human rights reparations, and participatory planning.

Sometimes this meant seeing success in discursive shifts, with the hope that substantive change might come later. I knew one civil society activist who articulated this perspective especially clearly. Brahim was a schoolteacher from a well-placed family. Like many younger activists from notable families, he had transitioned his high status from the traditional domains of landownership and commanding the labor of others to more contemporary status markers: a civil service position, consulting work for development agencies, and a close familiarity with participatory development and "gender in development" discourses. He straddled different worlds in local politics, navigating customary politics through his connection to the local saintly brotherhood as well as new initiatives such as European Union democratization programs. Brahim was also on the board of the agricultural cooperative founded after the human rights reparations meeting described earlier. In expressing satisfaction at the progress made through the reparations program, he knew that more self-identified leftist or Amazigh activists in the region would see him as accommodationist or self-promoting. However, the fact that people like Brahim continued to see hope, meaning, and substance in these sometimes small changes after working for years in local and regional politics signaled something more than empty optimism or self-aggrandizement. That hope represented a pragmatic sophistication about the possibilities of local activism, that perhaps they could push the state to honor its declared commitment to serving individual, rights-bearing citizens, or at minimum, to institute a bureaucracy that followed its own official procedures. This pragmatism self-consciously eschewed radical goals but held out a possibility for reform because it recognized how power operated in local government. Brahim was one of the "regulars" who attended local government meetings, and he invited me along to even the driest workshops or planning sessions. As he saw it, these were important sites for the conduct of local politics.

"Who runs the world? The politicians or the experts?" Brahim asked this rhetorical question when he facilitated a training session for local civil society activists and sympathetic elected officials in the empty restaurant of one of the two local hotels. We all sat on the low banquettes typical of Moroccan salons as Brahim explained the 2008 local government charter that required communes to use participatory processes to craft development plans. The Ministry of Interior had jurisdiction over these plans, but elected officials were tasked with drafting and executing them. The slippage between elected institutions and the unaccountable authority of the ministry produced general confusion about how the planning process was supposed to proceed. Activists were concerned that local ministry officials would subvert meaningful participation in favor of their preferred projects. However, when the Ministry of Interior published a manual for doing participatory needs assessments, the activists saw an opening for bringing some accountability to the planning process (Bouhdou 2009). Brahim was able to use his connections as a development consultant to get a sneak preview of the manual. This would allow civil society activists and reform-minded officials to strategize before the planning process was undercut by ministry operatives or the intransigent old guard at the communes.

When he asked, "Who runs the world?" Brahim was echoing Mitchell's (2002) argument that politics and, by extension, politicians do not always hold the real power. It was the experts, technicians, and bureaucrats who could master procedural obfuscation and direct policies to their own ends who ran the world that was local politics in the southeast. Civil society activists had seen that the new guard of officials elected from their ranks could make real, if incremental, change in the ways potable water, development permits, waste management, and other government functions would be managed. They made change when they forced the state to act more like the bureaucracies of liberal states, even if Moroccan bureaucracies were not held accountable through credible electoral politics. They were essentially rejecting the informality of indirect rule, less by staking overtly political claims, although sometimes they did that too, than by being more statelike than the state itself.

Politics for these activists was as much about bureaucratic maneuvering as it was about claims for rights and representation. Their vision of political participation countered the arbitrary or irregular nature of the state by expanding governance based on individual rights and citizenship. They sought to "find real ethical spaces" that sometimes invoked lofty ideals but more often privileged political pragmatism on the premise that "actual transactions over the everyday distribution of rights and entitlements [can] lead over time to substantial redefinitions of property and law within the actually existing modern state" (Chatterjee 2006, 25, 75). This political approach was a fraught project for the activists—a state bureaucracy based on legible citizenship may be used to control or oppress, but it could also promote accountability and a routinization of government.

Customary Authority in a Plural Political Landscape

As I moved between local government meetings in Kelaa and my rural fieldwork, however, I had the nagging feeling that few people I knew in villages throughout the valley were aware of or invested in the civil society activists' project. In these contexts, the dominant register for conducting politics eschewed rights language in favor of the communal identities and institutions that were so important to the economic and political transformations described in chapter 1. Land and communal affiliation remained so important in the Mgoun Valley in part because they constituted a distinctive political idiom that resonated with rural residents' social and economic aspirations. I do not want to overstate the differences between their approach to politics and that of the civil society activists. The same people, for example, could operate in different political registers, such as when Brahim moved from his civil society activism to the gatherings of *shurufa'* (saints) that involved symbolic offerings to the local Islamic brotherhood.

However, the contrast between these different political idioms would occasionally erupt on the surface with notable clarity. This happened one day in August when I was interviewing a small group of farmers in the village of el Harte. A man burst into the room, warmly greeting everyone but clearly agitated. I could tell from the way he spoke Arabic—no one in el Harte spoke Arabic unless they had to—that he did not live in the village. After a quick series of inquiries about everyone's health and families, he asked, "Do you know anyone who can build an adobe wall?" Everyone's eyebrows went up, and my host said, "After the *'aid al-kabir* [the major religious holiday was approaching] you can get someone, but not now. Everyone is too busy." "But I need it now," he retorted. "If I do not build the wall, they will take the rest of our land." "*Mushkil* [that is a problem]," my host responded noncommittally. The ensuing conversation illustrated the pragmatic, unspoken contestations over what institutions and practices of rule should predominate in local politics. Indeed, the man, Khaled, did not live in el Harte. He was born and raised in the distant metropolis of Casablanca, but in the previous decade, his elderly father had retired to his natal home in el Harte and Khaled returned every year during the summer, as he had done since he was a child. Now in his fifties, Khaled had requested an allotment of communal land as a native son of the village even though he had never lived there. He would build a summer home and possibly retire there himself, although his karate school in Casablanca was keeping him in the city for the time being.

When Khaled visited his land during this last stay, he noticed it had been divided in half by small cairns and was told that the collective-land representatives had assigned that land to another petitioner. Khaled was indignant: "How can they give it and take it away? My family has not taken our rights in land here yet. Don't we have our rights? Our ancestors are buried here, and this is where we will be buried!" By enclosing the plot, he thought he could protect the remaining land since walls were respected as markers of ownership. There had apparently been some confusion about the boundaries of plots given to different people. Although this kind of confusion was usually not difficult to resolve, for Khaled it represented a contravention of his rights as a native member of the community. So many people wanted land in the village these days that he suspected corruption among the land representatives.[10] Khaled urged the men in the room to speak out for their rights against the representatives' arbitrary decisions. The others were sympathetic, but one noted: "No one here speaks up in that way"—to which Khaled responded, "Elect young people who can stand up to them!" The other men seemed amused by this sentiment, and my host closed the conversation with a quiet, "In the village, it is hard. It is not like you imagine."

Khaled, visibly frustrated, appeared to interpret this response as quiescence. However, I saw in the men's barely perceptible smiles a sense that they knew better. Rights talk had little resonance for the men in that room. They were aware of, and in some cases had family members involved in, the civil society activism that engaged local government officials in debates over plans and programs. But by and large, they were farmers, manual laborers, and tradesmen with limited access to and interest in the discourse of liberal rights-bearing citizenship. My host's response that "it is not like you imagine" was less a sign of resignation than a polite way of saying that Khaled had missed the point. Like the civil society activists, these men understood that real power did not reside in elected institutions, but they did not respond by engaging in the push-and-pull of formal politics. They felt more comfortable with customary institutions and the personalized authority of leaders who may or may not hold official roles in local government, although they were not averse to using the courts or the qa'id to advance their claims.

When civil society activists used the language of rights or citizenship, they rejected the idea of communal identities as the reference point for political participation. The activists sometimes described their goal as challenging the old guard, customary authorities like the collective-land representatives, or even the formerly subjugated groups who had acceded to local elected office but practiced "old style," personal politics. Such political practice did not conform to the activists' conception of modern citizenship, one that foregrounded individual rights but also located sovereignty exclusively in the state, even if the state was not yet willing to guarantee democratic participation. In some respects, this was a generational struggle between the elderly men who had served as leaders in the jma'a and continued to regard land and livestock as the primary sources of prestige or wealth, on the one hand, and younger activists who tended to be teachers and civil servants, on the other. Many activists had spent time working or attending school elsewhere in Morocco and sometimes abroad. In my discussions with them, they described the progress they had made in local and regional politics by listing the communes where older elected officials who had ruled uncontested for years had been unseated by younger challengers committed to government accountability. Kelaa Mgouna was not among these communes. There, activists rued how politics was still conducted through favors and informal relationships. This did not diminish the activists' involvement in programs such as human rights reparations or participatory communal planning, but it did inform their strategies: using bureaucratic procedure rather than overt political claims.

However, their efforts were more than a generational struggle against older men who had held on to power for too long. They also challenged an unroutinized form of government that relied on customary authority located "outside" the state and the arbitrary intrusion of the Ministry of Interior into daily life. To be sure, customary institutions were located outside the state only in a formal sense; in the daily practice of government, they operated in symbiotic relationship with state institutions and ministry officials. In some respects, customary and local government institutions mutually constituted one another, a legacy of the indirect rule detailed earlier. As Mamdani explains, the colonial system "ascribed rights and duties to groups, not to individuals. . . . Not surprisingly, where the legal and administrative order remain unchanged, these practices were only exacerbated by the introduction of representative political institutions at independence" (2012, 125). The result is ongoing tension between practices of rule based on individuals and groups. In southeastern Morocco, this tension was expressed in sophisticated state strategies, sometimes exemplified by the king himself, that pitted elected institutions of government against customary sources of authority. These customary authorities were not easily glossed as "traditional." They both facilitated a transformation of the social and economic order and reconstituted themselves in relation to the modern state. In fact, one of the reasons formerly subjugated groups' use of customary law to resist the Imazighen was so effective was that it recognized the ways the postcolonial state imbued customary land tenure with a new political relevance.

Customary leaders like Khaled's hosts in el Harte may not have been motivated by discourses of accountability based on rights-bearing citizenship, but they still made claims on the state. They developed personalized relationships with officials who supported their authority, and they made substantive claims to advance the needs of their communities. Some of the most influential people in the valley did not attend meetings at the municipality and were unaware of the human rights reparations program. Haj Ahmed, whom I introduced in the previous chapter as the collective-land representative of el Harte, expressed surprise that some in el Harte and Kelaa Mgouna had started complaining about the local commune president and the "old guard" style of politics he represented. The president was effective in bringing government funds to the area, he said. "Why would we complain that he is getting things done for us, for the region?" He either did not comprehend or accept activists' critique that government should represent citizens using transparent and democratic processes, rather than use their influence to negotiate for more funds from government ministries.[11] The most relevant terrain of political contestation for leaders like Haj Ahmed was land, not participatory development plans. However, the old guard and the civil society activists did not simply talk past each other. Most activists I met understood and felt personally invested in land as a pressing issue in the area. They respected customary institutions but regarded them as a style of governance that needed to be superseded or was already in decline.

Time and again, academic observers, officials from the interior and agriculture ministries, and community leaders emphasized to me that land was among the most urgent political issues not only in the Mgoun Valley but all over rural Morocco. However, the fact that land governance in this region was largely in the purview of customary tenure institutions "outside" the state located these politics in unformalized sites of authority that often bypassed the discourses of civil society activists. Those activists sometimes got involved in land disputes, but they were often on the sidelines of a politics they tended to code as "traditional" or "unfocused."[12] By "unfocused," they meant that claims were not articulated with coherent political goals but simply aimed to acquire land or advance personal objectives over explicitly political ones. This posed a challenge for activists working toward the rule of law and democratic participation. Ziyad, the head of the regional human rights commission introduced earlier, explained that the majority of claims the commission was now hearing were related to land: individual contraventions of land rights, unlawful allocations of collective holdings, corrupt land deals, and others. This was difficult, he said, because claimants could not articulate a human rights dimension to their complaints, and he worried that the groundswell of mobilizations and claims around land was not being directed for a common purpose or to make any broader political point.

At the same time, Ziyad felt that the human rights commission had to act because "land is the people's main concern here." Although land constituted the central political issue for so many, formal political sites such as the local commune remained on the margins of many land conflicts. Some people took land disputes to court, but customary tenure regimes and the Ministry of Interior officials who had inherited the role of "mediator" from their colonial predecessors remained the locus of authority for those disputes. Civil society activists talked about the need to work with people to make their land claims more "political," translating them into the language of rule of law and citizenship. In approaching land struggles in this way, activists effectively ceded leadership of mobilizations that invoked customary authority and substantive rather than procedural rights. As a result, activists often found themselves on the periphery of the new politics of the commons as an alternative approach to governing communal life.

Conclusion

It was undeniable that customary institutions such as the jma'a and tribal confederations saw their sovereignty eroded by the protectorate and the state territorialization strategies of the postindependence monarchy. However, the traces of indirect rule in contemporary governance had transformed, not eradicated, the political authority embedded in customary institutions. These institutions were imbricated with the state, which alternately resisted formalization and experimented with new efforts to territorialize its authority. In this context, land remained a site of trenchant political contestation between state actors, civil society activists, customary leaders, and groups marginalized from all these sites of political authority. When civil society activists labeled land claims as "pre-political," when I saw the knowing smiles of el Harte's farmers in response to the rights claims of their metropolitan visitor, and when state actors simultaneously overwhelmed residents with bureaucracy while distancing themselves from the responsibilities of daily governance, I understood that these stances also had implications for those with no visible presence in the formal conduct of politics—the "maids, widows, and orphans, and all weak and distressed persons whomsoever."[13] These were the poor women, formerly subjugated groups who had not been able to secure upward mobility, outsiders, and others whose status left them on the periphery of the sites of authority I have outlined in this chapter. Their political claims may have appeared invisible from the vantage point of dominant political actors, but they were as engaged with the valley's political pluralism as anyone else. They drew on some of the same discourses I have already described—communal identities and customary governance institutions—but for different ends. Those who had been excluded from access to land developed notions of commoning based on broader notions of reciprocity and ethical obligation. These emergent politics upset the balance that had been struck since the colonial period between a state interested in sustaining elements of indirect rule and customary leaders committed to protecting their authority over land. As people on the margins of formal political practice questioned their exclusion from land rights and access to other resources, their claims began to coalesce around a distributive politics that invoked idioms of obligation and dependency often rooted in the same customary institutions that historically excluded them. Their challenges may be called "political society," in Chatterjee's (2006) terms, or "everyday forms of resistance," in Scott's (1985) renowned formulation. In chapter 3, I weigh the possibility that these claims may represent something else: an emergent politics of the commons.

3
LAND AND THE NEW COMMONING

In 2008, residents of Ichihn watched as bulldozers began leveling land across the national road from their village, a small community on the steppe ten kilometers outside Kelaa Mgouna. An Arab businessman from Casablanca had rented the land on a ninety-nine-year lease through the Ministry of Interior, although the land was formally owned by the Aït Sedrate tribal confederation (which includes Ichihn). Ben Tounsi, the businessman, first enclosed the land by bringing in local adobe craftsmen to construct a low wall around the hundred-hectare concession. I visited the *firma* (commercial farm) in its third year of operation. Ben Tounsi gave me a tour of the drip irrigation system, the olive saplings, and the tall breaks designed to slow the harsh winds coming off the steppe. When I asked what inspired his agricultural investment in this challenging environment, he replied that he had fallen in love with the southeast—in his words, "its pure air and dramatic landscape"—when his construction company executed a government contract in the area. He also described the occasional bursts of anger toward him from residents of surrounding villages. Concluding that the anger stemmed from their poverty, Ben Tounsi employed local women on the farm and paid substantially more than the going rate. He was puzzled, though, that the anger continued. Ben Tounsi thought the land had been unused; his firma was the only built structure on the empty steppe, and the villages with claims to the land were tucked out of sight along a narrow riverbank. When I conducted interviews in the villages, I learned that residents had shifted from transhumant pastoralism to wage labor some decades ago, with some farming along the Dadès River. They did not use the steppe to pasture herds anymore, but they did not regard it as empty either.

They saw the makhzan exercise unaccountable authority over their land and dismissed the relevance of colonial laws that passed sovereignty, ownership, or authority—they were not concerned with legal definitions—from the tribal confederation to the state. As they saw more of their land enclosed for the benefit of outsiders, they fought back with an enclosure of their own.

One day in early 2010, a bulldozer appeared on Ichihn's side of the road and began leveling the land on another hundred-hectare concession granted by the Ministry of Interior according to colonial-era procedures for renting collectively owned land (Wizara al-Dakhiliya 2007). No one had consulted Ichihn's residents before a foreign investor took out a lease on the stretch of steppe adjacent to the village for another agricultural investment (rumor had it the concession was for a prickly pear farm). Word of the new concession traveled quickly. I heard about it through an acquaintance who sat next to an elderly woman on an overnight bus from Fès. She recounted how her son had called her back from a visit to relatives to help oppose the Ministry of Interior's allocation. After chasing away the scared bulldozer operator, residents countered the ministry's juridical enclosure with a physical enclosure of their own. They set up cairns at even intervals along the concession to stake their claims on the land. The scene looked like any of the hundreds of such cairns and low-slung adobe walls on the side of the national road: signs of land conflicts, negotiated land divisions, or individual appropriations (figure 12).[1] Ayoub, a retired migrant who had spent forty years in Belgium and helped lead the mobilization, told me that the land was not for the ministry to give away, because it belonged to them; it was part of their village's customary pasture land (hurm), not communal land belonging to the ethnic collectivity of Aït Sedrate. He explained that residents did not have anything against the *barrani* (foreigner or outsider; he used the Arabic term for this) who leased the land, but they felt that he should stay in *tamazirt inas* (his own homeland). He was referring in a literal sense to the businessman's home in Casablanca but also evoked the multivalence of the term *tamazirt*, a site for the construction of community and a social web through which people, place, and the cultural and material economies of belonging were reproduced (Hoffman 2007). Even if those lands were no longer being used to pasture livestock, the residents of Ichihn were, in Ayoub's words, "suffering, weak economically, and have the right to do whatever they want with their land. If they have the money, they could set up a firma like the foreigner, or a gas station, restaurant, stable, warehouse. Anything they need, but it is not the government's to rent. The boundaries between our land and the collective lands of Aït Sedrate may be customary [formally undefined] but we know what they are. And so, we did something. We were the first village in this area to do anything about all of the people coming to take land, and now other villages are following our lead."

FIGURE 12. A land division in the collective lands outside Kelaa Mgouna.
Photo by the author.

It was a quiet but bold opening salvo that put the *sulta* (government authorities) on notice. The authorities returned to the site in the middle of the night and removed the small piles of rocks. The next day, the villagers also returned, setting up encampments to guard the 122 allotments they had traced in the rocky earth. Men, women, and children—including the elderly woman arriving from Fès—moved full time into tents on the rocky expanse. Government authorities asked the village's elected representative to calm them down. The representative quoted the Ministry of Interior official who called him: "He told me, 'If it is land they want, we can give them land somewhere else.' I said they didn't want land anywhere else." After thirty-eight days of the standoff, a high-level provincial representative (the *secrétaire général*) called the elected representative and told him to warn Ichihn that the security forces would be dispatched to break up the encampments. The representative recounted his response: "I told the *secrétaire général* that there were 398 people there—I made up the number—and that the government should bring 398 ambulances because the people were not going to leave." The security forces did arrive, but with a limited appetite for intimidation. By the late afternoon, the qaʾid and Ichihn leaders came to an agreement with no violence. The agreement was an unmitigated success for the occupiers: the government retracted the concession and formally recognized Ichihn's land division. Ironically, it was in dividing that land, wresting it away from the juridical category of "collectively owned" by the larger tribal confederation, that Ichihn residents were able to express their own, more meaningful form of commoning.

This chapter demonstrates how emergent definitions of the *common good* worked out through land conflicts in places like Ichihn might produce a new politics of the commons. Land conflicts in and of themselves were certainly nothing new in the Mgoun Valley or anywhere else in Morocco. Historically, tribal confederations had elaborated sophisticated mechanisms for resolving such conflicts internally and with neighboring confederations. Tribal agreements did not always work, of course, and could lead to violence or simmering hostility (Chiche 2003). There was also great diversity in land conflicts, from long-standing personal rivalries, to resource access disputes, to proxy struggles over political power, among others (El Alaoui 2002). Similarly, villages divided their communally owned land among village or tribal rights holders for various reasons I detail below: some were the culmination of dissension, and others expressed a strong communal spirit. This chapter focuses on the subset of land conflicts, divisions, and mobilizations that used customary practices to challenge old hierarchies and make new political and subsistence claims. Contextualizing these conflicts in a genealogy of communal governance reveals how the mutual imbrication of colonial property law and customary land tenure simultaneously eroded one form of the commons and created an opening for marginalized groups to create a new one.

The fact that steppe land was collectively owned by tribal confederations in a formal legal sense did not imply that commoning was practiced in any meaningful way on that land. Collective lands evoked a unified tamazirt, but this presumptive social cohesion obscured long-standing inequalities, population mobility, and contingent relations between tribal governance and other political authorities (Hoffman 2007). It was this "traditional law rooted in discriminatory forms of social status" to which many of the mobilizations responded (Rachik 2016, 13). The commons had also been undermined when the French Protectorate absorbed collectively owned lands into the colonial juridical apparatus. That apparatus remained largely intact after independence in 1956, indicating why the most vociferous defenders of collective lands in 2010 were rural notables and state officials with a vested interest in their maintenance. Those most involved in land mobilizations like Ichihn were, by contrast, often the most marginalized: the poor, the formerly subjugated, women, and intraregional migrants without access to land. They challenged inherited practices of commoning that were communal only in name.

In resisting the state's concession of collectively owned land, then, Ichihn's residents were not trying to save a commons so much as forge a new one. When they learned that the Ministry of Interior had leased tribal confederation land for private use, they could have simply asked for the return of those collective lands.

They opted instead to divide the land among the village's households. Understanding how this decision could support commoning requires a historical and ethnographic analysis of how people maneuvered in the interstices of formal legal and political institutions. Because of ambiguities in collective-land law and villages' customary authority to manage their own communal lands without state involvement, most collective action around land occurred "outside" the law. Marginalized groups used this space of maneuver to make claims that simultaneously invoked their customary rights and resisted tribal confederation and, by extension, state authority. On the one hand, their actions on the land were often visible to officials or collective-land representatives who, as in the case of Ichihn, gave their formal imprimatur to residents' unilateral actions, simply ignored land mobilizations, or otherwise tried to interpret the law with minimal guidance from the Ministry of Interior. On the other hand, the commoning practices I document were largely invisible to official policy and data gathering on collectively owned land because the Direction des Affaires Rurales only monitored tribal confederation land under its purview, and, by the office's own admission, rarely conducted even this monitoring (Mousaif 2008). Land divisions at the village level and some that involved tribal confederations bypassed this national legal framework either because it did not apply or because it was simply not applied given local and provincial officials' irregular understanding of collective-land law (El Alaoui 2002).

The mobilizations in this chapter therefore worked through the ambiguous juridical status of collectively owned land to ethically refigure the commons for the benefit of those marginalized from formal politics. Aware that the institution of collectively owned lands had facilitated over a century of gradual enclosure, residents themselves used enclosure to break with the formal commons and develop a processual approach to commoning instead—working together to make political claims and jointly managing resources with a more egalitarian ethic. To be sure, there was a defensive element to this posture. As Massimo de Angelis notes, "It is either capital that makes the world *through commodification and enclosures*, or it is the rest of us—whoever that 'us' is—that makes the world through counterenclosures and commons" (2004, 61). The commons is a site of struggle, the strategic terrain on which the social, political, and material dimensions of commoning are worked out, sometimes without resolution. This pragmatic and unnostalgic understanding of common action reminds us that the "*latent commons cannot redeem us*. Some radical thinkers hope that progress will lead us to a redemptive and utopian commons. In contrast, the latent commons is here and now, amidst the trouble" (Tsing 2015, 255). Grappling with the commons that is "here and now" also troubles our conceptions of what the commons should look like. A counterenclosure, for example, might nurture a new commons regardless of the property form involved, using communal governance to secure subsistence rights and fashioning a moral economy to challenge past exclusions.

In what follows, I describe this emergent moral economy by first contextualizing it in the grand enclosure of a century ago: the colonial transformation of collective sovereignty into collective property under the tutelage of the state. By folding collective lands into the state space of positive law, the French Protectorate simultaneously created the commons and undermined it. The chapter then examines how the French colonial legacy shaped contemporary struggles around land. Ironically, the government's inability, or unwillingness, both during and after the protectorate to shepherd collective-land tenure along its "natural evolution" toward private property was principally responsible for eroding the "common" nature of collective lands (Lyautey 1927). This reframes the counterenclosures I documented in 2010 as a new approach to commoning rather than a straightforward drive to capitalist privatization. Dividing collectively owned land can represent the first step to commoditization and dispossession for marginalized landholders who subsequently succumb to distress sales.[2] This was a central dynamic in the littoral plains and agricultural areas around Meknes and Fès before and during the protectorate. In the contemporary period, rising land prices, increased speculation, and the growth of export agriculture has put similar pressures on landowners in commercial agricultural areas and urban peripheries. However, the spatially differentiated ways groups used land division in the Mgoun Valley underscore that we cannot assume commoditization and a dismantling of communal governance follow from counterenclosure. Following these cases ethnographically reveals how they created a nested form of private property that subjected individual holdings to communal governance and reinforced customary authority over social life. The claims and ethics of a new commoning articulated an alternative approach to rural politics that broke with traditional hierarchies and formal institutions of the state.

The Grand Enclosure of Colonialism

The strategic terrain for contemporary land conflicts can be traced to the French Protectorate's efforts to convert diverse forms of Moroccan collective sovereignty into a unitary juridical category of collective property ownership. The early colonial legal architecture governing collective lands is, with minor modifications, still in place today, and the assumptions underlying colonial attempts to fold collective lands into positive law continue to influence state land tenure policy. The legacy of this juridical framework produced the interesting alignments I observed during my fieldwork. I found that state agents and rural notables were often more invested in preserving collective lands than the economically poorer groups with whom I conducted most of my research. I was initially surprised when I heard staff at the Direction des Affaires Rurales, the Ministry of Interior agency charged with managing hundreds of thousands of hectares on behalf of their collective owners in the province of Ouarzazate, express dismay at contemporary pressures on collective lands. After all, post–World War II development orthodoxy had promoted individual or privatized land tenure as necessary to economic growth and containing the communist threat around the world.[3] In Morocco, official efforts to encourage private over collective landownership in pursuit of this orthodoxy are well documented (D. Davis 2006; Banque Mondiale 2008; Mahdi 2014). When I delved deeper into the history of collective lands during the protectorate period, however, it became apparent that state interest in retaining collective lands did not contradict colonial ideologies of enclosure or modernist preferences for private property.

This became clear to me one cold winter day at the directorate offices in the provincial capital, Ouarzazate. I had arranged a meeting with the director of rural affairs to request a map of the Mgoun confederation's collective lands. Sitting at a corner of a large conference table covered with maps, reports, and file folders, I had expected a short and unproductive meeting. It usually took many visits to track down these kinds of documents, if I could find them at all. Instead, I spent hours observing the staff's work and listening to the director take calls—and even hold meetings with complainants in land disputes—in between long discussions with him about the state of Ouarzazate's collective lands. The director was engaged, open, and critical. He and his staff at the directorate in Ouarzazate, which had authority over the Mgoun Valley until the new province of Tinghir was established in mid-2010, took their work very seriously. They scrambled with a meager budget and inadequate staff to manage the vast collective lands belonging to tribal confederations they worried were on the brink of dissolving. As the director explained, "Small appropriations and the piecemeal extensions of villages are eroding the integrity of collective lands." He expressed concern about the decline of communal identities: "When the collectivity does not have land, it is no longer a collective. It is not only a group of people that are threatened—history, customs, tradition are disappearing. We are talking about the future of our collectivities, our tribes."

The director's concern was genuine and informed, but it also extended a narrative present since the early colonial period that only the state could protect collective lands and the cultural integrity of the social formations (the tribes) that officially owned them. This narrative decried the rising individualism of rural Moroccans, quick to sell or divide their collective patrimony. From the precolonial French scientific missions to postcolonial retrospectives of the protectorate, the dominant official narrative was that makhzan corruption, peasant improvidence, and the dissolution of communal sentiments drove the decline of collective lands. Albert Guillaume, former French director of Morocco's collective lands during the colonial period and close confidant of the first resident general of the protectorate, Hubert Lyautey, summarized these concerns when he wondered why so many Moroccan peasants were "trying to appropriate collective rangelands" (1960, 74). He warned about the dangers of the "excessive individualism" driving these appropriations and emphasized the role of the protectorate in saving Moroccans from themselves by assuming tutelary authority over their collective lands (74). It was a narrative that, not surprisingly, occluded the first grand act of enclosure in the twentieth century, that of colonialism itself.

Producing Land Knowledge

French efforts to understand and shape collective rights in land began well before the imposition of the protectorate in 1912. Scholars analyzed the plural legal environment for land tenure in the sultanate as part of a broader effort to facilitate property transfers to Europeans in the speculative environment of the late nineteenth and early twentieth centuries. Understanding how the makhzan controlled land or otherwise exercised authority in the presence of alternative sovereignties (primarily in the form of tribal confederations) was also important for justifying the concentration and transfer of that authority to a territorialized central state controlled by the French. These arguments were developed in the pages of *Archives Marocaines*, the journal of the Mission Scientifique du Maroc, and *L'Afrique Française*, the bulletin of the Comité de l'Afrique Française (the main scientific societies that produced colonial knowledge on Morocco), as well as in the writing of French jurists, many of whom were trained or served in colonial Algeria.[4] They documented the difficulty of tracing property rights when the majority of Morocco's land was communally held with varying usufruct arrangements. Observers rued the vast tracts of fertile land they considered excellent for cultivation but seemed to go unused, "abandoned by the makhzan for pastureland" (Salmon 1904, 148). This echoed the official French position developed over the previous century in Algeria that pastoralism was not only unproductive but actively destroyed the land.[5] The notion that the makhzan abandoned productive land supported the colonial proposition that the sultanate had abdicated its responsibility for adjudicating land tenure. This abdication in turn created a speculative climate, which French scholars criticized because it encouraged Europeans and well-placed Moroccans alike to dispossess poor Moroccans for a quick profit on land transfers (Courageot 1934). They saw rampant dispossession as a threat to the peaceable implantation of French control. At the same time, and somewhat paradoxically, jurists described the makhzan's failure to adjudicate land as preventing the lawful land acquisition by Europeans because Moroccan officials and judges at the local level exercised unchecked power (Amar 1913). This was a central justification for the formal establishment of the protectorate in 1912 (Pennell 2000).

Understanding the nature of state sovereignty over land was therefore important for theorizing French authority to direct land transfers to Europeans, control populations resistant to French control, and territorialize government along the modern European state model. Collective lands posed a problem for these projects because they represented an alternative form of sovereignty that the makhzan never eradicated, especially in the areas traditionally considered *insoumis* or *siba*.[6] Scholars and jurists writing for the protectorate were preoccupied with finding the legal origins of collective property in a way that would vest ultimate sovereignty in the makhzan, and by extension, the modern state the French charged themselves with creating. One line of argumentation held that collective property was rooted in the long-standing anarchy of precolonial Morocco. By this reasoning, centuries of economic and social instability rendered the development of private property beyond the limited areas of central state control impossible because the weak legal and political infrastructure could not support individualized property rights (Berthault 1936; Courageot 1934). In the nomadic areas outside makhzan control, some French officers and scholars recognized ecological reasons for collective ownership given the difficulty of demarcating individual rights in the vast rangelands of the Atlas and pre-Sahara (D. Davis 2007). Once stability was secured, however, the need for collective land would disappear even there; the security of the colonial order would "help Moroccan individualism find its full expression" (Courageot 1934, 39).

Some of those same commentators decried Moroccan individualism as undermining the cohesiveness of rural society. That contradiction, among others, produced a legal architecture suffused with tensions about how to deal with Moroccans' property rights. Broadly speaking, there were four imperatives guiding early protectorate laws regarding collective lands: freeing land for state and private colonization, demonstrating respect for indigenous land tenure and customary law to quell political opposition, securing complete military control over the restive mountains and southern oases, and promoting the view that private property was fundamental to progress and civilization.

Preserve, Teach, Expropriate

There was another concern that framed all these governing imperatives: to avoid repeating the mistakes the French committed in Algeria. Michaux-Bellaire (1924), one of the premier French scholars of the period, summarized the objective of the protectorate as offering lands for colonization while avoiding the negative consequences of the Algerian approach. There, the French declared state sovereignty over all collective lands, facilitating the almost complete dispossession of Algerians through an aggressive colonization program and other policies that French officials in Morocco deemed *"inadaptés"* or insensitive to the basic needs of native residents (Courageot 1934; D. Davis 2007). General Lyautey, famously contemptuous of European colons after his own experience in Algeria, articulated a strategy of respect for indigenous institutions (Hoisington 1995). The land tenure policies he promulgated are often understood in light of this ideology of indirect rule (Bidwell 1973). However, Lyautey's disdain for colons should not, as some historical accounts warn us, be taken as disdain for colonial exploitation. He disliked the petty greed of colons, but his aristocratic and monarchical leanings were well known; he was happy to work with large agrobusiness entities acquiring vast tracts of land and with Moroccan notables eager to enrich themselves while supporting French rule (D. Davis 2007; Pennell 2000). Diana Davis (2007) notes that even if the legal and political strategies in Algeria and Morocco differed, the results were the same for indigenous dispossession and the transformation of collective lands into a property form that could be easily expropriated. Unlike in Algeria, however, the Moroccan approach sustained collective property regimes rather than imposing the French civil code outright (Berthault 1936, 211). Regardless, both approaches transformed tribal sovereignty over communal lands into a form of property that could accelerate the "natural evolution" toward privately titled land.

The reasoning permeating French land law drew on the Lockean assumption that whoever did not render their land productive did not deserve to own it (D. Davis 2007; Hoisington 1995). This justified enclosure on both economic and civilizational grounds. As Massimo De Angelis (2004) reminds us, enclosure does not simply dispossess but also shapes new subjects normalized to the capitalist market. Lyautey was explicit about how this pedagogical intent served the colonial mission: "We are arriving, we have already arrived, at making them understand, making them believe that the true form of property is individual property. And so, to the extent that we transform tribal collective lands into individual lands, and as we increase the value of the holdings [*domaine*] of each tribal member, we ask in return that they cede a part of their collective lands to the State. And it is precisely on this collective land that we create the state lands [*lots domaniaux*] to benefit colonization" (1927, 398). Lyautey's vision of colonial tutelage was rooted in the belief that private property represented civilization and progress, but in Morocco, it was also a pragmatic concern. There simply was not enough private property to satisfy French colonial ambitions: collective lands would have to be transferred as well (Bidwell 1973). This posed a political dilemma. Scholars asserted that in Morocco, unlike Algeria and Tunisia, "creating private property was delicate work because Morocco is, in effect, a country populated by a race of farmers attached to their soil" (Berthault 1936, 213). By French estimation, Moroccans may not have been adequately valorizing their land, but they nonetheless actively resisted expropriation and were unwilling sellers. A legal framework that formally acknowledged collective ownership in land and provided a mechanism for transferring portions of that land for colonial development could, the thinking went, sensitively address Moroccan reticence and promote European colonization at the same time.

The French legal framework was based on a positivist approach to governing territory, not social groups (Bouderbala 1996). This contrasted with the Moroccan understanding of social groups as "potential" objects of government rather than a standing unit of territorial control; their "existence was linked to the events that activated them," such as tribal conflict or a sultan's military expedition (Rachik 2016, 31). The protectorate dismantled this system through a series of laws that transformed tribal sovereignty from control over "territory" to ownership of "collective property." Immediately upon the declaration of the protectorate in 1912, legislation prohibited ethnic collectivities—a term used to indicate tribal confederations—from selling their land in an attempt to slow the rampant land speculation in the collectively held areas of the littoral plains (Milliot 1922). A 1916 dahir recognized the jma'a of a tribe as a "moral person," empowered to represent these collectivities by serving as a "consultative voice for all questions relating to common interest" (Milliot 1922, 60). If the jma'a presided over community interests in some vague sense, the legislation left the question of who actually owned collective lands unanswered (Zirari-Devif 2009–2010). The ambiguity of this early dahir and its ineffectiveness in stopping land speculation led to a 1919 dahir that specified ethnic collectivities as owners of land held in common. The collectivities as a whole were now deemed "moral persons" in the eyes of the law, which nonetheless never defined the legal features of "moral personhood" (Milliot 1922, 67). Property could be held collectively by tribal confederations over large swathes of land, at smaller scales by lineages, or locally by single communities. Historically, however, sovereignty over these lands did not nest smaller scales neatly into larger ones but could overlap; sovereign authority could also shift depending on the negotiating power of parties at any given time.

At the same time that protectorate legislation established formal collective ownership over land, it circumscribed that ownership through the creation of "tutelary authority" vested in a council for the disposition of collective lands housed at the Direction des Affaires Indigènes. The council was composed of the Directeur des Affaires Indigènes, a representative of the Gouvernement Chérifien (the relevant Moroccan official) or, importantly, a French functionary representing that Moroccan official, a French magistrate, and two Muslim notables (collective-land representatives) appointed by the grand vizir (Empire Chérifien/ Protectorat de la République Française au Maroc 1919). The committee weighed proposals for allocating collective lands for individual projects (usually private French agrobusiness or concessions for colonial settlers) or state-led infrastructure projects such as road building (Bidwell 1973). The state could also preside over the division of collective lands among the entirety of the ayants-droits, members of the ethnic collectivity due a share of communal land, using a fraught process described in chapter 1. In the case of formal division, the land would become the private property of the individual rights holders (although this provision was eventually reversed), while for concessions for individual projects, the fiction of long-term usufruct contracts resulted in the de facto transfer, and often eventual formalization, of ownership to foreign investors or Moroccan notables. These allocation procedures concentrated communal authority over land disposition in one office holder per ethnic collectivity (as opposed to the jmaʿa, which in the 1912 dahir had been tasked with representing common interest). With the 1919 dahir, collective ownership was essentially vested in the person of the collective-land representative, a liminal bureaucratic figure officially chosen through indigenous procedures by tribal members, but in reality a lifelong sinecure held by powerful regional notables, some with more popular legitimacy than others.[7]

Creating the Commons in Order to Dismantle It

Despite Lyautey's rhetoric about preserving indigenous institutions, colonial legal scholars recognized that protectorate land tenure policy was not simply a restitution of customary practice but a new configuration of rights. Georges Surdon, a noted French jurist, admitted in 1926 that collective lands were "nothing but an invention of the Protectorate" (quoted in Karsenty 1988, 445). These new tenure rights would transition collective property to private freehold in a departure from the French colonial treatment of customary law in West Africa, where the focus was on codifying collective usufruct rights rather than ownership (Le Roy, Karsenty, and Bertrand 1995). Moroccan collective-land representatives, by contrast, did not sign treaties as sovereigns governing territory but rather sold or ceded land as owners (Guillaume 1960). As in Pauline Peters's analysis of the Botswana case, "almost as soon as the commons was created [by colonial law] so it began to be dismembered" (1994, 3). Echoing the enclosure of American Indian lands in the United States, this legal maneuver did not just transfer property; it enacted a political project to transfer sovereignty (Chang 2011). As Mamdani describes for elsewhere in colonial Africa, tutelary authority in Morocco represented the incorporation of "natives into a state-enforced customary order" that vested ultimate authority in colonial government (1996, 18).

The law ostensibly declared collective land inalienable but placed the actual rights of disposition in the hands of the tutelary authority, not the collectivities themselves. The council convened by the tutelary authority would "assure that the collectivity possesses enough land for its own, normal development. . . . The council will substitute itself for the collectivity, taking on the responsibility of a diligent tutor and good father [*bon père de famille*]" (Guillaume 1960, 25). Tutelary authority drew on this paternal metaphor (which has roots in Roman law) to assert that the ethnic collectivity was a "minor" unable to govern itself, as witnessed by collectivities' inability to protect their lands from speculation in the period before and immediately after the creation of the protectorate. The Directeur des Affaires Indigènes, as head of this council, had the right to act on behalf of the jma'a, and council decisions were final (Milliot 1922, 79). The absence of an appeals process then—and in the contemporary period—fueled land disputes outside the framework of property law as claimants enacted their own forms of appeal on the land itself or otherwise tried to pursue cases in the courts (Zirari-Devif 2009–2010, 125). In the Wild West atmosphere of early colonial land grabbing, these procedures allowed for the wholesale transfer of large tracts of productive land to colonial concerns under the guise of respecting Moroccan institutions (Bidwell 1973; D. Davis 2007; Pascon 1986). A state-led enclosure process fueled intense land speculation in these early years, creating a reserve of collective land under state control to be doled out through opaque and unaccountable procedures while ostensibly retaining ethnic collectivities' formal ownership of that land.

These policies produced many conflicting imperatives, but one is particularly relevant to the contemporary context. Officials at the time recognized the tension resulting from how the tutelary structure imbricated different tenure systems—a reified version of customary and French positive law—with one another, although these were hardly unitary categories themselves (Bouderbala 1999). Colonial property law "created" collective lands not simply to expropriate them but to fulfill the impossible mandate of simultaneously preserving indigenous tenure and nudging Moroccans along an evolutionary path to private property (Karsenty 1988). The result was a contradictory set of policies that decried *melkisation*, the division of collective lands to produce mulk (private property in Islamic law), in some circumstances and actively promoted individualized tenure in others (Pascon and Ennaji 1986). A rural exodus feeding into politically restive and economically destitute shantytowns around major cities raised concerns about native improvidence in selling off collective lands (Gallisot 1964; Montagne 1952). Yet, the same legal framework that stoked fears of political instability had facilitated these sell-offs or otherwise allocated land for *pied-noir* farms with the reasoning that Moroccans were not fulfilling these lands' productive potential. Without resolving these contradictions, protectorate policy shifted after Lyautey stepped down as resident general in 1925. The guiding philosophy of the tutelary structure moved from Lyautey's associationist rhetoric of protecting collective lands for Moroccans to a more explicitly pedagogical one of retaining collective ownership as Moroccans "learned" the ways of modern landholding (Bouderbala 1996).

These tensions played out differently depending on the location and potential economic value of collectively owned land. In the littoral plains, melkisation accelerated as both official and private colonization transferred over a million hectares to European interests (D. Davis 2007, 138). Official colonization ended, however, just after the French conquered the remaining pockets of resistance in the southeast in 1933. Although private colonization continued, the policy of providing state allocations to French colons was controversially phased out in 1935 (Bouderbala, Chraïbi, and Pascon 1974). In the southeast, then, the juridical procedures that transferred collective land for official colonization were of little relevance during the colonial period. There was minimal foreign interest in directly colonizing these peripheral zones. Although my oral histories did surface accounts of land seizures, it was primarily the proxy rulers, the Glaoua, and their agents who capriciously took land outside any framework of property law. They did not bother to invoke any colonial dahirs, nor were they stopped by the French indigenous affairs officers who blandly noted the seizures in biweekly political reports to the regional directorate in Marrakech.

The juridical framework for collective lands may not have shaped people's experience of colonialism in the Mgoun Valley, but it was certainly relevant to the land conflicts I witnessed in 2010. It was the director of rural affairs who alerted me to the importance of this genealogy the day I visited his office in search of the map of Mgoun. When he expressed dismay that ayants-droits were dismantling their own collective patrimony, however, he was doing more than rehearsing the colonial narrative of Moroccan improvidence. He was also acknowledging the role of the state (and his own directorate) in undermining collective lands and the communal sentiments that he felt should accompany them. The director's desire to preserve collective lands for the benefit of their owners seemed quite genuine. However, by drawing my attention to how the state had essentially folded the commons into the bureaucratic apparatus, he shed light on why dividing the commons might constitute a new form of common action.

The Contemporary Legacy of Protectorate Land Governance

Despite some twists and turns in colonial and postcolonial property law, the 1919 dahir remains in force with only minor modifications (El Alaoui 2002; Zirari-Devif 2009–2010). Upon independence, Morocco did not enact sweeping land reforms or nationalization programs as in other decolonizing African or Middle Eastern countries (especially Egypt and, after its war of independence, Algeria). The limited land reform that was promulgated distributed less than four hundred thousand hectares to only twenty-three thousand beneficiaries (Pascon and Ennaji 1986, 97). Millions more that had passed to colons during the protectorate were either hastily sold to Moroccan elites in the immediate aftermath of independence or were folded into the makhzan and the king's personal holdings. None of the privately held colonized land was redistributed back to its original owners or tribal rights holders (Pascon and Ennaji 1986). The state and the king himself remain the country's largest landowners (Banque Mondiale 2008). King Mohamed V's deftness in managing the transition to independence to the detriment of left-leaning redistributive political programs undermined efforts to substantially refashion the colonial legal architecture for collective lands. He alternately crushed rural revolts against his newly centralized authority and co-opted rural notables (Hammoudi 1997; Leveau 1985).

There were some modifications to collective property law. In the postcolonial period, the first substantive modification came with the agricultural investment law of 1969, which mandated the distribution of collective lands to their rights holders in the large irrigated perimeters created through the official policy of large-scale dam building (D. Davis 2006; Swearingen 1988). There are two irrigated perimeters in the southeast: the Ziz and the Dra' Valleys. Most of the land within these perimeters was mulk even before the 1969 law, as most intensively cultivated oasis land had been for centuries. By contrast, the Mgoun Valley, dominated by rangeland, mountainous terrain, and narrow river valleys, falls under the 1919 dahir governing collective lands; as noted in chapter 1, the delimited status of confederation territory means that mulk along the riparian oasis is not officially recognized by the state. Landowners cannot get official title to their land. Another set of laws, 33–94 and 34–94 of 1995, superseded that of 1969 in an explicit attempt to render drylands "more productive" and to prevent the putative abandonment of rain-fed land in primarily collectively owned areas (Van Buu 1995). The laws provided for the categorization of these lands into agricultural improvement, pastoral amelioration, and soil conservation zones and updated the legal infrastructure for imposing market logics on Morocco's drylands (Davis 2006). Although these laws have had marked impacts elsewhere in Morocco—by 2005, over 1.3 million hectares had been declared as perimeters and therefore subject to the laws—no such perimeters or improvement zones have been declared in the steppe surrounding the Mgoun Valley or in Tinghir province more generally (Bajeddi 2000, 25).

The independent monarchy retained the legal and bureaucratic regime developed under the protectorate, renaming the Direction des Affaires Indigènes to become the Direction des Affaires Rurales. Housed within the Ministry of Interior, the directorate inherited the colonial state's tutelary authority and, to this day, coordinates the same protectorate-era council charged with allocating collective land. The directorate also manages the accounts of the ethnic collectivities receiving rent on the long-term contracts on their property and otherwise attempts to resolve disputes over collective lands.[8] The director of rural affairs in Ouarzazate was committed to protecting collective lands, but he also offered a disarmingly frank analysis of the state's own role in creating what he called the "land problem." He noted that the government had never codified procedures for determining individual rights in collective lands beyond the land allocation councils under the ministry's tutelage, as evidenced by the diverse procedures used by the ethnic collectivities listed in the Ministry of Interior's 1996 survey of collective land policies (Royaume du Maroc 1996). Nor did property law clarify the relationship between the state's juridical authority and the myriad ownership and usufruct rights layered over collective lands. The director recognized that the colonial-era tension between the stated objective of protecting collective lands and allocating those lands to outside investors had become even more untenable in the contemporary period, with so many groups claiming land in even the most peripheral fringes of the country. He worried about the large investment projects as well as the small encroachments that were eating away at collective holdings. However, unlike other officials I encountered, he readily admitted the role of the state in producing this situation. He located the problem in ambiguities in the law: "While the state promotes the mapping and delimitation of collective lands, we have never developed a consistent definition of what it means to be a rights holder in land. When collective lands are divided, many tribal members don't get their rights, like émigrés, women, and immigrants into the area." I was struck by the director's concern for equity, a sentiment few people I met associated with the Ministry of Interior. As a committed officer of the ministry, he struggled with the fact that the government's tutelary authority was a primary reason for this state of affairs.

It was a state of affairs that most actors involved—officials, land tenure scholars, human rights activists, and rights holders in collective lands—considered an impasse. If French colonial land policy aimed to move Moroccans along an evolutionary path toward private property, this evolution had hardly proceeded as planned. Despite the massive conversion of collective lands into privately held land in the littoral plains, the primary effect of colonial property law in the southeast was to ossify land tenure and the customary land tenure regimes that supposedly governed them. Virtually everyone agreed that this land problem was political, with periodic efforts in the postindependence period to clarify state policy on recuperated lands from colonization and collectively owned land. The first such national colloquium was held in 1969 and presided over by General Mohamed Oufkir, then minister of the interior; he was executed three years later for his alleged role in an assassination attempt against King Hassan II (Bouderbala, Chraïbi, and Pascon 1974). Another national colloquium on collective lands held in 1996 by the Ministry of Interior gathered land tenure experts and government officials, concluding that "today, everything is working against traditional collectivities. Time will only aggravate this drama.... It is evident that all reform must depart from the admission that these institutions are inadequate to the reality of the current situation" (Royaume du Maroc 1996, 9). Echoing earlier colonial discourse, the consensus of the colloquium was the need to stop piecemeal appropriations while at the same time encouraging the sedentarization of nomadic "collectivists" and the division of communal land so that they could develop their patrimony for greater economic productivity. And in an echo of post–World War II development orthodoxy, the final report emphasized the need to revisit a basic principle of collective land: its formal inalienability.

After the colloquium, however, this principle was not revisited, no reforms were passed, and surveying of collective lands remained stalled. In 2009, another national committee was convened with land tenure experts—some of whom had been vocal in their criticism of government land policy—to again address the collective land problem. This committee never issued a final report before it was quietly disbanded. Participants in that committee with whom I spoke were held to a nondisclosure agreement but ascribed the paralysis at least in part to the political sensitivity of defining official rights holders. All the ferment of land transfers, investment projects, piecemeal appropriations, and land occupations was therefore occurring on the margins of a property law that had remained in force since 1919. In Ouarzazate province, this activity was difficult to track in any systematic way because the Provincial Directorate of Rural Affairs had little capacity to gather data on the vast holdings under its purview (295,000 hectares). In a report to his superiors at the Ministry of Interior, the head of the directorate expressed frustration that his office did not have adequate documentation about cessions or collective-land division from the 1970s on, that the data supplied by the central tutelary authority did not provide enough detail for his office to locate the actual holdings, and that other state agencies claiming eminent domain on collective land refused to forward information on property in their possession (Mousaif 2008, 9). The Ministry of Interior itself, then, had virtually no data on what was happening on collectively owned land in Ouarzazate and was not confident about the limited data it did have.

This legal situation fueled intensifying conflicts and national scandals over the opacity of collective-land transfers (Berriane 2017). For years, but especially since a speculative and construction boom began midway through the first decade of the twenty-first century in major cities such as Tangier and Marrakech, the Moroccan press had been full of coverage regarding protests against land deals and corrupt transfers of collective lands for housing or other investment projects.[9] Housing shortages, land speculation, real estate projects for luxury tourism, industrial or agricultural initiatives, and other land uses drove intense activity on collective lands not already transformed into private freehold, especially in urban peripheries (Bogaert 2018). The main theme underlying the scandals and protests was the opaque transfer procedures whereby land allocation councils ceded land cheaply or at no cost to insiders. That land was subsequently resold or developed for outrageous profits, exacerbating already-existing land inequalities and precipitating new social mobilizations, especially from *soulaliyates*, women rights holders in collective lands (Aït Mous and Berriane 2016; Berriane 2015, 2017; Berriane and Rignall 2017). These developments indicate that the paralysis surrounding the legal status of collective land was not simply about the difficulty of defining rights holders. Rather, paralysis had the salutary effect of retaining vast reserves official actors could allocate to private or public interests, positioning collective land as a state-sanctioned "frontier of commodification" (Kelly and Peluso 2015).

Colonial property law and its postcolonial deployment therefore promoted enclosure in large part by *not* fulfilling its mission of transforming collective lands into private property. Retaining the institution of tutelary authority allowed the Ministry of Interior to hold collective lands in abeyance, dismantling indigenous systems for governance while ostensibly preserving their formal ownership of the land. This scenario may not conform to the formal definition of enclosure, the literal or legal fencing off of common lands for individual or private use.[10] The state did not parcel out land in a single act of enclosure—juridical or otherwise—but the effects were similar in the ways land was held in reserve to be distributed through opaque procedures. This sheds light on why state officials and elites were often the most vocal defenders of collective lands, decrying popular efforts to undermine communal holdings. Some officials, like the director of rural affairs in Ouarzazate, expressed commitment to preserving tribal patrimony. For others, not fully commoditizing collective land kept vast tracts out of the market; privatizing collective lands would have pulled this reserve out from the purview of the Ministry of Interior.

This situation is not unique to Morocco. Scholars in other parts of Africa have described how "government's ability to expropriate land was better served by the maintenance of customary tenure as controlled by tribal authorities than by any reform that provided statutory recognition (and need to negotiate compensation) for individual users' rights" (Chimhowu and Woodhouse 2006, 351). As Tania Li (2014b) emphasizes, fuzzy legal frameworks and incomplete markets are often the most profitable means of securing privatization and enclosing land. In Morocco, the state has gradually enclosed collective lands by maintaining communal tenure regimes rather than dismantling them outright. This strategy has enabled the state to promote the image of the makhzan and *la tutelle* as protecting the nation's collective patrimony while simultaneously creating a sanctioned institutional space for enclosing collective lands. The commons was the easiest, most profitable path to enclosure.

Counterenclosures as Common Action

If, in Morocco, the commons produced enclosure, then perhaps a counterenclosure could produce a new commons. The ever-looming prospect of potential enclosure for the benefit of outsiders worried residents of the Mgoun Valley and motivated occupations like that of Ichihn—when residents scared off the bulldozer operator and occupied the land for thirty-eight days before the state acceded to their demands. Whereas official observers interpreted the mobilizations as evidence that collective institutions were breaking down, others I spoke to in Mgoun described them as an alternative approach to commoning that defined their relation to the land on their own terms. When viewed from this perspective, the mobilizations I witnessed in 2010 evinced a complex relationship to the past: their strategies referenced a well-established dialectic between communal tenure and individualized property rights. Historically, the tenure status of land could shift between individual and collective ownership or control; these categorizations were not static over time and space (Rachik 2016). Despite these historical antecedents, however, the mobilizations of 2010 did not represent a return to a romanticized communal past. The contemporary counterenclosures rejected the way the modern state had appropriated collective lands and challenged the exclusions historically embedded in the commons, but they stopped short of a resistance movement. The vision of the good life articulated here was usually quite modest, emphasizing the right to a livelihood in the tamazirt instead of being forced to migrate for a precarious life in peri-urban shantytowns.

The Political Dimensions of Contemporary Land Mobilizations

The events in Ichihn that opened this chapter reverberated throughout the area, inspiring active debates and new mobilizations. Six months later, in October 2010, and emboldened by Ichihn's success, residents of el Bour n'Aït Yahya began staking claims in the steppe just a few kilometers from where the Ichihn standoff had taken place. El Bour n'Aït Yahya is the relatively new settlement described in chapter 1 founded approximately thirty years earlier in privately held land outside Kelaa Mgouna. In 2010, residents saw someone "signaling" (`alam in Arabic) a plot, laying out rocks in the collective lands beyond the settlement as though to claim territory, even though officials had halted land sales in the area because of alleged corruption. Angry residents set up encampments in the same style as those of Ichihn to drive off the furtive claimant and refused to leave until the qa'id gave each of them their own plot. Unlike the residents of Ichihn, the occupiers here were largely Imaghrani migrants with no land rights based on a historical affiliation with local tribal confederations. Their land claims in the occupation of fall 2010 were about the right to set up households and to subsist in their new homes. The encampments drew more and more claimants as local officials worked quickly to broker an agreement for land allocations outside the settlement. The land occupation in Ichihn that inspired this sit-in (people used the English term) had taken thirty-eight days and a standoff with the military to achieve success. The residents of el Bour, by contrast, had timed their occupation to coincide with an impending royal visit and the qa'id could not afford to have the king view a land protest as his motorcade passed by. They received their concessions in just two weeks. Everyone who had lived in the area for over five years could sign up to receive an allotment, which would divide up a wide swath of steppe between el Bour and the foothills of the Atlas. According to the elected representative of el Bour, the allotments were meant to help poor families set up households for themselves and their children, although he conceded that income level was not a criterion for acceptance on the list. Youssef, a livestock trader whom I interviewed in el Bour, signed up to receive a plot even though he was well off. "You always need more land," he shrugged.

I heard local officials express their dismay at this incursion into collectively owned lands, but they felt they had to concede to popular demands in the days before the king's visit. For participants, however, these mobilizations articulated communal sentiments in an emergent form of political expression. This was a very different site for political action than the local government meetings and civil society gatherings described in the previous chapter, where land divisions or mobilizations were often coded as pre-political. Nor did these mobilizations ally themselves with Amazigh activism or other social movements. Rather, they drew on a moral economy of subsistence and land rights as a basic feature of people's communal identities. In the face of challenges to their rights to land and livelihood, people came together not by operating on the field of law or formal political organization but by moving directly on the land. In the urban peripheries of Sao Paolo, James Holston (2008) describes how marginalized residents developed new conceptions of citizenship by both occupying space and working through the law. They mastered arcane bureaucratic procedures and used the legal opacity that for centuries had been used against them to legalize their property. In the Mgoun Valley, by contrast, participants in the land mobilizations disregarded or worked outside formal legal frameworks, claiming territory and waiting to see what kind of response their claims would elicit. The mobilizations were, in important respects, an extension of the slow action of villages like el Harte, described in chapter 1, where upwardly mobile former sharecroppers used customary law and patient investments in land to challenge the racialized dominance of the neighboring Amazigh village. Those investments were aimed at securing family well-being but also had political intent. The striking assertion of political voice in Ichihn, el Bour, and, as described in the introduction, Imzilne punctured the surface of that slow action with an explicit challenge to the dominance of rural notables and an unaccountable state.

I pieced together the political meaning of these mobilizations through extended discussions with participants and comparisons with other land conflicts. Not all parties to land conflicts expressed the same political intent. On the hard dirt road leading into Rbat, for instance, a large cement house slowly took shape during my first year of research. An infusion of income had allowed a family in one of Rbat's neighboring communities to "upgrade" from the adobe and rock that characterized the adjacent compounds. This home ignited, or extended, a local political controversy since it was pointedly located in the hurm of Rbat, not the neighboring village where the owner lived. Even people from the builder's own community were concerned about the confrontational move: the owner had simply started building at night in defiance of customary law and of Rbat's dominant family. Each night, a few more cement blocks were laid. The furtive home builder did not have rights to that land as an outsider with no customary claims, and in any case, Rbat had forbade construction in the hurm to preserve the spring that served as the village's primary water source. Observers interpreted the construction as the latest phase of a long-standing electoral dispute that had created enmity between the two families. Although Rbat could have made an entreaty to the local Ministry of Interior office—the director of rural affairs in Ouarzazate asserted that they occasionally removed illegal construction, but no one I spoke to recalled this being done in the Mgoun Valley—the parties began a long process of mediation and eventually court action got under way. Neighbors of the home builder, and even some of his extended family, disavowed the act as provocative. They described it as a personal dispute without the kind of communal referent that was so prominent in Imzilne's account of their own efforts to challenge that same family in Rbat.

Land was the "strategic terrain" through which various groups contested privilege, rights, and belonging (De Angelis 2004, 68). Land divisions did not need a specific opponent or clearly stated agenda to articulate a new politics of commoning. In fact, rejecting the more explicitly political language of resistance or redistribution in favor of discourses of custom may have been one reason this new politics of commoning was effective. The collective-land representative of Aït Khalifa, another village on the Aït Hamd plateau, underscored the sometimes-subtle political language involved in these divisions when he described their experience in 2001. Villages could divide communal lands within their customary boundaries without formally involving the Ministry of Interior. This practice drew on the jmaʿa's historical authority to govern both collective and privately owned land in the village. In the case of Aït Khalifa, the decision to divide an approximately two-hectare section of their hurm reflected new land-use imperatives: fewer households were using the hurm to pasture the livestock they kept intensively, and they needed that land for their expanding families. Rather than deal with requests piecemeal, the village allocated each household a uniform-size plot. The collective-land representative described their decision to divide as responding to poorer families' need for housing and rejected the idea that this diminished the power of their communal institutions: "Land division has increased our communal spirit, not lessened it. We all came together to solve a problem. Before, there was conflict over who had what land, but now all of that is clear, and we work better together to solve our problems." The key issue for him was not that all of the village's land should remain collectively owned, but that, as he phrased it, "we remain loyal to the traditional institutions that keep us together." This was not an explicitly oppositional move against one institution or powerful figure, but it did articulate a form of communal governance that broke with the past, when a few notable families would determine how land would be used and allocated.

The Communal Dimensions of Contemporary Land Mobilizations

Land divisions or occupations were more than the literal enclosure of land for private ownership and use. Moha ou Lahcen, the collective-land representative who spearheaded Imzilne's land division, expressed pride at this new show of collective solidarity against powerful notables they had never been able to challenge.

They were no longer dependent on a few ruling families because they now could earn their living elsewhere, even if they were still, by most standards, poor. He scoffed at the idea that their land division signaled the dissolution of communal attachments as native sons left to find wage work. He noted that "not everyone returns to stay, but we all remain connected to the tamazirt" through their communal affinities. Similarly, the process for dividing their land had a communal orientation that reinforced rather than dismantled customary governance institutions. In Imzilne, water scarcity framed strict rules about what households could do with the forty-five apportioned 10×20-meter lots in the village hurm. The jmaʿa worked closely with the village association that managed the well-based potable water system to limit the number of hookups households could extend to their new plots near the weekly market. Agriculture was forbidden in these plots, and the size of structures built there had to be approved beforehand. Moha ou Lahcen reported that the ghurm system, which established fines or other penalties for contravening customary land-use rules, was extended to this new zone. The jmaʿa also adjudicated new requests for plots for housing elsewhere in another section of the village hurm. Managing these requests to ensure equity among households was a complex project, but Moha ou Lahcen and his assistant noted that the new demands had reinvigorated their communal governance, especially after the energizing experience of using customary institutions to resist state appropriation of their land. Rather than individualizing ownership in a way that removed land from the purview of communal institutions, it increased those institutions' roles in land tenure, water, and other resource management.

Land divisions and mobilizations could reinvigorate and even support the emergence of a communal approach to governance beyond land tenure. In Ichihn, one of the leaders of the occupation was explicit about how a newfound sense of agency after their success began to inform other efforts to address the village's isolation and economic marginalization. Like Imzilne, the jmaʿa continued to exercise authority over how land allocated in the hurm could be used and transferred, and they retained a reserve of land to meet future needs. The jmaʿa also began to work with the elected official who helped them mobilize against the Ministry of Interior to bring public transit to the enclave. Situated only fifteen kilometers from Kelaa in the steppe, the village was nonetheless difficult to access. Private taxis refused to cover the difficult terrain, but local families could not afford the fare anyway. Demanding a regular transit, and then monitoring to ensure it actually made its scheduled run, was as much an outgrowth of the land occupation as the divided plots themselves. Even in el Bour n'Aït Yahya, the collective action that organized individual families' efforts to claim land produced lasting communal sentiments. Some involved in that mobilization who had never held communal governance roles in their home villages in Imaghran began working with their elected official to request the appointment of a collective-land representative to manage land disposition and use in the entire settlement. Although neither I nor the participants in these conflicts would attribute these communal actions solely to land division, participants emphasized that the communal orientation of the mobilizations spilled into other aspects of governance. They linked that experience of political agency with a sense that they could manage their resources and collective life on their own terms.

New Commoning

The series of counterenclosures that I encountered in 2010, then, did more than answer the grand enclosures set in motion by colonial capitalism. Each mobilization put forward specific concerns, and the marked variation in the situation of each village even within the narrow confines of the valley meant that land division could mean quite different things. In highlighting the possibilities for common action that might arise in this countermovement, I do not argue that land divisions throughout the pre-Sahara were always communal in orientation. But they could be, and in entertaining this possibility, a new configuration of politics in the valley becomes apparent. The vision for commoning articulated in the counterenclosures spoke to a generalized awareness that the commons had not operated communally for a long time, if ever. More than a demand for sharper rights in land, participants in the subset of occupations and land divisions I document here were organizing around communal attachments that challenged both state appropriation of collective lands and historical iniquities embedded in Mgouni social relations.

These claims also explained an apparent paradox in the land conflicts I witnessed in 2010. State actors—including the director of rural affairs, local elected officials (often those with rural notable backgrounds), agriculture extension agents, and the qa'id, among others—were the most prominent defenders of customary tenure regimes in the face of individual and collective challenges. These challenges rarely came from large agricultural interests or local elites; they had always been able to manipulate the rules to their advantage. Rather, the challenges came from the most marginalized members of ethnic collectivities. Their demand for land rights came from two kinds of claims: as members of the ethnic collectivities, they had a right to their share in communal lands, and for the Imaghrani immigrants without rights-holder status, it was an ethical claim about the right to subsistence. Rachik describes how outsiders without native land rights have, in other parts of Morocco, based their claims on the idea of citizenship supplanting the obsolete authority of the tribe (2016, 43). In the Mgoun Valley, I did occasionally hear these kinds of claims, but the mobilizations I witnessed largely eschewed rights talk. Most participants echoed a basic desire to be able to continue living in their home—one migrant worker poignantly described to me how everyone should be able to stay in their tamazirt if they want and that his goal was always to get back, to make enough money to be able to live with his family. The protesters in Ichihn expressed no personal hostility to the Arab businessman who set up his firma in the steppe, but the protest leader was firm, using the same phrase as the migrant worker: "Everyone should stay in their tamazirt. He should stay in his and we should have the right to ours." In this context, subsistence claims were moral economy claims linked to place, the right to make a living, and the right to maintain one's family in their homeplace.

Participants in the land divisions were unsentimental about the possibility that their claims might undermine the institutional infrastructure of collective lands. This led me to wonder if I was witnessing the beginning of the process that Tania Li (2014a) described for Sulawesi highlanders in Indonesia, recounted in the introduction to this book. She tells how a historically communal approach to land use and governance unraveled when highlanders experimented with private property to take advantage of a commodity boom that seemed to hold the prospect of strengthening their livelihood security. When that boom passed and the forces of capital overwhelmed their capacity to sustain their autonomy, structures of reciprocity and economic support could not recover. Similar forces had long pressured smallholders elsewhere in Morocco, especially as a result of colonial expropriation. De Haas describes a land division that occurred in the 1990s in the Ghéris plain, two hundred kilometers to the east of the Mgoun Valley. While this division did not have the same devastating impacts as Li's case, it illustrated the possible negative outcomes of dividing arid lands for capital-intensive, commercially oriented agriculture: unsustainable draws on groundwater and rising inequality as only those with access to foreign remittances or other sources of capital could work the land (de Haas 2007a). In observing how the land divisions in the Mgoun Valley at the center of this chapter unfolded, however, I saw another possible outcome. None of the participants I interviewed described the divisions as dissolving communal land and resource management regimes. Rather, they saw the divisions as the latest chapter for land tenure regimes that had always been mutable.

Residents acknowledged that communal governance had been weakened over the decades, but they located the reasons in how colonial policies, capitalist transformation, environmental stress, and political marginalization had reconfigured their livelihoods, not in the fact that land divisions were threatening communal identities. Demands for tenure changes to grant households land rights in the steppe were at least in part a pragmatic realization that new approaches to resource management were needed to make evolving livelihood systems work. People's lack of nostalgia for collective tenure regimes was therefore not a challenge to the "communal" as a basis for identity and action, an argument that scholars working on customary law elsewhere in Morocco are also making. Rachik notes, for example, that "there is broad agreement on the disaggregation of communal governance. But this should not obscure other processes through which communities organize themselves quite well, with or without the state's blessing, in managing collective goods. . . . It is important to attend to how communities adapt their local laws to changes that affect their governance structures and the new social situation of their members" (2016, 48). In the Mgoun Valley, this adaptation rejected a romantic view of communal governance or tenure regimes—after all, these regimes had oppressed many of the people now using them to advance their aspirations. Yet, these regimes could still provide a communal referent for navigating the transformations of the previous half-century.

We cannot know for certain how communal governance will fare over the long term in the cases I highlight here. However, there were indicators from previous experiences elsewhere in the valley and from developments since the 2010 divisions that point to the transformation of communal regimes rather than their straightforward eclipse by the forces of capitalism. For one thing, communal governance was imbricated with capitalist transformation, sustaining the relevance of customary institutions as a flexible way of responding to changing social and economic circumstances, albeit with mixed equity implications. In el Harte, for example, an emergent commercial agricultural sector reinvigorated the customary roles of irrigation and land managers at least in part because the state-sanctioned "modern" institutions charged with organizing land and water use were unresponsive, imposed a financial burden, or were simply too divorced from the social networks that actually governed collective life. El Harte's irrigation manager, Abdallah, explained this dynamic to me. The village's main irrigation canal originated three kilometers up the valley at a diversionary dam that directed water from the Mgoun River into a complex network of canals servicing five villages before it terminated in the steppe outside el Harte. Officially, the main canal had been managed by a water user association (WUA) since 2004. The Ministry of Agriculture required the creation of a WUA as a criterion for funding cement lining that ran the length of the main canal. But the WUA did not supplant the customary institutions governing irrigation. The urge to yawn in the middle of an interview prompted Abdallah to recount how he had been up in the middle of the night because the diversionary dam had broken, and he needed to rush upriver to resolve the problem. Was this not the responsibility of the WUA? I asked. He paused to consider the answer and said that the WUA was there for when they needed to deal with the Ministry of Agriculture, but the customary irrigation manager was there for actually making the irrigation system work for farmers and communities. "We respect what the other does, but we each do different things." The membership fees for the WUA were too high for many farmers and the bureaucracy too burdensome to make the association relevant for day-to-day management of the village's complex agricultural infrastructure.

I saw other evidence of the enduring relevance of communal governance in places that had divided land. The experience of Aït Khalifa, Imzilne's neighbor, indicated how land could transition between various governance regimes, from collective to individually owned land and in defiance of an evolutionary conception of land tenure, sometimes the reverse. After floods in the late 1990s damaged agricultural fields in Aït Khalifa, the jma'a organized the creation of a new wood lot to be held in common that could buffer remaining fields from sudden surges of water; this was at the same time they began organizing their land division. Landowners in the flood-prone areas donated their land, and residents gathered to plant a birch stand in the lot. Although the former landowners received a higher proportion of wood allocations for the first two to three years, subsequent allocations of wood gleaned from the stand were done by lottery. All households had the right to collect forage in the forested area, and other rules were developed to manage the new commonly held wood lot. This authority to manage land tenure transitions and other kinds of overlaying rights supported the legitimacy of encumbering even mulk to collective authority.

The people I interviewed in Aït Khalifa and other communities in the valley saw this authority as protecting newly divided lands from succumbing to distress sales. To be sure, distress sales had a long history in the plateau; recall Taleb's account in chapter 1 of how the Aït Zahirs accumulated their holdings in times of famine by buying land from the starving "for a handful of barley." However, the contemporary danger of distress sales was highly differentiated spatially and socially. In the plateau, where agricultural prospects were limited by water scarcity and distance to markets, residents reported an increase in demand for land for housing among native families but no sales of productive land given the limited possibilities for cultivation. Requests for communal allocations from the hurm for housing reflected the low level of transfers as a whole; while recipients of the land divisions had the right to buy and sell their allocations as mulk, few people were willing to do so. The irrigation manager for Imzilne explained that distress sales "were in the past" because people could travel for work to meet their needs and were no longer forced to sell land in times of difficulty. Distress sales could still happen; one family I knew sold land to pay legal fees and fines for an imprisoned son. However, a sense that subsequent generations might need the land for housing, that it could serve as a store of wealth, or a strong sense of attachment compelled households to retain their land even if its productive potential was limited.

In this context, then, land divisions did not strip land of its customary encumbrances. This was not privatization in the sense of enclosing land to produce a straightforward capitalist property form. On the one hand, there were no legal mechanisms in delimited collective zones to provide freehold title, a key step in transforming land from "dead capital" to a vehicle for capital accumulation—or dispossession (de Soto 2000, 2003). The inability to register land excluded landholders from using it as collateral in formal financial dealings or applying for Ministry of Agriculture subsidies (although there were some mechanisms for subverting this rule as well as spotty enforcement in some places) (Zirari-Devif 2009–2010, 121). On the other hand, land of any tenure status remained bound up in overlapping jurisdictions that included the collective authority of the jmaʿa, the tribal confederation, and the state. The land occupations I witnessed used these legal ambiguities to create a space for articulating alternative visions of common action and subsistence rights.

Conclusion

The state had subsumed collective lands for nearly a century, and the confusing juridical structure had little legitimacy for people struggling for access to land, if they understood the law at all. They simply saw outsiders, state or nonstate actors, appropriating their lands when it suited them. That does not mean that communal tenure regimes had no legitimacy. Even if some of the traditional practices associated with the commons declined or even disappeared in some places, they sustained their importance or were modified to suit new realities in others. Such practices offered a pragmatic vision of how a commons might work rather than a romanticized moral economy untethered from the reality of people's lives. The participants in land divisions whom I met may have wanted to dismantle certain elements of collective lands, but they did so with the aim of reimagining commoning, not dissolving it. Land mobilizations therefore undergirded ethical claims that belied a straightforward interpretation of individualized land tenure as the atomization of communal life. Collective action to divide up lands could become the basis for a new ethical community based on the right to subsistence rather than a state-sanctioned tribal affiliation that encoded long-standing social hierarchies and allowed marginalized people little or no control in the disposition of their collective lands.

This underscores how the communal referent point for popular enclosure movements was definitely not a return to an idealized past of collective governance. As I did life histories, people emphasized how the oppression and poverty of the past were rooted in rigid inequalities, and that however difficult life was now, there was more freedom. They could move for work, for example, rather than suffer the burden of indentured labor. In responding to these histories of dispossession, mobilizing for land rights and the right to subsistence could open new avenues for the expression of communal affinities. Certainly, intra- and intercommunity tensions abounded—around land, other natural resources, political power and many other issues—but the fact that people enacting land division could speak of increased communal spirit encourages a reconsideration of how individual rights, communal identities, and land related to one another. When this latent commons surged to the surface of political life, it also offered insights into the communal dimensions of other, perhaps less visible changes, such as patient investments in new kinds of farming and the emergence of new ways of making a living. The next chapter uses this communal referent to frame an analysis of livelihood transformation as socioecological change, linking the new ways people began to make a living in the valley to the broader environmental politics of land-use change and customary natural resource management.

4
ENVIRONMENTAL POLITICS AND THE NEW RURALITY

One morning in early spring, I accompanied Mohamed, the part-time employee of el Harte's development association, on his bimonthly tour of the village to read people's water meters.[1] We passed through the village center, beyond the densely planted plots of the oasis to the larger, less shaded fields in the outlying areas of el Bour. We continued past Imaghran, the neighborhood settled by migrants from the mountains in the 1980s, to the rocky steppe at the edge of the village hurm. I asked Mohamed why we needed to hike out to this empty expanse far from the homes provisioned by the deep communal well. He pointed to what looked like boulders in the distance but were, upon closer inspection, water hookups encased in concrete. I realized that these hookups dotted the landscape at regular intervals. A couple had faucets and hoses used to irrigate olive saplings that were the only sign of cultivation in the windswept steppe. Some families had engineered ad hoc drip irrigation systems, placing a plastic cooking oil bottle at the base of each sapling to slowly release water from a small hole punctured in the bottom. When the village association first set up the potable water system in 1998, there was heated discussion about whether to extend the hookups into the hurm (Attar 1994). While some felt that it would encourage people to move into the steppe and place unsustainable demands on the association well, others felt they needed to plan for the inevitable growth of the village. Only one family had moved there, but a small group had begun the long process of rendering the land arable even if it meant using expensive association water, charged by the ton, until they could dig their own wells or perhaps extend the irrigation canals fed by the Mgoun River even farther (figure 13).

FIGURE 13. The sole domestic compound in the steppe outside el Harte, with a resident of el Harte in the foreground.

Photo by the author.

The hookups offered visual confirmation of el Harte's new status as the agricultural hub of the Mgoun Valley. However, local agriculture officials worried about the effects of water pumping on the water table, even if there was little motorized pumping in Mgoun compared with Dadès, the eastern portion of their zone. One official told me: "Drought has become structural here; people should not extend fields or plant trees in the steppe. The water table cannot guarantee the sustainability of these extensions; during the last major drought [in the 1990s], many people let their lands go and back then, the extensions did not go as far as they do now." Attempts to expand the area devoted to cultivation surfaced the tensions in narratives about the environmental consequences of land-use practices here. Despite their concern about the water demands of new extensions, these same officials administered subsidies designed to encourage commercial agriculture—often for the very same projects that they described as unsustainable. Most changes to the landscape, however, unfolded outside the purview of government policies or programs; they resulted from the socially and spatially differentiated shifts in livelihoods, settlement patterns, and agrarian practice that I have described throughout the book.

These shifts "reterritorialized" populations and land use by "reworking [. . .] the fabric of everyday interactions and exchanges to include new persons, places and relations" (Mutersbaugh 2002, 475). The results were visible on the landscape: the movement of villages from the oasis valley toward the national road, the expansion of the built environment, new agricultural projects in the steppe, and the geometric patterns of cairns and low-slung adobe walls marking land divisions. As Jacques Berque describes for another landscape in the High Atlas: "The morphology of the land emerges directly from the human," although contemporary socioecological analyses would describe this relationship as mutually constitutive (Berque and Pascon 1978, 17).[2] Official declensionist narratives attributed these changes to rising individualism and the dissolution of communal governance. This chapter, however, details how new land-use practices reterritorialized what was already a highly anthropogenic landscape by refiguring, not dissolving, the moral and political economies associated with customary natural resource management regimes. Struggles over how land should be used simultaneously drew on and reconfigured customary practices to engage the changing realities of people's livelihoods and sociopolitical aspirations. These struggles also produced different interpretations of the environmental consequences of land-use change in the region, especially whether extensions into the steppe were degrading the land or enriching it in new ways. Through an ethnography of environmental narratives circulating in the region, I document the disjuncture between dominant notions of degradation inherited from the colonial period and the socioecological understandings that informed residents' land-use practices. I do not seek to adjudicate the scientific basis for their alternative understandings but instead draw on critical environmental history and political ecology of North Africa and the Middle East to demonstrate how environmental narratives framed divergent perceptions of changing land-use practices.[3] In this socioecological approach, movements of labor, capital, and ideas that promoted certain land uses over others did not simply have implications *for* the environment. Rather, these processes produced landscapes and social life together.

This chapter extends my argument that a pragmatic and grounded understanding of communal governance is necessary to disentangle peasants from the burden of preserving an idealized version of the commons. One way this romanticism works is by transforming agrarian rurality into an object of ecological desire— for a land and food sovereignty where social justice, communal sentiments, agricultural productivity, and agroecological sustainability all align (Li 2015). Such ecological desire also infuses calls to preserve or return to socially embedded agroecologies as the basis for sustainable agrofood systems and an oppositional politics rooted in "the commons as resistance." Romantic imaginaries, however, can obscure how rural residents creatively adapt existing governance arrangements and livelihood strategies to craft their own visions of agrarian rurality. Conversely, counterposing dominant narratives of peasant improvidence with accounts of how smallholders do, in fact, nurture sophisticated ecological knowledges can reify their inherent resourcefulness in seemingly undifferentiated resource-poor environments (Bernstein and Woodhouse 2001). This runs the risk of its own kind of functionalism—an assumption that if peasants are not good environmental stewards, the cause must be located in the "outside" of capitalist transformation and other global pressures.

A preservationist approach to peasant livelihoods and lifeways seems particularly ill conceived when rural residents are themselves elaborating land use and governance regimes to respond to the changing imperatives of contemporary rural life. Such processes are "bottom-up as much as top down," challenging statecentric and functionalist approaches that automatically assume the powerful wrest control over resource management from the subaltern (Bassett and Gautier 2014; Smith [1984] 2008, 240). Territorial strategies may "emanate from a variety of social locations and aspirations," underscoring the agency of even the most marginalized groups in the social production of landscapes (Bassett and Gautier 2014, 6; Bernstein 2010; Watts 2012). It is therefore important to detail the "actual historical relations of socially differentiated land use practices" to question how any received wisdom (negative or positive) can draw on universalizing assumptions about the sources and consequences of land degradation (Fairhead and Leach 1996, 12).

There is ample scientific evidence from rangeland ecology and research on pastoralism that details the ecological resilience of drylands and the adaptability of land uses such as the transhumant livestock production that historically dominated the steppe around the Mgoun Valley.[4] Similarly, Moroccan and Moroccanist scholars have detailed how oasis farmers have developed fine-tuned production and water management systems to meet the agroecological challenges of dryland farming. Bencherifa's work, for example, spans both oasis and pastoralist systems to demonstrate how sophisticated agroecological knowledges have sustained high levels of productivity in both (Bencherifa 1988; Bencherifa and Popp 1990). This research has challenged dominant discourses of deserts as sterile wastelands subject to human-induced desertification at the hands of "traditional" land managers, instead pointing to historical land use patterns as the most productive use of variable, uncertain, and yet resilient ecologies (D. Davis 2016). Scholars have long noted that these land-use systems, in Morocco and other arid lands, are broadly networked as pastoralists move herds across large distances through a wide diversity of political and social arrangements (Johnson 1969; Lefébure 1979; Nelson 1973). Even the functionalist models of tribal organization that have been so thoroughly critiqued underscore the interconnection between productive and sociopolitical dimensions of pastoralism (Gellner 1969; Hammoudi 1980; Hart 1981; Marx 1977; Munson 1993).

The Mgoun Valley forms part of these wide regional networks. To the south lies the Saghro Mountains, the historical domain of the Aït Atta tribal confederation (Lefébure 1979). These networks extend through the Saghro Mountains toward the Draʿ Valley and Algeria, northward to the igdaln of the High Atlas, and the vast eastern high plateaus, where nomadic systems historically predominated (Hart 2000; Johnson 1969). However, transhumance and oasis agropastoralism were the dominant livestock systems in the Mgoun Valley, and households I interviewed reported no direct contact with or historical involvement in nomadic pastoralism. In the Saghro and surrounding steppe, Aït Atta households had for some years been assigning individual members the task of settling a homestead in informally claimed communal land to begin cultivation in a livelihood diversification strategy common to arid land pastoralists (McCabe 2003; Yessef and Aït Hamza 2007). Unlike the land-use changes I have described for the Mgoun Valley, where former transhumants settled primarily in or around oasis villages, these tended to be smaller, isolated settlements in the collectively owned lands of Aït Sedrate (El Alaoui 2002). For logistical reasons, I was not able to extend my research to these isolated settlements or, as development officials termed them, *empiètements* (encroachments) in the steppe.

Intensive land uses in the oasis were also a part of networked systems involving transhumant pastoralists (Berque and Pascon 1978; Miller 1984; Skounti 2012). My research focused on the intensively cultivated oasis of the lower valley and one plateau in the foothills that served as a staging ground for herds traveling to the igdaln at higher altitudes. In this chapter, I explain the dynamics in the borderlands between the steppe and the historical oases to suggest how we can recognize the historical resilience of natural resource practices in places like the Mgoun Valley without reifying or romanticizing those practices.

The scholarship on transhumant pastoralism—especially on the agdal, the renowned customary institution governing highland pasture—offers insights for analyzing this dilemma in the borderlands that are the subject of this chapter (Auclair and Alifriqui 2012; Ilahiane 1999; Venema Mguild 2002). Laurent Auclair et al. (2013), for example, contextualize the agdal of the High Atlas in contemporary conservation and natural resource management policies that aim to preserve the institution as natural and cultural patrimony. They describe how the agdal was historically effective because it could be mobilized to address numerous forms of climatic and political insecurity (Auclair and Alifriqui 2012). Rules that regulated pasture use supported local economies, promoted biodiversity by selectively closing off rangeland from grazing, and promoted social solidarity through an integrated approach to governance in mountain zones (Auclair et al. 2013; Ilahiane 1999). However, Auclair et al. (2013) critique a notion of patrimony that privileges abstract design principles over the agdal as socioecological practice. They cite Ollagnon's definition of *patrimoine*: "An ensemble of material and intangible elements that come together to maintain and develop the identity of their 'holders,' and promotes autonomy across time and space by enabling their adaptation to an evolving universe" (cited in Auclair et al. 2013, 112). Their analysis resists the notion that socioecological patrimony is a static condition. The competing logics that govern the actually existing agdal complicate and politicize the concept of natural patrimony as a tool for conservation and natural resource management.

In what follows, I extend this analysis of the agdal as socioecological patrimony to other practices and institutions at the heart of environmental narratives in the Mgoun Valley. Official efforts to revive or preserve customary natural resource management institutions assumed the decline of custom in the face of outside economic pressure and rising individualism. These accounts also implied that residents were incapable of protecting biodiversity and environmental sustainability. The central government and multilateral donors would therefore have to step in to save the institutions that now constituted the region's natural and cultural patrimony. This preservationist project narrowed customary institutions that historically governed many aspects of life to the functional role of "natural resource management." I then map the social geographies of new land-use practices to describe an alternative set of narratives that nonetheless expressed its own contradictions and exclusions. In the final section, I return to how dominant discourses "patrimonialized" customary institutions—domesticated them as patrimony to be protected like a nature reserve after they had been politically contained and divorced from their wider roles. This discourse of patrimonialization obscured the political economy of shifting land-use practices and the changing role of customary institutions in governing socioecological systems.

Environmental Change and the *Longue Durée* of Degradation Narratives

The most prominent narrative framing official discussions of land-use practices in Mgoun emerged from early French colonial history and Morocco's participation in global discourses about desertification and deforestation. When the French invaded Algeria in 1830, military officers, Orientalists, and other apologists for colonial expropriation used purely literary sources to develop a story of previously lush lands despoiled over centuries by Arab nomads (D. Davis 2007, 4). Diana Davis terms this "the French colonial environmental declensionist narrative, that is, a tale of environmental decline since what was presumed to have been the fertile and forested Roman period. This colonial narrative primarily blamed the pastoralists, especially nomadic pastoralists, and their 'ancestors,' the 'invading Arabs' of the eleventh century, for deforesting and desertifying North Africa" (2007, xii). Davis traces how French colonial policy and scholarship facilitated the dispossession of Algerians, Tunisians, and Moroccans. In the process, the declensionist narrative mutated from a romantic account into the authoritative language of an emerging ecological science. French scholars first used the term "desertification" to describe the Sahara in 1927, and, deploying spurious methods and literary sources, they constructed potential vegetation maps to show that the entire region should have thick forest cover but was instead denuded and degrading even further (Davis 2007, 4). While the narrative took shape in Algeria, it reached its apogee in Morocco, the last French colonial acquisition in North Africa when the protectorate was declared in 1912.[5] Davis details how the difficulty of conquering restive mountain and desert regions led to particularly draconian forest and range management policies. As scholars have noted for other colonial contexts, repression and dispossession were often cloaked in the language of resource conservation (Grove 1996; Neumann 2002; Peluso 1994).

In Morocco, these colonial narratives also elaborated cultural or ethnic distinctions between the putative destructiveness of Arab nomads and the more salutary environmental practices of Berbers, which in turn fed broader civilizational distinctions aimed at co-opting Berber sympathies (Gellner and Micaud 1972; D. Davis 2007; Hoffman 2008; Hoffman and Miller 2010). The reality was that many Berbers, such as the transhumant pastoralists of the Mgoun Valley, utilized similar strategies as Arab pastoralists when they opportunistically moved herds to access variable and uncertain rangeland resources. Colonial narratives homogenized such ethnic fluidity and the striking diversity of livestock management systems throughout Morocco, but at the same time, protectorate authorities well understood the power of regional networks linking tribal confederations. That understanding informed policies to fix tribes in restrictive zones to make way for colonial land expropriation and otherwise contain mobile populations (D. Davis 2007; Miller 1984; Skounti 2012). Livestock producers required permits to move herds in demarcated tribal territories—historically subject to negotiation in the framework of customary law and governance—a policy that discouraged mobility and deprived pastoralists and agropastoralists of their livelihoods (D. Davis 2007, 263).

Following independence in 1956 and paralleling the trajectory of collective property law described in the previous chapter, there was no decisive break in the environmental narratives or the legal apparatus that supported them. Instead, the declensionist perspective joined up with global discourses of desertification to inform contemporary Moroccan environmental and agricultural policy. This despite ample empirical evidence that indigenous range management practices are not responsible for land degradation, and that there is "no definitive overall pattern of massive deforestation on the order of the frequently claimed 50 to 85 percent [in North Africa] over the last two millennia" (D. Davis 2007, 10). To be sure, recurrent drought is a persistent problem in the disequilibrial agroecology of Morocco (Benassi 2008; D. Davis 2016; Swearingen 1992). Several scholars have documented land degradation in Morocco, but the primary drivers are agricultural, land tenure, and environmental policies that have effectively dispossessed pastoralists and smallholders, particularly in the littoral plains and foothills of the Middle and High Atlas that were drawn into commercial agricultural development schemes during the colonial period (Glantz 1994; Pascon 1986; Swearingen 1988). In the pre-Saharan region, pastoral improvement programs have tended to draw on entrenched assumptions that herders overstock the range and otherwise degrade the land. However, the primary pressures on the land actually stem from other land uses: the expansion of urban centers, rangeland conversion, and intensive use of pastoral resources because of concentrated livestock production in smaller areas (Gertel and Breuer 2007; Jaafar, Yessef, and Ramdan 1996). Diana Davis notes, for example, that the area devoted to cereals in Ouarzazate province increased from fifteen thousand hectares in 1975 to fifty-six thousand hectares in 1995, with most of the new cultivation located in the steppe (2006, 98).

The narrative that indigenous natural resource management causes land degradation has shown great resilience since its inception, but the narrative has also shifted across time and space, sometimes in contradictory ways. In the Mgoun Valley, I observed a mutation of the declensionist narrative that transferred blame for land degradation from pastoralism to the decline of community-based governance that had traditionally protected the arid steppe. Instead of causing degradation, customary institutions and traditional land-use practices were now at fault for not preventing degradation. This interpretation undergirded a nine-year, nine million dollar United Nations Development Programme (UNDP) initiative entitled Biodiversity Conservation through Transhumance in the Southern High Atlas (known by its French acronym, CBTHA), which was coming to a close when I arrived for my fieldwork in 2010. The aim of the program was to "conserve biodiversity in the productive landscape of the southern High Atlas through sustainable land use and relaunching transhumance" (PNUD [Programme des Nations Unies pour le Développement] 1999, 36). However, in a departure from previous range management programs, the initiative identified the vectors of degradation not as transhumant pastoralists themselves but rather "rupture with the traditional management of common property" (17).

Project designers explicitly adopted the "fundamentals of the new paradigm for transhumance," devoting an appendix of the project document—the official agreement between the UNDP and the Moroccan government—to a summary of the revolution in rangeland ecology (PNUD 1999, 64–66). The appendix cites the key texts of the new paradigm (especially Behnke, Scoones, and Kerven 1993) to declare: "Transhumance is a sustainable production system that is adapted to arid lands and that, at the same time, contributes to globally important biodiversity" (PNUD 1999, 64). It goes on to describe how the new paradigm completely reverses old models of pastoral development, "discrediting the myths of irrational economic behavior, assumptions of over-pasturing, and the equilibrial nature of arid ecosystems" (64). However, integration of the new paradigm into one, albeit prominent, project does not signify a government-wide policy shift. As Diana Davis (2007, 2016) details, colonial misrepresentations of dryland ecology and pastoralism had important political uses that so permeated the state apparatus it would take more than a new approach to development projects to reorient the forest code, the juridical framework for land tenure and agricultural policy, and the culture of generations of officials trained to view pastoralism through outdated paradigms. This parallels how new theories of range ecology have successfully influenced official discourse and policy in other countries without substantive progress "on the ground" because of durable biases among officials tasked with implementing new approaches, environmental pressures, and a changing political economy that has undermined pastoralism (Turner 2011).

A modified narrative about the environmental impacts of pastoralism threads through the technical and social scientific studies commissioned by the CBTHA project. These studies tell a similar story as the interdisciplinary literature on pastoral development in the country since the colonial period. Some of these changes are broadly applicable to the diverse livestock production systems in Morocco's arid lands, but others are specific to the socioecological dynamics of the Mgoun Valley and surrounding project area. Scholars, officials, and consultants' reports document a general shift to more intensive systems, such as agropastoral production less reliant on mobility (Bencherifa and Johnson 1991; Gertel and Breuer 2007; Swearingen and Bencherifa 1996; Yessef and Aït Hamza 2007). They describe how the legacy of colonial policy increased pressures on marginal grazing lands while newer pressures, such as the border closure with Algeria, limit access to traditional grazing grounds or deepen smaller producers' vulnerability to economic or climatic shocks. The use of feed supplements and changing husbandry practices to bring livestock to weight quicker have, according to some observers, produced higher stocking rates in concentrated areas and degraded rangeland resources, although this pressure is unevenly distributed (Bourbouze and Gibon 2000, 295). These issues have been exacerbated by rangeland improvement programs that install deep wells and subsidize feed, sometimes explicitly, sometimes inadvertently encouraging sedentarization of extensive producers and reducing transhumant mobility (Skounti 2012; Steinmann 2001; Yessef and Aït Hamza 2007).

However, the CBTHA project design and supporting literature did not integrate an analysis of the long-term effects of capitalist transformation, instead presenting a new variation on the declensionist narrative. In this formulation, social factors led to a disarticulation of land uses and the institutions governing resource management, with negative effects for biodiversity and the ecology of the steppe. Specifically, changes in the pastoral sector were due to "the striking rise of individualism, which privileges the individual over the group and all forms of collective organization"; this, in turn, produced a "de-responsibilization of these actors in relation to their patrimony" (Yessef and Aït Hamza 2007, 74). In the portrait painted in project documents, the jma'a, tribal agreements for resource sharing, and other customary institutions were no longer capable of managing land use, especially in the face of "chaotic and unsustainable appropriation of marginal lands" (PNUD 1999, 18). A "rupture in common property management, along with localized over and under-pasturing are the principal threats and root causes of biodiversity loss in an ecosystem dependent on pasturing" (19). Communal identities dissolved when households appropriated plots in the steppe or left their natal homes to settle elsewhere in the region. Customary authority could no longer regulate pasture use in the high-altitude plateaus. The result, in this analysis, was an upsurge in land conflicts between tribes, the extension of cultivation and other modes of appropriating rangeland, individualized natural resource use, and further erosion of community-based institutions.

If the dominant narrative of environmental change had previously hinged on the improvidence of herders, this story of decline emphasized the dissolution of customary institutions and how farmers and pastoralists alike had eschewed communal identities for individual self-interest. Herders and farmers were now blamed for not being mobile *enough*, or at least not being mobile in the right way. Moving herds through the semiannual transhumant circuits was now promoted as a sustainable natural resource practice without an explicit analysis of, or strategy for addressing, the pressures on transhumance for the most vulnerable households. Nor did this new declensionist narrative contextualize pastoralism in an analysis of other land uses and forms of mobility, such as labor migration and household investments in land, agriculture, or housing. I heard complaints in the Aït Hamd plateau about how the project assisted primarily larger producers, evoking another major pastoral development project in Morocco's eastern high plateaus, the Projet de développement des parcours et de l'élevage dans l'Oriental (PDPEO). Although operating in a different context and with its own distinct approach—creating cooperatives based on "ethno-lineage" relationships alongside a suite of rangeland improvement interventions—the PDPEO evaluation and other documentation note that benefits were skewed to larger producers better able to afford the supplementary costs now required to sustain herds on the range (such as the use of trucks or purchasing feed supplements) (FIDA [Fonds International de Développement Agricole] 2002). Whereas large producers saw their incomes from livestock increase 128 percent during that project, the most vulnerable families experienced a 36 percent loss in the face of "socioeconomic changes that tend to exclude the small herd owners [those owning fewer than one hundred head of sheep, or 75 percent of livestock producers in the project zone] from the pastoral sector" (FIDA 2002, xiii; 2008, 19). These kinds of divergent results are common for development projects of any kind. Here, I am focused less on the relative efficacy of pastoral improvement projects than on how environmental narratives in the Mgoun Valley sustained and reworked longstanding explanations for perceived degradation. The process of demarcating certain institutions as responsible for safeguarding the environment, whether a reinvigorated jma'a or a newly created cooperative, privileged certain forms of mobility over others and divorced those governance regimes from broader changes that were refiguring what forms of mobility people or livestock could practice.

Lived Experience of the Oasis and Steppe

The quotidian realities of people's engagements with the land in the Mgoun Valley complicated these dominant environmental narratives. As described in chapter 1, the governing mandate of customary institutions went beyond natural resource management or adjudicating pastoralist land uses. Determining what those roles should be in the contemporary period produced contestation, maneuvering, and alternative narratives. From the vantage point of the oasis residents who were the focus of my fieldwork, these narratives were bound up with changes that had reworked socioecological relationships in both the oasis and the steppe.

Oasis residents were impacted by changes in the livestock sector regardless of whether they had a background in transhumance. In our survey, only 4 out of 306 households reported involvement in transhumant pastoralism, even though livestock ownership was important across the board (table 6). The dominant livestock system for households we interviewed was intensive agropastoralism. Alfalfa was an important crop both for feeding livestock and for sale; 30 percent of households (92 households) marketed at least some of their production. Households rarely pastured the sheep and cows they kept in enclosures attached to their domestic compounds, but collecting weeds and other agricultural residue was an important source of forage. Most (63 percent, or 190 households) still had to purchase feed.

TABLE 6. Livestock ownership for households in the Mgoun Valley and surrounding steppe, 2013–2014

LIVESTOCK	TOTAL HOUSEHOLDS THAT OWN LIVESTOCK	TOTAL NUMBER OF LIVESTOCK OWNED	AVERAGE NUMBER OWNED	RANGE WITHIN A HOUSEHOLD
Cows	135	315	2	1–15
Sheep	203	1,234	6	0–100
Goats	16	179	11	1–33
Mules	33	38	1	1–4
Donkeys	30	34	1	1–5
Bees	4	30	8	1–20
Chickens	36	247	7	1–20
Rabbits	1	10	10	10

Source: Household survey, 2014–2015 (author in partnership with Reseau Associatif de Tinghir pour la Démocratie et le Développement).

Note: This table presents data on livestock owned by households, but entrustment was also practiced, whereby individuals or households would leave livestock in the care of a family member or a trusted ally under arrangements similar to sharecropping, with in-kind payments or a share of profits. We specifically asked about livestock owned by the household and were not able to assess the extent of these entrustment practices in the household survey.

Broader shifts in the pastoralist sector in the foothills and lower altitudes of the High Atlas reflected the compounding effects of long-term capitalist transformation and the droughts of the 1980s and 1990s. These droughts intensified a bifurcation that enabled larger herders to rely on feeding supplements and trucked-in water; overall patterns of movement simplified and either shortened, as producers minimized herd mobility, or lengthened, as others with access to capital began trucking their herds to maximize range resources at progressively farther distances (Bourbouze and Gibon 2000; Yessef and Aït Hamza 2007). Smaller livestock producers from Imaghran, in particular, could not absorb the losses sustained during the droughts, and many sold what remained of their herds, leaving the region to settle in the Mgoun Valley (Yessef and Aït Hamza 2007).[6] Imaghran and other mountain areas adjacent to Mgoun had fewer prospects for livelihood diversification than the intensively cultivated riparian oasis of the valley, which had more sustained access to both surface water and groundwater and was less geographically isolated. Just as oasis residents were extending farming and housing into the steppe surrounding their villages, then, migrants were arriving from Imaghran in search of wage-labor opportunities and land on which they could build their new homes. However, regarding these shifts as a "chaotic encroachment" on the steppe—as dominant narratives tended to hold—simplifies how residents used governance regimes to manage these changing land-use practices.

The Social Construction of the Oasis

Although there were many kinds of "encroachment" on the steppe, the ones that received the most official attention were agricultural extensions. Whether a project was a commercial operation in the collectively owned steppe or a smaller extension into the hurm by village residents influenced how different actors perceived extensions. For smallholders with remittances or wage income, extensions out of the historical oasis were hard work, expensive, and risky. But that was nothing new. Aware of the environmental and economic risks, many felt the investment made sense given the contemporary economic, political, and ecological realities they encountered. Agriculture had always been unpredictable here, and a large part of the labor that constructed and reshaped the anthropogenic landscapes of the oasis was devoted to managing that uncertainty (Sahli 1997). I sat with Haj ou Zayd one day to talk about the extensions that had added a whole new agricultural "neighborhood" to the village of el Harte. He returned from the French coal mines in the early 1990s and together with his large family had amassed substantial holdings—either through purchase or by developing plots allocated by the collective-land representative—in el Harte's historical oasis and el Bour. He was among a small group that extended agriculture into el Bour (the village hurm); those extensions were now a well-established feature of the agricultural landscape.

When I interviewed him in 2010, the haj was again joining a handful of families preparing land even farther outside the historical oasis for cultivation. He had applied to the Plan Maroc Vert, the flagship Ministry of Agriculture development initiative, for a drip irrigation system, the only person in the village to have done so. We talked about his investment in this land—rocky, dry, and so far from the irrigation canals and the densely fertile plots of the oasis. I asked the haj what people did in the extensions when there was drought. He paused as though considering whether there was something more profound to the self-evident nature of my question and then decided there could not be. "Well, if you do not have water to sow, you do not sow. There is nothing." I pressed him on why people were working the land so far from the irrigation canals given this risk. Why would people go out there? The haj was now visibly puzzled. "It is about your means. Those who have the means to do it will. Those who do not, will not." Mbarak, my research assistant, jumped in to clarify: "This is what it is to be *benadam* [human]. We have to increase our land." The haj laughed, saying, "Yes, we all want to increase land. Man wants to take everything. It is greed." He noted the centrality of land in the social mobility of many families from el Harte, including his own. In his view, the reason for their climb in status was land, not migration, even though migration may have brought the resources enabling them to acquire property. "Everything is in land. You can have all the money in the world, but if you don't have land you are nothing. It will never go down. You will never lose money. The returns are more than you could get from a bank. Look at you—in the US, you became great because of your agriculture." The haj's explanation invoked land's historical importance as a marker of status but in decidedly novel terms: land had acquired new economic meaning as a productive asset and object of investment.

The changing significance of land shaped the social production of el Harte's landscape, but it did so in the context of a historical understanding of oases as inherently flexible, human creations. Oases are constantly adjusting to social, environmental, and legal imperatives, and their borders are fungible as a result. The centrality of elaborate irrigation systems and the minute detail of production techniques lend themselves to an image of human-controlled equilibrium. But as Battesti (2005) explains in his study of North African oases, there is nothing necessary, determined, or even all that stable in this agricultural system. Oasis farmers have always relied on experimentation to negotiate changing environmental conditions, manipulating water and land to adjust to the same climatic variability that influences the dynamics of mobile pastoralism on the steppe. These diverse systems have persisted not because farmers have found a way to overcome this variability but because they actively manage landscapes to work with the disequilibrial dynamics in these arid environments. "Oases are animated by shifting spaces and reveal diverse practices and discourses. These moving spaces are produced by the encounter of socio-historical and ecological factors. . . . When we ignore the intricate character of oases they seem like monolithic spaces, but an oasis is the infinite recombination of its constituent spaces and fluctuating borders" (38). The careful management of water and land has, over centuries, produced intensive, anthropogenic landscapes that persist precisely because they are always changing.

In the Mgoun Valley, the frontiers between oasis and steppe were embedded in social and productive relations that brought the zones together as part of a regional land-use system. The static categorizations of land typical of official environmental narratives ignored people's own epistemological categories and the commonalities in risk and resource management strategies across ecological boundaries. Residents of the valley did not distinguish the social dynamics that determined appropriate land uses from ecological dynamics that might favor one use over another. Ideas of environmental degradation or enrichment were embedded in sophisticated understandings of how land use was a social *and* ecological question. To Haj ou Zayd, then, the oasis and steppe did not represent categorically separate ecological domains but together formed part of a landscape that was fundamentally social in nature and always changing. Like others expanding their farming operations around el Harte, Haj ou Zayd did not perceive changing land-use practices as environmentally questionable. This was not out of ignorance; how one farmed made all the difference for how ecologically sustainable one's efforts would be. When Haj ou Zayd said matter-of-factly that "if you do not have water, you do not sow," he was echoing a refrain I heard repeatedly: extensions represented an investment in the land's fertility, even if one did not necessarily get a harvest every year. If you did not have water one year, you did not sow, but that did not mean investments in soil fertility were a waste.

Another farmer in el Harte displayed the same confusion as Haj ou Zayd when I asked about the possible environmental ramifications of the extensions. "What would be the downside? I have never heard anyone say there was anything bad about the extensions. The only thing with extensions is that you need to make sure they do not create problems for other people's land, like their access to the canal. There are no downsides. No, the reverse is true. This is good for the land." Like the Guineans Fairhead and Leach interviewed in their study of environmental change, this farmer described how "peopling and everyday practice tends to improve, enrich and render productive the landscape" (1996, 116; Fairhead and Scoones 2005; Tiffen, Mortimore, and Gichuki 1994). Although the overwhelming sentiment I encountered viewed human activity as enriching the landscape, farmers drew a distinction between the deep wells that depleted water tables and new lands developed with surface water delivered by irrigation canals or the more modest wells sunk manually by local well diggers. They criticized some neighbors, most of them absentee farmers still in migration, whose wells adversely affected the water table, and pointed to the unsustainable draws on groundwater farther east in Dadès and Tinghir, where mechanized pumping had severe effects on water supply (de Haas 2001).

These distinctions were clear in part because farmers understood how customary law guided who could access land for agriculture in the changing political economy of farming. Because irrigation was gravity based, customary law in Mgoun historically zoned land below irrigation canals for agriculture to preserve scarce land for cultivation. Changes in farming practice had complicated this zoning regime. By 2010, many of el Harte's most productive lands were called *isuhad*, high land on the edge of the village effectively "made by man." Families with the money to rent bulldozers were cutting into the uneven landscape to bring it down below the irrigation canal, at which point gravity-based irrigation and all the rules associated with it would apply. Beyond the work of moving the earth, these extensions required heavy doses of patience as landowners incorporated organic matter over successive seasons to make the land productive (figure 14 depicts fields developed this way). Customary law gave individual landowners the right to extend secondary canals on their land as several families in el Harte did

FIGURE 14. Recently developed agricultural fields in el Bour of el Harte.
Photo by the author.

after the initial extension in the 1970s. Over five hectares of additional land were brought under cultivation in el Harte, a substantial area in this region.

However, these extensions were not, strictly speaking, "out in the steppe"—the rangeland collectively owned by tribal confederations and previously used to pasture transhumant herds. They were in the village hurm. They were off limits to passing transhumants, and while they were used for pasturing small domestic herds in the past, few residents took their animals out to the hurm anymore. Since the land used for extensions in el Harte had never really served as rangeland, at least not for transhumant pastoralism, no one imagined the extensions as conversions at all, regardless of the land's ecological features. People understood the boundaries between oasis and steppe—and the most appropriate uses of each type of land—in social and juridical terms: what kind of law governed the use of that land. Collective-land representatives made land allocations in the hurm based on historical precedent about who had land rights and for what purpose. When land was fed by irrigation canals, rules about water use that governed the rest of the oasis applied. In these areas, customary rules regarding land zoning, such as the prohibition against housing construction in agricultural fields, were also in force. These new land uses did not represent extensions in the steppe so much as an expansion of the oasis itself. Just as an oasis could historically expand, so, too, might it at some point retract.

Differing perceptions of the extensions' ecological impacts therefore stood at the heart of the conflicting environmental narratives circulating in the valley. The tensions were evident in how the same person could espouse seemingly contradictory positions depending on the time and place. One day during tree planting season, I talked with a local agricultural extension official at the weekly market as he denied petitioners' requests for subsidized olive trees if they failed a verbal test of how much space there should be between saplings. He was frustrated at what he saw as the shortsighted nature of many extensions, not only because of their high water requirements but also because of what he perceived as the farmers' inadequate technical knowledge. The officer explained to me that these farmers were using olive trees to make a land claim rather than seriously grow olives. This same official helped farmers in the "modern" operations (firmas) apply for subsidies to support mechanized pumping out in the steppe. His performance was assessed in part by the levels of support he administered to these farmers, but he also expressed admiration for the firmas' technical approach to drip irrigation.[7] In the service area of the agricultural extension office in Kelaa, official data reported four large projects, one hundred hectares each, leased on Mgouni or Aït Sedrate land through the Ministry of Interior, and thirty-three smaller projects ranging from one to fifteen hectares. Officials estimated two-thirds of the smaller projects were located on private or village collective land developed for agriculture, and the remaining one-third on tribal collective land, although they were not confident about the accuracy of these records. Records likely undercount the number of projects on the steppe because agents conceded their data gathering was irregular, and questions about the land tenure status of some agricultural projects meant their owners tried to avoid official attention.

While expressing general concern about extensions into the steppe, even these officials did not expect an explosion of commercial farms on the level of agricultural export regions such as the Souss or Saïss. Water was too scarce here even with reliance on deep wells. The main impact of the firmas was twofold. They converted the land tenure status of collective lands so that speculation and new forms of valuation could take hold in the steppe. They also consumed far more groundwater than the smallholders' more gradual extensions from the oasis. However, the firmas were officially sanctioned uses of collective land and rarely figured in dominant narratives about land degradation or environmental decline. Ministry officials struggled to reconcile their positive views of high productivity and agricultural modernity in these firmas with the potential environmental costs of farming in the steppe. I suspected they regarded the use of drip irrigation as rationalization for government support to projects that, were they to be smaller "encroachments" for building a home or cultivating a modest plot, would be the object of official critique. The groups involved in the latter kind of extension were among the most vulnerable in the region, and their settlements in the collectively owned rangelands figured prominently in degradation narratives that decried the dissolution of traditional natural resource management institutions.

Tracing changing land use practices in the Mgoun Valley, then, offers another example to add to the extensive political ecology literature on how dominant narratives single out vulnerable, subaltern groups as precipitating environmental degradation. However, these narratives did more than assign blame, mystifying the "true" environmental dynamics at work in Mgoun. The narratives also revealed the contradictory ways in which the region's new rurality was remaking the landscape. The large projects approved by the Ministry of Interior on collectively owned land and usually owned by foreign interests (whether Arab or non-Moroccan) were deemed a productive land use, exempt from charges of environmental degradation because they conformed to the productivist model of state agricultural policy. However, these firmas represented a relatively minor component of land-use change in the region. Most expanded cultivation occurred at the village level, a form of capital accumulation linked to global processes but "bottom-up" more than "top-down" (Smith [1984] 2008, 240). This accumulation moved through the "capillary action" of migrants and low-wage workers, enabling some households to transform migration remittances into local assets and livelihoods. Others were not able to make these investments, limited by their own resources and land tenure dynamics that used customary law to limit access to the new opportunities.

New Geographies of Social Reproduction

In their emphasis on formally productive uses of land, dominant environmental narratives focused on the tension between pastoralist land uses and cultivation as well as the role of customary institutions in preserving an environmentally sustainable balance between the two. However, these changing land-use practices were only part of a broader transformation in the geography of social reproduction in the valley. In fact, most of the extensions had nothing to do with agriculture but with urbanization and population resettlement. These movements were no less embedded in land tenure governance than agricultural land uses. Where one could settle to gain access to wage labor was dependent on customary land rights and on having the resources to purchase privately owned land; the combination of limited land rights and poverty prevented most intraregional migrants from practicing farming as a primary livelihood. The social differentiations of the migration era were therefore also a spatial differentiation produced by tenure institutions that permitted certain groups access to land while restricting the rights of others. When Haj Ahmed, the collective-land representative of el Harte, told me bluntly that "we do not give land to foreigners," meaning anyone not native to the village or the Mgoun tribal confederation, he was signaling how customary tenure regimes both guided the direction of land-use change and policed who could participate in opportunities for upward mobility.

These regimes may have been rooted in customary governance, but they did not operate according to the logic of what Auclair et al. describe as "global patrimony" (2013, 106). Just as local institutional regimes were "de-patrimonialized" in the process of managing the demands of diversifying livelihoods and changing land uses, new global forms of patrimonialization emerged that reified historical natural resource management practices (121). This approach to global patrimony isolated particular scientific, aesthetic, and cultural values to be managed for local sustainability and marketed to foreign audiences, but the new geographies of social reproduction in the Mgoun Valley did not readily conform to these values. The disjuncture between dominant notions of patrimony and the realities of social life became apparent to me when I returned to the Aït Hamd plateau in the summer of 2012. The UNDP initiative protecting biodiversity through pastoralism (CBTHA) had been closed for over two years and the traces of project activities had begun to fade. The project had funded local associations to promote the region's natural and cultural patrimony as part of its broader conservation effort. A new *gite* (hiking shelter) in Rbat, for example, would attract foreign ecotourists, educate them with a small museum, and display a seed bank of local landraces of heritage crops and steppe vegetation that were in danger of disappearing. The gite was adjacent to the domestic compound of the Aït Zahirs, the powerful family that historically dominated the plateau. Residents of the plateau had little interest in getting involved in the association; they left it to the Aït Zahirs since the latter had spearheaded the effort. The association fell dormant soon after the project ended. No tourists had ever stayed there, and although the Aït Zahirs did occasionally plant a field of *ikikr*, a traditional variety of millet, the seed bank was now a collection of dusty bowls on a shelf in the shuttered gite (figure 15). Even the Aït Zahirs, still practicing transhumant pastoralism, had little use for recuperating customary institutions as cultural patrimony. They were among the few families in the Aït Hamd plateau that fielded a herd in the steppe in part because they had the capital to adapt to the current ecological and economic realities of livestock production. They trucked their herds to productive pasture as far away as Bouarfa or the Souss.

There may have been other considerations informing the Aït Zahirs' involvement in this aspect of the UNDP project. I heard an unsubstantiated rumor that they supported the gite to prevent donor money from going to the only other gite that was actually active in the plateau. This gite belonged to a divorced woman, Khadija, and her widowed mother, who began the venture in an effort to secure their independence. With no family to support them—their extended relatives were also struggling—they had been forced to sharecrop for the Aït Zahirs. Khadija,

FIGURE 15.   A field of *ikikr* (millet) surrounded by maize, Rbat.
Photo by the author.

the gite owner, described how the powerful family held it against her when she and her mother refused to sharecrop for them anymore. She surmised that they were trying to sabotage her tourist venture. Her partnership with a tourist operator from el Bour n'Aït Yahya and her time spent tending to foreign tourists even led to her being labeled a prostitute, a comment more on the social opprobrium of her independence than her actual comportment. Khadija rued that the UNDP project had passed her over, describing the intense work and irregular income associated with the tourist trade. One evening when I was visiting her in the gite, the regular rhythms of conversation waned, and we paused over tea as a news story on television caught our attention. A volcano was erupting in Iceland, spewing dramatic plumes of ash into the atmosphere over continental Europe. Khadija sighed with disappointment: "This volcano. You see what it will do to us? The airplanes cannot fly from Europe with all that ash. We will get no business this month, our busiest period of the year. It will be a lean time," she said, looking at her mother with noticeable worry. She was intimately tied to new conceptions of rurality that linked Mgoun's cultural and natural landscapes to the movements of European tourists who would appreciate and monetize the region's global patrimony. Khadija understood this process well. She spoke ambivalently about the government's effort to pave the road from Kelaa Mgouna all the way up to the isolated villages farther up the mountain: "It is good to be able to travel the road so easily," she said, "but tourists do not want paved roads. It is not authentic for them. Now that the pavement runs all the way through Rbat Aït Hamd, we are not as appealing anymore. They want to go higher and further away."

For Khadija, the concept of natural or cultural patrimony constituted a livelihood strategy tied more to global movements of capital and tourists than the practices the UNDP project was trying to protect. It was a useful concept, helping her navigate life in the mountains to preserve her place at home. She and her mother did not want to move down to the steppe as so many residents from the high mountain plateaus had done. However hard their life in Rbat, Khadija considered an isolated existence in the anonymous neighborhoods of el Bour n'Aït Yahya even less appealing. For many of the new arrivals down in the steppe, though, this intraregional mobility constituted a productive land-use strategy; it enabled the migrants to at least stay connected to their natal villages as they assumed the new role of a rural wage-labor force or looked for work in the city. For those who could not stay in the mountains, the move to the steppe around Kelaa Mgouna was one way to avoid an even worse prospect: moving to a shantytown on the fringe of a major city.

Geographies of social reproduction also shifted with the transformation of household dynamics throughout the valley. Historically, households brought together brothers and their families to manage their collective holdings and pool their labor under the direction of a patriarch. Brothers would create independent households upon the passing of the patriarch and division of his assets. Even in this circumstance, however, many families often stayed together under the new authority of the eldest son, keeping their assets undivided and potentially maintaining a joint domestic compound. When brothers did establish an independent household, it was usually in the village, although sometimes men would travel for work as shepherds, well diggers, or soldiers before labor migration gathered steam in the 1960s and 1970s. Although a movement toward "nuclearizing" the family, with brothers taking their nuclear families into independent households earlier and more often, did happen, a large household that operated as a collective unit was still the social and economic ideal. Moving down to the steppe or "bursting" out of the tightly grouped housing of the qsur represented a way for households throughout the valley to simultaneously achieve distance from one another and stay together as a productive unit.[8] The availability of land in el Bour n'Aït Yahya offered opportunities for brothers to set up an independent household and reduce the pressure on their natal families while remaining "one household." The result was that offshoots of families from villages within the valley were interspersed among the Imaghran, the migrants from the mountains. Whether I was interviewing a vulnerable family in Imzilne or wealthy notable in el Harte, discussion invariably turned to a family member who had moved to el Bour n'Aït

Yahya. There were different reasons for moving out into the steppe: it could be a concerted effort to remove pressure on the household or to ease a family conflict without causing "separation," the formal division of household assets. One man from a wealthy family in el Harte moved into a house in el Bour belonging to his sister who had migrated to France (he was essentially a caretaker), while his brother moved his nuclear family from the homestead in el Harte to the uncultivated steppe surrounding the village. The family had not divided its holdings but conflict over financial management drove the brothers to seek some independence without striking out completely on their own, which they all realized would diminish their collective wealth considerably.

This breaking off of a portion of the family by moving to el Bour was part of a larger shift in domestic arrangements and construction norms. The shift was visible in the contrast between the adobe housing in the qsur and new construction on the edges of villages and out in the steppe. Extensions for domestic construction were not limited to the steppe but occurred throughout the valley where villages had room to grow. Newer houses were larger, with more space between domestic compounds. Some research participants suggested that people were adopting urban styles of consumption by opting for bigger homes with more private spaces. Whereas previously only married couples in a household would have their own bedroom, families had begun building larger homes that gave individual family members such as unmarried sons their own rooms. It was also a question of construction quality. People did not want to build vertically anymore, as in the historical fortified settlements, because they felt construction standards had declined and the thinner adobe walls common now could not bear the weight. Skilled craftsmen who could build such walls were difficult to find and expensive, one reason why people turned to cement construction.[9]

Moving out into the steppe or the edges of a village was appealing because plot sizes could be larger, unimpeded by surrounding homes that had been grouped together for safety in times of greater insecurity.[10] Standing on an escarpment overlooking the village of Imzilne one day, I asked a former metal worker turned wage laborer why houses had spread out from the traditional boundaries of the village. He attributed the increase of construction on the periphery to people's search for freedom. Before, everyone lived in the fortified settlements out of fear, but the increased security that came with independence in 1956 had ambivalent implications for him. He lamented that people had begun to "separate"; they did not want to live together anymore and were "letting go of their traditions." And yet, I also saw in my visits to these new settlements that building large homes on the edges of villages also enabled households to stay together comfortably. In offering a release valve for portions of the family to break off, the new settlements helped keep families together.

The spatiality of changing domestic arrangements remade the landscape of mountain communities as well as the steppe. Despite economic pressures and experiences of drought, mountain villages did not depopulate. If anything, rural populations in the valley and mountain plateaus were increasing as the global financial crisis depressed urban job opportunities toward the end of the first decade of the twenty-first century, especially for clandestine migrants in southern Europe. I encountered a few such men who had returned from Spain and were making a go of life in the mountains. They told me there was no more work abroad and, perhaps apocryphally, that even Spaniards were coming down to Morocco in search of jobs. Returning migrants and growing households claimed unused land in their village hurm for expanded housing. The Aït Hamd plateau, for example, witnessed unprecedented growth in settlement after 2000 despite a contraction in agriculture. El Houcine, a blacksmith in Imzilne, explained: "A family like ours that used to have twenty now has fifty. Before maybe four children out of eight or ten born survived and now, all the children will survive. They cannot all stay here. There is no work for them."[11] Labor migration and setting up a satellite household in the steppe allowed households to remain in their communities by providing an outlet for the family members that the tight village economy could not support.

For vulnerable intraregional migrants, a new form of mobility rooted in wage labor and migration allowed them to maintain their family in a place with affective significance and a more affordable cost of living. In satellite images, new housing settlements ringing the towns along the national road stood alongside the extensions of cultivation in villages like el Harte as contrasting blocks of color. An ethnographic perspective, however, reveals the social complexity of new land-use practices and uneven development in the region. Certain land uses, such as the agricultural extensions of el Harte, represented new strategies of accumulation, while others—housing in el Bour n'Aït Yahya—were associated with precarity and the mobility of a rural labor reservoir. Some residents of el Bour *were* able to use their new homes as a staging ground for a wider array of accumulation strategies, expanding the "productive space" of their livelihoods by farming in multiple locations or selling at diverse livestock markets. These strategies kept their families together socially even as they separated them spatially. People were remaking the landscape through their labor, but who could practice what kind of labor was mediated by customary institutions that governed these new geographies of social reproduction.

The Mystifications of Patrimony

Just as extensions into the steppe for housing or agriculture reached a crescendo, so, too, did official interest in traditional land-use practices and the resource management institutions that historically guided them. This interest was analogous to, or perhaps an extension of, the process described in chapter 3, whereby state officials and rural notables were the most vocal defenders of collectively owned lands against land divisions spearheaded by the most marginal ayants-droits. Concern about maintaining the integrity of these lands was usually couched in terms of protecting the communal identity of tribes and preventing illegal appropriations. These efforts to preserve an idealized image of communal ownership obscured how the French colonial legacy effectively guaranteed state control over those lands. Similarly, declensionist environmental narratives—especially among Ministry of Agriculture officials and multilateral donors—focused on preserving collective natural resource management institutions as essential to reversing degradation in the steppe. In the case of the UNDP project introduced earlier, the intent was to support the return or revitalization of transhumant pastoralism as the environmentally optimal use of rangeland. Official discourse held that traditional livelihoods and natural resource management practices needed to be resuscitated as part of a collective—Moroccan and global—responsibility to protect our ecological patrimony. Extolling the cultural and natural patrimony of the region also became a key element of sustainable development discourses. Conferences and reports in and about the region framed patrimony as an asset that "guarantees economic equilibrium and protects identity and social cohesion," an asset whose value could be extracted, monetized, and marketed (Centre International ERSG-SDDOM 2017, 3). A nostalgic narrative took shape that was largely out of step with the dynamics underpinning land-use change and the way government agricultural policies supported exactly those kinds of land uses that conservation projects were trying to counteract.

I encountered a stark example of this narrative at the closing conference for the UNDP project, held in the ballroom of a luxurious five-star hotel in Ouarzazate. I was one of over 150 audience members from the provincial government, civil society organizations, development agencies, and project participants. Like many development projects, the nine million dollar initiative generated divergent reactions from observers, participants, staff, and uninvolved residents in target communities, some of whom questioned the project's impact, some of whom knew little about its activities. These disparate perspectives were muted as pastoralists were ushered into the hotel and seated at the front of the audience as they waited to offer their testimonials about the project. They were clearly uncomfortable in this setting, put on display to represent a "way of life" that the provincial governor declared was our collective responsibility to preserve. A sophisticated multimedia production interspersed lounge music with traditional Berber instrumentation. The music accompanied a film juxtaposing images of wild flora and fauna (gazelles, wild oregano) preserved by the project with images of pastoralists moving their herds across the landscape, seemingly preserved in the same way. Speakers from the various ministries involved in implementation described how, in the words of the UNDP country director, the project "marked a new stage in Morocco's development: a consciousness that biodiversity and transhumance are not contradictory." By integrating local knowledge into biodiversity plans and celebrating traditional natural resource management practices, this project and the new ethic it represented would revive the pastoralist institutions tasked with sustainably managing the landscape.

Testimonials followed. Project participants spoke in Tashelhit with Arabic translation for the largely nonresident, non-Tashelhit-speaking audience. Pastoralists recounted how, in the words of one, they "had been ignorant, but were no longer" now that they understood the importance of biodiversity. They spoke of local development associations established to support livelihood activities or reduce fuelwood collection, although I knew from my fieldwork that several associations were no longer active. Each speaker knew the global language of development, aware of the power of terms like "participation" and "sustainability" while also retaining enough rural authenticity to elicit occasional audience laughter for slips of protocol or awkward speech. I felt deeply uncomfortable and complicit. The program concluded with audience comments, largely stylized expressions of appreciation to show respect for government authorities. I was struck by one speaker—a member of parliament—who thanked the project for guarding against the *malfaits de la civilisation* (the dangers of civilization) that she said imperiled the region by bringing paved roads and television. Ironically, she echoed Khadija's concern about the paved road ruining her tourism venture, although from a very different perspective.

The idea of preserving an idealized past as a bulwark against the corrosive effects of civilization is, of course, as old as the colonial domination this narrative helped support. However, my discomfort was about more than the disjuncture between the world depicted in the space of the ballroom and the landscapes I had come to know. The project had laudably valorized lifeways and land uses that had officially been repressed for so long, but the narrative on display at that ceremony and in project documents was still suffused with assumptions of decline. As one program evaluation notes: "Changes in pastoral landscapes are accompanied by a strong rise in individualism and a focus on individual interests at the expense of the group or any form of collective organization. As a result, pastoralists' new relationship with their environment rejects any responsibility for their patrimony" (FIDA 2008, 75). Initially, I found it ironic that the same government agencies that tried for a century to eradicate these ways of life had turned to reviving them but only after those lifeways had been irrevocably transformed. Attempts to revive putatively traditional livelihoods seemed at best a misrecognition of how people were constructing their livelihoods and adjusting their land-use practices in a changing regional economy. Valley residents negotiated emergent pressures and opportunities, to be sure, although they did so not by abandoning the institutions or practices that historically governed land use. Instead, they used those institutions to inhabit the land in new ways (Guyer et al. 2007). They were concerned less with resurrecting a patrimony that was slipping away than trying to manage a changing rurality through practices and institutions that continued to organize social and economic life. Customary natural resource management institutions had undeniably narrowed in scope, but this was not because of involution or some isolated process of institutional decline; it was a culmination of the political and economic processes I have described throughout this book. Those institutions still played an important role in managing the course of change—albeit with mixed equity implications—by shaping who could access land and for what purposes. Like Fairhead and Leach in their findings for Guinea, I, and some of the scholars providing analysis to the CBTHA project (Aït Hamza 2002b; Chiche 2003; El Alaoui 2002), found "little evidence to suggest that [customary] authority structures are, or have become, incapable in [the] role" of natural resource management (Fairhead and Leach 1996, 236). Historically, these regimes have been both flexible and responsive, with most major disruptions coming from political repression and broader shifts in the political economic context.

Something more than official misrecognition of the political economy of environmental change was at work in the Mgoun Valley. The irony of the state and multilateral donors holding up traditional institutions as patrimony needing protection makes sense as the institutional analogy to the romanticization of nature in industrializing Britain, nineteenth-century North America, and colonized landscapes around the world. Drawing on Americanist environmental history, Smith emphasizes how romanticizing nature was "a direct response to the successful objectification of nature in the labor process," a nostalgia that only became possible after human activity had subordinated nature (2008, 25). Similarly, customary institutions like the jma'a, tribal agreements for rangeland access, or the agdal could only be romanticized as Morocco's collective patrimony after they had been politically contained and officially stripped of their wider governance roles. A century of colonial and postcolonial declensionist narratives blaming traditional land uses and institutions for environmental degradation neutralized the political autonomy embedded in those institutions. The turn to preserving such institutions in the framework of "community-based natural resource management" was simultaneously an acknowledgment that they did not pose the same political threat they once did and an effort to further insert the state into this peripheral zone by narrowing their functional authority even more. Project goals of "relaunching transhumance ... [by] limiting the weaknesses of customary resource management regimes" and "redynamising pastoralist institutions created especially for transhumance and land management" downplayed the broader governance authority these institutions historically enjoyed (El Alaoui 2002, 9). The notion that protecting the land required the state to either sustain or hold watch over customary natural resource management institutions was a way to extend the state's *tutelle* (tutelary authority). This shifted the declensionist narrative that blamed traditional resource practices and institutions for environmental degradation in favor of a narrative that claimed degradation was due to the *decline* of those resource practices and institutions. However, both narratives reflected a similar ideology of state rule. As in the case of collective-land law described in the previous chapter, the colonial and then postcolonial state positioned itself as tutelary authority over tribal confederations and rural residents deemed incapable of managing their own resources. This logic reified people's relationship "to the environment" through a romanticized view of traditional practice, obscuring the socioecological coproduction of livelihoods, land use, and environmental change as well as the role of state policy in exacerbating uneven development in the marginalized pre-Saharan provinces.

Conclusion

Peasant farms in marginalized environments such as the Andes, Meso-America, and North Africa have been the object of repressive policies for centuries but are now widely acknowledged to be repositories of globally important crop genetic diversity (Aït Hamza and Popp 2005; Graddy 2013; Zimmerer 2006). In oases, the socioecological intricacy of production systems and social institutions has led to the designation of North African oases as a "globally important agricultural heritage system," a legacy to be preserved as much for its agroecological attributes as for its cultural ones (Koohafkan and Altieri 2011). Extensive and transhumant pastoralist systems, historically maligned by colonial and postcolonial governments alike for degrading arid lands, are now officially supported at least by some of the state agencies and donors that actively undermined them in the past. These examples illustrate how long-standing scholarly and political critiques of official environmental discourses have helped shift dominant narratives about smallholder or indigenous environmental practices. In Morocco, scholars have documented severe environmental pressures on oases, but they have also explored the quotidian practices of oasis farmers to highlight the ingenuity and adaptability of these complex socioecological systems. Recognizing this rich heritage, even designating it as national or global patrimony, can be an important way of valorizing livelihoods and life ways that have historically been repressed.

However, a cautionary tale about this acknowledgment of peasants' rich heritage unfolded when I observed the way "socially differentiated land use practices" intersected with the new orthodoxy surrounding environmental change in Mgoun (Fairhead and Leach 1996, 12). Migrants, pastoralists, farmers, and wage workers negotiated their land-use strategies through the mediating authority of customary land tenure institutions. These institutions were neither intact—a reflection of unchanging tradition—nor dissolving in the face of corrosive individualism, as the new dominant narrative asserted. Customary institutions did manage change, although often in inegalitarian ways, by limiting access to different categories of land. When contextualized in this way, the differentiated landscapes I encountered showed how the viability of agrarian rurality depended at least partially on shifting some land away from previously agricultural uses in ways that supported the increasingly diversified livelihoods of the valley's residents. Agrarian livelihoods for some (upwardly mobile el Harte famers with access to land and water, for example) were made possible by a contraction in agriculture elsewhere in the valley, as when others (migrants from the mountains who worked as day laborers in the fields of el Harte) repurposed land for housing.

When official policy engaged with these customary land tenure institutions, it did so by adopting preservationist discourses rather than pragmatically accounting for how these institutions worked given the changing ecological and economic realities of life in the valley. State and development actors simultaneously blamed environmental degradation on the failure of putatively traditional institutions and assigned responsibility for environmental conservation to those same institutions. Importantly, the state would have a central role in authorizing, funding, and monitoring these efforts within the framework of community-based natural resource management, reifying and circumscribing the broader governing authority these institutions once had. As the critical literature on heritage regimes emphasizes, invoking collective ownership of cultural or natural patrimony can be a way of commoditizing heritage and shifting control away from those designated as stewards of that patrimony, although these strategies do not go uncontested (Geismar 2015; Peutz 2011). In the Mgoun Valley, residents from various social locations expressed little interest in reviving traditional ways, whatever that might mean. Their intimate ecological knowledge and ability to adapt communal governance to new realities allowed them to negotiate environmental change with a nuanced, if contested, understanding of the risks and costs involved. Their strategies to repurpose customary institutions and a communal orientation to social life extended beyond land use to include the ways people made their living on and off the land, the subject of chapter 5.

5

MAKING A LIVING ON AND OFF THE LAND

In the Aït Hamd plateau, people often sat out on the rocky outcroppings that overlooked the river or on the mounded edges of irrigation canals bisecting the fields. They actually looked at the landscape and talked about its features. They did not take it for granted. Elderly men in particular described their attachment to the tamazirt, perhaps because many had spent so much time away—in the mines of France, on construction sites in Casablanca. One fall day, my research assistant Saïd and I joined Taleb, the returned migrant I introduced in earlier chapters, on the outcropping overlooking his adobe home. As the sun dipped behind the peaks surrounding the plateau, I could hear the voices of people working in the fields, women especially. It was crowded, bustling, even loud. People started to make their way home in the quickly diminishing light. The angled rays illuminated the dried maize stalks that rustled in the hard dirt alleys of the village, crackling underfoot as Saïd and I walked to greet Taleb and another returned migrant, Aït Zolit. Whereas Taleb's family was a large, raucous group always at work, Aït Zolit's home was muted. His migration experience in France had left him disillusioned. He went to work in the mines hoping to return and farm the land he had bought over the years. He came back to find that his children did not want to work the land. According to him, they did not want to work at all. I wondered if it was Aït Zolit's son I had seen earlier as we approached the outcropping—a young man dressed in stonewashed jeans who appeared to be wandering the fields, listening to music on his cell phone, and looking distinctly bored. The men talked about the landscape below as a space of labor, fields to be worked in a carefully balanced arrangement with the other labor they needed to keep their families going in the mountains: construction work in the city, livestock sales in Kelaa Mgouna, the butcher stall at the Imzilne market, the small transactions and constant movement of people in and out of the household. Their discussion illustrated the extent to which the Mgoun Valley's new rurality had reshaped how people made a living. Changing livelihoods also figured prominently in the debates over communal governance I have traced throughout this book. Labor, both on and off the land, tied people together and sowed new distinctions by refiguring the balance between communal identities and individual aspirations.

I thought back to another afternoon earlier in the agricultural season when I sat on the same outcropping with Karima, Taleb's niece. She had stopped to rest after thinning out one of the family's maize fields. A generation ago they were one of Rbat's poorest sharecropping families. Taleb's eighteen-year stint in a French mine had enabled them to acquire large landholdings and a herd that Karima's father kept on the range. Karima was sixteen, starting to wonder when she would get married and where her husband would take her. When I commented on the beauty of the river below, she grimaced and said, "No, the river is ugly. We go there to clean our clothes. Kelaa Mgouna is the beautiful place." Kelaa, with its cement block houses interspersed with mechanics' shops on rocky dirt roads, always seemed like the ugliest place in the valley to me. But Karima would have loved to move there, where there was less work and so much more going on. She regretted that the rare times she went to Kelaa to see a doctor or get official papers, she was able to stay only one night at a time in the house her uncle kept there. The women in her family always had to rise early and catch the transit (communal van) to the plateau, never experiencing the market town for more than a day. Their labor was tied to those fields by the river where they washed their clothes. Fully aware of other women's experiences but not able to access them, Karima hoped her future husband would take her down to Kelaa, or at least to Bou Thagrar, a larger village halfway between Kelaa and the mountain plateau where she lived. During a visit to Taleb a couple of years later, I learned that she had married, but her husband lived in Ouzighimt, higher up in the mountains than even the Aït Hamd plateau—a village with cold winters, hard agricultural labor, and little access to health services.

This chapter takes these personal experiences of work, familial ties, and social change as a window into the profound transformation in the meaning and practice of labor in the Mgoun Valley. I link an ethnography of people's affective and economic investments in land and communal life to agrarian practice, tracing how new labor relations simultaneously transformed and sustained the social reciprocity that undergirded moral economies in the valley. Rather than simply eroding the communal basis for Mgoun's agrarian rurality, new forms of wage labor represented sites for negotiating "entrustment": relations of dependence, obligation, and autonomy (Shipton 2007). The commons had always been constituted through labor—the literal working of the land as well as the work of sustaining communal governance. As new forms of labor emerged in the latter half of the twentieth century, communal identities and governance mediated access to resources and social authority in new ways, although land remained vitally important to social and political life. Migration was central to these changes, but as this chapter details, a wide range of social and economic processes influenced how people worked and to what ends, with priorities such as maintaining access to land, experiencing the dignity of cash wages for the first time, securing relations of dependency with powerful patrons, and experimenting with new strategies for upward mobility, among others.[1]

The integration of North Africa's rural periphery into global circuits of capital and labor has framed narratives decrying the erosion of the traditional order. These narratives parallel and reinforce declensionist narratives about customary governance described earlier in this book. For Pierre Bourdieu, forced submission to colonial capitalism represents irrevocable rupture, a "cleaved habitus" (*habitus clivé*) against which the Algerians at least had no cultural resources to resist.[2] The violent suppression of peasant rurality in colonial Algeria was extreme, but many observers have described a swell of rural proletarianization around the world that traps the "laboring poor in a world of relentless microcapitalism," destroying traditional moral economies in the process (M. Davis 2006, 181). For Neil Smith, the dominance of the wage form erases other labor relations: "Capital's drive toward universality . . . bludgeons, connives, and insinuates the wage-labor relation into virtually every crevice of the pre-capitalist systems it encounters" ([1984] 2008, 186). Others have found that a moral economy of mutual support, autonomy, and meaning can survive this onslaught. Viviana Zelizer rejects the idea that markets necessarily undermine intimate social life or affective relations; instead of trying to keep out an "invading, predatory, economic world," she contends, people use "economic activity to create, maintain, and renegotiate important ties—especially intimate ties—to other people" (2005, 3). Anthropologists have long accounted for the culturally embedded nature of economic activity, but Zelizer shows how the money nexus permeates social life rather than opposing or lurking outside the boundaries of sociality. In the Mgoun Valley, residents sustained moral economies by actively engaging with broader capitalist processes, not attempting to withdraw from them. Their habitus was not "split" or "cleaved"; it was becoming more elaborated, expanding to include new livelihoods and agrarian relations.

The new rurality of the Mgoun Valley therefore extended beyond agriculture to include diverse social, economic, and political arrangements (Enríquez 2010; Hecht 2010; Kay 2008; van der Ploeg 2008). Even if the formal contribution of agriculture to household income had declined, residents affirmed their commitment to a specifically agrarian rurality through investments in land and farming. Residents did not simply invest migration remittances or wages "back" into farming as though capitalist labor simply buttressed an archaic form of agriculture. As Ferguson argues for southern Africa, people did not "oppose the 'logic' of the market to the 'logic' of communal solidarity, [with] resources . . . accumulated in the cash economy (according to one set of rules) and distributed in the moral economy (according to another)" (2015, 121). Rather, imperatives of maintaining social networks, managing risk, and diversifying sources of income and other support informed farming *and* wage labor—and transformed both in the process. What may have appeared as traditional peasant farming was in fact quite new, a response to how integration into new markets reshaped labor relations within and outside of agriculture (van der Ploeg 2010). Small-scale commercial agriculture represented an important element of many households' livelihoods, but this was not a continuation of historical farming systems marked by rigid social hierarchies. As van der Ploeg argues, peasants are far from being remnants of the past; they exercise a very contemporary form of agency in the ways they negotiate ecological processes, capital investments, and labor dynamics on and off the farm (2014, 999). In the Mgoun Valley, this negotiation formed the infrastructure extending commoning into domains beyond land governance: to urban work sites, for example, where laborers reinforced social ties or secured access to land back in the village.

In what follows, I present a snapshot of the transformations in livelihoods and agriculture through the initially deceptive results of our household survey. Measured in terms of income, agriculture in 2014 contributed only marginally to household livelihoods. Measured in terms of nonmarket or in-kind support, however, agriculture assumes much greater importance. I then explain this discrepancy through an ethnographic account of labor transformations, tracing how wage-labor strategies in Kelaa and urban Morocco supported communal life and productive activities in the rural hinterland and vice versa. Obligations in the village could place great demands on migrants committed to keeping up with communal life. Many of these obligations centered on the new dynamics of oasis agriculture; agrarian practice simultaneously drew on centuries of knowledge about oasis agroecology and reoriented that knowledge to new economic, political, and social imperatives. The last part of the chapter addresses the exclusions produced by the communal orientations that framed both agriculture and wage labor, from the gendered experience of work to the marginalization of households without access to certain kinds of labor. Labor transformations over the past half century in Mgoun were therefore not a linear conversion from noncapitalist relations—an idealized time during which communal life flourished—to commoditization and the dissolution of collective life. Wage labor offered new spaces and networks to extend communal attachments that were neither inherently democratic nor egalitarian but nonetheless sustained a communal referent for rural life.

New Livelihoods and Agrarian Change: A Statistical View

Our household survey data offer *one* perspective on the region's livelihood transformations, especially the kinds of labor that sustained households as the role of agriculture changed and new livelihoods became available. For one thing, these data are specific to the twelve communities along Mgoun's riparian oasis where cultivation dominated, as well as the six communities in the Aït Hamd plateau and the steppe around Kelaa where at least some households practiced transhumant pastoralism. Since the Mgoun Valley was a receiving area for regional migrants who had left pastoral livelihoods, our data showed a movement out of livestock production in the High Atlas and pre-Saharan foothills. Although our sample gathered data about people who left these regions, it did not include those who stayed. Other areas where transhumant pastoralism has remained central to livelihoods, such as the plateaus and mountains at higher altitude than my research area, would likely tell a different story. Table 7 shows the primarily agrarian

TABLE 7. Occupation of father of current head of household, 1960

OCCUPATION	NUMBER OF INDIVIDUALS	PERCENTAGE
Agriculture	136	46
Pastoralism	42	14
Migrant wage labor	21	7
Skilled trade	18	6
Other	18	6
Butcher	11	4
Commerce	11	4
Local salaried work (not government)	10	3
Inactive	6	2
Fqih/taleb (religious scholar)	6	2
Metalworker	5	2
Manual labor	6	2
Government/soldier	6	2
Total	296	100

Source: Household survey, 2014–2015 (author in partnership with Reseau Associatif de Tinghir pour la Démocratie et le Développement).

TABLE 8. Primary occupation of adults, 2014

OCCUPATION	NUMBER OF INDIVIDUALS	PERCENTAGE
Services, sales, commerce	185	31
Building trade	156	25
Craft and skilled	69	14
Transport	50	8
Teaching, health, religion	43	8
Industrial, mechanic	31	8
Government	18	3
Services and management	4	2
Agriculture	4	1
Total	560	100

Source: Household survey, 2014–2015 (author in partnership with Reseau Associatif de Tinghir pour la Démocratie et le Développement).

occupations of current household heads (or their fathers, depending on the age of the current household head) at our baseline date of 1960, before large-scale migration began.

In contrast, table 8 shows the predominance of wage labor in services, commerce, and the building trades, especially the lower-paid sectors of construction, among active adults in 2014. Many of these activities did not even exist in the valley in the previous generation. Over the previous fifty years, then, changes in households' primary occupations were marked by a notable decrease in the role of agriculture. However, the tendency of respondents (both men and women) not to report women's work meant that the importance of agriculture as a primary form of labor was substantially underreported.

Data on income sources support the overwhelming importance of wage labor and the concomitant decline in the importance of agriculture to household income in the contemporary period. We collected data on revenue sources for all household members, combining methods from the Moroccan Household Living Standards Measurement Survey with my own understanding of how people accounted for their income (table 9). When we tabulated sources of income, wage labor not surprisingly led with nearly 47 percent of household income derived from wages or salary, with migration remittances representing nearly 30 percent and only 4 percent coming from agriculture.[3]

The data seem to confirm the decline of agriculture, a story resonant of Neil Smith's description of capitalism insinuating the wage-labor relation into every crevice of contemporary life. I frequently heard that farming in the region was primarily "nostalgic," because it represented such a small portion of household income. This is not, however, the whole story. When we accounted for the con-

TABLE 9. Sources of cash income by household, 2014

SOURCE OF CASH INCOME	MEAN INCOME (DIRHAMS)	PERCENTAGE OF TOTAL
Wage labor	59,278	47
Cash income from agriculture (marketed production)	4,771	4
Migration remittances	36,400	29
Business	23,127	18
Other revenue	2,023	2
Total	125,600	100

Source: Household survey, 2014–2015 (author in partnership with Reseau Associatif de Tinghir pour la Démocratie et le Développement).

tribution of agriculture to household income by imputing a market value to production that was consumed or donated (*zakat* and *'ashur*, religious tithing), the relative importance of agriculture jumps to 34 percent of mean household income (table 10). We also calculated the value of in-kind labor, especially the exchanges women organized on the fields of relatives and patrons for portions of the harvest. These more expansive data show that agriculture continued to play an essential role in the livelihood security of households, contributing food, income, nonmarket inputs, and, as this chapter argues, keenly valued social connections linked to households' communal affiliations.

Taken alone, then, income and occupational data offer a partial, even misleading, perspective on the role of agriculture in livelihoods and agrarian transformation in the valley. It is not simply that subsistence agriculture and nonmarket means of acquiring labor and food remained important. Rather, the logics guiding labor and resource allocation worked with a much broader notion of land and labor productivity than neoclassical economics would allow. These logics revealed how individual aspirations, communal obligations, and the socially embedded nature of labor informed one another, even in the context of capitalist transformation. To explain these logics in the historical arc of the previous half century, I turn to ethnography, starting with the market town of Kelaa Mgouna as the exemplar for how livelihoods were changing.

Transformations of Labor in the Market Town

As a hub of regional economic activity, the market town of Kelaa revealed the intricate networks of labor and exchange that crisscrossed the valley (map 5).

TABLE 10. Sources of total income (including imputed values for nonmarketed labor and agricultural production), 2014

SOURCE OF INCOME	MEAN INCOME (DIRHAMS)	PERCENTAGE OF TOTAL
Wage labor	59,278	32
Total agricultural production (imputed value and sales)	65,545	34
Migration remittances	36,400	19
Value of in-kind labor	2,313	2
Business	23,127	12
Other revenue	2,022	1
Total	188,685	100

Source: Household survey, 2014–2015 (author in partnership with Reseau Associatif de Tinghir pour la Démocratie et le Développement).

Through their purchases, patronage, and even leisure choices, people made investments of labor that cultivated relations of debt and obligation (Geertz, Geertz, and Rosen 1979). Labor, then, enacted communal affinities, drawing wage work, commercial apprenticeships, and new trades spurred by the migration economy into relations characterized by reciprocity as well as commercial gain. These dynamics were on display at the *suq* (weekly market), an expansive rectangular space enclosed by walls that had warehouses and stores built into them—a standard organization for periodic markets in Morocco. It was located at the exit to town, moved from the center of Kelaa less than a decade before because of beautification efforts and because it had simply outgrown its surroundings.

One of my first visits to the market in Kelaa happened during one of the rare soaking rains that rolled over the valley, turning side streets—unpaved because the hard earth normally served just as well as asphalt—and the market into a thick, red mud (figure 16). A closed and isolated feeling settled onto the landscape, maybe because men nestled their arms in their woolen burnouses and pulled their hoods down over their heads. The sky was shifting gray, black, and blue, with the sun occasionally emerging to cast a silver sheen on the wet terrain and debris cast outside the tarpaulins upon which vendors mounded their vegetables. The market was busy and full despite the mud, as men and a few women made their purchases while connecting with friends and business alliances. Geertz describes the urban bazaar as the "promiscuous tumbling in the public realm of varieties of men," but this was not only a promiscuous tumbling of *men* (Geertz, Geertz, and Rosen 1979, 141). Although women from the mountains like Karima primarily passed through Kelaa on their way to their rural homes and local women commonly avoided the weekly market, others participated in the market by necessity and sometimes by choice (Kapchan 1996). Whether or not they attended the

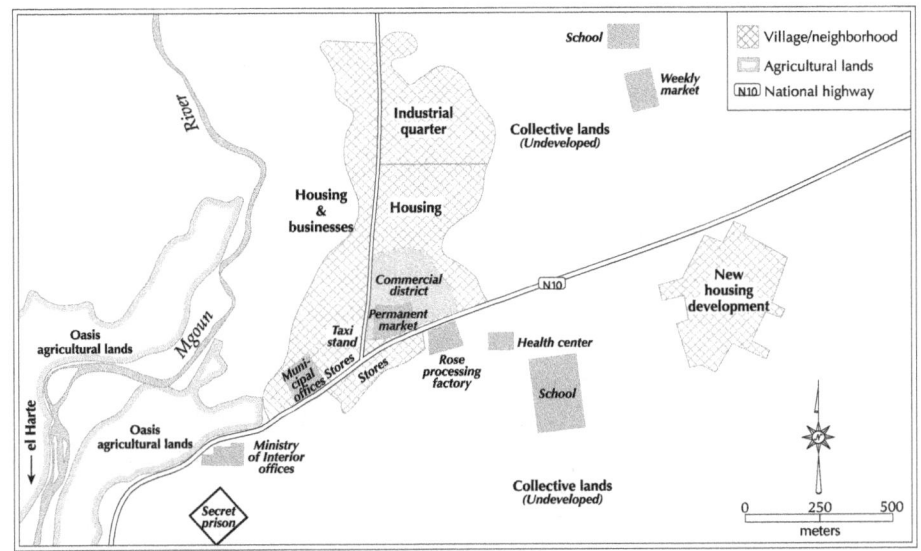

MAP 5. Kelaa Mgouna.

Map by Richard Gilbreath, independent cartographer.

FIGURE 16. Kelaa's weekly market after a rain.

Photo by the author.

weekly market, women's labor was as important to the social infrastructure that linked the rural hinterland to the market town as that of men.

During that first visit, I wondered if the historical importance of weekly open-air markets as a place for social interaction and provisioning had been undermined by more formal, corporate distribution channels. It quickly became clear that not only had the weekly market persisted, it had expanded to absorb the new trades and labor relations produced by the region's fuller integration into the national economy. The market's standard organization, however, masked the reconfiguration of where and how people practiced those trades. In my subsequent shopping trips, I often saw Mohamed, the son of Hamid, whom I introduced in chapter 2 as Imzilne's oldest metalworker. Hamid was the last to maintain his workshop in the village using the old system: repairing tools for clients who traveled to his home and often spent the night as guests. When Kelaa emerged as an important regional market town, Imzilne's position as center for the trade faded and Mohamed began taking his hand-forged tools down to the weekly market. Metalwork represented only a small portion of his income. As a younger man, he had traveled for irregular construction work—"traveling" was the term people tended to use for periodic migration to Moroccan cities. As he grew older and had his own children, he stayed in Imzilne but went to the Kelaa market to sell his tools and purchase dates that he would resell in the smaller Imzilne weekly market.

Kelaa had drawn Mohamed down from the mountains as it had so many others from rural communities in the valley. Formerly dispersed economic activities began to concentrate in Kelaa, especially for adjacent villages like el Harte that had become bedroom communities for men who earned their wage income or ran businesses in town. I had difficulty tracking down Abderrahmane, one of el Harte's customary leaders, in the village, but he could be found every week selling vegetables at the market. He employed a poor relative from the village to manage sales while he conducted other business as an influential political figure and entrepreneur. He would often hold equipment at the stall for his brother, Brahim, who was a plumber in town and was particularly busy on market days with both repairs and a regional trade in plumbing supplies. Several families in el Harte vied to get their adolescent sons in the service of the brothers as apprentices to carve a path to a remunerative career in the skilled trades. While I heard a frequent complaint that youth no longer wanted to work, I saw no shortage of young men apprenticing as mechanics, plaster workers, carpenters, electricians, and plumbers, among other trades. Families used kinship or patronage ties to secure an apprenticeship for their sons, cementing relations of obligation far into the future.

Virtually everybody in the valley moved through Kelaa, following trajectories that reinforced networks anchored in their villages or extended alliances to new spaces and types of work. I began to notice who was interacting with whom in Kelaa, not just at the market but in the coffeehouses, at the counters of construction supply stores, and at the municipal offices. Kelaa had become a regional economic center in a process that de Haas calls "rural urbanisation," the growing density of economic activity around market towns (2009, 1583). One factor driving this process was the tendency of migrants who maintained ties to the valley to invest outside their natal villages but within the region. Populations coalesced around market towns, transforming the regional economy through various multiplier effects: changing consumption patterns, new trades, and other commercial activity (de Haas 2006). Remittances monetized the local economy in novel ways, fueling a local construction sector that served as the primary employer for men without access to higher-paying skilled trades, a driver's license and taxicab medallion, or, if they had the requisite education and connections, a civil service position. Returned migrants who lived close to Kelaa usually invested both in agriculture and in Kelaa's new economic vibrancy. One returned migrant I knew from el Harte, Abdelhafid, spent his early years in France sending back remittances (like so many others) to buy agricultural land in the village. When he was satisfied with his holdings, he built two houses in Kelaa as investments and places for his expanding family to move should they want to leave his compound. Two of his sons ran shops on the ground floor of the homes in Kelaa because, as Abdelhafid phrased it, "not everyone wants to farm, and the land cannot hold everyone anyway." The land never really had sustained everyone, but infant and child mortality rates used to be higher and families historically sloughed off members through marriage and migration. If the land could not support those who stayed, they could open a perfume shop, work as a mechanic, or search out a position in one of the many new businesses that had opened in Kelaa.

These multiplier effects enabled many nonmigrants to secure upward mobility or transition their already-high status to the new realities of a monetized economy. Our landlord, Youssef, was one of the wealthiest and most influential men in the valley and perhaps the region. According to an elderly Amazigh patriarch from a historically dominant family, though, Youssef began by "stealing corn from our fields," a pejorative reference to the latter's family's historically low status as sharecroppers. Youssef had begun amassing his wealth by receiving remittances from workers in France and delivering the money to families dispersed throughout the valley. Kelaa had no bank in those early years and transport was poor, allowing him to hold on to the cash for a time and use it as working capital to start his own construction business. Everyone got their money—part of why he was so revered—but he wisely parlayed that experience into a diversified enterprise. In addition to large contracts for schools and government buildings elsewhere in Morocco, *al-Beid* (the White one), as the very dark-skinned Youssef was called, opened a *hammam* (public bath) and coffeehouse, two key social institutions as well as profitable businesses. Coffeehouses such as al-Beid's were as important as the weekly market as sites for conducting business, and which coffeehouse one frequented was a political choice. The wide array of stores, workshops, and coffeehouses—more than I would have anticipated the relatively small town could sustain—had less to do with what abstract market demand could bear than with the social relations undergirding the businesses and the people working in them.

Migration was an important part of this story, but it was not the exclusive driver of the transition to predominantly wage-based labor markets. These markets linked old commercial traditions to new trades and economic imperatives. Some trades had certainly died off at the hand of industrially mass-produced goods. Plastic mats, for instance, had replaced the reed mats women had previously specialized in making, depriving them of this source of cash and economic independence. However, new specialized trades also emerged. A whole sector of the local economy was devoted to the sale and repair of satellite dishes, decoders, cell phones, and other electronics. The men involved in this trade were highly skilled at installing and repairing off-brand electronic and computer equipment from Korea and China, cobbling together solutions using largely self-taught technology skills. The language of "capitalist transition" felt inappropriate here, for it was less a linear shift from uncommoditized labor to new wage-labor regimes than a proliferating repertoire that added new types of work and labor relations onto old ones or combined them in novel ways.

Labor and the Production of Communal Life

Wage labor and the emergence of new trades transformed work in the valley, but people still found a way to tailor the amount and nature of work they did to balance various economic and social imperatives. They were not only earning a living; they were using new labor arrangements to produce communal life, adjusting the time they devoted to specific jobs to sustain relationships and networks. Abderrahmane, the customary leader from el Harte, set up his stand at the weekly market to sell vegetables, but he also used the stall as a staging ground to adjudicate land disputes, assist his brother in his plumbing business, and otherwise negotiate the various economic and social relationships that maintained his high stature. What constituted "labor" for him could not be easily identified by occupational categories (vegetable merchant, farmer, official) or the pace and intensity of his daily rhythms in Kelaa and at home in el Harte. He adjusted his work routines to accommodate the increasing density of economic activity in Kelaa, el Harte's prominence in small-scale agricultural production, rising land values, and the persistent importance of customary leaders in mediating these various economic and political processes. His livelihoods therefore enabled his political life and undergirded collective-land governance back in el Harte.

Abderrahmane was a perfect example of how collective life seeped into individual projects of capital accumulation. His time at the vegetable stall was valuable, so he hired relatively cheap wage labor in the form of a poor extended relative while he conducted important personal and collective business at the market and in town. Relying on the paid labor of others gave him flexibility to shift between his various roles. For Abderrahmane, as for so many others in and around Kelaa, irregular schedules were the norm and certainly preferable. Leisure was not "residual," something to be sacrificed if work duties became too onerous (Guyer 1992, 475). On the surface, then, it could be difficult to tell how people made their living in the valley. Abderrahmane's time in the café on market day, sitting for a late afternoon tea with friends in el Harte, and lingering outside the mosque after prayer were, in fact, an important dimension of the labor process. So, too, was the time he spent working on others' behalf outside of any monetary transaction. These exchanges in Kelaa, monetized or not, supported relations of debt and obligation that sustained collective life back in el Harte. At the same time, these relations supported Abderrahmane's decidedly self-interested goal of securing labor for his agricultural operations. This labor was unpaid more often than not.

The rising commoditization of labor not only changed communal life; communal life also shaped how people engaged in wage labor or otherwise conducted commercial transactions in the market. This was as true for merchants and other business owners—owners of their time like Abderrahmane—as for wage workers with less control over their time. I came to know Filali first as one of Kelaa's taxi dispatchers. Although small in stature, he struck an authoritative figure, necessary for managing the chaotic space of the taxi stand and the frequent disputes that occurred there. Filali was there six days a week, working long hours in often difficult weather, maintaining his serious, efficient demeanor. He stood out. As I began my fieldwork in el Harte, I came to know Filali in another capacity, as respected community leader because of his family background as a *murabit* (saintly family) and his reputation as an astute livestock trader. His work as a taxi dispatcher provided important income and stability. He was only thirty-three but had been responsible for his family for many years after his father's untimely death over a decade earlier. Filali's wages were not high, but with substantial land holdings and his mother's strong farming skills (she managed the farming operation with Filali's wife), subsistence production limited their expenses. He was able to use part of his wages as working capital to buy and sell livestock around the valley; but given the impressive size of his operation, Filali's working capital clearly did not come from invested wages alone. His livestock trading was renowned, and he had extensive networks that invested, gifted, and otherwise kept capital in circulation through various arrangements with him. Filali had little control over most of his time; he had to be at the taxi stand for ten hours a day, six days a week. He chose Tuesday, the day of the weekly livestock market, as his day off so that he could devote himself to his first love and the business he felt secured his social position. Filali used his evenings to maintain his various communal commitments. Mbarak and I waited for him at his home on more than one occasion as he mediated a dispute late into the night or consulted with el Harte's jma'a on a land allocation issue. He said he was not ready to leave his dispatch job—the stable income of a job he had essentially inherited from his father was too important to give up—but if the job started to impinge on his other activities, he might eventually choose to leave.

Filali's job was more structured than most of the work people did in the valley. Generally, the time discipline of wage labor here did not conform to the rigidity usually associated with capitalist labor regimes, in terms of both the regularity of the work conducted and its payment. Most of the wage labor I encountered in the market town was flexible because it integrated communal imperatives often rooted in the rural communities to which laborers returned or in which they lived. In my walks across the river to el Harte, I began to question whether it was only "rural urbanization" that was occurring in the Mgoun Valley. Kelaa was also witnessing an "urban ruralization," as communal imperatives and other rural-focused dynamics infused the way people labored in the space of the market town, in urban Morocco, and sometimes abroad.

In Search of Dependency

Our household survey therefore captured only a slice of the livelihood transformations that had remade social and economic life in the valley. By asking for "primary occupation" we necessarily simplified the diversity of livelihood activities not only within households but as practiced by individuals over the course of the year and their lifetimes. At any given point, people might be engaged in wage labor, skilled or unskilled trades, trading on their own account, and unpaid help for family, friends, or patrons. Often, they were doing several activities at the same time, or appearing not to do anything at all. And that appearance of inactivity could be the most productive labor of all; for example, by buying a coffee at a particular café, one could display one's loyalty or indebtedness to the café owner from one's natal village (Rignall 2013). Some of our survey questions were aimed at describing people's multiple activities, but I knew they were an imperfect means of capturing the full import of livelihood diversity: many of the most important benefits could not be quantified as income. They embedded people in relations of dependence that provided social support, validated communal membership, and sustained the infrastructure for what I have called the new politics of commoning.

At the end of Wednesday market days, I would often greet Mohamed, the blacksmith from Imzilne, as he gazed out from the transit idling next to our house. He and the other passengers waited to leave for the mountains as Taleb, the returned migrant from France who had built substantial holdings in Rbat, loaded nylon sacks with provisions onto the roof of the van. Mohamed and Taleb often moved through the same spaces—in the market, on the transits—but they represented very different social locations. Mohamed still struggled to make ends meet as a blacksmith in Imzilne, while Taleb had used his remittances to buy land and put a midsize herd on the range. For someone like Mohamed, Kelaa's rural urbanization facilitated an irregular income from small-scale trading but also offered employment opportunities with people who may have been as poor as him thirty or forty years ago but whose upward mobility allowed them to start businesses and hire others from their natal communities. For Mohamed, even low-paid day labor in Kelaa was preferable to his time working construction in Casablanca, Tangier, and Agadir. He described the loneliness of pitching tents on construction sites or sharing rented rooms in faraway cities and how "it is always better to work in the tamazirt, to live close to your home." He never earned enough to invest in the kinds of businesses some other migrants did, but Mohamed was able to earn a living because others did return with this kind of investment capital, creating new labor markets that could employ people like him.

For Mohamed, returning home meant new uncertainty in the regularity or level of his income, but it also secured autonomy and another form of certainty: the ability to maintain social relations in the valley. The importance of maintaining those relations underscores the particular kind of autonomy to which people like Mohamed aspired. It was not an individualized notion of independence or self-sufficiency but came from a "plurality of opportunities" for dependence and was fundamentally relational (Ferguson 2015, 146). James Ferguson resists fetishizing individual autonomy as a universal goal, noting that "material dependence on others is not a passive condition—it is a valued outcome of long, hard social labor"; it is a "mode of action" and "an achievement" that does not treat hierarchy as inimical to autonomy but rather as constitutive of it (2015, 97). As in southern Africa, relations of dependence in the Mgoun Valley that enmeshed people in networks of debt and obligation were not a failure of autonomy; they supported it (Ferguson 2007). This kind of dependence was preferable to having to rely on anonymous employers in distant wage-labor markets.[4] Those markets were, perhaps, unavoidable, but even for those working in urban Morocco, communal logics and an aspiration to dependence meshed with the imperative to make a living. As in most migration streams around the world, people used local networks to secure jobs in distant cities. Mobilizing social networks not only was an instrumental means of finding work; it was a strategy for sustaining communal attachments in the tamazirt and extending relations of dependence to new spaces of labor.

Agrarian Transformations: New Forms of Labor and "Traditionalist" Farming

In rural zones like the Mgoun Valley, it is tempting to see out-migration as driving capitalist transformation at the expense of nonmarket or communal approaches to organizing work and social life. Migration was undeniably transformative, but it also folded into an agrarian rurality that, like the economic dynamics of the market town, both shaped and was shaped by new forms of labor. Our survey data confirmed that agricultural production remained important to household livelihoods even if relatively small quantities were marketed for cash income. However, this persistence was not "an undifferentiated quality" of oasis farming; it was a product of changing labor regimes (Guyer 1992, 483). Understanding how wage-labor relations repurposed communal affinities to meet new economic and social imperatives also compels a reappraisal of oasis agriculture as a repository of tradition. When migration began on a large scale in the 1960s, small farmers inaugurated a methodical process of unassisted "indigenous intensification," experimenting with new cropping combinations to produce an emergent commercial agricultural sector in the lower-lying steppe (Adams and Mortimore 1997, 151). At the same time, farming contracted in the water-scarce plateaus farther up the valley. This uneven development in the fields was predicated on the same logics that organized labor relations and networks of obligation in the market town and urban job sites. The fact that these strategies were embedded in and yet reworked long-standing oasis farming practice rendered them invisible to the productionist logic of many official observers. As in the example of men sitting at cafés in Kelaa appearing to do nothing and yet doing quite a lot, we need to explain changing farming systems in the oasis through the communal imperatives framing the social organization of production.

Productionism and the Logic of Oasis Farming

The logic of these farming systems was hidden in plain sight as tourist buses idled on the national road outside Kelaa. It was the beginning of May, and the lower Mgoun Valley was in bloom. Visitors photographed small clusters of pink roses weighing down branches that created a wall of color around the wheat fields. Decades ago, the Ministry of Tourism seized on rose production here to label Mgoun "the Valley of the Roses" and scheduled an annual harvest festival to turn this brand identity into revenue. Promoted initially during the French Protectorate, the odiferous *rosa damascena* was the region's only export crop. It was processed in Kelaa Mgouna by a factory owned by the king's personal holding company, which had expropriated the operation from its original colonial French founder. The factory in turn sold the essence to European cosmetics and perfume manufacturers. In town planning meetings, officials repeated the mantra that roses *were* the Mgoun Valley, its *ra's al-mal* (economic capital) and the region's cultural and natural patrimony. Officials in the provincial capital identified the rose as the next *produit de terroir* that would achieve international renown and high prices just as argan oil and saffron had in other parts of the south. But farmers were showing progressively less interest in growing roses. Local extension officers charged with increasing production worried about the decline in linear meters planted from four thousand in the 1970s to just over three thousand in 2010 (Centre de Mise en Valeur Agricole 2010). In the words of one official: "People just do not want to work on the rose."

Women, who were responsible for the harvest, hated roses. In el Harte, women left for the fields at five in the morning to begin picking before the sun wizened the ready blooms. They used a *tamghurt* (hand sickle) to pull down the thorny branches, swiftly picked off the blooms, and tucked them into their folded *tajdat* (large overdress that women knotted and draped over their shoulders to carry harvested crops). Few could afford gloves, meaning the sticky resin from the roses seeped into cuts from the thorns and turned their raw hands a deep orange. When their tajdats were full, women guided them into a burlap sack, hoisted the sack on their shoulders, and walked through the fields to the *bu mizan* (the weigher), a village notable and agent of the rose processor who set up a weigh station in his garage for the month. He paid the women on the spot. The money glided into pockets in their underdresses—sometimes to be handed to the family patriarch at the end of the day, sometimes quietly saved for a personal purchase—as they worked their way back to the fields. Women did this circuit for five hours every day; the rest of the day was devoted to their usual agricultural and domestic tasks. Over the one-month harvest, they revisited the same bushes as new blooms emerged, and moved to the fields of extended family members with whom they did labor exchanges. Rose bushes were planted around the edges of plots—only a handful of people in the valley planted roses *in* the fields as a primary crop—meaning the agricultural landscape was in constant motion as large work groups wended their way through the complex patchwork of holdings. Entire families that had immigrated from Imaghran in the mountains walked into fields looking for a day's wages, while beggars stood in the pathways asking for alms in the form of a handful of blooms. The fields were noisy and crowded, an intensely social space that brought all the contradictions, solidarities, and transformations of agriculture into swirling contact.

Women were hard at work in the fields when the inaugural rose colloquium opened the May 2010 harvest festival. Officials, teachers, civil society activists, and male farmers from the villages around Kelaa Mgouna filed into the town auditorium for technical presentations from university agronomists and marketing experts about how to refine production techniques for greater profitability, even though it was the monopoly of the king's processing factory that kept farmgate prices low at annual price-setting meetings held in the municipal office. Echoing local narratives that farmers did not pay enough attention to the rose, PowerPoint presentations detailed the negative impacts of tearing roses off the stems, how people either did not prune or were "brutal" in their cutting, and how the use of roses as boundary hedges meant that they did not get the irrigation or fertilization regime suited to their needs—they only received the water intended for the field crop. A few weeks after the rose colloquium, I was interested to hear local agricultural extension officers speculate about the impending failure of a hundred-hectare rose farm established in the steppe by the king's processing company. The goal of the farm was to demonstrate modern production techniques to local farmers while securing a stable supply of roses for the plant. After seven years, the monoculture farm had yet to match yields in the oases, and extension agents debated how long it would take before the company shuttered the effort. They explained that the alternately frigid and hot winds coming off the steppe buffeted the shrubs. The roses needed the protection offered by the microclimate of a diversely planted oasis system (figure 17).

The women largely responsible for rose production understood this better than anyone. Friends in el Harte laughed when I relayed the agronomists' assessment that they were "brutal" in their cutting, joking that their aggression was retribution for the pricking during harvest time. For them, the real object of pruning was to cut back the plants so they did not catch their dresses when they walked through the fields and to use the cuttings as forage (apparently, livestock did not mind the thorns). Roses were a welcome source of cash, but for most households, they played a minor role in the diverse repertoire of crops and ancillary products they derived from their fields. Farmer strategies enacted what observers of the hundred-hectare rose farm had taken seven years to conclude: the overriding importance of diversity in oasis agroecologies means the productionist tactics of agronomy often yield poor results. In fact, their strategies were viable precisely because they eschewed productivist approaches in favor of an agroecological and social diversity that drew on communal affiliations as well as individual artistry (Guyer 1996, 1997). Households did not prioritize the yield of any one crop at

FIGURE 17. The oasis landscape in el Harte: wheat, roses, and almond trees.
Photo by the author.

the expense of other considerations: food security, spreading risk, using labor to balance the need for income and agricultural production, and participating in the communal life supported by farming, among others.

An Agroecological Landscape in Transition

A genealogy of contemporary farming systems illustrates how farmers experimented with new techniques by integrating changing labor relations into, rather than dispensing with, the established rhythms of oasis farming (Battesti 2005). These were the rhythms to which the wage labor I described earlier in this chapter adjusted, but farming styles also experienced profound change as a result of migration and economic integration. Historicizing these agrarian landscapes revealed that despite the apparent continuity with archetypal oasis systems, the landscape I encountered in 2010 was in fact fairly new. Oral histories of farming described a marked transition in agriculture in the early 1980s. Before this, cropping was primarily focused on a winter wheat and summer maize rotation. Sharecroppers farmed for the benefit for their landlords and often maintained small subsistence plots for their own households. Grain was never marketed, and vegetable production (for example, fava beans, turnips, squashes, and herbs) was also for household subsistence. Barley was grown both for fodder and for human consumption. Although there were horticultural trees—primarily almond, olive, fig, quince, and apricot—their production was rarely marketed. "We did not know trees, then," said one successful farmer in el Harte. "We did not have the knowledge or the trees to plant. There was nothing then." Cattle and sheep were central to this agropastoral system. Intensive home-based livestock production provided steady supplies of manure to the fields—a distinct system from transhumant pastoralism, although some households were involved in both.

Some observers describe the region's agroecosystem as historically self-sufficient, with limited integration into the national or world economies (Gregg and Geist 1988). While it may have been more self-sufficient than it is now, only the wealthiest and politically powerful households I interviewed in Mgoun claimed a historical ability to produce all their needs. The dominant narrative was one of desperate poverty, an agricultural landscape that could barely provide. Memories of this penury were intricately bound up with the dominance of sharecropping, a labor regime that allowed people few opportunities to grow anything beyond grains that did not always provide adequate sustenance and offered little variety in the diet. This emphasis on grain production as a mode of labor exploitation contrasts with an idealized image of oasis agroecological diversity, indicating how inequitable social relations of production may have actually compromised the sociospatial heterogeneity typically associated with oasis farming.

In the early 1980s, all of this started to change. Haj Ahmed, el Harte's collective-land representative, noted this period as the time that people switched from a wooden to a metal scratch plow. Others talked about it as when they started planting trees, when the sharecropping shares went from one-fifth to one-third (and subsequently to one-half), when people started selling vegetables in the market, when they started buying land for money instead of grain, and when they started using chemical fertilizers, among other changes. One unpublished ethnography of the neighboring valley to the west completed in the mid-1980s captures this moment of transition: Gregg and Geist (1988) describe low fertilizer usage, low levels of commercialization, the dominance of barley production, and an emergent arboriculture that had only just taken off among the richer farmers. This was a farming system on the cusp of change. The investments farmers had made with migration remittances in the 1970s were starting to yield results when Gregg and Geist wrote their ethnography. Purchasing one or two plots a year and experimenting with new cropping mixes as cash started to flow into the valley was a gradual process whose full impact only became visible in the 1980s. The same man who described how "we did not know trees then" started planting them in 1972 when he saw migration remittances begin to arrive. Those with the foresight to plant then did particularly well as almonds, olives, figs, and other high-value fruit became important cash crops. In interviews, people described the widespread adoption of tomatoes, potatoes, lettuce, and apples, verbally listing the progressive diversification of crops. Despite varying emphases, no one opted for a purely specialized operation. For el Harte, these changes were transformative. Agriculture had expanded into the steppe, a diverse array of horticultural trees came to maturity, and the town's vegetables were in demand. Haj Ahmed described how "people come from all over to get our vegetables. They are great quality. They come for our quince, figs, tomatoes, potatoes, and watermelon. There was not any of this before. I was the first to grow mint [in the 1980s] and when I took it to market, people gathered around me out of curiosity. We were not known for that. Bit by bit, we became known for our farming." The same changes that produced new labor relations in Kelaa facilitated this transformation of the agroecological landscape.

Contemporary Logics of Oasis Agriculture

In the Mgoun Valley, then, diverse oasis landscapes did not represent custom, tradition, or continuity in any straightforward sense. The status quo—what looked like oasis agriculture as it had always been practiced—was a sociopolitical as well as technical outcome. Farming households remade the agricultural landscape in the oasis by adapting ostensibly nonmodern techniques to new commercial imperatives. The logic of their strategies meshed uneasily with dominant approaches to commercial farming. Earlier in this book, I introduced an Arab businessman, Ben Tounsi, who had leased one hundred hectares from the Ministry of Interior to establish a commercial olive plantation, or firma, in the steppe outside Ichihn. Since the firma was established in 2008, Kelaa agricultural extension agents had made regular visits, offering advice as well as subsidized prices on equipment and inputs. One agent invited me along to meet Ben Tounsi during one of the businessman's periodic trips from Casablanca to check on the operation. The bank of windows on the second floor of the farm office looked out on olive saplings at various heights, planted in regular intervals with drip irrigation tubing running the length of the rows. Ben Tounsi had no agricultural experience, but he hired a farm manager from the Souss, an agricultural export region to the west. Since beginning the project, Ben Tounsi had committed nearly 5 million dirhams (US$625,000), an unheard-of sum in this region, and conceded that it would take some time to bring the firma to profitability. When I visited, only thirty-five hectares had been leveled and planted with olive trees. Ben Tounsi planned to gradually turn over the remaining land to olive production and press his own oil. He also intended to establish a commercial honey operation. When I saw a plot growing vegetables on the property, I asked him if they figured in his commercial strategy. He shook his head. "The vegetables are for the workers and for bee pollination. People in this area are too poor for commercial vegetable production to succeed." Perhaps Ben Tounsi's conclusion made sense in the context of the scale and returns necessary for a profitable operation given his capital outlay for the farm. Less than fifteen kilometers away, however, farmers in el Harte were diving headlong into commercial agricultural production. They would have been surprised to hear that they or their customers were too poor for their farming systems to succeed.

Ben Tounsi did not get it wrong simply because he was an outsider. His goals had little in common with farmers in el Harte, whose farming styles did not evince all the obvious hallmarks of "modern" agriculture in terms of scale, mechanization, or spatial management. However, it was precisely because agriculture in el Harte's oasis did *not* look modern in the sense of Ben Tounsi's firma that it was viable for commercial vegetable production. This is evident in how they negotiated the small plot size and dispersed holdings throughout the oasis, a hallmark of agriculture in the pre-Sahara. Since colonial times, policy and agronomic discourse has labeled this fragmentation an impediment to growth, and contemporary assessments of Moroccan agriculture continue to emphasize the drag on productivity (Royaume du Maroc 2005). In the oasis context, however, farmers regarded the diversity in growing conditions that fragmentation produced as a situation to manipulate, not eliminate.[5] One of the largest landowners in el Harte had a two-hectare operation dispersed across thirty plots, typical of Mgoun and the pre-Saharan oases in general (Battesti 2005). Farms were not delimited spaces anchored by a homestead but instead consisted of a patchwork of plots dotting the oasis. Farmers worked with this spatial organization, weighing the advantages of each plot according to a myriad of considerations: plots bordering the larger irrigation canals benefited from seepage and were best for crops with high water requirements; those closer to the home were best for crops such as tomatoes that either needed greater care or were a high-value candidate for theft; land with an even slope and means of ingress for a tractor were suitable for crops benefiting from mechanized turning of the soil; and different degrees of shade from the trees planted in or along the borders of plots created microclimates and adjusted sunlight to suit the needs of different crops (not to mention cropping decisions based on regular assessments of soil fertility, which led to the adjustment of a rotation to accommodate legumes or to cycle out of a multiyear rotation of alfalfa).

Factors that suppressed yields in one location in any given year could bolster yields elsewhere; farmers used this diversity as an essential element in developing their cropping strategy over time and space. Trees often blocked the sun from reaching ground crops, different plantings crowded together in small fields, and vines sprawled across the pathways between plots. The fact that el Harte farmers replicated these spatial strategies in the newer farming extensions as well as the historical oasis underscored them as intentional practice, not a simple holdover from the past (Richards 1985). In any case, farmers were well aware that many capital-intensive approaches typical of the "modern" agricultural operation would have been inappropriate to the oasis. For instance, farmers here were dismissed as traditional in part because of low levels of mechanization, but people had mixed feelings about the use of tractors. I was impressed to see how expertly farmers were, in fact, able to negotiate tractors through tight spaces and in between trees. Everyone used tractors on at least some of their holdings; common practice was to hire a tractor to turn the soil every two years (there were only a few wealthy households in the valley who owned a tractor, which they rented out). However, most were wary of using tractors regardless of the cost because they compacted the hard clay soil. Filali, the taxi dispatcher whose mother ran their farming operation in el Harte, attributed their high yields to the fact that they never used tractors to turn the soil. The use of tractors, then, did not represent a progressive or linear move toward greater mechanization and away from hand tools or animal traction. All harvesting was conducted by hand, an expression of the availability of labor—unpaid female labor and other waged labor. People weighed their use of any given technology versus a labor-intensive approach after deliberating the consequences for quality, soil fertility, and yields, and responding to their labor availability at any given point in the year. There was always a "margin for maneuver, socially, in space, time, work and techniques," a social complexity making it difficult to isolate one economic or ecological rationale for any given practice (Battesti 2005, 52). These spaces were in constant movement, much like the women moving through the fields to pick roses off the thorny bushes.

These spatial strategies complemented temporal strategies that made use of what I came to understand as the "life cycle" of the land. That life cycle was evident in Abdallah's farm in el Bour, the steppe on the edge of el Harte that since the 1970s had been gradually converted from pasture for village livestock to cultivation. When his family moved out to el Bour, they already had significant landholdings in the oasis inherited from his grandfather. However, it was Abdallah's uncle's departure to the Netherlands that allowed the family to double their holdings over the course of three decades through incremental purchases and the development of the steppe around their new home. During the years they waited for these new lands to produce, their established holdings provided subsistence while regular infusions of cash from the Netherlands enabled the family to improve their consumption. These were agricultural investments that extended far beyond any given growing season, working with time horizons that extended years into the future. The household's slow, methodical investments in land reflected the availability of capital in small amounts over a long period of time, but they also meshed with the agroecological requirements of rendering land productive in the arid steppe. Land could only be valorized over an extended period since it took time to raise its productivity, working organic matter into the soil over successive seasons.

These extensions did not stand in opposition to the intricate farming systems of the oasis in the stark way that Ben Tounsi's firma did. They certainly had different characteristics than the established oasis fields, but these differences were integrated into the temporal and spatial logics governing oasis farming, not set apart from them. Households like Abdallah's had begun working the land out in the steppe only gradually, planting trees with low water requirements, such as olive trees, and ensuring the trees became well established before committing additional resources (figure 18). They understood that they may see strong yields only one out of several years. The spatial heterogeneity of farming here meant that sometimes newer areas would have better years than the old, depending on the lay of the land, the distribution of rain and temperatures over the growing season, wind, frost, and other factors. People invested in the long-term productivity of their land, not any one crop or season. Their strategy of timing incremental investments often over many years enabled them to wait the long "gestation" period before new lands saw yields and to cope with the irregularity of those yields when the land did begin to produce. When I asked a returned migrant, Abdelhafid, whether agriculture in the new extensions differed from that of the histori-

FIGURE 18. Abdallah's brother works the soil in an extension in el Bour of el Harte.

Photo by the author.

cal oasis, he answered, "Of course. The new fields give strong yields because there are no trees yet." I asked whether he could just cut down trees in the old fields when the shade got too heavy. "I guess you could," he responded. "But it is *hashuma* [shameful] to pull up a tree. It is like you killed a person. It takes ten years for a tree to grow. You cannot just cut it down." Abdullah offered the same analysis when I asked him why he kept the thirty walnut trees he planted some two decades ago, even though he had determined that the climate was too hot to sustain good production: "Sometimes I think of cutting them down, but I never do. It is shameful to cut down trees." This was not only a cultural injunction. It also reflected the real economic value of trees; even the ones that did not produce fruit for marketing could at least offer a sustainable source of wood.[6]

In the historical oasis, a "mature" landscape featured well-established trees that in some areas shaded out crops in need of steady sunlight. People pruned trees in an effort to strike the desired balance between sun and shade, but no one entertained the idea of ridding a plot of trees for economic and agronomic reasons; they would lose the income from trees and the microclimate they provided. Nor did people refrain from planting trees in the new extensions to maintain an area devoid of shade. Planting trees was seen as an important step in bringing new land into production. In addition to their agroecological and commercial importance, trees were an important way to solidify a claim to land. Despite their reluctance to cut down trees, people did take advantage of each plot's different position in the life cycle of their holdings. They planted more shade-tolerant crops in the mature sections and sun-loving crops in the "younger" plots. Eventually, these plots would also enter maturity. If there were new lands to bring into production, all the better; but if not, they would again turn to pruning as the dominant strategy for striking the right balance in growing conditions.

The purposive nature of these strategies underscores how people in the region produced the land in order to work with, not overcome, agroecological conditions. Adjacent to Ben Tounsi's firma in the steppe, there was a slightly smaller effort by Hmou, a local farmer who had achieved local prominence with his commercial success. There were a few native sons who had established operations out in the steppe; Hmou was revered in the valley for his work ethic, his business acumen, and the technical knowledge he accrued over three decades of farming despite his functional illiteracy. People lauded him for practicing "organized agriculture" (*falaha biltartib* in Arabic), which he attributed in part to weekends spent observing Dutch farmers while he worked as a driver in the Netherlands. Like Ben Tounsi's operation, Hmou's farm was called a firma, denoting a modern, commercial operation; but unlike the linear organization of Ben Tounsi's olive trees, Hmou's firma was structured to replicate the layout of oasis farming. He combined tree and ground crop production, using the diverse conditions of his land to subdivide plots, and maximizing ancillary products and the recycling of biomass on the farm. The deliberate way in which he reproduced the oasis exemplified the extent to which spatial management here was not simply an adaptation *to* environmental conditions (Brookfield et al. 2002). It also produced those conditions—produced the land itself.

Labor and the Transformation of Agriculture

These anthropogenic landscapes took shape in the context of changing labor relations. Labor migration had essentially created a third agricultural season, as least in communities such as el Harte that had three crucial endowments: land, water, and proximity to markets. Saïd, the patriarch of a family I frequently visited in el Harte, explained this over lunch one summer day. As tea was being served, he sat in a wooden chair and placed a bucket of coriander seeds in front of him. He doused the seeds in water and ran his hands through the bucket, every once and a while taking a handful and inspecting it. "This is coriander," he explained, but even without his explanation the scent released from immersion in water was unmistakable. It was mid-June and Saïd noted that he was planting cilantro, tomatoes, and potatoes for Ramadan and the return of labor migrants from Europe or urban Morocco, an annual ritual that coincided with the European summer vacation. "Prices are good and demand is high" at this time, although Saïd regretted that Ramadan and the migrants' return overlapped this year in August. Normally one could expect separate spikes in demand and prices: religious holidays such as the month of Ramadan, 'aid al-kabir, and 'ashura shifted each year in accordance with the lunar calendar, while the migrants' return occurred the same time every summer.

The winter wheat and summer maize rotation was still prominent in the landscape, but a short, third season intervened toward the end of summer as farmers adjusted their strategies to meet the expected increase in market activity coinciding with the migrants' return. August had become wedding season, when families took advantage of the migrants' presence to conclude marriages and other important rites of passage. The increased consumption was visible in the bustling market and lavish meals offered during celebrations. Farmers timed their planting to coincide with these rhythms and, when they could, held on to dried or processed foods to sell when prices were high. Saïd reported that olive oil yielded 25 dirhams (US$3) a liter immediately after the olive harvest (in the late winter of 2009) but had climbed to 50 dirhams (US$6) a liter during the summer migrant season. "They buy everything, and they do not care about the price," he explained, citing the case of one migrant who famously spent a reputed 6,000 dirhams (US$750) in one day at the weekly market during one of his vacations from the Netherlands. Migration had not only spurred increased demand for produce; it was at least partially responsible for changing consumption patterns through higher incomes and the creation of new tastes. From its somewhat exotic profile as an "import" from the Middle East, olive oil was being consumed in increasing amounts. Historically, residents of the valley would purchase oil from itinerant traders or in the weekly market, but in the 1980s, farmers began planting more trees with the express intent of commercial production and self-provision. Now, every meal, every work break, and every social visit necessarily involved the senior man or woman in the room breaking off pieces of freshly baked (and sometimes stale) bread to distribute to everyone seated around the low round table for dipping into a tea plate filled with olive oil.

The introduction of a new agricultural season was only one of the many ways that new labor relations shaped the "family farm" as a mixed subsistence and commercial enterprise. Migration created new opportunities for households whether they had relatives away or not. Saïd had no family members working in the city, but his family was able to build a viable agricultural livelihood because of their neighbors who did. In discussions with local agricultural officials and Moroccan researchers about the impact of migration, they frequently emphasized a new openness to agricultural experimentation that the migrants brought back with them from Europe. Abdelhafid, for example, had returned from fifteen years in the mines of northern France to create one of the largest farming operations in el Harte. He claimed to have been the first in town to use a metal plow in place of the traditional wooden plow, and he pointed to two possessions that he felt symbolized his achievements as a returned migrant: the 1980s' Renault automobile he brought back from France and parked in the central courtyard of his adobe compound, and the metal cultivator that he designed and fabricated on his own. He had not only built financial assets abroad, but he developed what he described as a new mentality that informed his approach to farming.

It would be difficult to pinpoint the importance of farmers such as Abdelhafid in introducing new techniques and attitudes in agriculture. I suspected observers seized on mechanization, the use of chemical inputs, or other technical measures as the most important indicators of innovation, because to them, these practices signified "modern" agriculture. However, given the kinds of strategies farmers like Saïd deployed, I resist ascribing the propensity for experimentation to migrants alone. Some of the most innovative strategies were not as visible as new cultivators or drip irrigation systems. An ahistorical analysis of Saïd's farming style would hold it up as the ideal type of oasis agriculture: a highly diverse cropping regime focused on managing the interactions between livestock and cultivation, tree and ground crops, spatial and ecological variation, and complex labor mobilization strategies. However, Saïd was more emblematic of agriculture's transformation than its traditional orientation. Small farmers like him received no government assistance as they invested migration remittances, or capitalized on others' remittances, to produce an "indigenous agricultural revolution" (Richards 1985). Migration had not helped to preserve this oasis system; it had precipitated the creation of a new agroecological regime.

The fact that these processes were embedded in long-standing practices of oasis agriculture meant that purely quantitative indicators or other conventional measures of agrarian change would not fully describe how agriculture was changing here. Our data showed a high level of crop diversity across households (table 11), although as I describe below, diversity was often the preserve of wealthier households. I also knew from my extensive interviews with farmers that their cropping decisions could vary substantially from year to year depending on climatic conditions, labor availability, access to inputs, and other factors. In any case, aggregate

TABLE 11. Agricultural production (grains, horticultural crops), 2013–2014

CROP	TOTAL PRODUCTION	NUMBER OF HOUSEHOLDS CULTIVATING	PERCENTAGE OF HOUSEHOLDS CULTIVATING	LAND AREA GROWN ('ASHIR, 1/40 HECTARE)
Alfalfa	29,039 (qarda)	180	59	1,418
Wheat	8,906 ('abra)	155	51	1,363
Maize	4,918 ('abra)	97	27	925
Barley	3,416 ('abra)	55	18	321
Turnip	3,145 (kilo)	23	8	122
Cabbage	2,373	14	5	47
Potato	1,772	22	7	193
Cilantro	1,555	8	3	1,555
Onion	1,355	7	2	37
Misc. vegetables	1,333	10	3	132
Mint	845	5	2	26
Carrot	570	9	3	54
Tomato	533	9	3	39
Squash	457	8	3	60
Pumpkin	400	1	1	2
Parsley	255	2	1	12
Fava	200	1	1	2
Pepper	60	1	1	8

Source: Household survey, 2014–2015 (author in partnership with Reseau Associatif de Tinghir pour la Démocratie et le Développement).

Note: Qarda is a local measure for bundled alfalfa (a dried, tied bunch); 'abra is a local measure roughly equivalent to ten kilograms; vegetables and herbs were measured in kilograms.

production statistics yield an incomplete picture because of marked spatial differentiation in where cultivation could be intensified or expanded into the steppe. The emergence of commercial farming and new cropping strategies coexisted alongside a contraction in agriculture in many areas. While farmers in el Harte harvested an expanding repertoire of vegetables, most people in Imzilne could not sow a summer crop of maize, were fallowing for long periods, or even abandoning fields because of water scarcity that no one anticipated would let up. De Haas documents how these countervailing processes essentially canceled each other out in official statistics in the nearby Todgha Valley, noting that the "apparent stagnation of agriculture here conceals important changes in cropping patterns," with upwardly mobile households cultivating a larger array of crops than those without access to capital or other resources (2003, 273). Those who could not surmount the financial and political obstacles to sustaining agriculture or acquiring land in other communities relied on wage labor or internal migration down to the steppe, becoming part of a nascent agricultural labor force in the more productive areas.

Labor Process in the Oasis

The intense work of planting diverse crops and then storing, processing, transporting, and marketing them in small quantities was in many respects made possible by broader transformations in labor markets. Somewhat paradoxically, a labor-driven agricultural intensification unfolded at the same time that migration was drawing labor away from the region. I have described how the departure of workers for Europe and urban Morocco undermined the institution of sharecropping. This produced labor shortages for some households, primarily Imazighen who had previously relied on indentured labor. Some of them sold land, reduced their involvement in farming, or left farming altogether. However, the collective refusal of sharecroppers who migrated and the rising shares demanded by those who remained also freed up labor. Households were able to focus labor time on their own land, purchase or develop land with remittances, and make long-term investments because remittances removed the survival imperative that pushed households to farm on others' account. Normally, it was one son or brother, perhaps two, who left, meaning large households remained to continue farming and manage increasingly complex livelihoods as the region's economy became monetized. Their families usually remained in the tamazirt to manage agricultural work, take on additional livelihood activities, and, importantly, maintain the migrants' active presence in the community.

The scholarship on how migration affects smallholder agriculture emphasizes how remittances remove credit and liquidity constraints, allowing households to invest in more capital-intensive approaches to farming to raise productivity in a context of labor scarcity (Taylor and Lopez-Feldman 2010). The trajectory of agrarian change in the Mgoun Valley defies this formulation: remittances allowed households to organize their labor as peasant producers for the first time. They used family labor and minimized the use of external inputs instead of directing those remittances to mechanization or other capital-intensive investments (Netting 1993). Commercial viability was located not in levels of mechanization or scale—having more capital to produce more crops with less labor—but in the expert ways that farmers managed their labor to locate profits in the margins. I cataloged a diverse array of strategies that captured small profits afforded by different ways of handling crops, market pricing, and labor. Abdallah and his family, the most commercially oriented household I interviewed in el Harte, marketed over twenty crops in any given year (table 12). While there were some prominent high earners, Abdallah emphasized that their success lay in the accumulation of smaller profits from selling crops at different times of the year. The size of his operation did not lessen his interest in extracting value where he could. It was, for example, more profitable to pay to press their olive harvest and sell the oil than sell the olives directly, even though the additional step of processing took extra labor. Available labor was used to process a steady supply of ancillary products that cut input costs and provided additional income. Apricot trees seeded themselves out all over the oasis, to farmers' chagrin, and the price of apricots sometimes dipped so low that farmers would let the delicate fruit rot on the ground. However, if trucks belonging to jam producers in Marrakech came through the village in late spring to gather the harvest as they did in 2010, most people would fill plastic crates and take them to the buyer to earn whatever they could.

When I sat down with Saïd the day he cleaned the coriander seeds, he had just hauled four large bags of charcoal into his storehouse. In addition to planting vegetables for the migrants' return, he had made charcoal from wood on his holdings to sell during the migrant season and Ramadan, when grilling meat is an important aspect of celebratory meals. Stopping in to see Abdallah later that fall, I encountered him and his brothers using wood and dried reeds from their land to repair the roof on their house. Late fall (after the wheat had been sown but before the olives were harvested) was devoted to cutting down the twenty-foot-tall reeds growing along irrigation canals, which could then be sold as construction material, used for home repair, or shaped into trellises for vines and tomatoes. When Abdallah lost his tomato crop in the summer of 2010 because of a heat wave, at least he had not paid for the trellises, since he had constructed these from the collected reeds. Weeds gathered from the fields and along irrigation canals reduced forage expenses, while virtually everything produced or even discarded,

TABLE 12. Abdallah's household agricultural production and income, 2009–2010

CROP	PRODUCTION	NET INCOME (DIRHAMS)
GRAINS/FORAGE (ALL FOR HOME CONSUMPTION)		
Wheat	120 'abra	4,500 (imputed)
Barley	60 'abra	1,100 (imputed)
Maize	100 'abra	2,000 (imputed)
Alfalfa	650 qarda	2,250 (imputed)
TREE AND OTHER CASH CROPS		
Rose	1 metric ton	9,000
Almond	40 'abra	2,800
	(10 'abra home consumption)	700 (imputed)
Fig	60 'abra	2,080
	(18 'abra home consumption)	720 (imputed)
Pomegranate	1 metric ton	8,000
Apple	20 'abra	1,000
Olive oil	150 liters	4,500
	(150 liters home consumption)	4,500 (imputed)
VEGETABLES		
Tomato		16,000
Fava bean		8,400
Turnip		6,000
Potato		4,800
Carrot		3,500
Greens (cilantro, parsley)		3,000
Mint		1,500
Squash		1,500
Peas		1,500
MISCELLANEOUS		
Butter		1,400
Livestock sales		8,000
Additional input costs (livestock costs, tractor fees, and other) expenses) fertilizer and seed costs are embedded in net income for each crop)		(38,600)
Total		60,150

Source: Author's fieldwork.

such as almond shells, rose cuttings, and the residue from olive pressing, found another use.

Lulls in the work schedule offered other opportunities for increasing the income from crops. Abdallah's family's almond harvest was large enough that they would usually sell the nuts unshelled even though they yielded a lower price than shelled nuts. One sunny day, though, I approached the compound to see his mother, wife, sister-in-law, and two brothers seated on a plastic mat and cracking almonds as they chatted and took advantage of the late autumn warmth. Some of the almonds were for their own consumption, but they also wanted to take advantage of higher prices. They planned to take some to market for sale by the kilo (as opposed to the ʿabra, the standard measure for unshelled almonds). This was a common strategy throughout the valley, as households of varying wealth status used the incremental sale of dried fruits and nuts to garner small amounts of cash. People placed a premium on crops they could dry, store, and sell at different times or places as both a savings strategy and an effort to increase their margins (figure 19). Sliman, who headed the poorest household in my research in el Harte, would store hay, dry alfalfa, and gather residues from others' fields to use as a safety net throughout the year. He would hold on to them as long as possible to take advantage of higher prices at different times or in different markets. Sometimes, taking hay across the river to sell in the Kelaa market, where prices could be slightly higher than in the village, was worth the effort or cost of transport. These measures were not only the strategies of the poor. To the contrary, they composed a core strategy of successful commercial farmers. At the other end of the socioeconomic spectrum, Haj Ahmed, el Harte's collective-land represen-

FIGURE 19. Drying roses for sale later in the season, Rbat.

Photo by the author.

tative, described his version of the same strategy. He said they never have had to sell land when they needed money, because "we have trees: we have olives, figs, almonds. We eat from them and every time we need money, we take a bit from our storehouse and sell it."

Communal Referents for Agriculture

These intense investments of labor relied on networks of support and obligation extending beyond the village, into Kelaa, and beyond. As in the workshops and cafés of the market town, labor here included the time and material obligations needed to maintain social relations across diverse spaces. By sustaining relations of obligation in one domain—a plumbing apprenticeship in Kelaa, for example—they could call on them in another, such as when they needed to mobilize labor for a particularly large harvest. One of the reasons Ben Tounsi, the Arab businessman, could never have marketed his vegetables profitably in the valley was that he did not have the dense social networks that would enable him to extract the profits that the oasis farmers did. Successful farmers like Abdallah and Haj Ahmed sometimes took their produce to market, but they often had clientele come to their fields and storehouses to buy crops directly. They selected the market venue by weighing prevailing prices against the prices they could negotiate with their networks after accounting for past obligations and exchanges.

Securing the benefits of communal affiliation, however, was itself hard work, and results were not always guaranteed. My research assistant Mbarak and I were walking in el Harte after a morning of interviews when we saw Kebira, the matriarch of a prominent family, directing a small herd of sheep down the pathway toward us. Mbarak and I greeted her, although he quietly shook his head after we passed. I knew Kebira through my social interactions in the village, and the family's challenges were well known, but I was puzzled by his reaction to the scene. Mbarak explained that her family owned a lot of land and livestock but were not "good managers" and did not have the labor to harvest enough fodder for the herd they kept intensively at home. They must have run out of purchased fodder, he conjectured. So Kebira had to walk the herd out to the hurm, the town's buffer zone that historically served as the pasture for village herds. Few used it for that purpose now; instead, they preferred to grow alfalfa, collect weeds or crop residue, and buy fodder, which was why residents were able to extend cultivation into the steppe. It was embarrassing for a wealthy woman such as Kebira to have to pasture her herd. It indicated that the family could not command the labor, either within the household or through networks that would permit them to call on the help of others. The family of Kebira's husband, Ahmed, started out as one of the town's poorest fifty years ago to become one of its wealthiest. In a familiar story,

Ahmed's brother had migrated to the Netherlands, sending back remittances for years to buy land. Although two brothers remained to manage the operations, personal differences meant that their collective enterprise would sometimes break down, with women like Kebira filling the gaps by taking sheep to the hurm. For a while, the family engaged a sharecropper on a portion of their land. Ahmed himself had been a sharecropper as a youth, but no one in the village described the family's contemporary arrangement with a White Amazigh sharecropper from Imaghran as the use of indenture to perform social hierarchy. Rather, it was an effort to cobble together the labor necessary to work their expansive holdings. Their sharecropper eventually left for other work, and the family was now struggling to manage. Mbarak was not the only one to shake his head at this situation. Others in el Harte spoke of Ahmed's holdings with awe while also ruing the family's inability to properly care for their investments.

Most men I encountered would have jumped at the chance to work in Europe like Ahmed's brother, but international migration had its costs. Conflicts, poor management, and a clumsy handling of social networks could render a steady stream of remittances moot if they produced labor shortages and an inability to work the land. Even if domestic migration or working in Kelaa did not bring the same income, it was easier for people to sustain their networks so that a relationship cultivated in, say, Casablanca would ensure a steady supply of agricultural labor back home. Kebira's desultory walk with her herd indicated what could happen when networks of reciprocity embedded in the apprenticeships, wage labor, and other forms of obligation enacted in Kelaa and urban centers broke down or did not take shape as intended. Beyond the dyadic relations of debt and obligation embedded in commercial transactions and labor relations in the market town, people were also investing in communal membership that would enable them to call on labor and other forms of social support in the village. Their urban dealings signaled presence in absence.[7] Those dealings took many forms, from sustained displays of generosity during summer vacation in the village to financially supporting close family, extended relatives, and other community members in need.

However, financial contributions alone could not cement community membership. While it is true that Kebira's family probably could have hired agricultural laborers to cover the shortfalls, consistently relying on wage labor (rather than hiring people for a day or two to supplement family labor, which was common) would eat into slim earnings and have other, more serious social costs. It would further distance the family from communal norms that emphasized labor sharing as a sign of commitment to the social life of the village. Investing labor and time was more difficult for international migrants than it was for those who were able to frequently return to the village. Men who migrated for work therefore supported their families at home not only through their remittances but also by sustaining communal ties essential to securing labor for farming. By sending a son or brother to work for a powerful figure in town—whether in Kelaa or Casablanca—a family might secure access to tools, draft animals, or labor during harvest time. It was rarely a direct quid pro quo, but claims on labor in town could reinforce claims on labor in the tamazirt. By employing a poor relative in his vegetable stall in Kelaa, for example, a powerful figure like Aberrahmane deepened the obligations of that relative's family to work his land, reducing his labor costs and maintaining a safety net for more vulnerable households that was nonetheless predicated on their continued marginalization. The space of rurality had extended into urban areas as much as the reverse.

Participating in communal networks allowed absent members who committed the right kind of resources and effort to remain a part of their rural communities. During my visits to his large complex in el Bour, I often sat quietly as Haj Ahmed received calls from Haj Bou Saaden, who owned a successful company in Casablanca. Few people could offer details on what exactly the company did, but I came to understand that it was an engineering firm focusing on waterworks and large sanitation projects. Like many migrants, Haj Bou Saaden left as one of the town's poorest sons; he had been abandoned by his father before he was born and was raised alone by his nearly destitute mother. What set him apart was his success in building a business empire in Casablanca. This success did not lessen his attachment to el Harte and the region. He built three mosques in the area, several apartment buildings in Kelaa, and a large firma in el Bour, on the outskirts of el Harte. Other gestures were less grandiose. He called Haj Ahmed regularly to find out what was happening in town, how the rains were, what this year's harvest was looking like, and who had married or passed away. He would donate a sheep for a wedding or help someone with medical expenses. Haj Bou Saaden visited infrequently—sometimes only once a year—but he sustained his presence through Haj Ahmed and through his long-standing commitment to hire as many young men from the village as he could. Only a few, like Haj Ahmed's son who had a college degree in engineering from Marrakech, could rise to highly paid positions. Others provided manual labor on the company's job sites around the country. For Haj Bou Saaden, the relationship with Haj Ahmed linked him to communal life in material and intangible ways.

Several successful migrants built homes in el Harte, came back regularly, or otherwise contributed to the financial and social life of the town. Not all of them were considered active members of the community. The quality of presence mattered. Beyond his sheer wealth, there were other dimensions to Haj Bou Saaden's prominence in town despite his long absence. For one thing, he farmed in el Harte, finding a way to continue participating in what remained the region's most important social and productive activity. Selling one's productive land, even if the family kept a house in the village, usually signified that the family was withdrawing from collective life, that they were truly leaving even if they did return for occasional visits. The implications of this withdrawal extended beyond farming itself. It also meant the withering of networks that offered all sorts of support. One young man from Qlaʿa's most influential family complained to me one day that he was a *chomeur* (unemployed), a word people rarely used to describe their employment situation in the valley. This particular young man had studied at a hotel management institute in Agadir and was prepared to work in the finest tourist establishments, as he recounted, but no one in Kelaa could help him find a job. The family had long retreated from farming and the patriarch's other sons had become high-placed government officials in Marrakech and Rabat. Their withdrawal from the daily back-and-forth of community life left that young man isolated, unwilling to work in more "traditional" capacities, and unconnected to the social life around him. Most migrants, and families with men who earned their living primarily through wage labor closer to home, tried to keep at least some land under production. It was a source of food and income to be sure, but it also was the most important way in which families participated in rural communal life. For poorer families, sustaining some level of agricultural production was particularly important, permitting their continued participation in networks that guaranteed other forms of social support.

The Limits of Farming

This new rurality, a combination of petty commodity and subsistence production geared to local markets, represented a way forward for many in the valley: a type of agriculture that was productive, commercial, and suited to the region's climatic uncertainty. But it was not a way forward for everyone. It was predicated on the proletarianization of certain kinds of labor (migrant industrial labor abroad and casual agricultural labor in the valley) and the insulation of other kinds of labor (women's labor and informal exchanges) from commoditization. Nor did migration always translate into upward mobility, as in the case of Hassan, a well-liked construction worker in el Harte. Hassan's grandfather had immigrated to el Harte from another oasis valley, meaning he was not considered a native resident with land rights. However, he married a woman from one of the village's most prominent families and purchased twelve ʿashir. The family's land acquisition stopped there, however, and Hassan's father migrated to Casablanca when Hassan was an infant in the early 1970s. His father's work as a waiter never resulted in any substantial remittances, and when his father divorced his mother a few years later to start another family in Casablanca, Hassan's family's fortunes sank further. At an early age, he helped support his mother and their small household. As an adult, Hassan had achieved some much-sought-after stability: he had learned the construction trade and had fairly steady work in Kelaa. He continued to farm the family's twelve ʿashir, although he rued his low production.

Hassan did not know why his production was so low, but he offered a thoughtful assessment of what someone like him could realistically hope to accomplish in agriculture. As a head of household with only young daughters and the need to do full-time nonfarm work to keep the wages coming in, he had limited options. "For a man by himself, like me," he elaborated, "it is very difficult to base yourself in farming. You need to have a lot of land, like fifty to sixty ʿashir." Hassan and the village as a whole were well aware that he should have larger holdings because he was due an inheritance that his grandmother never received. There was little Hassan could do about the problem. He could have theoretically accessed more land by petitioning the collective-land representatives for an allotment from the village's communal reserves but one of those representatives was the same relative holding the land due Hassan as his inheritance. In any case, owning land was useless without the people to work it, and Hassan knew that he could not mobilize the necessary labor. This was the primary reason he did not grow vegetables (they took too much work and time), and in any case, planting wheat was the priority to ensure his family's basic needs. Even with his exclusive focus on wheat, his yield was not sufficient, and the previous year he had to purchase substantial amounts. "I know that for the amount of money I put into agriculture, I could just buy the wheat, but I have to cultivate the land. There are other benefits to farming that bring money and food: like figs and almonds." He did an accounting the previous year and was discouraged by what he found: it cost him approximately 2,200 dirhams ($US275) to grow the amount of wheat that he could have bought for approximately 1,000 dirhams (US$125). But on that same land, he was able to garner an additional 2,300 dirhams (US$287) from the sale of his tree crops and roses, none of which had input costs other than the labor he and the women in the family expended. Hassan did not feel as though he had any other choice. He could not grow vegetables and could not imagine leaving the land uncultivated; planting wheat kept the land in production, maintained his social networks, and provided for basic needs, even if the cost-benefit analysis on that crop alone was negative. The fact that Hassan was forced into a simplified cropping regime illustrates how diversity was a privilege, a strategy that reflected one's position in inequitable social relations of production.

To be sure, subsistence grain production remained the central feature of everyone's rotation, and no one marketed wheat, barley, or maize for historical reasons. Famines were not such a distant memory, even if only the eldest residents lived through the last one in the 1930s. People placed a high priority on ensuring subsistence needs, and even the largest producers did not sell their grains, often stocking a large surplus. Filali, the livestock trader and taxi dispatcher, would regularly harvest eighty ʿabra (eight hundred kilos) of wheat, more than his nine-member household (five of whom were children) could consume in a given year. But he never sold, he said, "because there are children." He also quietly distributed more than his share of grain as *zakat* and other forms of mutual aid. Beyond grain cultivation, however, farmers did not apply different logics to commercial and subsistence production. The most vulnerable households might only be able to keep a kitchen garden to supplement their diets, but they could market even small quantities of a crop if prices climbed particularly high. The dominant strategies of larger, commercial farmers were not so different. Abdallah, who regularly netted an impressive 20,000 dirhams (US$2,500) on his tomato harvest, made his cropping and marketing decisions with the understanding that his family needed to be fed first. If prices of a particular crop climbed, he would market a greater percentage of that crop, but he did not plant any crops purely for sale.[8] Farmers managed their resources and developed their marketing strategies with this broader set of priorities in mind (van der Ploeg 2008).

However, the ability to move between subsistence and commercial production when the opportunity for profit arose was not available to everyone. For people such as Hassan, who planted wheat even though he knew that vegetables would be more profitable, being the only adult male in the household and having small landholdings prevented him from experimenting with commercial agriculture. But labor was not simply an "endowment," a factor of production determined by the lottery of demographics. Access to capital combined with social and political factors—and the contingencies of family life such as divorces, health crises, and household conflicts—to differentiate which households would be able to buy or develop new lands, wait long periods until that land sustained good yields, weather the risk of farming in the oasis, and commit to the commercial strategies that emerged in the 1980s and 1990s. Households capable of mobilizing the right mix of labor for the changing demands throughout the year were better able to develop commercially viable operations. The key to maintaining flexibility during the agricultural season was not to command all the labor one might need within the household but to mobilize social networks to bring in that labor without having to pay scarce cash to workers. Poorer farmers like Hassan were more likely to hire paid agricultural labor than wealthier ones, because they had few claims on others' in-kind labor and male household members needed to work in the city for wages themselves. Hiring labor for peak periods made more sense than forgoing urban remittances. But for successful farm households, relying on family and unpaid labor exchanges that retained clients in their orbit was the preferred way of mobilizing agricultural labor.

Moving between Commoditized and Uncommoditized Labor

Smallholder agriculture could serve as an anchor for these households' livelihoods at least in part because it played with the boundaries between market and nonmarket relations, or commoditized and uncommoditized labor. The lines between subsistence and commercial production were not blurred simply because of a putatively traditional aversion to risk—that blurring is what made farming economically viable and culturally meaningful. In important respects, the cash from wage labor slowed the monetization of agricultural labor markets because informal labor exchanges supported the new commercial imperative while keeping input costs low. In sharing meals, washing wheat in the river, and walking along winding pathways through the fields to visit friends, I learned that a central tension in this story about the shifting meaning of work revolved around what and whose labor would get commoditzed. Wage labor may have irrevocably transformed how people worked, but this transformation was not linear or total. Wage labor also helped set limits to commoditization, or at least set the stage for contestations over who should get paid for their work. When people used their wage-labor relations to reinforce communal networks, they invested in norms of reciprocity that included claims on unpaid agricultural labor.

Wage labor helped sustain spheres of uncommoditized labor, and vice versa, in distinctly gendered ways. Women's labor remained largely uncommoditized, although many men were also drawn into relations of dependency that played with the boundaries between waged and in-kind labor through, for example, new forms of sharecropping or employing a poor relative in the vegetable stall. These relations were sometimes rooted in exploitation, but they could also have strong affective significance and sustain relations of social support for vulnerable residents. When women exchanged work on each other's fields, they were reinforcing friendships and family ties, supporting a neighbor in need, and singing together in the hot sun. Although all the women I knew valued these relationships, many expressed ambivalence about or even an overt desire for waged work, either in the fields or, better yet, in town. The persistence of uncommoditized labor, then, produced tensions over how labor was gendered within households and across networks of extended families. Wage labor for women still carried a stigma in most parts of the valley, but the more time I spent there, the more I saw how young women in particular often furtively angled for wage payments for their agricultural work. I learned, for example, that all the women in one well-respected family that lived on the edge of el Harte would skirt over the embankment next to their home and trek across the plateau to a firma in el Bour n'Aït Yahya for agricultural wage labor. The firma's owner told me this during an interview about his farm operation. He said the women asked that he keep their employment secret from others in el Harte. Their family was relatively well off, but everyone needed cash and a few days' work by the large contingent of women would provide substantial support to the family. I doubted that it was truly a secret in the village, but keeping it quiet maintained the family's reputation. Even though women's labor was broadly understood as important to a household's functioning, earning cash wages was socially compromising and could cast doubt on the patriarch's management skills. Another friend, who at twenty-eight assumed that she would never find a husband, usually received in-kind payment for work she did for others; but increasingly, she asked for cash wages so that she could quietly keep money for herself rather than hand over a sack of wheat to her father. As she said: "I want to buy things for myself, to have some independence. I am not a young girl anymore to give my father all my earnings."

Other women actively searched for wage-labor opportunities in town but usually found that their lack of education or specialized skills meant they could work for only very low wages in socially suspect situations such as cleaning in cafés or in the homes of teachers and civil servants. Most male relatives would not allow such work anyway. Even with norms limiting women's access to waged labor, their diverse strategies for managing in-kind labor exchanges and searching out opportunities for cash income revealed the subtle contestations over what kind of work would remain uncommoditized. The result was a striking diversity in labor arrangements involving male and female family members in different kinds of work over time and space, complicating any notion of a unitary, patriarchal household I may have started out with. Who would engage in what kind of work was a product of necessity *and* negotiation, reflecting one's relative position in the household as well as the unique circumstances of the family. Divorced women often returned to their family's household, for instance, but I knew a number who developed quasi-independent livelihoods within their family households. Other divorced or widowed women maintained completely independent households, managing their economic vulnerability by skillfully moving between wage work and other relations of obligation in the village and in town.

When they contested the assignment of their uncommoditized labor to a "protected" sphere signifying communality, women underscored how labor arrangements involved more than balancing household economic and communal imperatives. They believed strongly in how they contributed to the household but knew their personal aspirations were intricately woven into the diverse labor regimes that involved them and their family members. A few people I knew in the valley (usually men) talked about women's increasing involvement in wage labor as a sign that individualism had reached the point of no return, corroding not only communal attachments but also family bonds. Most women who engaged in this work saw the dynamic differently. For them, these labor opportunities created new possibilities for mutuality, expanding their social relations in ways that evoked the back-and-forth between the city and the country I described earlier. Receiving wages also became a marker of personal dignity that valorized the work they did and made relations with employers more transparent than they had been in the past. This emphasis on the dignity of waged work applied to men as well as women. It was a clear break with the era of indentured sharecropping, when uncommoditized labor represented oppression more than a moral economy based in mutuality. Taleb, the returned migrant from the Aït Hamd plateau, described this break as an act of refusal: "When colonialism was finished, people like me were free to go. I went to France to work in the mines. The overlords could not control us anymore. We said *safi* [enough]." When he told me this, Taleb waved his hand across his chest in a gesture of refusal. Perhaps women were engaging in their own act of refusal. For them, earning wages could represent a path to autonomy, a new independence that could support both individual aspirations and a communality rooted in equivalence rather than hierarchy.

Conclusion

Agriculture in the Mgoun Valley both produced and was enabled by a communal infrastructure that informed everything from local politics, to wage-labor opportunities in town, to quotidian decisions about how to manage the farm. These communal affinities resolved an apparent paradox that I encountered in my discussions with farmers. From the beginning of my fieldwork, people told me, "If you did any accounting, you would see that agriculture does not pay." One man elaborated: "We never do [cost-benefit] calculations here. It would never work out. We say that agriculture is just *baraka* [a blessing] from God and you have to rely on that blessing to continue." One of the most successful commercial farmers in the whole region threw up his hands when I asked him about this, chuckling that "agriculture does not want you to do accounting. If you did, you would close your farm. Calculating profits and costs would make you crazy, so I do not do it." He said he used baraka to guide his farming and hoped for the best. Many making that claim did, in fact, earn a decent living from agriculture by local standards. It was a more understandable stance for the poorer families I interviewed.

Their farming operations were usually simpler, and a surface accounting indicated that it cost more to plant wheat than to buy it on the market, as in Hassan's example earlier in this chapter. However, when all the ancillary products of farming, such as wood, forage, and reeds, among others, and the importance of maintaining networks of social reciprocity through the act of farming were considered, the cost-benefit analysis came out differently. Declaring that agriculture "did not pay" was an acknowledgment that reducing this diverse farming system to economic calculation could not account for the social embeddedness of how people made a living.

The persistence of small farming in the Mgoun Valley and in so many places around the world has challenged long-standing assumptions that agriculture's main function lay in "facilitating a process of accumulation of physical, financial and wage goods [that] can become the basis of the emergence of capital," feeding growth in other economic sectors (Akram-Lodhi and Kay 2009, 193). Historically, this accumulation usually happened at the expense of smallholders, dispossessed of their land and forced into wage labor. Contemporary incarnations of such dispossession have undeniably ravaged many landscapes and livelihoods around the world, as in the oil palm plantations in large swathes of South America, West Africa, and Southeast Asia. In Mgoun, where farming arguably never constituted an adequate livelihood for vulnerable sharecropping households, it was not dispossession *from* a viable agricultural livelihood that pushed them *into* wage labor. Rather, it was wage labor that enabled them to remain in agriculture at all, to not have to migrate definitively to the city with the unpalatable prospect of living in a shantytown. Migrants and their families in the tamazirt managed their mobility, job commitments, and agricultural investments together, each contributing to individual aspirations and communal imperatives of maintaining belonging. For families with access to capital, labor, and land, farming anchored a new autonomy. For others, small-scale commercial agriculture and other wage-labor opportunities enabled their continued involvement in farming and sustained their communal affinities. The result was a landscape of labor and production that embodied all the possibilities, contradictions, and exclusions of the transformations I have described in this book.

CONCLUSION

Each year when I return to the Mgoun Valley, I look expectantly at the river skirting the road leading into Kelaa Mgouna to see if el Harte has built its bridge, thereby easing the transport of goods and people into the market town. I check in with old friends about the status of the debates (discussed in chapter 1) with the Amazigh families of Qla'a who resisted the bridge as an emblem of el Harte's rising prominence in commercial agricultural production. In preparation for the 2021 communal elections, the president of the commune took on the bridge project as a pledge to the village and as part of his program for infrastructural improvement. And yet residents were still skeptical. "We will see what happens, if that bridge will ever get built," my friend Fatima mused in 2017. "In the meantime, we still walk into town, the river still floods and washes out our bridge, and we make do." In 2019, I arrived two days after the inaugural ceremony for a new bridge. In smartphone videos of the event, cars and motorcycles waiting to cross revved their engines behind the president of the commune as he made his speech and cut the ribbon. Some residents, however, noted that it was not "a real bridge," as one friend, Abdallah, pointed out. It was more of a causeway, a low-lying bridge common in southern Morocco that involved building a raised, reinforced road over large pipes to allow water to flow under the road. To be sure, Abdallah was happy about the bridge. As one of the village's largest commercial producers, his family could now use their pickup truck to transport goods to market. But he explained that this bridge could also be washed out: "It would just take a bit more water and more force. We will see how it works."

A healthy skepticism had long inured residents of marginalized communities like el Harte to repressive policies and other obstacles. That skepticism could also downplay the transformations they had lived through or achieved themselves. The bridge did not pass in front of the notable Amazigh family's house that had, for years, blocked the project. Haj Hsain, that family's patriarch who welcomed me into his home to talk about his experiences opening el Bour to cultivation in the 1970s, had passed away in 2016. Although his family still blocked the construction of the road, engineers from the public works ministry worked with residents of el Harte to find an alternate route. The new dirt road passed over an arid hilltop that constituted the hurm for the cluster of villages in the area. Because of its topography, the hilltop was unsuited for cultivation.

That bridge and unpaved road precipitated a new service and livelihood in el Harte: the trimotor. A staple source of transport in southeast Asia, the trishaw, auto rickshaw, or tuk-tuk is a three-wheeled motorcycle with a bed that can carry goods or people. In Morocco, it was called the trimotor. Someone—I could not find out who—saw the market for a vehicle more affordable than a car or truck and more practical than a scooter or motorcycle. Soon, there were a half dozen trimotors serving the cluster of communities on the opposite side of the river from Kelaa. Although transporting people from el Harte to Kelaa in a trimotor was officially forbidden, it quickly became a standard means of getting to town. The president of the commune vowed to establish regulations for this new transport sector. Hassan, the struggling construction worker and farmer I introduced in chapter five, used his savings and pulled informal sources of credit together to buy a trimotor and now earned a good and stable living making the run between town and country. They may have been a new addition to the landscape, but the bridge, the road, and the new economic and social relations they helped fashion seemed to fold into rural life as though they had always been there. David Crawford (2008) describes how the old trail that used to lead him into the High Atlas village where he previously conducted fieldwork had disappeared when he returned some years later. However, a new trail had etched a different path with the same air of weathered use as the old, illustrating how "places that seem to remain are in fact constituted anew" (43).

In this book, I have told a story of change by stopping a place in time. I have recounted individual stories of making do, collective mobilizations asserting new claims, and the gradual reworking of the landscape as social, political, and agricultural acts. These accounts do not describe the current reality of the Mgoun Valley, which, like all places, seems to shift too quickly to be captured in the deliberate work of academic writing.[1] The accounts do, however, represent a genealogy of the present, an analysis of how residents in the Mgoun Valley have refigured a vibrant, if conflicted, rurality. I have argued for their creative agency in repurposing customary law and communal governance institutions to engage with emergent processes and reassert their attachment to the tamazirt. Eschewing a romantic nostalgia that would hold a peasant traditionalism as the way forward out of contemporary crises—whether of industrialized agriculture, the new extractivism of capital accumulation, or disinvestment in rural areas, among others—I have pointed to the ambivalent dynamics of this new politics of the commons. Residents foregrounded the communal as a referent for social life, but their approaches reworked rather than dismantled systems of inequality. These strategies for securing autonomy were unstable and contested, and no one described them as a refuge or an unbroken link to the past.

In searching for the patterns and historical legacies that would allow me to interpret these snapshots in time, I have identified more durable dynamics informing how people in this rural space constructed their social and economic worlds as fundamentally political projects. A grounded understanding of these dynamics decenters the state, the development industry, or global capital as the only or even primary agents in reconfiguring rural zones. Residents' rootedness in the tamazirt allowed them to use the seemingly out-of-the-way attributes of this place, such as state neglect and investors' relative lack of interest, to assert new forms of autonomy that were nonetheless embedded in relations of dependency and obligation. In fact, the Mgoun Valley had always been cosmopolitan in one way or another. That cosmopolitanism and people's ability to use their engagements with broader processes to articulate a new politics of the commons can help reframe our understanding of how urban and rural politics relate to one another in North Africa, the Middle East, and beyond.

As my initial period of fieldwork came to a close, my spouse and I took our children to visit my own tamazirt in Egypt: my mother and father-in-law were born and raised in Egypt. I had not visited in over a decade, and moving from the expansive rural spaces of southern Morocco to the urban pressures of Cairo brought Egypt's own economic inequalities and political repression into sharp relief. One month after our visit, a massive popular mobilization toppled President Hosni Mubarak; but nearly a decade later, those pressures have only deepened for poor and dissident Egyptians. The dominant frame for understanding political dissent in the region, at least from a Euro-American perspective, quickly became the Arab Spring after the Tunisian revolution of early 2011 inspired uprisings across the Middle East and North Africa (Beinin and Vairel 2013). Land rarely figures in accounts of the modest Moroccan response to the uprisings in 2011, which was concentrated in urban areas but also echoed throughout small towns and some rural areas (Bergh and Rossi-Doria 2015). These rural zones, however, did not simply follow the lead of urban protesters. They represented a growing swell of disaffection regarding rural inequalities and political exclusion (Mahdi 2015). The fact that Mohamed Bouazizi—the young man who self-immolated to spark the Tunisian revolution—was from the rural hinterland of Sidi Bouzid, that displaced peasants and factory workers in rural zones played an important role in ousting Egypt's Mubarak and Tunisia's Ben Ali, and that rural repression and marginalization contributed to the early uprisings in Syria all underscore the need to account for rurality in the post-2011 political mobilizations around the region (Abu-Lughod 2012; Bassiouni 2016; Fautras 2015; Gana 2013).

A turn away from Orientalist tropes that reify "peasant" and "tribe" and the sheer difficulty of getting permits to conduct research in many rural areas may be one reason for the sparse contemporary literature on rurality, agrarian change, and rural political expression, at least in the anthropology on the region (Deeb and Winegar 2012). Scholarship of North Africa and the Middle East is now grappling with these alternative understandings of political mobilization, especially the increasing importance of land-based politics in Morocco and elsewhere in the region.[2] The task is to identify how people themselves figure political action in ways that are meaningful to them. The idea of an Arab Spring, for example, had little resonance in the Moroccan south. There, the touchstone for activists was Algeria's Berber Spring of 1980 that inaugurated the Amazigh rights movement. The Algerian government canceled a conference on Berber poetry in Tizi-Ouzou, sparking a series of strikes and demonstrations that it then violently suppressed. The events and political consciousness they inspired have since been commemorated in Berber song, poetry, and political discourse throughout the Maghreb (J. Goodman 2010; Maddy-Weitzman 2011; Silverstein 2004).

However, Amazigh activism is only one possible frame for understanding collective expressions of dissent in the Moroccan southeast. Hoffman (2007) notes that many of the most educated, urbanized Amazigh activists tend to hold romantic notions of the tamazirt that inflect their language ideologies and political expression. Attending to how people themselves crafted meaning and asserted claims in the Mgoun Valley brought other forms of political expression—the latent commons that lay below the surface of formal political institutions—into view. Some of this expression coalesced around the popular mobilizations described in chapter 3, but much of it involved slow, patient work on the land. Women, for instance, developed subtle strategies for claiming land and, by extension, authority. They commonly laid their bundles of collected brush and wood (used for cooking) to dry in progressively larger circles outside their domestic compounds. As use of the land became attached to their household, claims on that land became legitimated. The practice was unspoken, but the effects were not lost on observers. On more than one occasion, I heard fellow riders on the transit van to the Aït Hamd plateau comment on how far this or that household's brush had been placed from their adobe enclosure.

These gestures were just as constitutive of a new commoning as more recognizable forms of political action: the sit-ins and occupations that juxtaposed old grievances with new claims. I interpret the communal referent underlying these claims as commoning in part because the concept helps us navigate the fuzzy boundaries between individual aspirations and the governance of collective life. These fuzzy boundaries complicate a romance of the commons that hinges as much on narratives of decline—the nostalgic need to recuperate a lost past—as on the desire for a utopian alternative to contemporary crises of capitalism. It was commoning because it often involved land and the collective management of resources held in common, but it was also a way to experiment with how to live together while managing the inherent inequalities of social life. The quotidian struggles and long time frames for people's actions on the land reinforced that I was not only witnessing *resistance*, an effort to fight against subjugation, poverty, or marginalization. I also saw people *building* new social relations and forms of political action. This was a positive project that may have been labeled protopolitical or undeveloped by some observers but nonetheless reworked existing modes of governance to make new claims.

The dilemma of how to govern "life in common" in rural Morocco has become a progressively more urgent question since I began fieldwork in 2010. Land conflict was largely muted as an idiom of protest for dominant political actors or social movements when I arrived but has since erupted into national political discourse—everything from corrupt land acquisitions by politicians, to protests around mining concerns, to mobilizations around women's access to collective lands (Berriane 2015; Bogaert 2016). Historically, scholarship and journalistic accounts alike focused on urban exclusion as motivating the popular uprisings that, at various times since independence in 1956, have provoked alternately repressive and conciliatory government policies (Beinin and Vairel 2013). This focus on the urban threat of poverty elides a long history of insurrection and mobilization in Morocco's rural zones, particularly in the pre-Saharan southeast and the Rif (Seddon 1986; Wolf 2019). The conflicts and related mobilizations that have dominated Morocco's rural political landscape since 2011 did not emerge from the urban, rights-based claims that motivated the February 20th Movement or the regional uprisings. Rather, they expressed simmering frustration with longstanding repression and persistent inequality in the southeast, northern Rif, and numerous provincial towns (Bennafla 2011; Bogaert 2015; El Maliki 2017; Masbah 2017). The result has been the emergence of explosive political movements precipitating both violent government suppression and hasty attempts to invest in peripheral zones. Social mobilizations protesting the long-standing impacts of extractivism, such as silver, cobalt, and phosphate mining, have linked these state and corporate projects to new efforts to extract wealth and resources from the rural periphery, such as renewable energy mega-projects that deploy the same juridical strategies for dispossession as the state-led enclosures described in chapter 3 (Aoui, el Amrani, and Rignall 2020; Cantoni and Rignall 2019; Rignall 2016;).

These oppositional politics have unfolded outside the frame of civil society activism like that described in chapter 2, but state actors and activists alike understand the import of contemporary mobilizations like the Hirak Movement in the Rif, often spontaneous and without formal leadership from seasoned organizers (Lefèvre 2017). The activists I know have offered support, often in the background, to disparate groups of primarily young people attempting to harness the energy of street protests to make lasting change. My analysis of how state rule intersects with customary governance and rural inequality clarifies the roots of these rural political mobilizations. These mobilizations are not simply the ground on which formal movements are built in an additive model of political analysis that would see the land conflict in Imzilne or Ichihn eventually coalesce into organized political action. I have focused on rurality as an important object of scholarly and political analysis in and of itself, arguing that we need to attend to people's construction of productive systems—new ways of farming and making a living—as politically transformative in their own right. Rural populations continue to rely on agrarian livelihoods, and while their income may come from diverse sources, they do not go through their days as though the region can no longer sustain an agrarian sector (Zurayk 2012). Far from being mired in the past, rural populations are making a living and refashioning their relationship with the land and each other. In explaining how people make a living, farm, and produce meaning in rural landscapes, I hope to have expanded our understanding of what effective political agency in Morocco can look like, and honored the stories and struggles of people who so generously shared their lives with me.

Acknowledgments

My first thanks go to the friends and research participants in the Mgoun Valley and elsewhere in Morocco who made this research and my ongoing work in Morocco possible. I was touched by the generosity with which they shared their stories and by the myriad ways, both large and small, that people in Mgoun welcomed my family. Atman Aoui and Moulay Ahmed El Amrani have been research partners and friends for so long that this project reflects their perspectives as much as my own, although any errors of fact and interpretation are my own. The network of friendship and support I developed through the Near East Foundation and Catholic Relief Services goes back even further. Thanks to Fatima Aït el Hashimi and her family, Brahim Aït el Kassi, Taleb Aït Taleb ou Ali, Abdessadek Attar, El Houcine Attar, Lahcen Azghari, Mohamed el Bazi, Elphège Ghestem, Malika Nims, Saïd Samlali, Rachida Ouchaou, Moha ou Lahcen, Abdallah Ou Moh, Mastafa Zahir, and everyone at the *mahlaba* in Kelaa. The staff at the Centre de Mise en Valeur Agricole in Kelaa Mgouna offered support and valuable insights. There are many more people throughout the valley whom I cannot name but who generously welcomed me. I can only hope that the profound personal experience my long-standing research engagement represents finds some expression in this book.

Fieldwork and writing were made possible by the National Science Foundation (NSF), the Wenner Gren Foundation for Anthropological Research, the American Institute for Maghrib Studies, and the Qatar Post-Doctoral Fellowship at the Center for Contemporary Arab Studies at Georgetown University. I am grateful for graduate support funding from the University of Kentucky as well as the University of Kentucky Multi-Year Fellowship. The University of Kentucky Department of Anthropology and other faculty at the university offered institutional support and a rich intellectual environment. Special thanks to Lisa Cliggett, Deborah Crooks, Hsain Ilahiane, Diane King, Juliana McDonald, Tad Mutersbaugh, and Jerry Skees. Lisa Cliggett has been much more than an adviser, and I am grateful for her ongoing mentorship. Yoko Kusunose guided me into new intellectual territory through my NSF postdoctoral fellowship; I thank her for both the partnership and the friendship that grew out of our collaboration. I am grateful to Patrick Bigger, MaryBeth Chrostowsky, Allison Harnish, Maria Moreno, and Julie Shephard-Powell for their camaraderie and feedback in our writing groups. A subsequent writing group with Cristina Alcalde, Sarah Lyon, and Kristin

Monroe brought this project to completion, and I am profoundly grateful for their insights. Ilana Feldman, Mandana Limbert, Karen Strassler, and Jessica Winegar offered both warm encouragement as I reentered academia and models of anthropological scholarship to which I aspire. The same is true for the *shilla*: in addition to Ilana and Jessica, I thank Christina Civantos, Kenneth Garden, Parastou Hassouri, Lee Keath, Kate Kolstad, and Karim Mostafa. I have also valued sharing ideas with Fida Adely, David Balgley, Rochelle Davis, Nicole Fabricant, Mythri Jegathesan, Emily McKee, Jeremy Walton, Rami Zurayk, and many others along the way. My friends and colleagues in the Departments of Community and Leadership Development, Sociology, and Anthropology, as well as the Sustainable Agriculture Program, at the University of Kentucky have provided mentorship, support, and a welcoming environment to extend my scholarship into new areas of engagement and collaboration. Being a part of the College of Agriculture, Food and Environment has enriched my scholarship, teaching, and connection to Kentucky in ways I could not have imagined. Special thanks to Beth Reeder at the Agricultural Information Center at the University of Kentucky.

I appreciated the opportunity to present portions of the manuscript at lectures and symposia at the Centre National de la Recherche Scientifique (Paris), Georgetown University, Northwestern University, Rutgers University, the University of Cincinnati, Université Chouab Doukkali (el Jadida), l'Université Euro-Méditerranéenne (Fès), Université Ibn Zohr (Agadir), University of Kentucky, and Université Mohamed V (Rabat). Special thanks to Mona Atia and the Institute for Middle East Studies at George Washington University for hosting a book manuscript workshop and to the College of Agriculture, Food and Environment at the University of Kentucky for sponsoring the event. Fida Adely, Ilana Feldman, Jane Guyer, Katherine Hoffman, and a group of graduate students read the entire manuscript and offered invaluable feedback. Katherine Hoffman and an anonymous reviewer's comments further enriched this book. I am grateful for the careful editorial stewardship of Michael Goldman, Nancy Lee Peluso, and Wendy Wolford. Richard Gilbreath produced beautiful maps, and I would like to thank Elizabeth Hallock and David Wishner for their illustrations.

I have valued the support and intellectual insights from the community of Maghribi and Moroccanist scholars, especially Mohamed Aït Hamza, Mona Atia, Mohamed Berriane, Yasmine Berriane, Koenraad Bogaert, Yahia Bouabdellaoui, Zhour Bouzidi, Graham Cornwell, David Crawford, Diana Davis, Souad Eddouada, Alice Elliot, Hein de Haas, Soraya el Kahlaoui, Nicolas Faysse, Ahmed Herzenni, Katherine Hoffman, Marcel Kuper, James Miller, Anne Montgomery, Madani Mountasser, Elkebir Ouhajou, Raja Rhouni, Zakia Salime, Paul Silverstein, Alice Wilson, and Jonathan Wyrtzen. Additional thanks go to James Miller and Saadia Maski of the Moroccan American Commission for Educational and

Cultural Exchange, John Davison of the Tangier American Legation, Myriem Noussairi and Aziz Rahou of the United Nations Development Programme, and the many local, provincial, and national government officials in Morocco who facilitated this research.

My more recent involvement in the Appalachian Land Study Collective and in Martin County, Kentucky, has deeply informed my research in Morocco and vice versa. Special thanks to Ricki Draper, Mary Hufford, Allison Leip, Mickey McCoy, Nina McCoy, Madison Mooney, Christin Roberson, Lindsay Shade, Charice Starr, Lyndsay Tarus, Betsy Taylor and fellow Likeneers, and the community of Appalachian scholars and activists who have taught me so much. I will always consider myself an apprentice of their moving and committed praxis.

I thank my parents, Raymond and Raymonde Rignall, whose sense of empathy, ethics, and cosmopolitanism shaped my trajectory in this research and in my life. I am grateful to my other parents, Sami and Elizabeth Kalliney, for supporting us in our wanderings through so many stages of life and work. Eric Rignall and Yasmina Keller, Charles and Lorraine Rignall, the Agias, and the extended families of the Kallineys and Ghebreals have all encouraged me as I make a go of academia. Peter Kalliney is present on each and every page of this book. He has generously given intellectual counsel and unwavering support, a model for how to find joy in scholarship and be fully present in our family. I thank Nedjma and Zayd for encouragement and reassurance beyond their years and moments of laughter I will never forget. Athena patiently saw this project through to its conclusion.

Portions of chapters 1 and 5 have appeared in Rignall, "Land and the Politics of Custom in a Moroccan Oasis Town," *Anthropological Quarterly* 88, no. 4 (2015): 941–968, and Rignall, "The Labor of Agrodiversity in a Moroccan Oasis," *The Journal of Peasant Studies* 43, no. 3 (2016): 711–730. They have been heavily revised for this book.

Glossary

Note: I indicate the primary linguistic identification for each term, though any given term may be used by speakers of all three languages (Ar: Arabic; Ta: Tashelhit, the Amazigh language predominant in southeastern Morocco; Fr: French).

agdal (pl. igdaln, Ta): Collectively managed pasture in the highlands of the Atlas Mountains.

'ashir (Ta): Local land measure equivalent to 1/40 hectare.

ayants-droit (Fr): Rights holders; members of a tribal confederation or ethnic collectivity with rights to communal property.

bour (Ar): A rain-fed agricultural zone. In some cases, the term has become a proper placename, as in el Bour, the outlying steppe around the village of el Harte, and el Bour n'Aït Yahya, both field sites for this research.

dahir (Ar): Moroccan government decree.

hurm (pl. hurum, Ar): Communally owned buffer zone separating villages from collective lands owned by tribal confederations.

jma'a (Ar): Customary governing council for villages and tribal confederations.

makhzan (Ar): Literally "storehouse," traditional name for Morocco's central government as represented by the sultan and the notables or institutions immediately surrounding him. It remains a common term for the state, referring primarily to the palace and central bureaucracy rather than the elected institutions of government.

melkisation (Fr): Process of privatizing collectively owned lands to produce *mulk* or private property.

mulk (Ar): Private property in Islamic legal traditions.

na'ib (Ar): Collective-land representative; customary official responsible for adjudicating the disposition of communally owned lands for villages and tribal confederations.

qa'id (Ar): Ministry of Interior representative with a local jurisdiction.

qsar (pl. qsur, Ar): Fortified village historically designed to offer residents security.

tajdat (Ta): Overdress, usually black, worn by Amazigh women.

tamazirt (Ta): Homeland, homeplace.

transhumance (Fr and English): Form of livestock production that involves the seasonal movement of herds between winter and summer pasture.

Notes

INTRODUCTION

1. Imazighen have been historically labeled "Berbers," and although this book foregrounds the term "Amazigh," I occasionally use "Berber" to follow the convention of the writer or speaker being discussed.

2. As detailed in chapter 1, most sharecroppers in the southeastern oases were racially Black, but in the transitional zone of the Mgoun Valley, where oases, foothills, and the Atlas Mountains meet, sharecropping could also indenture racially White Imazighen.

3. The literature on the contradictions of the global food regime, including the use of the term "regime," is extensive. Key sites for the ongoing debates are the *Journal of Peasant Studies*, the *Journal of Agrarian Change*, and the publications of social movements such as *La Vía Campesina*, among others. See, for example, Edelman et al. 2014; McMichael 2009; van der Ploeg 2008.

4. This book uses the term "peasant" to refer to smallholder agriculturalists who farm on their own account using primarily family labor (they may hire workers) and sometimes sell their production on the market (Narotzky 2016; Netting 1993). I also use "peasant" to refer to people who earn most of their income in the wage-labor market but retain a foothold in agrarian livelihoods, drawing on the long anthropological tradition that foregrounds critical political economy approaches to studying peasant livelihoods and lifeways (Kearney 1996; Mintz 1960; Wolf 1968, 1982, 2001).

5. Makhzan, literally "storehouse," is the traditional name for Morocco's central government as represented by the sultan and the notables who surrounded him (Park 1996). It remains a common term for the state, more in the sense of the palace, enduring state institutions, and bureaucracy than the elected institutions of government.

6. These idealized notions emerged from the functionalist study of segmentary systems. In the context of broader anthropological critiques, functionalist approaches gave way to a lively debate about the history, political economy, and social dynamics of Moroccan tribal formations and rural areas. See, for example, Asad 1979; Chatty 2006; Fabietti and Salzman 1996; Gellner 1969; Hammoudi 1980; Hart 1981; Marx 1977; Munson 1993; Nelson 1974; Salzman 1971; Seddon 1981.

7. This understanding draws on the vast literature, spanning diverse theoretical and methodological orientations, on common property and related resource management regimes. Key texts include Agrawal 2003; McCay and Acheson 1987; Ostrom 1990; Ostrom et al. 1999.

8. Defining precipitation thresholds in Morocco is difficult. Whereas the threshold for rain-fed cereal cultivation is often set at two hundred millimeters per annum, given the potential for extreme variability in precipitation in Northwest Africa, the four hundred millimeter average annual precipitation line (isohyet) is considered to be the threshold for viable rain-fed cereal production there (Swearingen 1992, 406). Morocco has always experienced frequent drought and the climatic uncertainty characteristic of disequilibrial systems, but drought has become an increasingly pressing problem. Benassi describes how "the frequency of periods, the intensity and duration of drought have increased over the past three decades," while the "average annual precipitation . . . experienced a decrease of about 15% nationally during the period 1971–2000" (2008, 85). Although there

is no official threshold for drought, the government bases its statistics on an agricultural definition linked to cereal production rather than absolute precipitation amounts. By this method, Morocco experienced drought for ten out the twenty-five years preceding 2005 (rains between 2005 and 2010 were relatively strong) (World Bank 2007, iv).

9. Household consumption is largely met through wells in the Mgoun Valley; a campaign for potable water provision beginning in the 1980s supported the establishment of local associations that manage water systems in partnership with the state utility. The smaller population in the Mgoun Valley relative to Dadès, high water availability, and modest size of the tourist sector mean that few considered household consumption to be a major pressure on groundwater supplies.

10. See the expansive literature on Moroccan natural resource management systems (for example, Ater and Hmimsa 2008; Auclair and Alifriqui 2012; Auclair, Aspe, and Baudot 2006; Auclair et al. 2011; D. Davis 2005, 2007, 2016; Elloumi 1997; Genin and Simenel 2011; Ilahiane 1999; 2001; 2004; Le Polain de Waroux and Chiche 2013).

11. These changes are described in greater detail in chapter 4; see Gertel and Breuer 2007 for a general assessment of contemporary livestock production in Morocco.

12. These integrated socioecological systems have been documented in mountain zones around the world. In the context of the Peruvian Andes, Zimmerer (1999) argues for replacing a "zonation" model that identifies the discrete ecological and social function of each geographic zone with the notion of overlapping patchworks, socially defined by populations who adapt their land uses to changing historical and agroecological circumstances.

13. See Jones 2005 for an introduction to transhumant pastoralism.

14. I first visited the region in 1992 in the context of my work for an international nongovernmental organization (NGO). Although I was based in Rabat, the capital city, the organization's programs supported an emergent local NGO sector around the country.

15. "Ethnic collectivity" is the official term for a tribe. First introduced during the French Protectorate, the definition was never fully elaborated. It was unclear whether it referred to larger tribal confederations made up of independent though allied tribes or smaller configurations such as fractions or both. It was also not clearly defined according to either geographic or social criteria, making the question of what constituted membership in a collectivity a difficult one. This ambiguity has created problems for contemporary land law regarding rights holders in collective lands, as discussed in chapter 3.

16. The terms often used to denote these groups (*haratin*, *isouqiyin*, or *iqbliyin*) are pejorative. I therefore refer to them as Black populations in an attempt to use a descriptive term that does not have as much of a politically charged local meaning.

17. Thami el Glaoua, the most powerful of the Glaoui family, was one of the "grands qa'ids" who consolidated power in the High and Anti-Atlas regions before and during the protectorate. The Glaoua drew on well-established strategies for developing local power bases, extending that power through alliances, and using their "calculated loyalty" to the makhzan—and then the protectorate—to secure broad authority over the territories they had conquered or otherwise brought under their control (Ilahiane 2006, 51). Their role in the lead-up to and consolidation of the protectorate has been a major subject of academic and popular history; see, for example, Burke 1976; Hoisington 1995; Maxwell 1966. The Glaoua used their stronghold in Telouet, a strategic location in the High Atlas between Marrakech and the Sahara, as a springboard for regional control and a broader campaign to garner national and even international influence. Although the French pressured Sultan Moulay 'Abd al Hafiz to sever ties with the Glaoua prior to the imposition of the protectorate, colonial authorities subsequently allied with the Glaoua when they real-

ized they could not conquer and then rule over the High Atlas or the southeastern foothills without proxies. As Pacha of Marrakech, Thami al Glaoui became a stalwart supporter of French rule while amassing extensive wealth and landholdings, often through violence and outright expropriation. The Glaoua presence in the Mgoun region is described in chapter 2.

18. Berber Studies has shifted from a focus on the relationship between Amazigh identity and nationalism to include contemporary Amazigh rights movements, cultural production inequality, and a rethinking of the historiography. See, for example, Crawford 2005; Feliu 2004; Gellner and Micaud 1972; J. Goodman 2005; Hoffman and Miller 2010; Maddy-Weitzman 2011.

19. One man, Félix Mora, was responsible for organizing this migration wave, at least in the south. A former French colonial official, he was hired by several coal companies to recruit labor in Morocco in the early 1960s (Atouf 2011). He has been memorialized throughout rural Morocco in song, poetry, and stories that continue to circulate throughout the region through aged cassette tapes, CDs, and still-vibrant oral traditions.

20. Throughout this book, I use actual place-names but use pseudonyms and otherwise anonymize individuals in how I render the details of their stories. I identify with Crawford's (2008) sentiment that anonymity is impossible—and usually undesirable—in these rural settings but opted for this compromise approach because many of the land and political issues I discuss are sensitive for the individuals involved. I use people's actual names when they specifically requested I do so.

21. I use the term "civil society activists" as the translation for the dominant French term *miliants associatifs* in Morocco for people active in formal nonprofits, local associations, or other NGOs—although the term *acteurs associatifs* (civil society actors) is also widely used. It can refer to activists in political movements but does not necessarily imply a radical or oppositional political stance. Chapter 2 describes how these activists in the Mgoun Valley focused primarily on government accountability and rule of law.

22. Determining population numbers is difficult not only because the census can be inaccurate but also because household members are constantly moving in and out of the village as their labor demands require, and people who have long lived away from a village may still form part of a household and contribute in important ways to village life. Present residents may well include these absent individuals in population numbers.

23. My rationale for the case studies followed McCabe (2004), who examines four Turkana (Kenyan) pastoralist households' decision making about mobility and herd management and then relates their strategies to macroenvironmental, political, and economic processes. For McCabe, such a small sample size renders the question of representativeness moot: he does not claim that these provide a window into Turkana decision making as whole. However, in amassing such detail about household movements, livestock ownership, and other variables over more than two decades, he is able to detail the pressures and considerations that frame household decision making. I took a similar approach to developing detailed portraits of the livelihoods and land-use practices of households in Mgoun.

24. I worked with three research assistants throughout my research. The first, Lahcen, helped me get started with his extensive networks and recognized social status in the region, although he did not have the time to work closely with me on the case study interviews. During this intensive period of interviewing, I worked with a resident of el Harte, Mbarak, who was widely respected and had himself conducted field research there for his bachelor's degree in geography nearly fifteen years before. In Rbat and Imzilne, I worked with a schoolteacher, Saïd, who was not from the mountains but was also well respected as a neutral presence in the community.

1. CUSTOM AND THE AMBIVALENT ROMANCE OF COMMUNITY

1. *Haj* is an honorific given to elderly or senior men (and women, fem. *Hajja*). Although the term literally refers to someone who has completed the *haj* (pilgrimage to Mecca), Moroccans often use the term regardless of whether the addressee has been on the pilgrimage.

2. I distinguish the village of Qlaʿa from the neighboring market town of Kelaa Mgouna by spelling the former using the transliteration system outlined at the beginning of the book (this spelling also approximates the numerous variants in official maps and documents). Qlaʿa literally means fortress in Arabic, reflecting the village's historical importance as the seat for notable families whose governing authority extended across the region. When the French founded the garrison and market town across the river from Qlaʿa, it was named Kelaa Mgouna (fort of Mgoun) and the francophone transliteration system still holds official weight, as it does for many place names throughout Morocco.

3. Jane Guyer, personal communication, December 15, 2017. See also Merry 1988.

4. Much has been written on the Berber Dahir of 1930, a French attempt to co-opt Amazigh sympathies and disable nationalist activity by establishing distinct legal systems for putatively Arab and Berber regions (see Ilahiane 2006 for an overview). Hoffman (2010) complicates historiographic accounts of its quick rescinding to show the lasting impact of Berber customary courts as spaces where distinctions between customary and shariʿa law were sustained well into the 1950s and also provided a space for rural residents of the southwest, including women, to advance their claims in diverse disputes and inheritance matters. There were no Berber courts in the Mgoun Valley, although one was active in the nearby *cercle* of Boumalne Dadès.

5. See Abaza 2009 for an overview of ʿada throughout the Middle East and Southeast Asia.

6. See the work of Lawrence Rosen (especially 1984, 2000, 2008) for a treatment of legal pluralism and the cultural dimensions of Islamic legal practice in Morocco.

7. The literature on igdaln is extensive, documenting the highly elaborated management regimes, social and political dimensions of communal governance (the agdal as commons), and the ecological dynamics associated with highland pasture management regimes. Scholars working in the High Atlas (some just a few hours' trek up a still-unpaved road from the area I conducted my research) provide a complementary analysis of how migration, environmental change, capitalist transformation of the livestock sector, and a legacy of repressive policies have pressured the agdal. At the same time, they have highlighted how this governance regime adapts to changing circumstances even as the agdal has become dormant in some places. See, for example, Auclair and Alifriqui 2012; Lérin 2010; Mahdi 1999; Mahdi and Dominguez 2009; Miller 1984; Niamir-Fuller 1999.

8. Hart 1981 details this structure; Skounti 2012 also provides an overview of this history for the region neighboring the Mgoun Valley.

9. The tutelary council had ultimate authority over land disposition despite formal tribal ownership of the lands; it is described in detail in chapter 3.

10. Outsiders or nonmembers could also petition for land in special cases. I describe this situation and detail the formal legal structure governing collective lands at the tribal confederation level in chapter 3. This and the next section describe the kinds of land division that occurred in the Mgoun Valley, but there are other mechanisms for dividing collectively owned land in other parts of Morocco. For example, in large irrigated perimeters, the agricultural investment codes of 1994 and 1996 developed a procedure for privatizing land as a condition for receiving government subsidies and technical assistance (D. Davis 2006).

11. Zirari-Devif 2009–2010, 122, although see Denoix 1996 for how diverse property forms have been addressed in Islamic legal thought.

12. See Bouderbala 1999 for an overview of the different legal regimes for governing property.

13. Estimates of the hurm's size in el Harte were disputed amid speculation among some residents that the hurm was informally expanding into tribal confederation territory with the tacit approval of customary land representatives.

14. This statistic does not mean that 46 percent of households did not possess any land or that the family had never inherited land but just that the household members had not received an inheritance in the period covered by the survey (1960–2014); they could be working land that had been undivided from the previous generation.

15. Like most families that had lived in the village for the past two generations or longer, Mohsin's family had a home in the old qsar. Most had moved out of the closely built agglomeration of adobe houses in the past forty years for new, more expansive homes on the outer edges of the village. Mohsin's family had a similar desire for more spacious grounds, so they also moved. Like the others, they maintained their adobe home in the qsar, allowing an Imaghrani family newly arrived from the mountains to stay there for nominal in-kind payments. Few attempted to sell their ancestral homes because of disputes among the many heirs and a sense that the homes were not worth much.

16. Imzilne means "blacksmiths" in Tashelhit.

17. Youssef and his family had high status, but in a reflection of this region's peripheral status in the country as whole, he still engaged in what would be considered low-status work for most urban Moroccans: manual well digging.

2. POLITICAL PLURALISM, LOCAL POLITICS, AND THE STATE

1. "Years of lead" is a translation of "Les années de plomb." See Slyomovics 2005 on human rights violations during this period and their ramifying effects for contemporary Moroccan society.

2. See Allal 2007 for an assessment of this process. Critiques of the rhetoric and reality of democratization were early in coming, although multilateral donors and foreign government observers have consistently praised Morocco's "moderate" politics and approach to religion without acknowledging the extent of Moroccan authoritarianism.

3. This chapter builds on Moroccanist scholarship that reevaluates state formation during colonial rule and its legacy for the contemporary period in the context of political pluralism (Bogaert 2015; D. Davis 2006, 2007; Hoffman 2010, 2015; Maghraoui 2013; Salime 2011; Wyrtzen 2015). Hassan Rachik (2012, 2016) has reevaluated Morocco's colonial past through two parallel projects: a critical intellectual history of Moroccanist anthropology and an examination of contemporary contestations over law, community, and property that accounts for the complex legacy of colonial rule. This scholarship, and other inquiries into colonial legal and religious policy, describes how colonial governmentality and knowledge production contributed to the "Moroccan colonial vulgate," reifying social identities and laying down the discursive formations and institutions that have continued to influence contemporary politics (Burke 2014; Hoffman 2010).

4. I am indebted to Ilana Feldman for this formulation.

5. Following Africanist historiography and anthropology on the enduring legacy of colonial approaches to customary law, I define pluralism as the coexistence, even coconstitution, of different institutions and practices of governing authority (Berry 1993; Biebuyck 1963; Chanock 1985, 1991; Gluckman 1965; Mamdani 1996, 2012; Merry 1988; Moore 1978; Peters 2004). The term has assumed a particular meaning in scholarly treatments of postindependence Morocco as a strategy of the monarchy to consolidate power through a "pluralization" of the political field: encouraging multiple political parties and centers for governing authority to consolidate the monarchy's ultimate authority (Bourqia and Miller 1999; Hammoudi 1997).

6. Subsequent resident generals modified Lyautey's philosophy as world wars, a burgeoning nationalist movement, internal French disputes over colonial policies, and other pressures on protectorate rule emerged (Rivet 1999). However, the architecture of indirect rule was enshrined in Morocco's administrative and juridical institutions. Mamdani notes, for example, how the Dutch jurist responsible for elaborating indirect rule in Indonesia, Snouck Hurgronje, advised French Protectorate officials on the Berber policy that codified Berber customary law as the dominant juridical framework for rural zones (2012, 41).

7. This positioning did not necessarily imply disinterest in local affairs; Native Affairs officers received intensive, formal training on (what was constructed as) customary and Islamic law, ethnology, and other aspects of the "social science" of native affairs (Hoffman 2008; 2010, 854). See also Hoisington 1995.

8. This analysis circulates in even the moderate opposition press and is a widely recognized state strategy. See Bennani-Chraïbi 2017.

9. I frequently encountered the metaphor of policies, programs, and laws making the long voyage from the capital to the southeast. Once, while waiting at a mechanic's shop, I asked a motorcyclist who was getting his engine fixed what he thought of a new national law mandating helmets for motorcyclists. Would he get one as a result? He laughed and said, "I am not worried about it; it takes ten years for a law passed in Rabat to make it down here."

10. As my presence in the village slipped to the back of people's consciousness, I heard progressively more discontent about corruption or, at minimum, favoritism in the management of collective lands. I suspected this was not because the situation had gotten worse during my time there but because people felt more comfortable discussing conflicts with and in front of me.

11. Bergh (2009) describes a similar dynamic in the High Atlas Mountains.

12. While my research showed this to be true in the Mgoun Valley, I hesitate to make this claim for rural Morocco generally. Land struggles around the country have become more overtly political in tone. Although scholarship reflecting this change is just emerging, cases such as the mobilizations around the silver mine in Imider (Tinghir province) are increasingly receiving national and even international attention and are allying themselves with broader social movements (Bogaert 2016).

13. This list is from a Robin Hood tale describing the medieval commons in Britain; Peter Linebaugh uses this and other references from British history and literature to describe how the Charter of the Forest, the forgotten supplement to the Magna Carta, guaranteed "estovers" (fruits of commonly held resources) to the poor, marginalized, and distressed (2008, 141). Here, I evoke that definition of the commons to consider how excluded groups developed their own registers for political practice in the Mgoun Valley's plural political environment.

3. LAND AND THE NEW COMMONING

1. "Land division" was the term for allocating collectively owned land among tribal ayants-droits with rights to the land. As described in chapter 1, these divisions were usually informal because of the bureaucratic complexities of formally dividing up collective lands.

2. This indirect dispossession has been well documented as part of land titling and other efforts to regularize land tenure. See, for example, Benjaminsen and Lund 2003. Other ways that land reform or state tenure policy can create unforeseen effects are documented in Atasoy 2017; Peters 2004, 2009; Platteau 1996; Sikor and Müller 2009, among others.

3. See Platteau 1996 for an overview of the evolutionary theory of land tenure that undergirded this development orthodoxy. International finance institutions have moder-

ated this position and since the first decade of the twenty-first century have officially supported diverse tenure regimes, including collective or customary landholding. However, development projects, lending facilities, and tenure reform initiatives operationalize the new orthodoxy in uneven ways, still foregrounding private property as the most secure—and economically preferable—form of land tenure. Even formalizing collective tenure can have the result of dispossessing the most marginalized groups of communal title holders through dynamics similar to individual titling efforts.

4. There is a substantial literature on how the production of colonial knowledge framed protectorate governance. See Burke 2014; Hoffman 2008; Lafuente 1999; Maghraoui 2013; Rachik 2012; Rivet 1984, 2012; Wyrtzen 2015. Burke notes how the colonial archive "generated the myth of the peaceful conquest of Morocco and of a beneficent monarchy under French authority. The discourse on Moroccan Islam made the violence and depredations that accompanied the imposition of French rule fade into the background, while diverting attention from the gigantic transfer of Moroccan resources to the Compagnie marocaine" (2014, 12). This discursive operation extended beyond colonial analyses of Moroccan Islam to Moroccan land tenure regimes and other domains.

5. See D. Davis 2007 for a full discussion of this assumption. In chapter 4, I delve into the environmental dimensions of these narratives and how, in criticizing farmer and herder improvidence, they "misread" the Moroccan landscape (Fairhead and Leach 1996).

6. Theorists of French colonization elevated a historically malleable distinction between *blad al-makhzan* (regions/land controlled by the makhzan or central government) and *blad al-siba* (regions/land of dissonance or outside the direct control of the makhzan) to governing trope (Rivet 1988; Hoisington 1984, 1995). This distinction reified the two zones, much like colonial knowledge reified other aspects of Moroccan society and continues to resonate in discourses of governance in Morocco. See Eickelman 2001 for how this trope migrated to serve as a metaphor for governance elsewhere in the Middle East and North Africa.

7. Collective-land representatives still played the same role when I began fieldwork in 2010. Some were considered staunch defenders of collective lands against outside investment projects, while others were dismissed in private as weak and easily manipulated by the state. These collective-land representatives were at the center of many land conflicts in Mgoun in 2010 and of scandals throughout Morocco involving land transfers to private investors or public officials reaping profits from their advantageous positions.

8. As the director of rural affairs in Ouarzazate explained, while the ministry oversees the funds collected on behalf of the ethnic collectivities, those collectivities have no access to or control over their accounts, and most have never received the money due for contracts on their land since those contracts started being issued in 1919. In the province of Ouarzazate, the first efforts to disburse the millions of dirhams that had accumulated over the previous century to the many collectivities began in 2003. The ministry's inability to trace exactly how much money was due to each tribe or to resolve the controversial issue of identifying eligible rights holders meant the ministry did not attempt to distribute cash directly to the ethnic collectivities. Instead, it established a community development fund to finance economic and social projects around the province, regardless of the target area's actual balance due.

9. One journalistic account that addresses these scandals as they relate to the king has produced court cases and even prosecution for alleged extortion on the part of the journalists (Graciet and Laurent 2012), which some claim is a state-led effort to target this kind of criticism.

10. As one of the central stories in the rise of industrial capitalism, enclosure has engendered powerful myths celebrating the power of private property or critiquing its

destructive effects. Raymond Williams notes how in England, "the idea of the enclosures ... can shift our attention from the real history and become an element of that very powerful myth of modern England in which the transition from a rural to an industrial society is seen as a kind of fall, the true cause and origin of our social suffering and disorder. It is difficult to overestimate the importance of this myth in modern social thought. It is a main source for the structure of feeling ... the perpetual retrospect to an 'organic' or 'natural' society" (1975, 96). Similar ideas of organic or natural society undergirded discourses of community I encountered, such as that of the Ministry of Interior official quoted earlier.

4. ENVIRONMENTAL POLITICS AND THE NEW RURALITY

1. The potable water system was installed in 1998 (and extended in 2000 and 2003) with the financial and technical support of the National Office of Potable Water (the state-owned utility at the time), but the village development association managed water distribution independently, collecting bimonthly fees based on water usage levels.

2. Jacques Berque's phrasing is evocative: "la morphologie [de la terre] touche ici directement à l'humain."

3. This interdisciplinary literature is growing, contributing empirically and theoretically to global debates in critical environmental studies. See, for example, Davis and Burke's volume on environmental imaginaries (2011), Mikhail's critical perspectives on how environmental dynamics figured in Ottoman rule (2011, 2014, 2017), and broader historical treatments of environmental change, disease, land politics, water management, and environmental governance, such as Barnes 2014; McKee 2016; Mikhail 2013; and White 2011. For brief overviews of the field of environmental history in North Africa and the Middle East, see D. Davis 2010 and Trumbull 2017.

4. Summarized in the introduction to this book, this research represents a paradigm shift in rangeland ecology with broader ramifications for social science and historical understandings of socioecological dynamics in arid lands. Scholarship on pastoralism in Morocco was documenting the importance of mobility and other adaptive management strategies as the new paradigm of rangeland ecology was taking shape—and even before. See, for example, Bencherifa and Johnson 1991; Galaty and Johnson 1990; Johnson 1969; Miller 1984; Swearingen and Bencherifa 1996.

5. Although this account focuses on North Africa, similar declensionist narratives, often drawing on the same sources, figure in the dominant narratives of environmental change elsewhere in the Middle East. See, for example, Burke 2009 and D. Davis 2012, 2016.

6. I do not have estimates of what percentage of Imaghranis exited pastoralism during the drought of the 1990s. Our household survey was limited to the Mgoun Valley, which means that our sample included those Imaghrani households that left and migrated into our research area. This does not capture those households that stayed in Imaghran to continue livestock production or other livelihoods, or the Imaghranis who migrated elsewhere. Two primary destinations were the city of Khenifra, on the northern side of the mountains from Imaghran, and the city of Ouarzazate, to the west of Imaghran and the Mgoun Valley.

7. It is important to note that drip irrigation does not in and of itself signify water-use efficiency; if it is being used to extend cultivation into a hundred-hectare concession, for example, the overall draw on the water table might still be very high.

8. Mohamed Naciri's influential 1986 article describes this *éclatement* (bursting) as a spatial reorganization of the qsar resulting from migration, drought, and related social changes in the household (355). See also Ilahiane 1999.

9. Home construction and maintenance represented major financial and labor burdens. Some scholars and other observers have decried Moroccan migrants' tendencies to use remittances to build large cement homes, abandoning traditional adobe construction, which they see as more culturally authentic (see de Haas 2009 for a critical discussion), but there were important reasons for their decisions. While more suited to the alternatively hot summers and cold winters, adobe required constant maintenance with a particular need for repair after the fall and spring rains. This represented either a financial drain given the shortage of skilled adobe builders or a burdensome time commitment for men who were often working away from the home.

10. See Ilahiane 2001b and 2004 for more on how security concerns historically shaped community dynamics and architecture.

11. Infant and child mortality rates are still very high in mountain regions and rural areas underserved by the public health system. In 2008, Morocco had a maternal mortality ratio of 110 per 100,000 and an under-five mortality rate of 39 per 1,000 live births, ranking it 130 out of 187 countries listed in the Human Development Index (UNDP 2012).

5. MAKING A LIVING ON AND OFF THE LAND

1. I discuss migration as a largely male phenomenon because few women in the valley were directly involved in contemporary labor migration. Although the controversial phenomenon of sending girls and young women to work as domestic labor in Moroccan cities is well documented, it was not common practice in the Mgoun Valley (Barraud 2011; Bendradi and El Aoufi 1996; Guessous 2002; Moujoud and Pourette 2005). In the few years before the 2008 global economic downturn, a small number of women received seasonal agricultural contracts in Spain, but this temporary migration arrangement had largely dried up by the time I began my fieldwork in 2010. Some women joined their migrant spouses in the city or abroad, although it was more common for the household to be maintained in the valley. Historically, though, women have been very mobile in part because marriage involved moving out of the natal home and into the husband's household, which could be quite far away (Crawford 2008; Hoffman 2007). These migration dynamics unfold differently in other parts of Morocco, where young women actively search for migration opportunities through marriage, education, or increasingly their own undocumented journeys to the city or abroad. See Elliot 2016 for more on this alternate experience.

2. Bourdieu 2008, 103; Bourdieu and Sayad 1964. See Goodman and Silverstein 2008 for an extended critique of Bourdieu's ethnography of colonial Algeria.

3. We distinguished wage labor from migration remittances by whether the wage earner lived for most of the year in the household or sent wages home from a work site elsewhere; in both cases, the wage earner would have been considered part of the household.

4. Numerous people I interviewed explained that they never took out loans from banks because of this desire to rely on people they knew. While credit was widely used throughout the valley, very few people carried formal loans from financial institutions, which they considered anonymous, foreign, and uninterested in their well-being. Different debt arrangements embedded in social relationships not only eased a credit crunch but strengthened those relationships.

5. This fragmentation also deepened the sociability of farming. The ways people moved through space to access their plots created regular patterns of social intercourse throughout the day and growing season as people greeted each other, worked alongside each other, and often sang together to ease the burden of labor. See Ilahiane 2004 for another discussion of the productive uses of fragmentation in an oasis context.

6. Maintaining a stable supply of wood and other building materials was a high priority for families because of the nearly constant need to maintain or repair homes. Most homes

in el Harte and in the other rural communities in the valley were still adobe or had portions of adobe in combination with cement structures. The cost of maintaining homes in terms of material and labor was substantial. This cost, along with the need to secure a stable supply of firewood for baking bread and preparing couscous (propane tanks were widespread for other cooking purposes), explained the importance of trees not only for the crops they harvested but also for the wood they produced.

7. See Hoffman 2002 for how migration in southwestern Morocco did not erode identity but led to understanding "community as comprising present and absent members" (929). Cliggett 2003 details the ambivalence of the social and economic ties that bind migrants to their home communities in Zambia.

8. One of Abdallah's brothers managed a stall at the weekly vegetable market, less for the income than to secure wholesale prices for the produce they needed to supplement their own production.

CONCLUSION

1. One national development with implications for land tenure dynamics throughout the country is the passage of a series of laws in 2019 (as this book was entering production) restructuring the legal framework for collective lands. Changes include recognizing women as rights-holders on par with men, incentives to privatize collective land in rain-fed areas (previously incentives were limited to irrigated perimeters), and the creation of regional tutelary councils replacing the centralized council described in chapter 3. As these laws become operational, it is not yet clear how they will shift the calculus of power between state institutions, well-placed economic actors, and the rights-holders who have long been marginalized from collective land governance.

2. Several anthropologists of the region have joined an interdisciplinary field of critical agrarian scholars addressing the neoliberal restructuring of rural economies over the past two decades: the rollback of land reform, a reorientation of agriculture to high-value exports, and cuts to support for rural producers and workers. See, for example, Ajl 2018; Barnes 2009, 2014; Bush 2007; Bush and Ayeb 2012; D. Davis 2006; Dixon 2014; Métral 2000; Mitchell 2002. These approaches, some inspired by political ecology, offer insights into how environmental change and natural resource dynamics were enmeshed with the neoliberal restructuring that began to take hold in the 1990s.

References

Abaza, Mona. 2009. "'Ada/Custom in the Middle East and Southeast Asia." In *Words in Motion: Toward a Global Lexicon*, edited by Carol Gluck and Anna Lowenhaupt Tsing, 67–82. Durham, NC: Duke University Press.

Abu-Lughod, Lila. 2012. "Living the 'Revolution' in an Egyptian Village: Moral Action in a National Space." *American Ethnologist* 39 (1): 21–25.

Adams, William M., and Michael J. Mortimore. 1997. "Agricultural Intensification and Flexibility in the Nigerian Sahel." *Geographical Journal* 163 (2): 150–160.

Agrawal, Arun. 2003. "Sustainable Governance of Common-Pool Resources: Context, Methods, and Politics." *Annual Review of Anthropology* 32: 243–262.

Aït Hamza, Mohamed. 1993. "Migration internationale du travail et urbanisation des espaces oasiens: Kelaat Mgouna." *Revue de Géographie Marocaine* 15 (1/2): 127–141.

———. 2002a. *Mobilité socio-spatiale et développement locale au sud de l'Atlas marocain (Dadès-Todgha)*. Maghreb-Studien. Heft 12. Passau: L.I.S. Verlag GmbH.

———. 2002b. *Étude sur les institutions locales dans le versant sud du Haut Atlas*. Ouarzazate: CBTHA (Programme de Conservation de la Biodiversité par la Transhumance dans le Versant Sud du Haut Atlas), Programme des Nations Unies pour le Développement.

Aït Hamza, Mohamed, and Herbert Popp, eds. 2005. *Pour une nouvelle perception des montagnes marocaines: Espace périphérique? Patrimoine culturel et naturel: Stock de ressources dans l'Avenir? Actes du 7ème Colloque Maroco-Allemand*. Rabat: Publications de la Faculté des Lettres et des Sciences Humaines.

Aït Mous, Fadma, and Yasmine Berriane. 2016. "Femmes, droit à la terre et lutte pour l'égalité au Maroc: Le mouvement des soulaliyates." In *Contester le droit: Communautés, familles et héritage au Maroc*, edited by Hassan Rachik, 87–173. Casablanca: La croisée des chemins.

Ajl, Max. 2018. "Auto-centered Development and Indigenous Technics: Slaheddine el-Amami and Tunisian Delinking." *Journal of Peasant Studies* 46 (6): 1240–1263.

Akesbi, Najib, Driss Benatya, and Noureddine el Aoufi. 2008. *L'agriculture marocain à l'épreuve de la libéralisation*. Rabat: Économie Critique.

Akram-Lodhi, A. Haroon, and Cristóbal Kay, eds. 2009. *Peasants and Globalization: Political Economy, Rural Transformation and the Agrarian Question*. New York: Routledge.

Allal, Amin. 2007. "'Développement international' et 'promotion de la démocratie': À propos de la 'gouvernance locale' au Maroc." *L'Année du Maghreb* 3: 275–296.

Altieri, Miguel A., and Victor M. Toledo. 2011. "The Agroecological Revolution in Latin America: Rescuing Nature, Ensuring Food Sovereignty and Empowering Peasants." *Journal of Peasant Studies* 38 (3): 587–612.

Amar, Émile. 1913. *L'Organisation de la propriété foncière au Maroc: Étude théorique et pratique*. Paris: Paul Geuthner.

Aoui, Atman, Moulay Ahmed el Amrani, and Karen Rignall. 2020. "Global Aspirations and Local Realities of Solar Energy in Morocco." Middle East Research and Information Project, October 6, 2020.

Asad, Talal. 1979. "Equality in Nomadic Social Systems? Notes towards the Dissolution of an Anthropological Category." In *Pastoral Production and Society*, edited by Équipe Écologie, 419–428. Cambridge: Cambridge University Press.

Atasoy, Yildiz. 2017. "Repossession, Re-informalization and Dispossession: The 'Muddy Terrain' of Land Commodification in Turkey." *Journal of Agrarian Change* 17 (4): 657–679.

Ater, Mohamed, and Younés Hmimsa. 2008. "Agriculture traditionnelle et agrodiversité dans le bassin versant de l'Oued Laou." *Travaux de l'Institut Scientifique (Rabat)* 19 (5): 107–115.

Atouf, Elkbir. 2011. *L'histoire de l'émigration marocaine au bassin minier du Nord-Pas-de-Calais (1917–1987)*. Rabat: Publications de l'Institut Royal de la Culture Amazighe.

Attar, El Houcine. 1994. *Al-hijra wa ta'thiriha 'ala al-majal: namudaj duwar al-Hart Jama'a Mguna Iqlim Warazazat. Bahth madani. Jam'a Muhammad al-Khamis*. Rabat: Jam'a Muhammad al-Khamis.

Auclair, Laurent, and Mohamed Alifriqui, eds. 2012. *Agdal: Patrimoine socio-écologique de l'Atlas marocain*. Paris: IRD Éditions.

Auclair, Laurent, Chantal Aspe, and Patrick Baudot, eds. 2006. *Le retour des paysans? À l'heure du développement durable*. Aix-en-Provence: Édisud.

Auclair, Laurent, Patrick Baudot, Didier Genin, Bruno Romagny, and Romain Simenel. 2011. "Patrimony for Resilience: Evidence from the Forest Agdal in the Moroccan High Atlas Mountains." *Ecology and Society* 16 (4): 24.

Auclair, Laurent, Pablo Domínguez, Mohamed Alifriqui, and Didier Genin. 2013. "Un monument pastoral à l'épreuve de la patrimonialisation: L'*Agdal* du Yagour dans le Haut-Atlas marocain." In *Effervesence patrimoniale au Sud: Entre nature et société*, edited by Dominique Juhé-Beaulaton, Marie-Christine Cormier-Salem, Pascale de Robert, and Bernard Roussel, 105–128. Marseille: IRD Éditions.

Bajeddi, Mohammed. 2000. *Évolution de la politique de développement agricole et analyse des contraintes au Maroc*. Rabat: Organisation des Nations Unies pour l'Alimentation et l'Agriculture.

Banque Mondiale. 2008. *Marchés fonciers pour la croissance économique au Maroc*. Rapport No. 49970-MA. Washington, DC: World Bank.

Barathon, Jean-Jacques, Hassan El Abbassi, and Claude Lechevalier. 2005. "Les oasis de la région de Tata (Maroc): Abandon de la vie oasienne traditionnelle et adaptation à la vie urbaine." *Annales de Géographie* 644 (4): 449–461.

Barnes, Jessica. 2009. "Managing the Waters of Ba'th Country: The Politics of Water Scarcity in Syria." *Geopolitics* 14 (3): 510–530.

———. 2014. *Cultivating the Nile: The Everyday Politics of Water in Egypt*. Durham, NC: Duke University Press.

Barraud, Émilie. 2011. "L'adoption au prisme du genre: L'exemple du Maghreb." *Liens Familiaux* 34: 153–165.

Bassett, Thomas J., and Donald Crummey, eds. 2003. *African Savannas: Global Narratives and Local Knowledge of Environmental Change*. Oxford, UK: James Currey.

Bassett, Thomas J., and Denis Gautier. 2014. "Regulation by Territorialization: The Political Ecology of Conservation and Development Territories." *EchoGéo* 29 (July/September): 2–7.

Bassiouni, M. Cherif, ed. 2016. *Chronicles of the Egyptian Revolution and Its Aftermath: 2011–2016*. Cambridge: Cambridge University Press.

Battesti, Vincent. 2005. *Jardins au désert: Évolution des pratiques et savoirs oasiens*. Paris: IRD Éditions.

Behnke, Roy H., Jr., Ian Scoones, and Carol Kerven, eds. 1993. *Range Ecology at Disequilibrium: New Models of Natural Variability and Pastoral Adaptation in African Savannas*. London: Overseas Development Institute.

Beinin, Joel, and Frédéric Vairel, eds. 2013. *Social Movements, Mobilization, and Contestation in the Middle East and North Africa.* 2nd edition. Stanford, CA: Stanford University Press.
Benassi, Mohamed. 2008. "Drought and Climate Change in Morocco: Analysis of Precipitation Field and Water Supply." In *Drought Management: Scientific and Technological Innovations. Options Méditerranéennes: Série A(80),* edited by Antonio Lopez-Francos, 83–86. Paris: Centre International de Hautes Études Agronomiques Méditerranéennes.
Benchemsi, Ahmed R. 2010. "Tous pourris, sauf Sa Majesté." *Tel Quel,* September 4, 2010.
Bencherifa, Abdellatif. 1988. "Demography and Cultural Ecology of the Atlas Mountains of Morocco: Some New Hypotheses." *Mountain Research and Development* 8 (4): 309–313.
———. 1991. *Migration internationale et changement agricole: Extensification, agriculture sentimentale, ou intensification? A propos d'observations divergentes récentes. Le Maroc et l'Allemagne.* Actes de la Première Rencontre Universitaire. Rabat: Faculté des Lettres et des Sciences Humaines.
Bencherifa, Abdellatif, and Douglas L. Johnson. 1991. "Changing Resource Management Strategies and Their Environmental Impacts in the Middle Atlas Mountains of Morocco." *Mountain Research and Development* 11 (3): 183–194.
Bencherifa, Abdellatif, and Herbert Popp. 1990. *L'Oasis de Figuig: Persistance et changement.* Passavia: Passavia Universitätsverlag.
Bendradi, Malika, and Noureddine El Aoufi. 1996. *Les enfants au travail: Cas du Maroc— Une enquête d'étape qualitative.* Rabat: Ministère de l'Emploi et des Affaires Sociales and UNICEF.
Benjaminsen, Tor A., and Christian Lund, eds. 2003. *Securing Land Rights in Africa.* London: Frank Cass.
Bennafla, Karine. 2011. "Enjeux et gestion de la protestation dans une marge territoriale: Le mouvement local de Sidi Ifni (Maroc)." *Maghreb et Sciences Sociales* 1: 105–115.
Bennani-Chraïbi, Mounia. 2017. *"Le roi est bon, la classe politique est mauvaise": Un mythe à bout de souffle?* Beirut: Asfari Institute for Civil Society and Citizenship, American University of Beirut.
Bergh, Sylvia I. 2009. "Traditional Village Councils, Modern Associations, and the Emergence of Hybrid Political Orders in Rural Morocco." *Peace Review: A Journal of Social Justice* 21 (1): 45–53.
———. 2012. "'Inclusive' Neoliberalism, Local Governance Reforms and the Redeployment of State Power: The Case of the National Initiative for Human Development (INDH) in Morocco." *Mediterranean Politics* 17 (3): 410–426.
Bergh, Sylvia I, and Daniele Rossi-Doria. 2015. "Plus ça Change? Observing the Dynamics of Morocco's 'Arab Spring' in the High Atlas." *Mediterranean Politics* 20 (2): 198–216.
Berlant, Lauren. 2016. "The Commons: Infrastructures for Troubling Times." *Environment and Planning D: Society and Space* 34 (3): 393–419.
Bernstein, Henry. 2010. *Class Dynamics of Agrarian Change.* Sterling, VA: Kumarian Press.
———. 2014. "Food Sovereignty via the 'Peasant Way': A Sceptical View." *Journal of Peasant Studies* 41 (6): 1031–1063.
Bernstein, Henry, and Philip Woodhouse. 2001. "Telling Environmental Change Like It Is? Reflections on a Study in Sub-Saharan Africa." *Journal of Agrarian Change* 1 (2): 283–324.
Berque, Jacques. 1940. *Les Nawâzil el muzâra'a du Mi'yâr Al Wazzâni: Étude et traduction.* Rabat: Félix Moncho.

———. 1962. *Le Maghreb entre deux guerres*. Paris: Éditions du Seuil.
Berque, Jacques, and Paul Pascon. 1978. *Structures sociales du Haut-Atlas*. 2nd ed. Paris: Presses Universitaires de France.
Berriane, Yasmine. 2015. "Inclure les 'n'ayants-pas-droit': Terres collectives et inégalités de genre au Maroc." *L'Année du Maghreb* 13 (2): 55–72.
———. 2017. "Développement et contremouvements: Réflexions à partir des conflits nés de la marchandisation des terres collectives au Maroc." *International Development Policy| Revue internationale de politique de développement* 8: 247–267.
Berriane, Yasmine, and Karen Rignall. 2017. "La fabrique de la coutume au Maroc: Le droit des femmes aux terres collectives." *Cahiers du Genre* 62: 97–118.
Berry, Sara S. 1993. *No Condition Is Permanent: The Social Dynamics of Agrarian Change in Sub-Saharan Africa*. Madison: University of Wisconsin Press.
———. 2004. "Reinventing the Local? Privatization, Decentralization and the Politics of Resource Management: Examples from Africa." *African Study Monographs* 25 (2): 79–101.
Berthault, Pierre. 1936. "La propriété rurale en Afrique du Nord." *L'Afrique Française: Bulletin Mensuel du Comité de l'Afrique Française et du Comité du Maroc* 46 (4): 210–221.
Betts, Raymond. 2005. *Assimilation and Association in French Colonial Theory, 1890–1914*. Lincoln: University of Nebraska Press.
Bidwell, Robin. 1973. *Morocco under Colonial Rule: French Administration of Tribal Areas, 1912–1956*. London: Frank Cass.
Biebuyck, Daniel, 1963. "Systèmes de tenure foncière et problèmes fonciers au Congo." In *African Agrarian Systems*, edited by Daniel Biebuyck, 83–100. London: Oxford University Press.
Blondel, Jacques. 2006. "The 'Design' of Mediterranean Landscapes: A Millennial Story of Humans and Ecological Systems during the Historic Period." *Human Ecology* 34 (5): 713–729.
Bogaert, Koenraad. 2015. "The Revolt of Small Towns: The Meaning of Morocco's History and the Geography of Social Protests." *Review of African Political Economy* 42 (143): 124–140.
———. 2016. "Imider vs. COP22: Understanding Climate Justice from Morocco's Peripheries." *Jadaliyya*, November 21, 2016. http://www.jadaliyya.com/pages/index/25517/imider-vs.-cop22_understanding-climate-justice-fro.
———. 2018. *Globalized Authoritarianism: Megaprojects, Slums, and Class Relations in Urban Morocco*. Minneapolis: University of Minnesota Press.
Bouderbala, Négib. 1996. "Les terres collectives du Maroc dans la première période du protectorat (1912–1930)." *Revue du Monde Musulman et de la Méditerranée* 79–80: 143–156.
———. 1999. "Les systèmes de propriété foncière au Maghreb: Le cas du Maroc." *Cahiers Options Méditerranéennes* 36: 47–66.
Bouderbala, Négib, Mohamed Chraïbi, and Paul Pascon, eds. 1974. *La question agraire au Maroc*. Vol 1. Rabat: Bulletin Économique et Social du Maroc.
———. 1977. *La question agraire au Maroc*. Vol. 2. Rabat: Bulletin Économique et Social du Maroc.
Bouhdou, Moustafa. 2009. *Dalil al-ijra'at al-idariya al-khasa bi 'idad wa injaz al-mukhtat al-jama'ai lil tanmia*. Rabat: al-Idara al-'Ama lil Jama'at al-Mahaliyya, Wizara al-Dakhiliya, Mamlaka al-Maghribiya.
Boujrouf, Saïd, and Hassani Elmostafa. 2008. "Toponymie et recomposition territoriale au Maroc: Figures, sens et logiques." *L'Espace Politique* 5 (2): 40–52.

Boum, Aomar. 2013. *Memories of Absence: How Muslims Remember Jews in Morocco*. Stanford, CA: Stanford University Press.
Bourbouze, Alain, and Annick Gibon. 2000. "Ressources individuelles ou ressources collectives? L'impact du statut des ressources sur la gestion des systèmes d'élevage des régions du pourtour méditerranée." *Options Méditerranéennes*. Série A (32): 289–309.
Bourdieu, Pierre. 2008. *Sketch for a Self-Analysis*. Translated by Richard Nice. Chicago: University of Chicago Press.
Bourdieu, Pierre, and Abdelmalak Sayad. 1964. *Le déracinement: La crise de l'agriculture traditionnelle en Algérie*. Paris: Les éditions de minuit.
Bourqia, Rahma, and Susan Gilson Miller, eds. 1999. *In the Shadow of the Sultan: Culture, Power, and Politics in Morocco*. Cambridge, MA: Harvard University Press.
Brookfield, Harold. 2001. *Exploring Agrodiversity*. New York: Columbia University Press.
Brookfield, Harold, Christine Padoch, Helen Parsons, and Michael Stocking, eds. 2002. *Cultivating Biodiversity: Understanding, Analysing and Using Agricultural Diversity*. London: ITDG Publishing.
Burke, Edmund. 1976. *Prelude to Protectorate in Morocco: Precolonial Protest and Resistance, 1860–1912*. Chicago: University of Chicago Press.
———. 2009. "The Transformation of the Middle Eastern Environment, 1500 B.C.E.–2000 C.E." In *The Environment and World History*, edited by Edmund Burke and Kenneth Pomeranz, 81–117. Berkeley: University of California Press.
———. 2014. *The Ethnographic State: France and the Invention of Moroccan Islam*. Berkeley: University of California Press.
Bush, Raymond. 2007. "Politics, Power and Poverty: Twenty Years of Agricultural Reform and Market Liberalisation in Egypt." *Third World Quarterly* 28 (8): 1599–1615.
Bush, Raymond, and Habib Ayeb, eds. 2012. *Marginality and Exclusion in Egypt*. London: Zed Books.
Cantoni, Roberto, and Karen Rignall. 2019. "Kingdom of the Sun: A Critical, Multiscalar Analysis of Morocco's Solar Energy Strategy." *Energy Research and Social Science* 51: 20–31.
Centre de Mise en Valeur Agricole. 2010. *Monographie de la zone*. Kelaa Mgouna: Ministère de l'Agriculture et de la Pêche Maritime.
Centre International ERSG-SDDOM (Centre International des Études et des Recherches Stratégiques de Gouvernance Spatiale et Développement Durable dans les Oasis et les Montagnes). 2017. *Appel à communication: Le premier congrès sur Économie du Patrimoine—Quelles contributions au développement durable des espaces fragiles des oasis et des zones de montagnes?* Ouarzazate: Centre International ERSG-SDDOM.
Chang, David A. 2011. "Enclosures of Land and Sovereignty: The Allotment of American Indian Lands." *Radical History Review* 109: 108–119.
Chanock, Martin. 1985. *Law, Custom and Social Order: The Colonial Experience in Malawi and Zambia*. Cambridge: Cambridge University Press.
———. 1991. "Paradigms, Policies and Property: A Review of the Customary Law of Tenure." In *Law in Colonial Africa*, edited by Kristin Mann and Richard L. Roberts, 61–84. London: James Currey.
Chatterjee, Partha. 2006. *The Politics of the Governed: Reflections on Popular Politics in Most of the World*. New York: Columbia University Press.
Chatty, Dawn, ed. 2006. *Nomadic Societies in the Middle East and North Africa: Entering the 21st Century*. Leiden: Brill.
Chiche, Jeanne. 2003. *Étude des conflits pastoraux dans le versant sud du Haut Atlas*. Ouarzazate: CBTHA (Programme de Conservation de la Biodiversité par la

Transhumance dans le Versant Sud du Haut Atlas), Programme des Nations Unies pour le Développement.
Chimhowu, Admos, and Phil Woodhouse. 2006. "Customary vs Private Property Rights? Dynamics and Trajectories of Vernacular Land Markets in Sub-Saharan Africa." *Journal of Agrarian Change* 6 (3): 346–371.
Cliggett, Lisa. 2003. "Gift-Remitting and Alliance Building in Zambian Modernity: Old Answers to Modern Problems." *American Anthropologist* 105 (3): 543–552.
Cooper, Frederick, and Randall M. Packard, eds. 1997. *International Development and the Social Sciences: Essays on the History and Politics of Knowledge.* Berkeley: University of California Press.
Côte, Marc. 2002. "Des oasis aux zones de mise en valeur: L'étonnant renouveau de l'agriculture saharienne." *Méditerranée* 99 (3/4): 5–14.
Courade, Georges, and Jean-Claude Devèze. 2006. "Introduction thématique. Maghreb: Des paysanneries en sursis?" *Afrique Contemporaine* 219(3): 19–28.
Courageot, Pierre. 1934. *Les communautés agraires du Maroc et le Protectorat Français.* Toulouse: Imprimerie Touloise.
Crawford, David L. 2003. "Arranging the Bones: Culture, Time, and In/equality in Berber Labor Organization." *Ethnos* 68 (4): 463–486.
———. 2005. "Royal Interest in Local Culture: Amazigh Identity and the Moroccan State." In *Nationalism and Minority Identities in Islamic Societies*, edited by Maya Shatzmiller, 164–194. Montreal: McGill-Queen's University Press.
———. 2008. *Moroccan Households in the World Economy: Labor and Inequality in a Berber Village.* Baton Rouge: Louisiana State University Press.
Davis, Diana K. 2005. "Indigenous Knowledge and the Desertification Debate: Problematising Expert Knowledge in North Africa." *Geoforum* 36 (4): 509–524.
———. 2006. "Neoliberalism, Environmentalism, and Agricultural Restructuring in Morocco." *Geographical Journal* 172 (2): 88–105.
———. 2007. *Resurrecting the Granary of Rome: Environmental History and French Colonial Expansion in North Africa.* Athens: Ohio University Press.
———. 2010. "Roundtable: Power, Knowledge, and Environmental History in the Middle East and North Africa." *International Journal of Middle East Studies* 42: 657–659.
———. 2012. "Scorched Earth: The Problematic Environmental History That Defines the Middle East." In *Is There a Middle East? The Evolution of a Geopolitical Concept*, edited by Michael E. Bonine, Abbas Amanat, and Michael Ezekiel Gasper, 170–187. Stanford, CA: Stanford University Press.
———. 2016. *The Arid Lands: History, Power, Knowledge.* Cambridge: MIT.
Davis, Diana K., and Edmund Burke, eds. 2011. *Environmental Imaginaries of the Middle East and North Africa.* Athens: Ohio University Press.
Davis, Mike. 2006. *Planet of Slums.* London: Verso.
De Angelis, Massimo. 2004. "Separating the Doing and the Deed: Capital and the Continuous Character of Enclosures." *Historical Materialism* 12 (2): 57–87.
De Foucauld, Charles. 1888. *Reconnaissance au Maroc, 1883–1884.* Paris: Challamel et Cie, Eds.
De Haas, Hein, ed. 2001. *Migration, Agricultural Transformations and Natural Resource Exploitation in the Oases of Morocco and Tunisia.* Final Scientific Report. IMAROM Project. Amsterdam: University of Amsterdam, AGIDS Research Institute.
———. 2003. "Migration and Development in Southern Morocco: The Disparate Socioeconomic Impacts of Out-Migration on the Todgha Oasis Valley." PhD diss., Katholieke Universiteit.
———. 2005. "International Migration, Remittances and Development: Myths and Facts." *Third World Quarterly* 26 (8): 1269–1284.

———. 2006. "Migration, Remittances and Regional Development in Southern Morocco." *Geoforum* 37 (4): 565–580.

———. 2007a. "Gestion d'eau dans les oasis marocaines, migrations et le rôle de l'état: Crise ou transformation? L'exemple du Todgha-Ferkla." Actes de Colloque, 13–16 November 2005. Rabat: Université Hassan II.

———. 2007b. "Morocco's Migration Experience: A Transitional Perspective." *International Migration* 54 (4): 39–70.

———. 2009. "International Migration and Regional Development in Morocco: A Review." *Journal of Ethnic and Migration Studies* 35 (10): 1571–1593.

De Haas, Hein, and Roald Plug. 2006. "Cherishing the Goose with the Golden Eggs: Trends in Migrant Remittances from Europe to Morocco 1970–2004." *International Migration Review* 40 (3): 603–634.

De Soto, Hernando. 2000. *The Mystery of Capital: Why Capitalism Triumphs in the West and Fails Everywhere Else*. New York: Basic Books.

———. 2003. "Listening to Barking Dogs: Property Law against Poverty in the Non-West." *Focaal* 41: 179–186.

Deback, Zoé. 2010. "Kelaat Mgouna: L'enfer des roses." *Tel Quel*, April 10–16, 2010.

Deeb, Lara, and Jessica Winegar. 2012. "Anthropology of Arab-Majority Societies." *Annual Review of Anthropology* 41: 537–558.

Denoix, Sylvie. 1996. "Introduction: Formes juridiques, enjeux sociaux et stratégies foncières." *Revue du monde musulman et de la Méditerranée* 79/80: 9–22.

Diekkrüger, Bernd, Henning Busche, Simone Giertz, and Gero Steup. 2010. "Hydrology." In *Impacts of Global Change on the Hydrological Cycle in West and Northwest Africa*, edited by Peter Speth, Michael Christoph, and Bernd Diekkrüger, 60–64. Berlin: Springer.

Dixon, Marion. 2014. "The Land Grab, Finance Capital, and Food Regime Restructuring: The Case of Egypt." *Review of African Political Economy* 41 (140): 232–248.

Dunn, Ross E. 1977. *Resistance in the Desert: Moroccan Responses to French Imperialism, 1881–1912*. Madison: University of Wisconsin Press.

Edelman, Marc. 2005. "Bringing the Moral Economy Back In . . . to the Study of Twenty-First Century Transnational Peasant Movements." *American Anthropologist* 107 (3): 331–345.

Edelman, Marc, Tony Weis, Amita Baviskar, Saturnino M. Borras Jr., Eric Holt-Giménez, Deniz Kaniyoti, and Wendy Wolford. 2014. "Introduction: Critical Perspectives on Food Sovereignty." *Journal of Peasant Studies* 41 (6): 911–931.

Eickelman, Dale F. 2001. *The Middle East and Central Asia: An Anthropological Approach*. 4th ed. New York: Pearson.

El Alaoui, Mohammed. 2002. *Étude sur le statut juridique des terres collectives au Maroc et les institutions coutumières et locales dans le versant sud du Haut Atlas*. Ouarzazate: CBTHA (Programme de Conservation de la Biodiversité par la Transhumance dans le Versant Sud du Haut Atlas), Programme des Nations Unies pour le Développement.

El Hamel, Chouki. 2013. *Black Morocco: A History of Slavery, Race, and Islam*. Cambridge: Cambridge University Press.

El Maliki, Fatim-Zohra. 2017. "Morocco's Hirak Movement: The People versus the Makhzen." *Jadaliyya*, June 2, 2017.

El Manouar, Mohamed. 2004. *Le Sud-Est marocain: Réflexion sur l'occupation et l'organisation des espaces sociaux et politiques. Le cas du Dadès*. Rabat: Phediprint.

Elliot, Alice. 2016. "The Makeup of Destiny: Predestination and the Labor of Hope in a Moroccan Emigrant Town." *American Ethnologist* 43 (3): 488–499.

Elloumi, Mohamed. 1997. "L'agriculture familiale méditerranéenne: Permanence et diversité avec références particulières aux pays du Maghreb." *Options Méditerranéennes* Série B (12): 177–185.

Empire Chérifien/Protectorat de la République Française au Maroc. 1919. "Dahir du 27 Avril 1919 (26 Redjeb 1337) organisant la tutelle administrative des collectivités indigènes et réglementant la gestion et l'aliénation des biens collectives." *Bulletin Officiel Édition Française* 8 (340): 375–378.

Ennaji, Mohammed. 1994. *Soldats, domestiques et concubines: L'esclavage au Maroc au XIXe Siècle*. Casablanca: Editions Eddif.

———. 1999. *Serving the Master: Slavery and Society in 19th Century Morocco*. Translated by Seth Graebner. New York: Palgrave Macmillan.

Enríquez, Laura J. 2010. *Reactions to the Market: Small Farmers in the Economic Reshaping of Nicaragua, Cuba, Russia, and China*. University Park: Pennsylvania State University Press.

Ensel, Remco. 1999. *Saints and Servants in Southern Morocco*. Leiden: E.J. Brill.

Fabietti, Ugo, and Philip C. Salzman, eds. 1996. *The Anthropology of Tribal and Peasant Pastoral Societies: The Dialectics of Social Cohesion and Fragmentation*. Pavia: Ibis.

Fabricant, Nicole. 2012. *Mobilizing Bolivia's Displaced: Indigenous Politics and the Struggle over Land*. Chapel Hill: University of North Carolina Press.

Fairhead, James, and Melissa Leach. 1996. *Misreading the African Landscape: Society and Ecology in a Forest-Savanna Mosaic*. Cambridge: Cambridge University Press.

———. 1998. *Reframing Deforestation: Global Analyses and Local Realities: Studies in West Africa*. London: Routledge.

Fairhead, James, and Ian Scoones. 2005. "Local Knowledge and the Social Shaping of Soil Investments: Critical Perspectives on the Assessment of Soil Degradation in Africa." *Land Use Policy* 22 (1): 33–41.

Fautras, Mathilde. 2015 "Injustices foncières, contestations et mobilisations collectives dans les espaces ruraux de Sidi Bouzid (Tunisie): Aux racines de la 'révolution?'" *Justice Spatiale* 7: 1–22.

Faysse, Nicolas. 2015. "The Rationale of the Green Morocco Plan: Missing Links between Goals and Implementation." *Journal of North Africa Studies* 4 (20): 622–634.

Feliu, Laura. 2004. "Le Mouvement culturel amazigh (MCA) au Maroc." *L'Année du Maghreb* 1: 273–285.

Ferguson, James. 2007. "Formalities of Poverty: Thinking about Social Assistance in Neoliberal South Africa." *African Studies Review* 50 (2): 71–86.

———. 2015. *Give a Man a Fish: Reflections on the New Politics of Distribution*. Durham, NC: Duke University Press.

FIDA (Fonds International de Développement Agricole). 2002. *Projet de développement des parcours et de l'élevage dans l'Oriental (PDPEO) Rapport d'évaluation intermédiaire*. Rabat: Fonds International de Développement Agricole.

———. 2008. *Royaume du Maroc: Évaluation du programme de pays*. Rabat: Fonds International de Développement Agricole.

Fink, Andreas, and Barbara Reichert, eds. 2009. *IMPETUS West Africa: An Integrated Approach to the Efficient Management of Scarce Water Resources in West Africa: Case Studies for Selected River Catchments in Different Climatic Zones, Third Final Report*. Interdisciplinary project of the Universities of Cologne and Bonn.

Food and Agriculture Organization. 2002. *Land Tenure and Rural Development*. Rome: Food and Agriculture Organization.

Freier, Korbinian P., Manfred Finckh, and Uwe A. Schneider. 2014. "Adaptation to New Climate by an Old Strategy? Modeling Sedentary and Mobile Pastoralism in Semi-arid Morocco." *Land* 3: 917–940.

Fusillier, Jean-Louis, Hacib El Amami, and Pierre-Yves Le Gal. 2009. "Stratégies des agriculteurs des oasis du Nefzaoua: Entre logique patrimoniale et productive, une mise en valeur agricole orientée vers l'extension des palmeraies, malgré les risques pour la durabilité des oasis." In *Gestion des ressources naturelles et développement durable des systems oasiens du Nefzaoua*, edited by Serge Marlet and Insaf Mekki, 1–9. Montpellier: CIRAD.

Galaty, John G., and Douglas L. Johnson. 1990. *The World of Pastoralism: Herding Systems in Comparative Perspective*. New York: Guilford Press.

Gallina, Andrea. 2006. "Migration, Financial Flows and Development in the Euro-Mediterranean Area." *Journal of North African Studies* 11 (1): 17–34.

Gallisot, René. 1964. "La question ouvrière au Maroc (1931–1935): Le prolétariat marocain à sa naissance et l'attitude du patronat européen." *Les Cahiers de Tunisie* 43 (3rd Trimester): 5–36.

Gana, Nouri, ed. 2013. *The Making of the Tunisian Revolution: Contexts, Architects, Prospects*. Edinburgh: Edinburgh University Press.

Geertz, Clifford, Hildred Geertz, and Lawrence Rosen. 1979. *Meaning and Order in Moroccan Society: Three Essays in Cultural Analysis*. Cambridge: Cambridge University Press.

Geismar, Haidy. 2015. "Anthropology and Heritage Regimes." *Annual Review of Anthropology* 44: 71–85.

Gellner, Ernest. 1969. *The Saints of the Atlas*. Chicago: University of Chicago Press.

Gellner, Ernest, and Charles Micaud, eds. 1972. *Arabs and Berbers: From Tribe to Nation in North Africa*. Lexington, MA: Lexington Books.

Genin, Didier, and Romain Simenel. 2011. "Endogenous Berber Forest Management and the Functional Shaping of Rural Forests in Southern Morocco: Implications for Shared Forest Management Options." *Human Ecology* 39 (3): 257–269.

Gertel, Jörg, and Ingo Breuer, eds. 2007. *Pastoral Morocco: Globalizing Scapes of Mobility and Insecurity*. Wiesbaden: Dr. Ludwig Reichart Verlag.

Geschiere, Peter. 2009. *The Perils of Belonging: Autochthony, Citizenship, and Exclusion in Africa and Europe*. Chicago: University of Chicago Press.

Geschiere, Peter, and Stephen Jackson. 2006. "Autochthony and the Crisis of Citizenship: Democratization, Decentralization, and the Politics of Belonging." *African Studies Review* 49 (2): 1–14.

Ghiche, Farid. 2009. "Plan Maroc Vert: La révolution agricole commence." *La Vie Éco*, April 17.

Glantz, Michael H., ed. 1994. *Drought Follows the Plow: Cultivating Marginal Areas*. Cambridge: Cambridge University Press.

Gluckman, Max. 1965. *The Ideas in Barotse Jurisprudence*. Manchester, UK: Manchester University Press.

Goodman, R. David. 2013. "Expediency, Ambivalence, and Inaction: The French Protectorate and Domestic Slavery in Morocco, 1912–1956." *Journal of Social History* 47 (1): 101–131.

Goodman, Jane E. 2005. *Berber Culture on the World Stage: From Village to Video*. Bloomington: Indiana University Press.

———. 2010. "Imazighen on Trial: Human Rights and Berber Identity in Algeria, 1985." In *Berbers and Others: Beyond Tribe and Nation in the Maghrib*, edited by Katherine Hoffman and Susan Gilson Miller, 103–126. Bloomington: Indiana University Press.

Goodman, Jane E., and Paul A. Silverstein, eds. 2008. *Bourdieu in Algeria: Colonial Politics, Ethnographic Practices, Theoretical Developments*. Lincoln: University of Nebraska Press.

Graciet, Catherine, and Éric Laurent. 2012. *Le roi prédateur*. Paris: Éditions du Seuil.

Graddy, T. Garrett. 2013. "Regarding Biocultural Heritage: In Situ Political Ecology of Agricultural Biodiversity in the Peruvian Andes." *Agriculture and Human Values* 30 (4): 587–604.

Gregg, Gary S., and Alison A. Geist. 1988. "The Socio-economic Organization of the Aït Imeghrane: Final Report Prepared for the O.R.M.V.A. of Ouarzazate." Unpublished manuscript.

Grove, Richard H. 1996. *Green Imperialism: Colonial Expansion, Tropical Island Edens and the Origins of Environmentalism, 1600–1860.* Cambridge: Cambridge University Press.

Guessous, Chakib. 2002. *L'exploitation de l'innocence: Le travail des enfants au Maroc.* Casablanca: Éditions Éddif.

Guillaume, Albert. 1960. *La propriété collective au Maroc.* Rabat: Éditions La Porte.

Guyer, Jane I. 1992. "Small Change: Individual Farm Work and Collective Life in a Western Nigerian Savanna Town, 1969–88." *Africa* 62 (4): 465–489.

———. 1993. "Wealth in People and Self-Realization in Equatorial Africa." *Man* 28 (2): 243–265.

———. 1996. "Diversity at Different Levels: Farm and Community in Western Nigeria." *Africa* 66 (1): 71–89.

———. 1997. *An African Niche Economy: Farming to Feed Ibadan, 1968–1988.* Edinburgh: Edinburgh University Press for the International African Institute.

———. 2004. *Marginal Gains: Monetary Transactions in Atlantic Africa.* Chicago: University of Chicago Press.

Guyer, Jane I., Eric F. Lambin, Lisa Cliggett, Peter Walker, Kojo Amanor, Thomas Bassett, Elizabeth Colson, Rod Hay, Katherine Homewood, Olga Linares, Opoku Pabi, Pauline Peters, Thayer Scudder, Matthew Turner, and John Unruh. 2007. "Temporal Heterogeneity in the Study of African Land Use: Interdisciplinary Collaboration between Anthropology, Human Geography and Remote Sensing." *Human Ecology* 35 (1): 3–17.

Hammoudi, Abdellah. 1980. "Segmentarity, Social Stratification, Political Power and Sainthood: Reflections on Gellner's Theses." *Economy and Society* 9: 279–303.

———. 1997. *Master and Disciple: The Cultural Foundations of Moroccan Authoritarianism.* Chicago: University of Chicago Press.

Hardt, Michael, and Antonio Negri. 2009. *Commonwealth.* Cambridge, MA: Harvard University Press.

Hart, David M. 1981. *Dadda 'Atta and His Forty Grandsons: The Socio-political Organisation of the Aït 'Atta of Southern Morocco.* Cambridge, UK: Middle East and North African Studies Press.

———. 2000. *Tribe and Society in Rural Morocco.* London: Frank Cass.

Harvey, David. 2003. *The New Imperialism.* Oxford: Oxford University Press.

———. 2011. "The Future of the Commons." *Radical History Review* 109: 101–107.

Hecht, Susanna B. 2010. "The New Rurality: Globalization, Peasants and the Paradoxes of Landscapes." *Land Use Policy* 27 (2): 161–169.

Hecht, Susanna B., and Alexander Cockburn. 2010. *The Fate of the Forest: Developers, Destroyers, and Defenders of the Amazon.* Chicago: University of Chicago Press.

Hecht, Susanna, and Sassan S. Saatchi. 2007. "Globalization and Forest Resurgence: Changes in Forest Cover in El Salvador." *BioScience* 57 (8): 663–672.

Hecht, Susanna, Susan Kandel, Ileana Gomes, Nelson Cuellar, and Herman Rosa. 2006. "Globalization, Forest Resurgence, and Environmental Politics in El Salvador." *World Development* 34 (2): 308–323.

Hoffman, Katherine E. 2000. "Administering Identities: State Decentralisation and Local Identification in Morocco." *Journal of North African Studies* 5 (3): 85–100.

———. 2002. "Moving and Dwelling: Building the Moroccan Ashelhi Homeland." *American Ethnologist* 29 (4): 928–962.

———. 2007. *We Share Walls: Language, Land, and Gender in Berber Morocco*. Malden, MA: Blackwell.
———. 2008. "Purity and Contamination: Language Ideologies in French Colonial Native Policy in Morocco." *Comparative Studies in Society and History* 50 (3): 724–752.
———. 2010. "Berber Law by French Means: Islam and Language in the Moroccan Hinterlands, 1930–1954." *Comparative Studies in Society and History* 52 (4): 851–880f.
———. 2015. "Pratiques Juridiques et Idéologies Langagières dans un Tribunal Non Officiellement Multilingue." *Anthropologie et Sociétés* 9 (3): 29–50.
Hoffman, Katherine, and Susan Gilson Miller, eds. 2010. *Berbers and Others: Beyond Tribe and Nation in the Maghrib*. Bloomington: University of Indiana Press.
Hoisington, William A. 1984. *The Casablanca Connection: French Colonial Policy, 1936–1943*. Raleigh: University of North Carolina Press.
———. 1995. *Lyautey and the French Conquest of Morocco*. New York: Palgrave Macmillan.
Holston, James. 2008. *Insurgent Citizenship: Disjunctions of Democracy and Modernity in Brazil*. Princeton, NJ: Princeton University Press.
Holt-Giménez, Eric. 2009. "From Food Crisis to Food Sovereignty: The Challenge of Social Movements." *Monthly Review* 61 (3): 142–156.
Horlings, Ina, and Terry Marsden. 2011. "Towards the Real Green Revolution? Exploring the Conceptual Dimensions of a New Ecological Modernisation of Agriculture That Could 'Feed the World.'" *Global Environmental Change* 21: 441–452.
Houdret, Annabelle. 2012. "The Water Connection: Irrigation, Water Grabbing and Politics in Southern Morocco." *Water Alternatives* 5 (2): 284–303.
Ilahiane, Hsain. 1999. "The Berber Agdal Institution: Indigenous Range Management in the Atlas Mountains." *Ethnology* 38 (1): 21–45.
———. 2001a. "The Social Mobility of the Haratine and the Re-working of Bourdieu's Habitus on the Saharan Frontier, Morocco." *American Anthropologist* 103 (2): 380–394.
———. 2001b. "The Break-Up of the Ksar: Changing Settlement Patterns and Environmental Management in Southern Morocco." *Africa Today* 48 (1): 20–48.
———. 2004. *The Political Ecology of a Moroccan Oasis: Ethnicities, Community Making, and Agrarian Change*. Lanham, MD: University Press of America.
———. 2006. *Historical Dictionary of the Berbers (Imazighen)*. Lanham, MD: Scarecrow Press.
Iskander, Natasha. 2010. *Creative State: Forty Years of Migration and Development Policy in Morocco and Mexico*. Ithaca, NY: Cornell University Press.
Jaafar, Brahim, Mohamed Yessef, and Abderrahmane Ramdan. 1996. "Le partage des terres collectives dans la moyenne vallée du Dra (Maroc): Atouts et contraintes pour la réhabilitation des parcours." *Option Méditerranéennes* Série B (13): 169–197.
Jacques-Meunié, Djinn. 1958. "Hiérarchie Sociale au Maroc Présaharien." *Hesperis* 9: 29–43.
Jennan, Lahsen. 1986. "Mutations récentes des campagnes du Moyen Atlas et de ses bordures." *Méditerranée: Revue Échographique des Pays Méditerranéens* 59 (4): 49–62.
Joffé, E. G. H. 1985. "The Moroccan Nationalist Movement: Istiqlal, the Sultan, and the Country." *Journal of African History* 26 (4): 289–307.
Johnson, Douglas L. 1969. "The Nature of Nomadism: A Comparative Study of Pastoral Migrations in Southwestern Asia and Northern Africa." Department of Geography Research Paper No. 118, University of Chicago, Chicago, IL.
Joly, Fernand. 1954. "Le sud présaharien marocain." *Cahiers de l'Information Géographique* 1: 20–32.
———. 1979. "L'homme et le Sud au Maghreb Atlantique: Essai sur les rapports de l'homme et du milieu en bordure d'un désert." *Méditerranée* 35 (1/2): 27–37.

Jones, Schuyler. 2005. "Comment: Transhumance Re-examined." *Journal of the Royal Anthropological Institute* 11 (2): 357–359.
Joseph, Miranda. 2002. *Against the Romance of Community*. Minneapolis: University of Minnesota Press.
Kalir, Barak, and Willem van Schendel. 2017. "Introduction: Nonrecording States between Legibility and Looking Away." *Focaal* 77: 1–7.
Kapchan, Deborah A. 1996. *Gender on the Market: Moroccan Women and the Revoicing of Tradition*. Philadelphia: University of Pennsylvania Press.
Karmaoui, Ahmed, and Stefania Balica. 2019. "A New Flood Vulnerability Index Adapted for the Pre-Saharan Region." *International Journal of River Basin Management* 17 (4/5): 1–15.
Karsenty, Alain. 1988. "Les 'terres collectives' du Gharb et le Protectorat: Modèle et réalités." *Annuaire de l'Afrique du Nord* 27: 429–447.
Kay, Cristóbal. 2008. "Reflections on Latin American Rural Studies in the Neoliberal Globalization Period: A New Rurality?" *Development and Change* 39 (6): 915–943.
Kearney, Michael. 1996. *Reconceptualizing the Peasantry: Anthropology in Global Perspective*. Boulder, CO: Westview Press.
Kelly, Alice B., and Nancy Lee Peluso. 2015. "Frontiers of Commodification: State Lands and Their Formalization." *Society and Natural Resources* 28: 473–495.
Kerr, Rachel. 2012. "Lessons from the Old Green Revolution for the New: Social, Environmental and Nutritional Issues for Agricultural Change in Africa." *Progress in Development Studies* 12 (2/3): 213–229.
Koohafkan, Parviz, and Miguel A. Altieri. 2011. *Globally Important Agricultural Heritage Systems: A Legacy for the Future*. Rome: Food and Agriculture Organization.
Kusunose, Yoko, and Karen Rignall. 2018. "The Long-Term Development Impacts of International Migration Remittances for Sending Households: Evidence from Morocco." *Migration and Development* 7 (3): 412–434.
Lafuente, Gilles. 1999. *La Politique Berbère de la France et le Nationalisme Marocain*. Paris: Éditions L'Harmattan.
Le Polain de Waroux, Yann, and Jeanne Chiche. 2013. "Market Integration, Livelihood Transitions and Environmental Change in Areas of Low Agricultural Productivity: A Case Study from Morocco." *Human Ecology* 41 (4): 535–545.
Le Roy, Étienne, Alain Karsenty, and Alain Bertrand. 1995. *La sécurisation foncière en Afrique: Pour une gestion viable des ressources renouvelables*. Paris: Karthala.
Leach, Melissa, and Robin Mearns, eds. 1996. *The Lie of the Land: Challenging Received Wisdom on the African Environment*. Oxford, UK: James Currey.
Lefébure, Claude. 1979. "Accès aux ressources collectives et structure sociale: L'estivage chez les Ayt Atta (Maroc)." In *Pastoral Production and Society*, edited by L'Équipe Écologie et Anthropologie des Sociétés Pastorales, 115–126. Cambridge: Cambridge University Press.
Lefèvre, Raphaël. 2017. "'No to *Hoghra!*': Morocco's Protest Movement and Its Prospects." *Journal of North African Studies* 22 (1): 1–5.
Lérin, François. 2010. "Pastoralisme méditerranéen: Patrimoine culturel et paysages et développement durable." *Options Méditerranéennes* Série A (93): 73–78.
Leveau, Rémy. 1985. *Le fellah marocain: Défenseur du trône*. 2nd ed. Paris: Presses de la Fondation Nationale des Sciences Politiques.
Li, Tania Murray. 2007. *The Will to Improve: Governmentality, Development, and the Practice of Politics*. Durham, NC: Duke University Press.
———. 2014a. *Land's End: Capitalist Relations on an Indigenous Frontier*. Durham, NC: Duke University Press.

———. 2014b. "What Is Land? Assembling a Resource for Global Investment." *Transactions of the Institute of British Geographers* 39 (4): 589–602.
———. 2015. "Can There Be Food Sovereignty Here?" *Journal of Peasant Studies* 42 (1): 205–211.
Linebaugh, Peter. 2008. *The Magna Carta Manifesto: Liberties and Commons for All*. Berkeley: University of California Press.
Litvack, Jennie. 2007. "The Poverty Mapping Application in Morocco." In *More Than a Pretty Picture: Using Poverty Maps to Design Better Policies and Interventions*, edited by Tara Bedi, Aline Coudouel, and Kenneth Simler, 208–224. Washington, DC: World Bank.
Lyautey, Hubert. 1927. *Paroles d'action: Madagascar, Sud-Oranais, Oran, Maroc (1900–1926)*. Paris: Libraire Armand Colin.
Maddy-Weitzman, Bruce. 2011. *The Berber Identity Movement and the Challenge to North African States*. Austin: University of Texas Press.
Maghraoui, Driss. 2012. "The Perverse Effect of Good Governance: Lessons from Morocco." *Middle East Policy* 19 (2): 49–65.
———, ed. 2013. *Revisiting the Colonial Past in Morocco*. London: Routledge.
Mahdi, Mohamed. 1999. *Pasteurs de l'Atlas: Production pastorale, droit et rituel*. Casablanca: Fondation Konrad Adenauer.
———. 2014. "Devenir du foncier agricole au Maroc: Un cas d'accaparement des terres." *New Méditerranées* 4: 2–10.
———. 2015. "Revendiquer sa 'part' de ses propres terres!" Paper presented at the Conference of the Arab Council for the Social Sciences, Beirut, Lebanon, March 13–15, 2015.
Mahdi, Mohamed, and Pablo Dominguez. 2009. "Les *agdals* de l'Atlas marocain: Un patrimoine en danger." *Bulletin Économique et Social du Maroc*, July 2009, 327–350.
Mamdani, Mahmood. 1996. *Citizen and Subject: Contemporary Africa and the Legacy of Late Colonialism*. Princeton, NJ: Princeton University Press.
———. 2012. *Define and Rule: Native as Political Identity*. Cambridge, MA: Harvard University Press.
Marei, Fouad Gehad, Mona Atia, Lisa Bhungalia, and Omar Dewachi. 2018. "Interventions on the Politics of Governing the 'Ungovernable.'" *Political Geography* 67: 176–186.
Marx, Emmanuel. 1977. "The Tribe as Unit of Subsistence: Nomadic Pastoralism in the Middle East." *American Anthropologist* 79 (2): 343–363.
Marzin, Jacques, Pascal Bonnet, Omar Bessaoud, and Christine Ton-Nu. 2016. *Study on Small-Scale Family Farming in the Near East and North Africa Region: Synthesis*. Cairo: Food and Agriculture Organization, Regional Office for the Near East and North Africa.
Masbah, Mohammed. 2017. "A New Generation of Protests in Morocco? How Hirak al-Rif Endures." *Policy Alternatives*, November 2017, 1–7.
Maxwell, Gavin. 1966. *Lords of the Atlas: The Rise and Fall of the House of Glaoua, 1893–1956*. New York: E.P. Dutton.
McCabe, J. Terrence. 2003. "Sustainability and Livelihood Diversification among Maasai of Northern Tanzania." *Human Organization* 62 (2): 100–111.
———. 2004. *Cattle Bring Us to Our Enemies: Turkana Ecology, Politics, and Raiding in a Disequilibrium System*. Ann Arbor: University of Michigan Press.
McCarthy, James. 2005. "Commons as Counterhegemonic Projects." *Capitalism Nature Socialism* 16 (1): 9–24.
McCay, Bonnie J., and James M. Acheson. 1987. *The Question of the Commons: The Culture and Ecology of Communal Resources*. Tucson: University of Arizona Press.

McDougall, James. 2010. "Histories of Heresy and Salvation: Arabs, Berbers, Community and the State." In *Berbers and Others: Beyond Tribe and Nation in the Maghrib*, edited by Hoffman, Katherine E. and Miller, Susan Gilson, 15–38. Bloomington: Indiana University Press.

McKee, Emily. 2016. *Dwelling in Conflict: Negev Landscapes and the Boundaries of Belonging*. Stanford, CA: Stanford University Press.

McMichael, Philip. 2008. "Peasants Make Their Own History, but Not Just as they Please. . . ." *Journal of Agrarian Change* 8 (2/3): 205–228.

——. 2009. "A Food Regime Genealogy." *Journal of Peasant Studies* 36 (1): 139–169.

Mendes, Lloyd. 1988. *Private and Communal Land Tenure in Morocco's Western High Atlas Mountains: Complements, Not Ideological Opposites*. London: Overseas Development Institute, Agricultural Administration Unit.

Merry, Sally Engle. 1988. "Legal Pluralism." *Law and Society Review* 22 (5): 869–896.

——. 2006. *Human Rights and Gender Violence: Translating International Law into Local Justice*. Chicago: University of Chicago Press.

Métral, Francoise. 2000. "Managing Risk: Sheep-Rearing and Agriculture in the Syrian Steppe." In *The Transformation of Nomadic Society in the Arab East*, edited by Martha Mundy and Basim Musallam, 123–144. Cambridge: Cambridge University Press.

Mezzine, Larbi. 1980–1981. "Ta'qitt de Ayt 'Atman: Le recueil des règles de coutume d'un groupe de Qsur de la moyenne vallée de l'Oued Ziz." *Hespéris Tamuda* 19: 89–121.

Michaux-Bellaire, Édouard. 1924. "Les terres collectives au Maroc et la tradition." *Hespéris: Archives Berbères et Bulletin de l'Institut des Hautes-Études Marocaines* 4: 141–151.

Miers, Suzanne, and Igor Kopytoff, eds. 1977. *Slavery in Africa: Historical and Anthropological Perspectives*. Madison: University of Wisconsin Press.

Mikhail, Alan. 2011. *Nature and Empire in Ottoman Egypt: An Environmental History*. New York: Cambridge University Press.

——, ed. 2013. *Water on Sand: Environmental Histories of the Middle East and North Africa*. Oxford: Oxford University Press.

——. 2014. *The Animal in Ottoman Egypt*. Oxford: Oxford University Press.

——. 2017. *Under Osman's Tree: The Ottoman Empire, Egypt, and Environmental History*. Chicago: University of Chicago Press.

Miller, James A. 1984. *Imlil: A Moroccan Mountain Community in Change*. Boulder, CO: Westview Press.

Milliot, Louis. 1922. *Les Terres collectives (blad djema'a): Étude de législation marocaine*. Paris: Éditions Ernest Leroux.

Mintz, Sidney W. 1960. *Worker in the Cane: A Puerto Rican Life History*. New Haven, CT: Yale University Press.

Mitchell, Timothy. 2002. *Rule of Experts: Egypt, Techno-Politics, Modernity*. Berkeley: University of California Press.

Montagne, Robert, ed. 1952. *Naissance du prolétariat marocain: Enquête collective exécutée de 1948 à 1950*. Paris: Éditions Peyronnet.

——. 1973. *The Berbers: Their Social and Political Organisation*. Translated by David Seddon. London: Frank Cass.

Moore, Jason W. 2008. "Ecological Crises and the Agrarian Question in World-Historical Perspective." *Monthly Review* 60: 54–62.

Moore, Sally Falk. 1978. *Law as Process*. London: Routledge and Kegan Paul.

Moujoud, Nasima, and Dolorès Pourette. 2005. "'Traite' de femmes migrantes, domesticité et prostitution: À propos de migrations interne et externe." *Cahiers d'Études Africaines* 45 (179/180): 1093–1121.

Mousaif, Abderrahmane. 2008. *Contrat programme: Réalisation, entraves et perspectives.* Ouarzazate: Direction des Affaires Rurales, Ministère de l'Intérieur.

———. 2009. *Rapport soumis à Monsieur le Gouverneur: Apurement juridique des terres collectives.* Ouarzazate: Direction des Affaires Rurales, Ministère de l'Intérieur.

Munson, Henry, Jr. 1993. "Rethinking Gellner's Segmentary Analysis of Morocco's Aït 'Atta." *Man* 28 (2): 267–280.

Mutersbaugh, Tad. 2002. "Migration, Common Property, and Communal Labor: Cultural Politics and Agency in a Mexican Village." *Political Geography* 21 (4): 473–494.

Naciri, Mohamed. 1986. "Les ksouriens sur la route: Émigration et mutation spatiale de l'habitat dans l'oasis de Tinjdad." *Annuaire de l'Afrique du Nord* 25: 347–364.

Naji, Salima. 2001. *Art et architectures berbères du Maroc: Atlas et vallées présahariennes.* Aix-en-Provence: Édisud.

Narotzky, Susana. 2016. "Where Have All the Peasants Gone?" *Annual Review of Anthropology* 45: 301–318.

Nelson, Cynthia, ed. 1973. *The Desert and the Sown: Nomads in the Wider Society.* Berkeley: University of California Press.

Netting, Robert McC. 1993. *Smallholders, Householders: Farm Families and the Ecology of Intensive, Sustainable Agriculture.* Stanford, CA: Stanford University Press.

Neumann, Roderick K. 2002. *Imposing Wilderness: Struggles over Livelihood and Nature Preservation in Africa.* Berkeley: University of California Press.

Niamir-Fuller, Maryam, ed. 1999. *Managing Mobility in African Rangelands: The Legitimization of Transhumance.* London: Intermediate Technology Publications.

Obarrio, Juan M. 2010. "Remains: To Be Seen. Third Encounter between State and 'Customary' in Northern Mozambique." *Cultural Anthropology* 25 (2): 263–300.

———. 2014. *The Spirit of the Laws in Mozambique.* Chicago: University of Chicago Press.

Ostrom, Elinor. 1990. *Governing the Commons: The Evolution of Institutions for Collective Action.* Cambridge: Cambridge University Press.

Ostrom, Elinor, Joanna Burger, Christopher B. Field, and Richard B. Norgaard. 1999. "Revisiting the Commons: Local Lessons, Global Challenges." *Science* 284: 278–284.

Park, Thomas. 1996. *Historical Dictionary of Morocco.* Lanham, MD: Scarecrow Press.

Pascon, Paul. 1980. *Études rurales: Idées et enquêtes sur la campagne marocaine.* Rabat: Société Marocaine des Éditeurs Réunis.

———. 1986. *Capitalism and Agriculture in the Haouz of Marrakesh.* London: KPI Limited.

Pascon, Paul, and Mohammed Ennaji. 1986. *Les paysans sans terre au Maroc.* Casablanca: Les Éditions Toubkal.

Peluso, Nancy Lee. 1994. *Rich Forests, Poor People: Resource Control and Resistance in Java.* Berkeley: University of California Press.

Pennell, C. R. 2000. *Morocco since 1830: A History.* New York: New York University Press.

Peters, Pauline E. 1994. *Dividing the Commons: Politics, Policy, and Culture in Botswana.* Charlottesville: University Press of Virginia.

———. 2004. "Inequality and Social Conflict over Land in Africa." *Journal of Agrarian Change* 4 (3): 269–314.

———. 2009. "Challenges in Land Tenure and Land Reform in Africa: Anthropological Contributions." *World Development* 37 (8): 1317–1325.

Peutz, Nathalie. 2011. "Bedouin 'Abjection': World Heritage, Worldliness, and Worthiness at the Margins of Arabia." *American Ethnologist* 38 (2): 338–360.

Platteau, Jean-Philippe. 1996. "The Evolutionary Theory of Land Rights as Applied to Sub-Saharan Africa: A Critical Assessment." *Development and Change* 27 (1): 29–86.

Pouillon, François, ed. 1997. "Enquêtes dans la bibliographie de Jacques Berque: Parcours d'histoire sociale." *Revue du Monde Musulman et de la Méditerranée* 83–84 (1): 9–201.

Programme des Nations Unies pour le Développement (PNUD). 1999. *Document de projet (MOR/99/G33/A/1G/99): Conservation de la biodiversité par la transhumance dans le versant sud du Haut Atlas*. Rabat: Programme des Nations Unies pour le Développement.

Rachik, Hassan. 2012. *Le proche et le lointain: Un siècle d'anthropologie au Maroc*. Marseille: Éditions Parenthèses/Maison Méditerranéenne des Sciences de l'Homme.

———, ed. 2016. *Contester le droit: Communautés, familles et héritage au Maroc*. Casablanca: Éditions la Croisée des Chemins.

Reid, Herbert, and Betsy Taylor. 2010. *Recovering the Commons: Democracy, Place, and Global Justice*. Champaign: University of Illinois Press.

Reynolds, James, and D. Mark Stafford Smith, eds. 2002. *Global Desertification: Do Humans Cause Deserts?* Berlin: Dahlem University Press.

Richards, Paul. 1985. *Indigenous Agricultural Revolution: Ecology and Food Production in West Africa*. Boulder, CO: Westview Press.

Rignall, Karen. 2013. "Time, Children, and Getting Ethnography Done in Southern Morocco." In *Encountering Morocco: Reflections on North African Fieldwork and Ethnography*, edited by David Crawford and Rachel Newcomb, 40–55. Bloomington: Indiana University Press.

———. 2016. "Solar Power, State Power, and the Politics of Energy Transition in Pre-Saharan Morocco." *Environment and Planning A* 48: 540–557.

Rignall, Karen, and Mona Atia. 2017. "The Global Rural: Relational Geographies of Poverty and Uneven Development." *Geography Compass* 11 (7): 1–11.

Rivet, Daniel. 1984. "Exotisme et 'pénétration scientifique': L'effort de découverte du Maroc par les Français au début du XXe siècle." In *Connaissances du Maghreb: Sciences sociales et colonisation*, edited by Jean-Claude Vatin, 95–109. Paris: Éditions du Centre nationale de la recherche scientiques.

———. 1988. *Lyautey et l'institution du Protectorat Français au Maroc, 1912–1925*. Paris: Éditions L'Harmattan.

———. 1999. *Le Maroc de Lyautey à Mohammed V*. Paris: Éditions Denoël.

———. 2012. *Histoire du Maroc*. Paris: Éditions Fayard.

Robertson, A. F. 1987. *The Dynamics of Productive Relationships: African Share Contracts in Comparative Perspective*. Cambridge: Cambridge University Press.

Rose, Nikolas. 1999. *Powers of Freedom: Reframing Political Thought*. Cambridge: Cambridge University Press.

Rosen, Lawrence. 1984. *Bargaining for Reality: The Construction of Social Relations in a Muslim Community*. Chicago: University of Chicago Press.

———. 2000. *The Justice of Islam: Comparative Perspectives on Islamic Law and Society*. Oxford: Oxford University Press.

———. 2008. *Law as Culture: An Invitation*. Princeton, NJ: Princeton University Press.

Rosenberger, Bernard. 2001. *Société, pouvoir et alimentation: Nourriture et précarité au Maroc précolonial*. Rabat: Alizés.

Royaume du Maroc. 1994. "Recensement Général de la Population et de l'Habitat, 1994." https://www.hcp.ma/glossary/Recensement-General-de-la-Population-et-de-l-Habitat_gw115.html.

———. 1996. *Réflexion sur les terres collectives*. Colloque National sur les Terres Collectives. Rabat: Ministère de l'Intérieur, Secrétariat General, Direction des Affaires Rurales.

———. 2004. "Recensement Général de la Population et de l'Habitat, 2004." http://www.hcp.ma/Recensement-general-de-la-population-et-de-l-habitat-2004_a633.html.

———. 2005. *Dossier: Le foncier agricole. Situation de l'agriculture marocaine 2005*. Rabat: Ministère de l'Agriculture du Développement Rural et du Pêche Maritime.

———. 2006. *Prospective Maroc 2030. Exclusion, inégalité et pauvreté: La transition sociale et ses déterminants*. Rabat: Direction de la Statistique, Haut-Commissariat au Plan.

———. 2010a. *Carte de Pauvreté, 2007*. Rabat: Direction de la Statistique, Haut-Commissariat au Plan.

———. 2010b. *Discours de SM le Roi à la Nation à l'occasion de la fête du Trône*. https://www.maroc.ma/fr/discours-royaux/discours-de-sm-le-roi-%C3%A0-la-nation-%C3%A0-loccasion-de-la-f%C3%AAte-du-tr%C3%B4ne.

———. 2014. *Recensement Général de la Population et de l'Habitat, 2004*. https://www.hcp.ma/glossary/Recensement-General-de-la-Population-et-de-l-Habitat_gw115.html.

Sahli, Zoubir. 1997. "Risques et enjeux dans les agricultures familiales: Cas des zones montagneuses, arides et semi-arides." *Options méditerranéennes* Série B (12): 111–124.

Salime, Zakia. 2011. *Between Feminism and Islam: Human Rights and Sharia Law in Morocco*. Minneapolis: University of Minnesota Press.

Salmon, M. Georges. 1904. "Quelques particularités de la propriété foncière dans le R'arb." *Archives Marocaines* 2 (1): 144–148.

Salzman, Philip C. 1971. "Movement and Resource Extraction among Pastoral Nomads: The Case of the Shah Nawazi Baluch." *Anthropological Quarterly* 44 (3): 185–197.

Schilling, Janpeter, Korbinian P. Freier, Elke Hertig, and Jürgen Scheffran. 2012. "Climate Change, Vulnerability and Adaptation in North Africa with Focus on Morocco." *Agriculture, Ecosystems and Environment* 156: 12–26.

Scoones, Ian, ed. 1994. *Living with Uncertainty: New Directions in Pastoral Development*. London: Intermediate Technology Publications.

———. 1999. "New Ecology and the Social Sciences: What Prospects for a Fruitful Engagement?" *Annual Review of Anthropology* 28: 479–507.

Scoones, Ian, Marc Edelman, Saturnino M. Borras Jr., Ruth Hall, Wendy Wolford, and Ben White. 2017. "Emancipatory Rural Politics: Confronting Authoritarian Populism." *Journal of Peasant Studies* 45 (1): 1–20.

Scott, James C. 1985. *Weapons of the Weak: Everyday Forms of Peasant Resistance*. New Haven, CT: Yale University Press.

———. 1992. *Domination and the Arts of Resistance: Hidden Transcripts*. New Haven, CT: Yale University Press.

———. 1998. *Seeing Like a State: How Certain Schemes to Improve the Human Condition Have Failed*. New Haven, CT: Yale University Press.

———. 2009. *The Art of Not Being Governed: An Anarchist History of Upland Southeast Asia*. New Haven, CT: Yale University Press.

Seddon, David. 1981. *Moroccan Peasants: A Century of Change in the Eastern Rif, 1870–1970*. Kent, UK: Dawson.

———. 1986. "Riot and Rebellion: Political Responses to Economic Crisis in North Africa (Tunisia, Morocco and Sudan)." Discussion Paper 196, School of Development Studies, East Anglia, UK.

Sedra, Moulay Hassan. 2015. "Date Palm Status and Perspective in Morocco." In *Date Palm Genetic Resources and Utilization*, edited by Jameel M. Al-Khayri, Shri Mohan Jain, and Dennis V. Johnson, 257–323. Dordrecht: Springer.

Shipton, Parker. 2007. *The Nature of Entrustment: Intimacy, Exchange, and the Sacred in Africa*. New Haven, CT: Yale University Press.

Sikor, Thomas, and Daniel Müller. 2009. "The Limits of State-Led Land Reform." *World Development* 37 (8): 1307–1433.

Silverstein, Paul A. 2004. *Algeria in France: Transpolitics, Race, and Nation*. Bloomington: Indiana University Press.

———. 2010. "The Local Dimensions of Transnational Berberism: Racial Politics, Land Rights, and Cultural Activism in Southeastern Morocco." In *Berbers and Others:*

Beyond Tribe and Nation in the Maghrib, edited by Katherine E. Hoffman and Susan Gilson Miller, 83–102. Bloomington: Indiana University Press.

———. 2011. "Masquerade Politics: Race, Islam, and the Scale of Amazigh Activism in Southeastern Morocco." *Nations and Nationalism* 17 (1): 65–84.

———. 2013. "The Pitfalls of Transnational Consciousness: Amazigh Activism as a Scalar Dilemma." *Journal of North African Studies* 18 (5): 768–778.

———. 2015. "The Diaspora and the Cemetery: Emigration and Social Transformation in a Moroccan Oasis Community." *Journal of North African Studies* 20 (1): 92–108.

Skounti, Ahmed. 2012. *Le sang et le sol: Nomadisme et sédentarisation au Maroc*. Rabat: Institut Royal de la Culture Amazighe.

Slyomovics, Susan. 2005. *The Performance of Human Rights in Morocco*. Philadelphia: University of Pennsylvania Press.

———. 2009. "Reparations in Morocco: The Symbolic Dirham." In *Waging War, Making Peace: Reparations and Human Rights*, edited by Barbara Rose Johnston and Susan Slyomovics, 95–114. A report from the Reparations Task Force, the Committee for Human Rights, American Anthropological Association. Walnut Creek, CA: Left Coast Press.

Smith, Neil. (1984) 2008. *Uneven Development: Nature, Capital, and the Production of Space*. Athens: University of Georgia Press.

Steinmann, Susanne H. 2001. "Gender, Pastoralism, and Intensification: Changing Environmental Resource Use in Morocco." *Yale F&ES Bulletin* 103:81–107.

Subramanian, Ajantha. 2009. *Shorelines: Space and Rights in South India*. Stanford, CA: Stanford University Press.

Swearingen, Will D. 1988. *Moroccan Mirages: Agrarian Dreams and Deceptions, 1912–1986*. London: I.B. Tauris.

———. 1992. "Drought Hazard in Morocco." *Geographical Review* 82 (4): 401–412.

Swearingen, Will D., and Abdellatif Bencherifa, eds. 1996. *The North African Environment at Risk*. Boulder, CO: Westview Press.

Taylor, J. Edward, and Alejandro Lopez-Feldman. 2010. "Does Migration Make Rural Households More Productive? Evidence from Mexico." *Journal of Development Studies* 46 (1): 68–90.

Tiffen, Mary, Michael Mortimore, and Francis Gichuki. 1994. *More People, Less Erosion: Environmental Recovery in Kenya*. Chichester, UK: John Wiley and Sons for the Overseas Development Institute.

Tozy, Mohamed. 1999. *Monarchie et Islam Politique au Maroc*. Paris: Presses de la Fondation Nationale des Sciences Politiques.

Trumbull, George R. 2017. "The Environmental Turn in Middle East History." *International Journal of Middle East Studies* 49 (1): 173–180.

Tsing, Anna Lowenhaupt. 2015. *The Mushroom at the End of the World: On the Possibility of Life in Capitalist Ruins*. Princeton, NJ: Princeton University Press.

Turner, Matthew D. 2011. "The New Pastoral Development Paradigm: Engaging the Realities of Property Institutions and Livestock Mobility in Dryland Africa." *Society and Natural Resources* 24 (5): 469–484.

United Nations Development Programme (UNDP). 2011. *Sustainability and Equity: A Better Future for All*. New York: United Nations Development Programme Human Development Report.

———. 2012. *Africa Human Development Report 2012: Towards a Food Secure Future*. New York: United Nations Development Programme Regional Bureau for Africa.

Van Buu, Edouard. 1995. "Chronique juridique marocaine." *Annuaire de l'Afrique du Nord* 34: 687–700.

Van der Ploeg, Jan. 2008. *The New Peasantries: Struggles for Autonomy and Sustainability in an Era of Empire and Globalization*. London: Earthscan.
———. 2010. "The Peasantries of the Twenty-First Century: The Commoditisation Debate Revisited." *Journal of Peasant Studies* 37 (1): 1–30.
———. 2014. "Peasant-Driven Agricultural Growth and Food Sovereignty." *Journal of Peasant Studies* 41 (6): 999–1030.
Veltmeyer, Henry. 2006. "Introduction: Development and the Agrarian Question." *Canadian Journal of Development Studies* 27 (4): 445–448.
Venema, Bernhard, and A. Mguild. 2002. "The Vitality of Local Political Institutions in the Middle Atlas, Morocco." *Ethnology* 41 (2): 103–117.
Waterbury, John. 1970. *Commander of the Faithful: The Moroccan Political Elite—A Study in Segmented Politics*. New York: Columbia University Press.
Watts, Michael. 2003. "Development and Governmentality." *Singapore Journal of Tropical Geography* 24 (1): 6–34.
———. 2004. "Antimonies of Community: Some Thoughts on Geography, Resources and Empire." *Transactions of the Institute of British Geographers* 29 (2): 195–216.
———. 2012. Review of *Class Dynamics of Agrarian Change*, by Henry Bernstein. *Journal of Peasant Studies* 39 (1): 199–204.
Weis, Tony. 2010. "The Accelerating Biophysical Contradictions of Industrial Capitalist Agriculture." *Journal of Agrarian Change* 10 (3): 315–341.
White, Sam. 2011. *The Climate of Rebellion in the Early Modern Ottoman Empire*. Cambridge: Cambridge University Press.
Williams, Raymond. 1975. *The Country and the City*. Oxford: Oxford University Press.
———. (1976) 1985. *Keywords: A Vocabulary of Culture and Society*. Rev. ed. New York: Oxford University Press.
Wilson, Alice. 2015. "Refracting Custom in Western Sahara's Quest for Statehood." *Political and Legal Anthropology Review* 38 (1): 72–90.
Wizara al-Dakhiliya. 2007. *Dalil kira' al-aradi al-juma'iyya*. Rabat: Mudiriya as-Shu'un el-Qarawiya, Wizara al-Dakhiliya, Mamlaka al-Maghribiya.
———. 2008. *Dalil na'ib al-aradi el jumu'a*. Rabat: Mudiriya as-Shu'un el-Qarawiya, Wizara al-Dakhiliya, Mamlaka al-Maghribiya.
Wolf, Anne. 2019. "Morocco's Hirak Movement and Legacies of Contention in the Rif." *Journal of North African Studies* 24 (1): 1–6.
Wolf, Eric R. 1968. *Peasant Wars of the Twentieth Century*. New York: Harper and Row.
———. 1982. *Europe and the People without History*. Berkeley: University of California Press.
———. 2001. *Pathways of Power: Building an Anthropology of the Modern World*. Berkeley: University of California Press.
Wolford, Wendy. 2010. *This Land Is Ours Now: Social Mobilization and the Meanings of Land in Brazil*. Durham, NC: Duke University Press.
World Bank. 2006. *Kingdom of Morocco Country Economic Memorandum: Fostering Higher Growth and Employment with Productive Diversification and Competitiveness*. Washington, DC: World Bank.
———. 2007. *Kingdom of Morocco: Moving Out of Poverty in Morocco*. Washington, DC: World Bank.
Wyrtzen, Jonathan. 2015. *Making Morocco: Colonial Intervention and the Politics of Identity*. Ithaca, NY: Cornell University Press.
Yessef, Mohamed, and Mohamed Aït Hamza. 2007. *Étude nationale sur la transhumance*. Ouarzazate: Programme de Conservation de la Biodiversité par la Transhumance dans le Versant Sud du Haut Atlas, Programme des Nations Unies pour le Développement.

Zelizer, Viviana A. 2005. *The Purchase of Intimacy*. Princeton, NJ: Princeton University Press.
Zereini, Fathi, and Heinz Hötzl. 2008. *Climatic Changes and Water Resources in the Middle East and North Africa*. Berlin: Springer-Verlag.
Zimmerer, Karl S. 1999. "Overlapping Patchworks of Mountain Agriculture in Peru and Bolivia: Toward a Regional-Global Landscape Model." *Human Ecology* 27 (1): 135–165.
———, ed. 2006. *Globalization and New Geographies of Conservation*. Chicago: University of Chicago Press.
Zirari-Devif, Michèle. 2009–2010. "Les terres collectives au Maroc." *Yearbook of Islamic and Middle Eastern Law* 15: 115–132.
Zurayk, Rami. 2012. *Food, Farming and Freedom*. Beirut: Just World Books.

Index

Figures, maps, notes, and tables are indicated by *f*, *m*, *n*, and *t* following the page number.

accountability of government, 78, 94, 97, 98, 100
activism. *See* civil society activism
administrative redistricting (*découpage administratif*), 86–88, 102, 114–115, 119, 134–135, 139
agency, 8, 36, 126–127, 136, 164, 208
agriculture, 28–29; *bour* (rain-fed agriculture), 17, 29, 213; commercial farms (*firmas*), 26, 104–105, 128, 149, 181–182, 185–188, 198; communal referents for, 167, 193–196, 201–202; customary land tenure enabling, 61; fertilizers, 180; funding initiatives for, 91–93, 95, 134, 218n10; global food regime, 5–6, 215n3; land degradation and, 140, 141; limits of, 196–202; livelihood transformations and, 160, 164–167; metal scratch plows, 180, 187; steppe extensions and, 135, 137, 144–145; tractors, 183. *See also* crops; oases and oasis agriculture; sharecropping
'aid al-kabir (religious holiday), 20, 186
Aït Atta, 21, 23, 44, 82, 137
Aït Hamd plateau, 50, 63–68, 64*m*, 80, 87, 155. *See also* Imzilne; Rbat
Aït Khalifa, 64*m*, 125, 130
Aït Mgoun, 21, 23, 43–44, 46, 87
Aït Sedrate, 23, 87, 104, 137
Aït Toumert, 71–72
Aït Zahirs, 64–67, 82–83, 130, 151–152
Algeria and French colonial rule, 112–113, 118, 138–139, 163, 206
Ali, Ben, 206
Amazigh populations. *See* Imazighen
amghar u aman (leader of water), 48, 50–51, 129. *See also* water use and availability
amghar u igran (leader of the fields), 47–48, 50
Arab Spring, 205, 206
Archives Marocaines, 111
association. *See* indirect rule
Atlas Mountains, 16–17, 19, 65, 69–70, 137–138, 140, 216–217n17
Auclair, Laurent, 137–138, 151
authoritarianism, 88

Battesti, Vincent, 146
Berbers, 24, 42, 139, 206, 217n18, 218n4. *See also* Imazighen
Berber Spring (1980), 206
Berlant, Lauren, 11–12, 15
Berque, Jacques, 84, 135, 222n2
biodiversity, 20–21, 137–138, 140–142, 151, 157
Biodiversity Conservation through Transhumance in the Southern High Atlas (CBTHA), 140–142, 151
Black populations: Amazigh activism and, 96; collective land and, 4; labor migration and, 56, 60, 65; road construction and, 38; sharecropping and, 22, 60, 215n2; terminology of, 216n16
blacksmithing, 65, 80–83, 165*t*, 170, 219n16
Bogaert, Koenraad, 89–90
Bouazizi, Mohamed, 206
Bougafer, battle of (1933), 23, 82
Bourdieu, Pierre, 163
bridge construction. *See* road and bridge construction
Burke, Edmund, 44, 84, 221n4, 222n3

capitalism: communal governance and, 129; communities functional to, 75–76; customary governance institutions and, 41; enclosures of, 108, 113, 221–222n10; land divisions and, 128; moral economies and, 163–164; pastoralism and, 144, 218n7; romance of the commons and, 11–12; wage labor and, 163, 166, 174
Casablanca, 72, 73, 99, 161, 194–197
Charte de la Transhumance (Transhumance Charter), 83
Charter of the Forest, 220n13
Chatterjee, Partha, 103
civil society activism, 217n21; administrative redistricting and, 87; claims on state through, 95–98; communal identities and, 35, 100; customary governance institutions and, 14, 100–102; land mobilizations compared to, 123–124, 208; rights-based discourse and, 80,

245

civil society activism (*continued*)
94–96, 100–102; rule of law as demand of, 14, 80, 100–102; state power and, 95–98, 100
climate change, 18–19. *See also* environmental change
coffeehouses and cafés, 1–2, 172–174, 176, 193
collective lands: colonial enclosure of, 109–117; contemporary property law on, 118–122; counterenclosure mobilizations of, 104–109, 122–128; customary governance of, 29–30, 43–46, 61; exclusions from, 61–63; firmas's impact on, 149–150; postcolonial allocation of, 118, 121, 218n10; representatives (*na'ib*), 50, 67, 74–75, 108, 148, 197, 221n7; state power and, 109–111, 118, 121, 122, 131–132, 156, 221n8. *See also* usufruct rights
colonialism: agricultural development and, 28; *blad al-makhzan* and *blad al-siba*, 221n6; commons dismantled under, 115–117; contemporary legacy of, 84, 118–122, 219n3; customary governance institutions under, 14, 42, 44, 50; environmental degradation narratives and, 135, 138–141, 157–158; expropriation through preservation under, 112–115, 122; grand enclosure of, 109–111; indirect rule, 79, 83–84, 86–89, 97, 113, 220n6; land knowledge produced by, 111–112, 221n4, 221n6; pastoralism and, 25, 111–112, 139; political pluralism originating in, 79–86; tribal confederations under, 44–45, 107, 108
commoditization, 25, 108–109, 121, 160, 173, 196, 199–201
commons and commoning, 10–13; colonialism and, 107, 109, 115–117, 122; common good, 107; counterenclosure as, 107–109, 117, 122, 127–131; customary governance institutions and, 41, 107, 127–131, 204–205; defined, 16; fuzzy boundaries and, 207; inequality and, 14–15, 207; labor constituting, 163; latent commons, 12–13, 108, 132; livelihood transformation and, 164–165; marginalized populations and, 103, 107–109, 220n13; private property and, 12–13, 130–131; state power and, 78–79. *See also* politics of the commons
communal governance: of contemporary land mobilizations, 125–132; customary governance refigured by, 41, 48–49, 67, 75–76, 128–129; environmental change and, 135–136, 160; livelihood transformations and, 163; politics of the commons and, 35;

of private property, 48. *See also* collective lands
communal identities: civil society activism and, 35, 100; collective lands and, 110–111, 124, 156; customary authority and, 98; environmental narratives and, 142; indirect rule and, 83–84, 86, 88, 100; land mobilizations and, 128–129; pluralism and, 78–80, 132; state power and, 94
community: agricultural referents for, 167, 193–196, 201–202; debt arrangements and, 168, 173, 175, 194, 223n4; dependencies in, 174–176; functionalism and, 75–76; labor and production of, 162–165, 168, 172–176, 193–196, 201–202; reparations for human rights abuses, 91–95
Consultative Council for Human Rights (CCDH), 90–94; Ziyad (representative), 90–93, 101–102
counterenclosures: as common action, 108–109, 122, 127–132; communal dimensions of, 125–127; political dimensions of, 123–125
Crawford, David, 53, 204, 217n20
crops: alfalfa, 143, 182, 188*t*; almonds and almond trees, 20, 179, 180, 190–193, 191*t*, 197; apricot trees, 20, 179, 190; barley, 20, 179, 180; diversity, 138, 140–142, 151–153, 178–179, 187–188, 197; fig trees, 20, 179, 180, 191*t*, 193, 197; olive trees and olive oil, 20, 149, 179–181, 184, 186–187, 191*t*, 193; quince trees, 20, 179; roses, 176–178, 192*f*; vegetable production, 20, 179–181, 188*t*, 189, 191*t*, 197; wheat/maize rotation, 20, 179, 186, 188*t*, 197–198
customary governance institutions, 14–15; civil society activism and, 14, 100–102; colonial preservation of, 14, 112–117, 120, 122; contemporary land mobilizations and, 125–132; documentation of, 48; environmental change and, 135, 138, 140–143, 150–151, 158–160; geographies of social reproduction and, 150–151, 155; hierarchy in, 22–23, 40–41; at household level, 51–53; landownership distribution and, 4–5, 14, 29–30, 54–56, 61; livelihood transformation and, 160; new commoning and, 41, 107, 127–131, 204–205; overview of, 41–43; pastoralism and, 21–22, 43–44; pluralistic context of, 15, 76, 84, 98–103; at regional/tribal level, 43–46, 48; for resource management, 19, 147–148; state power and, 79–80, 84, 86, 89; at village level, 44, 46–51, 125

Dadès Valley, 17–18, 24, 82–83
dahirs: Berber Dahir (1930), 42, 218n4; collective land (1924), 45; defined, 213; ethnic collectivities (1919), 114; jma'a (1912, 1916), 114, 115; land tenure (1919), 50, 115, 118
Davis, Diana, 113, 138–141
De Angelis, Massimo, 108, 113
debt, 168, 173, 175, 194, 223n4
decentralization reforms, 14, 78, 88, 90, 92, 94–96
declensionist narratives. *See* environmental change
découpage administratif. *See* administrative redistricting
deforestation and desertification, 18, 136, 138–140
de Haas, Hein, 74, 128, 171, 189
democratization reforms, 78, 94, 96, 100, 219n2
Direction des Affaires Indigènes, 84, 108, 114–116, 119
Direction des Affaires Rurales, 110, 119
distributive politics, 5, 80, 90, 103
Dra' Valley, 22, 118
drip irrigation, 104, 133, 145, 149, 181, 187, 222n7
droughts and famines: agricultural policy and, 28; in environmental degradation narratives, 140; measurement and frequency of, 215–216n8; migration patterns following, 3, 73, 83; pastoralism and, 19, 25, 73, 144; risk management and, 197–198; water pumping and, 134, 147

ecotourism, 151–153
el Bour n'Aït Yahya: customary governance institutions in, 49, 68–75; as field site, 31–32; household transformations and, 153–155; images of, 69*f*; labor migration and, 68–70, 73–74; land mobilizations in, 123–124, 126–127; maps of, 31*m*, 39*m*, 70*m*; oases and oasis agriculture in, 70*m*, 71; pastoralism and, 69; wage labor in, 71, 73, 200; water use and availability in, 69–71
el Harte: agriculture in, 56, 60; Black populations in, 38–40, 56; customary governance institutions in, 56–63, 67, 98–99; customary land tenure in, 46–48, 124, 129, 150–151; as field site, 31–32; images of, 38, 134*f*, 148*f*, 179*f*, 184*f*; labor migration and, 56–63, 195–196; landownership in, 46–48, 62*t*, 124, 129, 150–151; maps of, 31*m*, 39*m*; new rurality in, 56–63; road construction, 37–40;

sharecropping in, 38, 56–57, 124; steppe agricultural extensions in, 145–149, 148*f*, 183–185; wage labor and, 170; water use and availability in, 57–59, 129–130, 133–135
elusive commons, 13–16
emboitement (nesting hierarchies of administrative units), 86–87
eminent domain, 9–10
enclosures. *See* capitalism; colonialism; counterenclosures
entrustment, 162–163
environmental change: agrarian labor and, 179–181, 186; degradation narratives of, 135, 138–143, 150, 158–159; ecological resilience and, 136–137; geographies of social reproduction and, 150–155; lived experiences of, 143–144; livelihood transformations and, 132; oasis social constructions and, 145–150; patrimony and, 137–138, 155–159; soil conservation zones and, 118
état civil (identity card system), 83, 87
ethnic collectivities: contemporary property law and, 119; defined, 216n15; land mobilizations and, 127–128; PDPEO and, 142–143; property law and, 119; state funds for, 221n8. *See also* tribal confederations
Europe/European Union: democratization programs, 92, 96; labor migration to, 25, 57–58, 65, 155, 161, 183, 189, 194, 201, 217n19; tourism from, 152
exclusion of marginalized peoples, 80; counterenclosures against, 108–109, 122, 131–132; emergent politics of commons from, 80, 107–109; in formalized land tenure, 220–221n3; pastoralism and, 81–82; politics of commons and, 103, 220n13

Fairhead, James, 147
famines. *See* droughts and famines
Ferguson, James, 175
finance institutions, 220–221n3, 223n4
financial crisis of 2008, 5
French Protectorate: battle of Bougafer and, 23; contemporary legacy of, 84, 118–122, 219n3; direct land transfers in, 112–117; identity card system of, 83, 87; justification for, 112; road construction and, 37–38; *tutelle* (tutelary authority), 14, 114–117, 119–122, 159, 218n9. *See also* colonialism
functionalism, 75–76, 136, 215n6

Geertz, Clifford, 168
Geist, Alison A., 180

Gilbreath, Richard, 17*m*, 31*m*, 39*m*, 64*m*, 70*m*, 169*m*
Glaoua, Madani, 82
Glaoua chieftains, 82–83, 118, 216–217n17
grazing. *See* pastoralism
Green Morocco Plan (PMV), 29, 90, 95, 145
Gregg, Gary S., 180
guich (precolonial royal concessions), 29–30
Guillaume, Albert, 111
Guyer, Jane, 15

Harvey, David, 12, 75
Hassan I (king), 28, 82
Hassan II (king), 77–78, 88, 91
Haut Commissariat au Plan survey, 33
Hirak Movement, 208
Hoffman, Katherine, 3–4, 206, 218n4, 224n7
Holston, James, 124
households: agricultural production of, 191–192, 191*t*; customary law mediation by, 51–53; geographies of social reproduction and, 153–154; home construction and, 223–224n6; land inheritance and, 219n14; methodology and, 217n23; migration and, 57*t*, 189–190; occupational survey of, 165–167, 165*t*, 166*t*, 167*t*; water consumption of, 216n9
housing: adobe and domestic construction, 154, 223n9, 223–224n6; cement construction, 154, 223n9; on collective lands, 121, 125, 126, 130; communal governance of, 48, 148; construction materials for, 154, 223n9, 223–224n6; geographies of social reproduction and, 153–155, 160; landownership and, 26, 54, 67; urbanization and, 70
human rights, 77, 90–96; civil society activism and, 80, 94–96, 100–102; contemporary land mobilizations and, 127–128; customary governance institutions and, 99

Ichihn, 104–109, 122, 123, 126
identity card system (*état civil*), 83, 87
Idriss, Moulay, 23
Ilahiane, Hsain, 22, 60, 223n5
Imaghran and Imaghran Confederation, 25, 58–62, 69–70, 73–74, 123, 126–127, 144, 177, 222n6
Imazighen, 215n1; Algeria's Berber Spring and, 206; civil society activism and, 24, 96, 206–207; labor migration and, 58–59, 65; landownership and, 58, 59; Mgoun Valley history of, 22–24, 37; racial hierarchy and, 32, 60, 124; rights-based discourses of, 217n18; sharecropping and, 60, 64–65, 215n2; tamazirt and, 3–4
Imzilne: Black populations in, 3, 9, 32, 65; customary governance institutions in, 63–68, 126; as field site, 31–32; Imazighen in, 65; labor migration and, 63, 65; landownership in, 9–11, 44, 49, 50–51, 67–68, 124–126; map of, 31*m*; pastoralism in, 63; scarcity and politics of custom in, 63–68, 189; sharecropping in, 64–65; water use and availability in, 63, 66–67, 189
income sources: agriculture, 164, 176, 179, 191–192, 191*t*; quantifying and statistical view of, 166–167, 167–168*t*, 174–175; remittances, 25, 56–60, 128, 150, 166–168, 171–172, 188–190, 194–196, 223n3, 223n9; tourism, 152; wage labor, 62, 174
INDH (National Initiative for Human Development), 89, 90, 93–95
indirect rule, 79, 83–84, 86–89, 97, 113, 220n6
individualism: capitalism and, 12; in environmental narratives, 135, 138, 142, 157; land mobilizations and, 131–132; in romance of the commons, 14, 110–112; women's labor and, 201
inequality: collective lands and, 107, 121; contemporary land mobilizations and, 127, 207–208; inherent to commoning, 14–15; landownership distribution and, 54–56, 61; land tenure and, 34–35; new commoning negotiating, 16, 207; oasis farming and, 180; in southeast Morocco, 26–28. *See also* exclusion of marginalized peoples
infant and child mortality, 223n11
irrigation. *See* drip irrigation; oases and oasis agriculture; water use and availability
Islam and Islamic jurisprudence, 48, 51–52, 221n4; *shari'a* law, 42, 218n4

jma'a (customary councils): civil society activism and, 100; under colonial rule, 84, 102, 114, 116; defined, 213; environmental narratives of, 142; exclusions through, 61–63, 66; land mobilizations and, 9, 125–126, 130, 131; non-state spaces of, 88; role of, 5, 8–9, 41, 47–51
Joseph, Miranda, 12, 15, 75

Kelaa Mgouna: as field site, 31, 33–34; French development of, 38; Hassan II's prison in, 77–78, 78*f*, 82, 91, 93; images of, 106*f*, 169*f*; labor migration and, 170–172; livelihood transformations in, 167–172; local politics in,

INDEX   249

90–95, 100; maps of, 17m, 27m, 31m, 169m; population/households in, 32t; rental property in, 54; socioecological introduction to, 17, 18; uneven development and, 26
Kusunose, Yoko, 33, 49

labor, 35–36; commoditized/uncommoditized transitions of, 199–201; communal life and, 162–165, 168, 172–176, 193–196, 201–202; dependency and, 174–176; emergence of new, 132, 160; landscape transitions and, 179–181; market town transformations of, 167–172; oasis farming and, 176–179, 181–186, 189–193; statistical view of, 165–167; transformation of agriculture and, 186–193. *See also* livelihood transformations; wage labor
labor migration: agriculture transformed by, 186–190; capital accumulation and, 76, 150, 164, 166; to Europe, 25, 57–58, 65, 155, 161, 183, 189, 194, 201, 217n19; geographies of social reproduction and, 150–151; racial hierarchy and, 39, 59–60; rurality and, 74, 176. *See also* livelihood transformations
landownership: agricultural development and, 28, 61; authority contested through, 40–41, 60, 67–68, 98–99, 101–102, 105–109, 125, 220n13; *ayants-droits* (rights holders), 45, 51, 115, 117, 156, 213, 220n1; *azref* (customary law), 41, 42; communal dimensions of, 125–127, 220n1; contemporary property law, 118–119; customary land tenure, 4–5, 14, 29–30, 54–56, 61; dahirs on, 50; distress sales, 109, 130; distribution of, 4–5, 14, 29–30, 54–56, 61; exclusion of marginalized peoples in, 220–221n3; freehold title, 115, 121, 131; ghurm (fine) system, 48, 126; *habous* (religious endowment land), 29–30; *hurum* (protected spaces), 48–50, 105, 124–126, 145, 148, 193–194, 213, 219n13; inequality negotiated through, 34–35; labor migration and, 56–57, 59–60; new commoning in, 108–109, 122, 127–131; pluralistic context of, 29–30, 76, 84, 98–103; political dimensions of, 123–125; prestige in, 15; privatization and, 11, 110; producing knowledge of, 111–112; rising value of, 67, 74, 109; sale/transfer of, 50, 58–61, 69, 111–112, 121; as social insurance, 4; *soualiyates* (women rights holders), 121; tribal confederations and, 43–46, 48, 49, 131; at village level, 46–51; women and inheritance, 46–47, 51–53. *See also* customary governance institutions; *mulk*

Leach, Melissa, 147
legal pluralism, 219n5; land governance and, 42–43, 50–51, 75; political pluralism and, 78
Li, Tania, 122, 128
Linebaugh, Peter, 16
literacy courses, 71
littoral regions, 27, 28, 109, 114, 117, 120, 140
livelihood transformations: agrarian labor, 176–179, 186–189, 208; commoditized/uncommoditized labor, 199–201; communal life and, 132, 162–165, 168, 172–174; dependencies in, 174–176; environmental change and, 160, 179–181; oasis agriculture and, 181–186, 189–193; pastoralism and, 137, 157–158, 222n6; statistical view of, 165–167. *See also* labor migration
livestock. *See* pastoralism
local politics: civil society activism in, 95–98; land mobilizations and, 124–125; political pluralism and, 79, 90–95, 98–102; state power and, 93–94, 205. *See also* customary governance institutions; *jma'a*
Lyautey, Hubert, 83, 113–114, 117

makhzan, 8, 105, 111–112, 118, 122, 213, 221n6. *See also* state power
Maliki school of jurisprudence, 48
Mamdani, Mahmood, 14, 100, 115–116, 220n6
marriage and landownership, 53
Maxwell, Gavin, 82
McCarthy, James, 14
McKinsey (consulting group), 29
melkisation, 116–117, 213
methodology of the study, 30–34, 217n23. *See also* participants in study
Mgoun Valley: colonial rule in, 82–84, 86; contemporary property law and, 118–119; environmental change in, 138, 140, 160; history on landscape of, 21–25; land mobilizations in, 124, 127–128; landownership distribution in, 54–56, 54t, 55f; livelihood transformations in, 165–167; livestock ownership in, 144t; maps of, 17m, 31m; migration experiences in, 57t; new rurality of, 75–76, 163–164, 201–202, 204–205; population/households of, 32t; socioecological introduction to, 16–21; state power in, 79–80, 87, 93–94; uneven development in, 25–30, 155, 159. *See also specific locations*
Michaux-Bellaire, Édouard, 112
microclimates, 19, 178, 182, 185
migration. *See* labor migration

mining, 66, 145, 161, 207–208, 217n19
Ministry of Agriculture, 48, 91, 129–130, 156
Ministry of Interior: CCDH and, 94; civil society activism and, 95, 102; colonial legacy in, 84–86, 118–122; customary governance institutions and, 49–51, 86; environmental narratives and, 150; Imzilne land divisions and, 10; INDH and, 94–95; land allocations by, 104–108, 110; land area managed by, 30*t*; *muqaddam* (representative), 50; qa 'ids (representatives), 22, 23, 44, 84–87, 94–95, 127, 213; Rural Affairs Directorate, 44–45; surveillance role of, 88–89; tutelary authority and, 44–45
Mitchell, Timothy, 97
Mohamed V (king), 23, 86–87, 118
Mohamed VI (king), 78, 88–89, 93
monarchy, 88–89, 102, 118, 119, 219n5
moral economies, 108–109, 124, 128, 135, 163
Moroccan Household Living Standards Measurement Survey, 166
Mubarak, Hosni, 205, 206
mulk (private property): collective land divisions and, 10, 61, 116–117; colonial law on, 107, 109–114, 116; in common actions, 12–13, 130–131; communal governance of, 48, 109, 130; in contemporary property law, 118–119; customary institutions' jurisprudence over, 48; defined, 213; delimitation and, 45–46; total land area of, 29–30, 29*t*
mutual aid. *See* community; reciprocity

na'ib. *See* collective-land representatives
National Initiative for Human Development (INDH), 89, 90, 93–95
nationalism, 220n6
natural resource management: colonial narratives of, 138–140; customary law on, 19, 147–148; environmental narratives of, 136, 138, 142, 157–160, 224n1; livelihood transformations and, 132, 167; patrimony and, 151, 155–159. *See also specific types of resources*
neoliberalism, 5, 10–11, 14, 28–29, 35, 224n1
new commons. *See* commons and commoning
new rurality, 6–9; Amazigh identity and, 24; economic marginalization of, 26–29; environmental narratives of, 135–136; limits of farming in, 196–199; livelihood transformations and, 160, 162–165; oasis agriculture and, 21; political agency in, 205–208; state power and, 79–80; in urban areas, 174, 195

oases and oasis agriculture: contemporary logics of, 181–186; environmental narratives of, 136–137, 159–160; labor processes and, 19–20, 189–193; lived experience of, 143–144; pastoralism and, 18–21, 137, 143, 180; PMV and, 28; productionism and, 20, 176–179; rurality shaped by, 21; social construction of, 145–150, 223n5; trees, 20, 179–181, 184–186, 190–193, 191*t*, 197
Orientalism, 20, 138, 206
Ouarzazate province, 87, 110, 120–121, 140, 221n8
Ouchtou, Haj, 43–45, 48
Oufkir, Mohamed, 120

participants in study: Abdallah (el Harte), 129–130, 183–184, 190–193, 198; Abdelhafid (el Harte), 171, 174, 187; Abderrahmane (el Harte), 170, 172–173; Ahmed, Haj (el Harte), 56–60, 101, 150–151, 180, 195; Fatima (el Bour), 72–74; Filali (el Harte), 173–174, 183, 198; Hamid (Imzilne), 80–81, 83, 170; Hassan (el Harte), 196–198, 204; Hmou (el Harte), 185–186; Hsain, Haj (Qla'a), 37–39, 58–60, 204; Itto (el Bour), 72–73; Kebira (el Harte), 193–194; Mbarak (el Harte), 85, 145; Mohamed (Imzilne), 170, 175; Moha ou Lahcen (el Harte), 1–3, 2*f*, 8–10, 11*f*, 125–126; Mohsin (el Harte), 62–63, 219n15; Saaden, Haj Bou (Casablanca), 195–196; Safiyya (el Harte), 52; Taleb (Rbat), 65–67, 82–83, 130, 161–162, 201; Youssef (el Bour), 72–73, 123, 219n17; Youssef (Kelaa Mgouna), 171–172
participatory processes and planning, 14, 77–78, 88–89, 94–101
pastoralism: agdal, 43, 84, 137–138, 158, 213, 218n7; agricultural policy and, 25, 28–29; colonial position on, 25, 111–112, 139; customary governance institutions and, 21–22, 43–44; ecological scholarship and, 25, 28–29, 136–138, 222n4; environmental narratives of, 136–137, 139–143, 159–160; feed supplements, 140, 143; French pass laws and, 83, 139; husbandry practices, 141; livelihood transformations and, 137, 157–158, 165–167, 222n6; livestock ownership and, 143–144, 144*t*; living conditions of, 71–73; oasis agriculture and, 18–21, 137, 143, 180; patrimony and, 137–138, 156–159; racial hierarchies in, 81–82; state expansion and, 25
patrimony, 137–138, 151, 152, 155–160

peasants: colonial narratives of, 110–111; defined, 215n4; environmental narratives of, 8, 135–136; heritage of, 159–160; livelihood transformation and, 164; migration remittances and, 190; Orientalist tropes of, 206
Peters, Pauline, 14, 115
place, sense of: communal orientation and, 13; cultural patrimony and, 153; identity cards and, 87; for migrants, 3, 71, 76; new rurality and, 5; stopping a place in time, 204–205; in struggle to maintain villages, 65; subsistence claims and, 3, 128. *See also tamazirt* (homeland)
Plan Maroc Vert (PMV, Green Morocco Plan), 29, 90, 95, 145
pluralism. *See* legal pluralism; political pluralism
political agency, 8, 36, 126–127, 136, 164, 208
political economy, 16
political pluralism, 219n5; civil society activism and, 95–98; colonial origins of, 35, 79–86; in customary governance institutions, 15, 98–102; indirect rule and, 89; legacy of, 89–95; politics of the commons through, 9; state power and, 78–80, 95
politics of the commons, 9–13; civil society activism and, 102; dependencies in, 174–176; dynamic approach to, 16, 205; land mobilizations and, 35, 125; political pluralism and, 90, 103; tradition and, 5
poverty, 26–28, 95, 102–103
pragmatism: in civil society activism, 96–98; in environmental narratives, 135–136; in land mobilizations, 131–132
precipitation, 16–18
prisons, 77–78, 88, 91
private property. *See* landownership; *mulk*
Projet de développement des parcours et de l'élevage dans l'Oriental (PDPEO), 142–143

Qla'a, 37–40, 58–60, 218n2

race and racial hierarchies: customary governance and, 41; French reinforcement of, 38; Imazighen and, 22, 38; pastoralism and, 81–82; road construction and, 37–40; sharecropping and, 65
Rachik, Hassan, 42, 127, 129, 219n3
Ramadan, 186, 190
Rbat: customary governance institutions in, 63–68, 126; as field site, 31–32; images of, 152*f*; Imazighen in, 65; labor migration and, 63, 65; land mobilizations in, 124–125; map of, 31*m*; pastoralism in, 63; scarcity and politics of custom in, 63–68; sharecropping in, 64–65; tourism and, 152–153; water use and availability in, 63, 66–67, 189
reciprocity, 61, 103, 128, 163, 168, 194, 198, 202. *See also* community
remittances, 25, 56–60, 128, 150, 166–168, 171–172, 188–190, 194–196, 223n3, 223n9. *See also* labor migration
reparations for human rights abuses, 91–95
research assistants: Mbarak, 193, 217n24; Saïd, 161, 217n24
Réseau des Associations de Tinghir pour le Développement et la Démocratie, 33, 49, 144*t*
reterritorialization, 134–135
risk management, 19, 20, 146, 164, 179
road and bridge construction, 37–40, 63, 70, 135, 152–153, 203–204
romance of the commons, 11–14; capitalist enclosures and, 221–222n10; environmental narratives in, 135–136, 158–159; new commons complicating, 122, 129, 131–132, 207
Rqia, Lalla, 46–47
rule of law, 14, 94, 95, 100–102
rurality. *See* new rurality
rural proletarianization, 74–75, 163
rural urbanization, 74, 171, 174

Scott, James, 13, 79, 103
shantytowns, 116, 122, 153, 202
sharecropping: Imazighen and, 60, 64–65, 215n2; labor migration and, 55–60, 65, 66; oasis agriculture and, 180, 194; pastoralism and, 22; racial hierarchy in, 4, 8, 22, 55; UNDP project and, 151–152
shaykhs, 44, 82–83
silver mine mobilizations, 220n12
Silverstein, Paul, 22, 88, 96
slaves and slavery, 22
Smith, Neil, 163, 166
sovereignty, 9, 10, 109–115
state power: civil society activism and, 95–98, 100; collective lands and, 109–111, 118, 121, 122, 131–132, 156, 221n8; colonialism and, 82–86, 109–110; customary law and, 42–44, 50, 75, 127–128, 160; environmental change narratives and, 158–160; indirect rule and, 86–89; land concessions and, 106–108; in local politics, 93–94, 205; political pluralism

state power (*continued*)
  and, 78–80, 95; social worlds refashioned by, 81–82
steppe ecology, 16–21, 43–44, 135, 137, 145–149. *See also* oases and oasis agriculture
subsistence and subsistence rights: communal governance and, 107, 109; contemporary land mobilizations and, 124, 127–128, 131; distributive politics of, 5; elusive commons and, 13; Imzilne and, 65, 67; limits of, 196–199; PMV and, 29; sharecropping and, 179
suq (weekly market), 168, 169f, 170
Surdon, Georges, 115

Taher, Moulay, 69
tamazirt (homeland): attachment to, 161, 176, 205; contemporary land mobilizations and, 122, 126, 128; contestation of, 3–4; migrants' presence in, 189, 194; nostalgic imaginary of, 51, 107; outsiders defined by, 105; wage labor and, 67
Tashelhit language, 22, 34
Tinghir province, 87, 110, 119
Tounsi, Ben, 104–105, 181–182, 184, 193
tourism, 151–153, 177
trades and trade skills, 170, 172. *See also* blacksmithing
transhumance. *See* pastoralism
transit systems, 81, 126, 162, 204
tribal confederations: colonial boundaries and, 86, 88, 114–115, 119, 139; colonial narratives of, 110–111; customary land tenure and, 43–46, 48, 49, 131; as ethnic collectivities, 216n15; land conflict mediation and, 107, 108; monarchy and, 87
Tsing, Anna, 12–13
Tunisian revolution (2011), 205–206

United Nations, 20–21
United Nations Development Programme (UNDP), 140–141, 151–153, 156–157
urbanization, 70, 150–151
urban ruralization, 174, 195
usufruct rights, 44, 48, 111, 115, 119

van der Ploeg, Jan, 164
villages: agricultural extensions and, 150; boundaries of, 88; customary land tenure in, 46–51; household transformations and, 153–155; labor obligations of, 164–165; land mobilizations by, 105–110, 125–127; *qsur* of, 59, 82, 153–154, 213, 219n15, 222n8. *See also specific villages*

wage labor: commoditization and, 199; communal referents for, 162–165, 168, 172–174, 194–195, 202; labor migration and, 153, 155, 223n3; oasis agriculture and, 176; statistical view of, 166–167; women and, 199–200. *See also* labor; livelihood transformations
water use and availability, 16–18, 25, 28; customary governance of, 48, 49, 126, 147–148, 222n1; dams and dam building, 28, 86, 118, 129; drip irrigation and, 222n7; of households, 216n9; in oasis agriculture, 144–150; water use association (WUA), 129–130; wells and well digging, 66, 73, 147, 153, 219n17. *See also* droughts and famines
Williams, Raymond, 13, 221–222n10
Wilson, Alice, 42
Wolford, Wendy, 12
women: agrarian labor and, 166, 167, 177–178, 223n1; commoditization of labor and, 199–201; customary land tenure and inheritance, 46–47, 51–53; land mobilizations and, 107, 121, 206–207; political pluralism and, 102–103; social infrastructure of labor and, 168, 170; *soulaliyates* (women rights holders), 121
wood as resource, 130, 185, 190, 202, 223–224n6

zakat (mutual aid), 198
Zawiya Abdel Malik (Islamic brotherhood), 69
Zawiya Aït Ba 'Amran (Islamic brotherhood), 56
Zayd, Haj ou, 145–147
Zelizer, Viviana, 163
Ziz Valley, 22, 60, 118